THE ROMANOV DYNASTY

by Ed Stephan

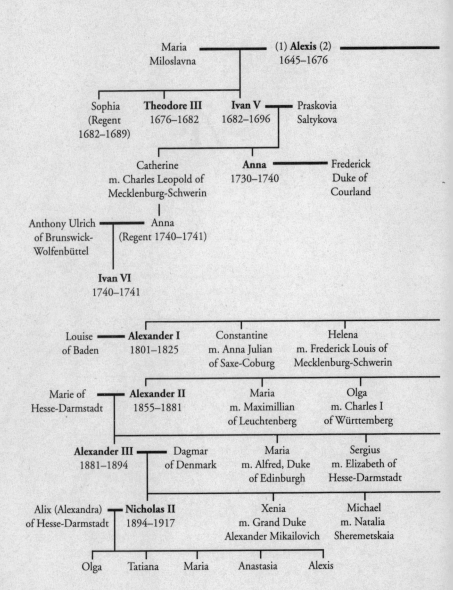

Maria Miloslavna ———— (1) **Alexis** (2) 1645–1676

Sophia (Regent 1682–1689)

Theodore III 1676–1682

Ivan V 1682–1696 ——— Praskovia Saltykova

Catherine m. Charles Leopold of Mecklenburg-Schwerin

Anna 1730–1740 ——— Frederick Duke of Courland

Anthony Ulrich of Brunswick-Wolfenbüttel ——— Anna (Regent 1740–1741)

Ivan VI 1740–1741

Louise of Baden ——— **Alexander I** 1801–1825

Constantine m. Anna Julian of Saxe-Coburg

Helena m. Frederick Louis of Mecklenburg-Schwerin

Marie of Hesse-Darmstadt ——— **Alexander II** 1855–1881

Maria m. Maximillian of Leuchtenberg

Olga m. Charles I of Württemberg

Alexander III 1881–1894 ——— Dagmar of Denmark

Maria m. Alfred, Duke of Edinburgh

Sergius m. Elizabeth of Hesse-Darmstadt

Alix (Alexandra) of Hesse-Darmstadt ——— **Nicholas II** 1894–1917

Xenia m. Grand Duke Alexander Mikailovich

Michael m. Natalia Sheremetskaia

Olga   Tatiana   Maria   Anastasia   Alexis

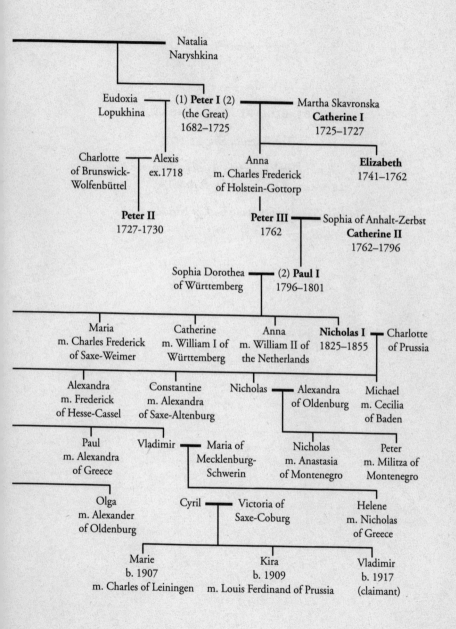

Natalia
Naryshkina

Eudoxia Lopukhina — (1) **Peter I** (2) (the Great) 1682–1725 — Martha Skavronska **Catherine I** 1725–1727

Charlotte of Brunswick-Wolfenbüttel — Alexis ex.1718

Anna m. Charles Frederick of Holstein-Gottorp

Elizabeth 1741–1762

Peter II 1727-1730

Peter III 1762 — Sophia of Anhalt-Zerbst **Catherine II** 1762–1796

Sophia Dorothea of Württemberg — (2) **Paul I** 1796–1801

Maria m. Charles Frederick of Saxe-Weimer

Catherine m. William I of Württemberg

Anna m. William II of the Netherlands

Nicholas I 1825–1855 — Charlotte of Prussia

Alexandra m. Frederick of Hesse-Cassel

Constantine m. Alexandra of Saxe-Altenburg

Nicholas — Alexandra of Oldenburg

Michael m. Cecilia of Baden

Paul m. Alexandra of Greece

Vladimir — Maria of Mecklenburg-Schwerin

Nicholas m. Anastasia of Montenegro

Peter m. Militza of Montenegro

Olga m. Alexander of Oldenburg

Cyril — Victoria of Saxe-Coburg

Helene m. Nicholas of Greece

Marie b. 1907 m. Charles of Leiningen

Kira b. 1909 m. Louis Ferdinand of Prussia

Vladimir b. 1917 (claimant)

ALEXANDER II

The Last Great Tsar

EDVARD RADZINSKY

Translated by Antonina W. Bouis

Free Press

NEW YORK · LONDON · TORONTO · SYDNEY

FREE PRESS
A Division of Simon & Schuster, Inc.
1230 Avenue of the Americas
New York, NY 10020

First Free Press trade paperback edition 2006
FREE PRESS and colophon are trademarks of Simon & Schuster, Inc.

DESIGNED BY PAUL DIPPOLITO

For information about special discounts for bulk purchases,
please contact Simon & Schuster Special Sales: 1-800-456-6798
or business@simonandschuster.com

Manufactured in the United States of America

10   9   8   7   6   5   4   3   2   1

Library of Congress Cataloging-in-Publication Data

Radzinsky, Edvard.
Alexander II : the last great tsar/Edvard Radzinsky; translated by Antonina W. Bouis.
          p. cm.
Includes bibliographical references and index.
1. Alexander II, Emperor of Russia, 1818–1881. 2. Russia—History—Alexander II, 1855–1881. 3. Emperors—Russia—Biography. I. Title.
DK220.R33 2005
947.08'1'092—dc22 [B]

ISBN 13: 978-0-7432-7332-9
ISBN 10:   0-7432-7332-x
ISBN 13: 978-0-7432-8426-4 (Pbk)
ISBN 10:   0-7432-8426-7 (Pbk)

A Note on Dates

Russia did not adopt the Gregorian calendar until January 31, 1918. Earlier dates, in the Old-Style Julian Calendar, are thirteen days behind Gregorian-calendar dates in the West. For example, the October Revolution of 1917, which took place on October 25, is now celebrated on November 7. All the dates in this book are in the Old-Style Julian Calendar.

Contents

Introduction

*This may be the most important era in the thousand-
year existence of Russia.*

—GRAND DUKE KONSTANTIN NIKOLAYEVICH
DIARY, JANUARY 1, 1861

If we perish, there will be others.

—TERRORIST ANDREI ZHELYABOV

The history of Tsar Alexander II is paradoxical. Alexander II dreamed of bringing Russia into the circle of European states, leading the country toward a European constitution. He gave the eternal Russian pendulum that swings between West and East a definite push to the West. Yet this Westernizing tsar is little known in the West.

Nevertheless, Alexander II was the greatest reformer tsar since Peter the Great. The Russian Lincoln, he put an end to a thousand years of Russian slavery by emancipating the serfs.

He did more than free 23 million Russian slaves; he reformed Russian life by changing the justice system, the army, and the very form of government. He was the father of the first Russian perestroika, which brought about a great spiritual awakening. "The Thaw" . . . "The Great Icebreaker" . . . "The Russian Renaissance" were some of the terms for Alexander's reign used by the press. Dostoevsky, Tolstoy, Turgenev, and Mendeleyev only begin the list of stars in the galaxy of famous writers and scientists who created their masterworks in the days of Alexander II.

"This may be the most important era in the thousand-year existence of Russia," wrote the tsar's brother, Grand Duke Konstantin Nikolayevich, in his diary.

"What a novel his life makes!" wrote a contemporary. His turbulent life encompassed everything from great reforms, to victorious wars, to the sexual exploits of a royal Don Juan, to his final, great love. Yet this hot blood in Russia's leader, echoed in that of his country, flowed dangerously. Once Alexander quickened Russia's pulse, he could not contain its circulation.

Like all reformers who followed him, including Mikhail Gorbachev, he failed to understand this basic truth: "Starting reforms in Russia is dangerous, but it is much more dangerous to stop them."

The young radicals, the children of his perestroika, decided to hasten Russian history. The great tsar was forced to see the bitterest change: His Russia became the home of terrorism, a terrorism previously unparalleled in scope and bloodshed in Europe.

Bombs and gunshots exploded all over the country. Tsarist officials were killed. Alexander II survived six attempts on his life. The terrorists managed to blow up his Winter Palace. The tsar saw the blood of dead and wounded victims in his own home.

For the first time the fate of the country was decided not only in the magnificent royal palace but in the impoverished hidden apartments of the terrorists.

Underground Russia, with its secret life and bloody exploits, is an important character in this book.

"Our work is destruction, a terrible, total, universal and ruthless destruction" proclaimed one of the fathers of Russian terrorism. "The revolutionary is a doomed man. He has no interests, no work, no feelings, no ties, no property, not even a name. Everything is consumed by the single, exclusive interest, the sole thought, the sole passion: revolution. Poison, dagger, and noose—the Revolution sanctifies everything."

The Russian terrorism of Alexander II's reign remarkably presaged the terrorism of our day. The words and slogans that agitated the long-buried and decomposed Russian terrorists can be read in newspaper articles today.

"The basic lesson of history is that people do not learn from history," is a trite but—alas—true aphorism.

Alexander II had to learn to fight against a previously unknown evil (the "new barbarians," as he called them). The tsar declared a war on terror, for the first but not the last time in history.

His war broke off in March 1881.

"Caesar, Beware the Ides of March"

The warning spoken two thousand years ago in ancient Rome would be an ominous prophecy for the Russian caesars as well.

The month of March turned out to be significant for Russian tsars. The greatest and most horrendous of the ancient Moscow tsars, Ivan the Terrible, died in March—perhaps poisoned.

Emperor Paul I was killed on March 11, 1801.

Nicholas II, the last tsar, abdicated from the throne in March, ending a three-century-old dynasty.

The first Bolshevik tsar, Josef Stalin, also died in March, perhaps killed by his comrades.

On March 1, 1881, one of the most mysterious events in Russian history took place.

St. Petersburg, 2:15 P.M., Emperor Alexander II leaves Mikhailovsky Palace, where he was visiting his cousin. The emperor is sixty-three. Even though he has aged in recent years, he is still in fine shape. Wearing a red cap, a red-lined overcoat with beaver collar, and gold epaulets with his father's crest, tall and with a guardsman's military bearing, he is the last handsome tsar in the Romanov dynasty.

The carriage is waiting before the marble columns of the palace, surrounded by unprecedented security for Russian sovereigns. Six Cossacks ride on horseback, another one with the coachman, and two sleighs with guards travel behind the carriage.

The imperial cavalcade—the carriage and two sleighs—pulls away from the Mikhailovsky Palace. The horses gallop merrily and the sleighs have trouble keeping up with the carriage.

The carriage turns onto the Catherine Canal. With it, turns Russian history.

The Venice of the North is still covered with March snows. Snow lies on the cobbled street along the embankment. There are few people out: The bone-chilling March wind has blown all the strollers away from the canal. Policemen patrol the sidewalk, guarding the passage of the imperial carriage.

For some reason they do not notice a young man hurrying toward the carriage. He is clearly nervous. He is carrying a suspicious package about the size of a box of Landrin chocolates, wrapped in a white handkerchief.

The young man waits for the approaching carriage. He throws the package under the horses' hooves.

The echo of the powerful explosion rocks along the canal.

In its wake, the body of a dead Cossack guard lies on the sidewalk. Next to the corpse is a boy who was carrying a basket with meat, screaming in pain. Blood and pieces of cloth lie on the snow-covered cobblestones.

The imperial cavalcade stops, and the unharmed sovereign leaves the carriage. The young man threw the bomb too late—he must have been very nervous.

Next comes something inexplicable. The guards and the tsar know that the assassin was probably not alone. The coachman and the guards beg the tsar to leave the canal as quickly as possible. But to their total amazement, the tsar, who has survived six assassination attempts, is in no hurry to go. On the contrary, he starts pacing along the Catherine Canal. As if waiting for something.

PART I

Grand Duke

CHAPTER I

The Harsh Fate of Heritage

Alexander was born in Moscow, in the Kremlin, on "the wonderful spring day of 17 April 1818 . . . during Easter Week, when the bells rang to glorify the celebration of Christ's Resurrection," recalls Alexandra Fedorovna in her memoirs. Despite her happiness and the holiday, the newborn's mother adds the surprising words, "I remember that I sensed something important and *very sad* at the thought that this tiny creature would someday be emperor."

There was reason for the former German princess to be strangely sad at the thought of her son becoming emperor of a boundless country. And there was reason why Alexander's future tutor, the celebrated poet Vassily Zhukovsky, in a poem dedicated to his birth, advised the infant "not to quail before harsh Fate."

Blood and violence accompanied the history of his ancestors, the tsars of the Romanov dynasty. Murdering their own tsars became a Russian tradition in the eighteenth century. Alexander inherited a secretive autocracy and an army that knew how to use force to get its way.

It all began with two events, not related at first.

At the very end of the seventeenth century, the great-great-grandfather of Alexander, Peter the Great, created the Russian guards. Then, in the very beginning of the eighteenth century, the great emperor invaded the Baltic region.

It was the occasion for a story that makes all Cinderella stories pale by comparison. It is probably the most magical tale of the magical eighteenth century.

In Liflandia, in a humble room in the house of Pastor Gluck, lived a cook named Marta, daughter of a local peasant. As expected from an extremely pretty maid, she washed, cooked, and provided other pleasant services. Marta was married, even though she lived without her husband. A passing dragoon had married her. The sly fellow had had his fun with the pretty cook and then gone off to war. He never returned, either dying in battle or having forgotten about her. Our little beauty would have grown old in the pastor's kitchen if not for the Russian troops, who conquered the area and took Marta prisoner.

Thus started the magical ride of the former cook—first into the bed of the commander, Count Sheremetyev, and then her buxom charms led her to a higher bed, belonging to Peter the Great's all-powerful favorite, Prince Menshikov. From there it was a straight (and very frequent) path to the tsar's bed.

There was a popular folk drawing on the subject. It depicted the tsar feasting, with a man bringing a big-bosomed, dumb beauty to his side. The caption read: "A loyal subject gives his most precious possession to the tsar."

Usually these passing fancies quickly moved out of the fiery Peter's bedroom. But Marta remained forever. Her charms and good nature wrought the impossible: The emperor of Russia married a married cook. Marta was baptized as Catherine Alexeyevna. Peter crowned her empress.

In 1725, Peter grew deathly ill. All the mighty gathered at his deathbed. The emperor could only manage to say: "Give everything—" But he did not have time to say to whom.

At the instant of his most important command, mocking Death took away the tsar.

While the body was being prepared, the courtiers gathered in the next room to decide who would get "everything," that is, the great empire that stretched across half the world, from the Baltic Sea to the Pacific Ocean. To their amazement, they found guards officers in that room. The commanders of the regiments founded by Peter the Great had come in.

The courtiers demanded, "How dare you!" The response was drumming from the street. They looked out the window and saw massed regiments in the courtyard. All the palace exits were manned by the guards. The guard commanders declared Catherine I, the former cook, empress of all Russia. (If the first husband dragoon had showed up then, it would have been quite a story.)

Catherine I's reign was extraordinary. Her account books remain. The expenditures on fools and feasts equal the expenses for the rest of the kingdom.

Yet her reign marks the entrance of Peter the Great's child—the guards regiments—into the political arena. They would not leave for the rest of the century. Not much later, the guards created yet another empress, Elizabeth, who was the daughter of Peter the Great and Catherine I.

After the death of Catherine I, her daughter, Elizabeth, found herself in reduced circumstances. The elderly associates of Peter the Great turned to the prince and princess Braunschweig, the children of Peter's brother, Ivan, to rule the country. Their infant son, Ioann Antonovich, still in his cradle, was pronounced emperor. The regent during his childhood was to be his mother, Princess Anna Leopoldovna.

The visitors from Braunschweig did not appreciate how dangerous the Russian guards could be, but the daughter of Peter the Great did. Elizabeth had been born before her parents' marriage. She was declared legitimate only after the wedding, as the legal daughter of Peter. The love child was very attractive, with thick red hair and divine porcelain skin with a rosy blush. Her figure was most tempting: she was tall, with a high bosom and long legs. One German diplomat fainted when he first beheld her.

She was extremely passionate. The Cossack Rozum, a handsome chorister in the palace church, captured her heart. She turned the ordinary Rozum into Count Razumovsky, who remained her lover for many years.

Elizabeth's portraits show a strong, willful jaw—her ruthless father's jaw. She gave herself up to love, but the red-haired Elizabeth did not forget about power. Peter's child did not want to live in obscurity. So she turned to the guards.

On a cold November night in 1741, a sleigh surrounded by three hundred guardsmen rode down Nevsky Prospect. Elizabeth was in the sleigh, headed for the royal palace.

Along the way, the guardsmen cheerfully arrested the sleepy aristocrats who lived along the palace embankment. With jokes and jibes, they sent Regent Anna Leopoldovna's main associates from their beds straight to prison. As they approached the palace, Elizabeth stopped the sleigh, to reduce the noise. The guardsmen carried the beauty the rest of the way to the palace. When the watchman tried to sound the alarm by beating his drum, an officer ran his sword through the drumhead. The palace was taken without resistance.

"Time to rise, sister!" Elizabeth said, awakening the regent of the Empire. The nocturnal revolution was victorious. The regent was sent to the fortress along with the rest of her family. Elizabeth herself brought the child emperor in her own sleigh. The boy laughed happily, reaching for the guardsmen. Elizabeth kissed him and sighed, "Poor child!" He suffered life imprisonment in the Shisselburg Fortress. The former emperor of all Russia grew up in a prison cell (a Russian version of the Man in the Iron Mask), not knowing why he had ended up there. The fortress guards eventually killed him. His wretched parents rotted to death.

The morning after the coup, Elizabeth declared herself empress and colonel of the guards regiment. She had respect for them. It was not to be their last taste of regime change.

Empress Elizabeth I ruled the country as a Russian landowner—in a willful, madcap, cruel, and yet simultaneously kind manner. She had no legal spouse or children, so Elizabeth decided to make her nephew the heir to the throne. He was the son of her older sister and a Holstein prince, Karl Peter Ulrich, who became known as Grand Duke Petr Fedorovich.

Elizabeth found him a wife, a German princess named Sophia Fredericke Augusta, the daughter of one of the innumerable German princes in the service of Frederick the Great. Little Sophia was sent to distant Russia. On the way to St. Petersburg, she passed through Riga where the unfortunate Braunschweig family, overthrown by Elizabeth, were imprisoned.

In St. Petersburg the Lutheran Sophia Fredericke converted to Russian Orthodoxy and became Grand Duchess Catherine Alexeyevna. Thus began the Russian life of the fourteen-year-old girl who was to become Empress Catherine II the Great, Alexander's great-grandmother.

Subsequently, she described her early years in Russia in her famous "Notes," which would be read after her death by all the following tsars of the Romanov line. As we will see, they read them with horror.

With a jealous female gaze, Catherine admired the beauty of Empress Elizabeth, and naturally, the object of general envy, her incomparable long and shapely legs. Usually they were hidden by horrible crinolines and skirts. But once empress, Elizabeth came up with a way to show the world her best feature. Nocturnal masquerades were held, and the empress bade the ladies to appear in masculine garb. Her ladies-in-waiting were turned into tubby short-legged boys, while Elizabeth reigned over them as a tall, long-legged, handsome man.

Little Catherine gradually came to understand another reason for the all-night masquerades: fear of the guards, and the memory of the nocturnal revolution.

The story of how Elizabeth took power was a tempting example for the intelligent girl. By the time she was fifteen, Catherine understood the mediocrity of her husband and began bribing courtiers with gifts to create her own power base. She also learned about ruthless will from the empress. Elizabeth knew how to follow through to the end, like her father. Starting a war with Frederick the Great, the empress spent hundreds of thousands of soldiers' lives on the battlefield.

A series of failed battles nonetheless brought her success—his army was decimated. She was poised to beat Europe's greatest military leader, but, once again, death, the great mocker, intervened, and took Elizabeth, on the eve of victory.

The empress who had determined the fate of Europe was an ill-educated Russian landowner. She was sure that there was a land route to England. For all her strength and confidence, she was ridiculously fearful. Once, Catherine observed Elizabeth dressing down her minister. To soften her dangerous wrath, the court jester came in with his hedgehog. Seeing the hedgehog, the empress turned pale. She screamed, "It's a mouse! It's a real mouse!" Lifting her skirts, the empress of all Russia ran out of the room.

Even as she observed the incongruous traits of Elizabeth, little Catherine learned the most important fact: Elizabeth had managed to seize the throne. Studying Russia's secret history, the smart little girl discovered the most important rule of the empire: Unlimited autocracy in Russia was limited. It was limited by the will of the guards. In ancient Rome the Praetorian Guard decided who the all-powerful caesars would be. With good reason, Russia proudly called itself the Third Rome.

But her wretched husband Peter did not understand that.

Catherine's husband, Emperor Peter III, ascended the throne after the death of his aunt. Peter and Catherine were the first Romanovs to live in the Winter Palace, which had just been completed. The late empress Elizabeth had brought the Italian architect Rastrelli to build it, but she did not live to see its completion.

The new Winter Palace became the symbol of the house of the Romanovs. Built on the embankment of the rebellious Neva River, its main reception and ball rooms and facade face the river and the Fortress of Peter and Paul. Tsars were buried in the fortress, and the greatest enemies of the dynasty were incarcerated in its cells. This strange view from the palace would upset foreign visitors. Alexander's nephew, Grand Duke Alexander Mikhailovich, later recalled, "We came to St. Petersburg in the period of usual fogs, which would have made London envious.

'Your room is pleasant because,' explained our tutor, 'when the fog dissipates, you will see across the Neva the Fortress of Peter and Paul, where all the Russian tsars are buried.' I felt sad. It wasn't bad enough to have to live in this capital of fog, but there was also the proximity of corpses!"

For Catherine's husband, Emperor Peter III, that view of the prison was a fatal omen.

Portraits of Alexander II's great-grandfather depict him as a strong, broad-shouldered man in military uniform. In fact, Emperor Peter III, who adored the army, was weak, cowardly, and very kind. The compassionate emperor had all the victims of earlier revolts, the victims of the guards' attacks on the palace, returned from exile. A festive ball was held for the returnees from Siberian exile. All the former time-servers, the great intriguers, the lovers of past empresses, many of whom had tried to destroy one another, danced in the thousand-square-meter, all-marble White Ballroom of the Winter Palace.

One of the returned exiles said to the new emperor, "You are too kind, Your Majesty. Russians do not understand kindness, you must rule by knout or axe, that is the only time everyone is happy." Another returnee told Peter III: "Your Majesty, your kindness will destroy you."

It was not kindness that destroyed him. It was his neglect of the guards regiments. The simple emperor was mistakenly confident in the unlimited nature of Russian autocracy. And he did what he wanted. He decided to serve the man who was his idol and the idol of all enlightened Europe, Frederick the Great. At the moment that the Russian army was about to vanquish the Prussian king, he gave orders to conclude a peace treaty with him.

Soon rumors began to spread in the regiment barracks: The emperor was going to disband the Russian guards and create new guards regiments from his homeland in Holstein. The rumors were disastrous for the emperor. It was not hard to guess who was spreading them. Peter III and his wife, Catherine, were great enemies. Alexander's great-grandparents were fashioning conspiracies against each other. He was planning to send her to a convent; she was planning to send him to the next world. She turned out to be the better planner.

She received her secret lover, guardsman Grigory Orlov, in the Winter Palace. Her lover had four brothers, who were all courageous and beloved officers of the guards. They became conspirators, thanks to her relationship with the handsome officer. However, her body almost betrayed her. Catherine became pregnant. Peter learned of this from his spies, and decided to catch her giving birth. With proof of her infidelity, he could put her away in a convent. But Catherine solved the problem. When her time was due, she ordered a valet to set fire to his own house. The childish Peter adored fireworks and fires. He took off with his retinue to watch the house burn down. The newborn was sneaked out of the palace, wrapped in a beaver skin coat. By the time Peter returned, the iron-willed little woman, hemorrhaging, met him calmly and even gave him coffee.

At last came the day of the third (this time, morning) coup headed by the guards. It took place on the saint's day of the poor emperor. Catherine was living at the Peterhof Palace, and the emperor and the court were in another country palace, in Oranienbaum. Peter set out to Peterhof to visit his spouse, but Catherine was not there.

Early that morning, Alexei Orlov, brother of her lover Grigory, came for her by carriage from St. Petersburg. Alexei Orlov was a giant of a man, who could fell a bull with a blow of his fist. He was a celebrated duelist, and a Don Juan. As a contemporary said of him, "I wouldn't trust him with my wife or daughter, but I could perform great deeds with him."

Alexei Orlov found the empress in bed. He awakened her with the famous words, "The time has come for you to reign, Madame." Catherine hesitated. But according to legend, Alexei Orlov "poured great determination into her womb."

The carriage driven by the audacious Alexei Orlov rushed Catherine to St. Petersburg, where the guards were waiting for her. The guards swore their loyalty to the former German princess. The creation of one Peter, Peter the Great, the glorious guards regiments, prepared to overthrow another, his grandson.

The attack began in the style of the age that was called "gallant." The charming Catherine rode on horseback, in regimental uniform, wearing a hat ornamented with oak leaves. She led the march of the imperial guards.

Alexander's wretched great-grandfather felt lost instantly. His courtiers fled shamelessly. Only the celebrated field marshal Khristofor Minikh remained steadfast. The seventy-year-old military man suggested sailing to the island of Kronstadt, to the impregnable naval fortress. They would stay there, gather loyal troops, and return to win back St. Petersburg. Peter was delighted by the plan. He was as easily enthused as he was depressed. They loaded up a galley and a small sailboat with the remains of the terrified court, those who had not had time to run away. Ladies in extravagant dresses, flashing precious stones and gold, gentlemen in parade uniforms, all sailed to Kronstadt. But Catherine had planned for that, and Kronstadt had been taken by her supporters. The soldiers shouted from the fortress walls at the lawful emperor, telling him to get lost.

Peter broke down and wept. According to a contemporary account, "Old Field Marshal Minikh, overcome with indignation, shamed him. 'Can't Your Majesty die like an emperor before his troops? If you are afraid of a sword blow, hold a crucifix in your hands, and they won't dare harm you!'" But the emperor did not wish to die and he surrendered obediently. Catherine imprisoned her spouse at the charming country seat of Ropsha.

She saved his letters from captivity, and Alexander II would later read them. In the letters, the emperor of all Russia begged permission to go to the toilet without watch guards and "pleaded humbly for a walk." He humbly signed his letters to his wife, the Prussian princess who usurped the throne of his ancestors, "your servant Peter." Catherine did not reply. She was apparently waiting for his guardians to figure out how this gallant revolution was to end. They finally did.

A contemporary wrote: "Alexei Orlov, the brother of Catherine's lover, a giant with a cruel scar across his cheek, two meters tall, offered the former emperor a goblet of wine with poison. The wretch drank it, and flames coursed through his veins. This aroused suspicion in the overthrown emperor and he refused the next glass. But they used force, and he defended himself. In that horrible struggle, in order to stifle his cries, they threw him on the ground and grabbed his throat. But he defended himself with strength that comes with final desperation, and they tried to avoid wounding him [the body would have to be displayed at the funeral—E. R.]. They placed a rifle strap on the emperor's neck. Alexei Orlov kneeled with both legs on his chest and blocked his breathing. He passed away in their hands."

The official announcement in St. Petersburg was that the emperor "passed away from hemorrhoidal colic." Few believed it. When Catherine later invited Jean Le Rond D'Alembert to St. Petersburg, the famous Encyclopedist refused. He wrote to Voltaire, "I am subject to hemorrhoids, and that seems to be a fatal disease in Russia."

As if in revenge, Alexander's great-grandmother would die pathetically: She suffered a stroke while in the toilet. Her servants barely managed to pull her out, for her body was heavy and they had aged along with her. The empress was laid on a mattress on the floor of her room. Her physicians did not want her disturbed further.

She had captivated Europe. The minds of the French Encyclopedists, Voltaire, Frederick the Great, all the European monarchs, the Crimean khan, and the nomadic Kirghiz had been engaged by her. She had controlled European politics like a puppeteer. "And when she tugged, Europe jumped like a cardboard clown," wrote a contemporary. One of her generals put it accurately when he said proudly, "Not a single cannon in Europe dared shoot without our permission!" Now there she was, dying on the floor. "Do not store up for yourselves treasures on earth, where moth and rust destroy, and where thieves break in and steal."

The empress breathed hoarsely. The rattle could be heard in the next room, where her son, the new emperor, Paul I, had decided to have his study. The courtiers who hurried to the new master's study ran past the bedroom of the helpless ruler. They would open the door and boldly stare at the dying woman.

At ten o'clock, the British doctor came into Paul's study and announced that the empress was dying. Only a few candles burned, and in the darkness Emperor Paul I and his courtiers awaited the sacred moment. The clock struck the quarter hour when the great-grandmother of Alexander II finally breathed her last.

The late empress's papers were gathered in her Privy Cabinet. It was there that her son, Emperor Paul I, found a large sealed envelope addressed: "To his Imperial Highness Pavel Petrovich, my dearest son." The envelope contained Catherine's "Notes," his mother's memoirs. He began reading avidly, and then with horror.

Catherine had written about her life with unabashed frankness, in the spirit of Rousseau. The main protagonist of the great empress's "Notes" was her miserable husband. She described Peter III ruthlessly—as a pathetic, infantile man who fell in love with every new lady-in-waiting. The only exception was his own wife. He would not sleep with her, simply because he did not know how it was done. Thus for nine years she could not give birth to an heir, though the interests of the empire required it. Her lady-in-waiting finally brought a message from the empress Elizabeth: "There are situations when the *interests of higher importance* demand *exceptions to all the rules.*" She proposed that Catherine select a lover, which she did. Soon after, she gave birth to a son, the future emperor Paul.

We can imagine Paul's feelings upon reading his mother's "Notes." He put them into another envelope and sealed them up with his seal, to be seen only by the next heir. When Nicholas I, Alexander's father, ascended to the throne, he read the memoirs right away. He then called the great Catherine "the shame of the family" and forbade even members of the Romanov family to read the disgraceful "Notes."

Alexander would read them once he became emperor upon his father's death. After that, Alexander II wrote on the envelope: "Seal until requested." Apparently, he realized the ghastly point: Were they not Romanovs at all?

In Catherine's Privy Cabinet, a fragment of a letter that she had not destroyed remained among her papers. It was from her wretched husband. Peter III wrote, "Madame, I ask you not to worry that you will have to spend this night with me, because the time for fooling me has passed. . . . The bed has become too crowded for the two of us. After a two-week separation from you, your miserable spouse, whom you do not wish to honor with that name. . . ." Here the text breaks off. But the date remains. The letter was written the year after their marriage. That means that he had slept with her, and that Peter was not indifferent to her at all! It was she who must have felt revulsion toward him. She did not want to sleep with him, and he suffered, but did not dare complain to his aunt the empress.

It was only after Empress Elizabeth demanded an heir that Catherine had to overcome her revulsion and bear a son. Most likely, Paul I was the biological son of Peter III, after all. That is why Paul had his father's looks, and character, and even his habits. That is why Catherine disliked him so much, born of a hated spouse. She likely made up the whole story about a lover being Paul's real father, so that after her death, her son would not try to avenge his father or persecute her associates—the ones who killed his father and whom she valued so highly. That would have sown confusion in the empire that was her only true love. In her "Notes," Catherine remained what she always had been—a ruler.

But what if she had told the truth?

After her "Notes," the Romanovs became a mystery even to themselves.

Once on the throne, Paul ordered that Peter III be reburied with great pomp, so that everyone could see how he honored his father. Peter had been buried in the Alexander Nevsky Monastery. Catherine had deprived him of the right to lie in the Cathedral of Sts. Peter and Paul at the Fortress, where Russian tsars were to be buried. Paul had the remains of his father moved to the cathedral.

First, Paul brought the family in black funereal carriages to the Alexander Nevsky Monastery. The coffin was raised and opened. Alexander's great-grandfather had decomposed—his bones were scattered, his uniform had rotted, leaving only gloves, boots, and the hat on the skull. Paul made everyone in the family bring their lips to the sorrowful remains. Paul, his beautiful wife, and the children all kissed the horrible skull. Alexander's father, Nicholas, was only a few months old at the time. Even he was brought to the opened coffin.

The next day Peter III was to be reburied at the Fortress. Paul ordered his father's murderer, Count Alexei Orlov, to follow the coffin and carry the crown of the emperor he had killed. The catafalque moved slowly in the freezing cold. Behind it, on gouty legs, strode the old giant with a vicious scar across his face, bearing the crown on a raspberry velvet pillow. Many said then that the scar was made by Peter in his final death struggle, that he had torn Orlov's cutlass away from him and left that mark on his face.

The gigantic and sickly old man walked through half the city in the cold, delivering the crown to the Cathedral of Sts. Peter and Paul.

Terrible and great people lived in that century. Count Alexei Orlov was not known only for killing the tsar. During the war with the Turks, he commanded the Russian squadron. In the Bay of Chesmen, during a fierce battle, he burned down the entire Turkish fleet. It was the bloodiest naval battle of the century.

They were special people. The grandfather of Alexander was right to fear them.

Paul had the Mikhailovsky Castle built in the center of the city, surrounded by impregnable walls, water-filled moats, and sentries. But even with the castle, Alexander's grandfather still did not completely appreciate the threat of the guards regiments. Like his abject father, Peter III, Paul I had faith in the power of the sovereign. He proudly stated that "an aristocrat in Russia is someone with whom I am now conversing and for only as long as I converse with him." But the ruler of millions of subjects and master of a vast empire had forgotten history: His autocracy was limited, not by a constitution or a parliament, but by the stranglehold of the guards. He had forgotten his mother's discovery.

When he was heir to the throne, living in his palace at Gatchina, Paul created a mini army, as had his murdered father, Peter III. His Gatchina troops were trained in strict Prussian discipline. He began instilling that Gatchina discipline in Catherine's pampered guards. With a passion bordering on mania, he ruthlessly punished the Catherine guards for the tiniest infraction in uniform or marching. Whenever officers went out on parade or on guard duty, they took cash with them because very often Paul sent officers who displeased him directly from the royal grounds to regiments on the outskirts of the empire. In the most elite Horse Guards regiment, out of 132 of Catherine's officers, only two remained. Throughout his four-year reign, Paul seemed to be taking his revenge against his mother's guards for the death of his father. Not surprisingly, a conspiracy formed in the guards regiments.

One of the participants was Alexander's uncle, the first Alexander, who would vanquish Napoleon. He plotted against his own father. The conspirators had promised him that Paul would be unharmed. He would be made to abdicate and nothing more. How could the heir have believed that, knowing the fate of Peter III? Alexander forced himself to believe them.

Before murdering the emperor, the guards had a festive dinner. They drank a lot of wine. Their speeches and toasts carried eerie omens of the distant future. Life Guards Colonel Bibikov (whose relative had brought Catherine II to the throne) expressed an opinion that there was no point in just getting rid of Paul, it would be better "to be free of the whole royal family." But the other conspirators did not support him then.

At midnight, the drunken guards officers approached the secret entrance to the Mikhailovsky Castle. Among them were Catherine the Great's last lover, Platon Zubov, and his brother, Nicholas. They were led by Paul's favorite adjutant. The conspiracy was headed by Count Petr Palen, another of the emperor's favorites.

In dress uniforms, swords bared, they burst into Paul's bedroom. The bedroom was empty. Paul seemed to have escaped, which meant the end for them. While the officers panicked, one of the leaders, General Leonty Benigsen, tall and phlegmatic, leaned on the mantelpiece and looked around calmly. There were drapes in the corner of the enormous room. The general saw the sovereign's bare feet sticking out from beneath the drapes.

"*Le voilà!*" General Benigsen said with a laugh and pointed to the drapes. The guardsmen pulled the tsar out.

As often happens with despots, he quickly turned pathetic and helpless. Small and snub-nosed, wearing long white underpants and a long-sleeved nightshirt, he looked like a frightened boy. The drunken crowd attacked Paul. He fought them off feebly, begging for mercy, asking for time to say a prayer.

Count Nicholas Zubov, red-hot, huge, resembling a butcher, struck the tsar of all Russia in the temple with the corner of a gold snuffbox. Paul fell to the floor. According to one version, Zubov's French valet sat on Paul's stomach. Guardsman Yakov Skaryatin took off his officer's sash and they strangled him with it. And then they mocked the corpse drunkenly—kicking and beating the lifeless body of Alexander's grandfather.

They came outside to the soldiers guarding the castle and announced merrily: "The emperor died suddenly of apoplexy." And the soldiers shouted, "Hurrah! Long live Emperor Alexander!"

Paul was dressed in guard's uniform, the tricorn pushed forward over his face to cover the bruise from the snuffbox. Only then was the weeping widow permitted to bid him farewell. General Benigsen forcefully asked her, "Please do not draw out the farewell scene, which could harm the precious health of Your Majesty."

As in the case of Peter III, the announcement stated that the emperor had died suddenly and peacefully. The emperor's body lay in state at the Mikhailovsky Castle. But as Madame de Stael had written, "In Russia everything is secret, but nothing is unknown." St. Petersburg society rushed to look at the suddenly departed. The body was displayed cleverly. The famous journalist Nicholas Grech recalled, "I went to Mikhailovsky Castle a dozen times and could see only the soles of his boots and the brim of his wide hat, pushed low on his forehead. No sooner do you come in the door than they point to another: 'Move along.'"

That is how Alexander's uncle became Alexander I, future vanquisher of Napoleon. The new emperor did not dare act against the regicide guards. When guardsman Skaryatin hung his officer's sash on the back of his chair when he played cards, everyone tried to guess whether that was the very sash with which they strangled the father of the new emperor. General Benigsen became one of the army commanders in the war with Napoleon. When Alexander called Napoleon "a bloodthirsty monster," Bonaparte mockingly reminded the tsar about "the exploits of his commander in his father's bedroom."

The Romanov family had many legends about the martyred Paul I. In his favorite palace, Gatchina, there was a room with a door nailed shut. Inside was the bed from the Mikhailovsky Castle with blankets and pillows stained by the murdered emperor's blood. Servants insisted that they had seen the emperor's ghost wandering the formal rooms of the Gatchina Palace at night. The ghost allegedly appeared on the eve of fateful events.

Little Alexander dreamed of seeing his grandfather's ghost whenever he visited Gatchina. Olga, sister of the last Romanov tsar, Nicholas II, recalled in her memoirs how she and Nicky walked through the palace hoping for and fearing the sight of the restless soul. Grand Duke Nikolai Pavlovich, father of Alexander, is supposed to have seen the ghost on the most terrible day of his life.

The murdered Emperor Paul I had four sons. Two older boys, Alexander and Konstantin, and two younger ones, Nicholas (Alexander II's father) and Mikhail. Unlike their father, short and snub-nosed Paul, Alexander and Nicholas were athletic and handsome, with faces that belonged on medals. There would be many more handsome men born in the Romanov family. Paul's wife, the fecund princess of Württemberg (she gave Paul eight children), brought the Württemberg looks and stature to the royal line.

There were almost two decades in age difference and an abyss in education between the older brothers and the younger ones. Catherine the Great took the two older boys, Alexander and Konstantin, away from their father. "The best grandmother" supervised their education and invented an amusing primer for them, wrote fairy tales, and even designed "clothing beneficial for the health."

Catherine turned bringing up children into a political project. She wanted to pass her throne to her grandson Alexander, rather than her despised son, Paul. She intended Konstantin to become emperor of a revived Byzantium with its capital in Constantinople (hence the choice of his name), which she planned to win from Turkey. Russia and the liberated Balkan Slavs would then create the world's largest empire, a Slavic one. But she died before putting her plan into action.

The murder of Paul I implemented "the best grandmother's" plan for Alexander posthumously. Her favorite grandson became Emperor Alexander I. He would gain worldwide glory with his victory over Napoleon.

The older the victor grew, the deeper he plunged into black melancholy. He was tormented by the murder of his father and his part in the conspiracy. In 1819 he told his brother Konstantin, "I have to tell you that I am tired and no longer can bear the weight of ruler." That meant that Konstantin, as next in line, had to wear the crown.

Konstantin had loved his father. He had his father's snub nose and big blue eyes. He also had his hot temper. He could never forget that March night, when Prince Platon Zubov, his grandmother's former lover, came to his room right after the emperor's murder. Zubov shook him awake and made him get dressed, without any explanation. Konstantin thought they had come to kill him. But he was taken from Mikhailovsky Castle to the Winter Palace, where the conspirators declared his brother emperor.

Konstantin told guardsman Sablukov, "My brother can be tsar if he wants. But if the throne were to come to me, I would refuse it!" When his brother made his offer in 1819, he replied that he "was prepared to ask for a place as his second valet, just not to be the tsar on the throne!" He hastily wrote an official renunciation: "I do not feel I have the gifts, or the strength, or the spirit . . . etc."

The next in line was Nicholas, father of Alexander. Nicholas adored his brother Alexander and had great respect for Konstantin. He had named his own sons Alexander and Konstantin in their honor. But Nicholas had not been prepared for the throne. His education consisted solely of military training, which he excelled at. He was considered the martinet of the extended Romanov family. Even more dangerously, that was his reputation among the powerful guards regiments. Many of the capital's intellectuals were in the guards, and it was fashionable to despise "martinet Nicholas." Emperor Alexander understood the danger for Nicholas if he took the throne.

But there was no choice, and Alexander I went to see Nicholas. The tsar did not discuss it with him, he simply announced his will to his brother: in the case of his death, the throne went to him, Nicholas. The emperor added, "However, it might happen much sooner. I keep thinking more frequently of freeing myself of responsibility and moving away from worldly things. Europe needs young monarchs, at the peak of their power and energy, and I am no longer what I was."

Alexander's mother described their startled reaction to the emperor's news. "We listened to the Sovereign, like two statues, with open eyes and shut mouths." Like Konstantin, Nicholas was also afraid of the offered crown, stained as it was by the blood of his father and grandfather.

Alexander I had to calm him down. "The moment that will suit you has not yet come . . . it may be another ten years," he said in farewell, and left.

"We were thunderstruck. . . . In tears and sobbing over this horrible, unexpected news, we were silent," recorded Alexander's mother.

All over the world, brothers fought over the crown, even committed crimes to attain it. In Russia, brothers dreamed of only one thing: to give up the great kingdom. That was the result of the guards' attacks on the palace.

Word soon reached Alexander that the guards were hatching another conspiracy, another attack on the palace. In 1820, General Alexander

Benkendorf, chief of the guards corps staff, wrote a note, that is, a denunciation, to the emperor about the conspiracy. The victory over Napoleon had brought a very dangerous turn of events: The intellectual officers had caught revolutionary fever in France and brought it home to Russia. "Without understanding how to bring order to their own affairs . . . they wish to rule the state," wrote Benkendorf. He appended a list of the conspirators.

Alexander I, the mystic tsar, must have decided that this was retribution. The guards that had put him on the throne were now removing him. He left his fate in God's hands. Expressing regret that the conspirators had fallen "victim to the same French air of liberty that had delighted me in my youth," the emperor put the denunciation in his desk drawer. "I shared and supported those illusions, it is not for me to persecute them," he later said.

This was a very new kind of conspiracy in the old guards regiments. For the first time in a century, no one in the royal family participated. Like the old conspiracies, the plan called for killing the tsar, but this time, not in order to put a different tsar in place. This time, they wanted to declare a republic.

One of the main conspirators was Colonel Pavel Pestel, son of the Siberian governor general. He had fought Napoleon bravely. This Russian Robespierre, who wanted to found a republic, decided that for the security of the future republic not only the tsar but the entire royal family had to die, in order to avoid a civil war. The majority of the conspirators were kinder: They decided to leave the emperor on the throne if he agreed to a constitution. Thus, in snowy Russia, began the path that led to the destruction of a dynasty, the Bolsheviks, and the great schism of the world into two camps.

Further news of the conspiracy led the tsar to hasten toward a solution of the dynastic problems. On August 16, 1823, Alexander wrote a secret manifesto on succession. It named Grand Duke Nikolai Pavlovich, Alexander's father, as the heir to the throne. It was placed in a sealed envelope for safekeeping in Russia's main church, the Cathedral of Assumption in Moscow, where Russian tsars were crowned. Only a very

narrow circle knew about the manifesto. Alexander must have had some
hope that Konstantin could be persuaded to accept the throne. He did
not forget the attitude of the dangerous guards toward Nicholas.

Alexander I was almost never in Moscow. He attended all the meetings of the monarchs in the Holy Alliance who had fought Napoleon,
and he traveled aimlessly around the country. A contemporary wrote,
"He rules the country from a carriage." The emperor avoided the capital,
where the regiments were based.

In 1825 the "nomadic despot," as the poet Alexander Pushkin called
him, set out on yet another journey, to the small town of Taganrog,
where the southern climate would be gentler on the empress's weak
lungs. Leaving St. Petersburg late at night, the emperor drove first to the
Alexander Nevsky Monastery. In the darkness by the gates he was met by
a black row of monks headed by the metropolitan, the leader of Russian
Orthodox Christians. That was the start of the last church service the
emperor would see in his capital. During the gospel reading, Alexander I
suddenly sank to his knees and asked the metropolitan to lay the Bible
on his head. He prayed for a long time, weeping as he prayed.

In Taganrog, the emperor died swiftly and unexpectedly. The official
diagnosis has been preserved, but it is so vague that it is difficult to guess
what disease killed Napoleon's conqueror. The rumor that reached
Moscow right after the news of his death has also survived the centuries:
Alexander I did not die. Another corpse was in the coffin, and the
emperor went off to be a hermit in Siberia, to pray and repent for his terrible sin against his father.

The arrival of the coffin bolstered the rumor, since the coffin was not
opened when the emperor lay in state. This was the first time that the
court said its farewells to a ruler without seeing his face. Even Peter III
and Paul I, who had marks of violence upon them, were laid out to be
seen.

The court was told that the heat in Taganrog had caused the body to
decay. But everyone knew that the body had been embalmed. People

repeated the strange words of Prince Volkonsky, that "the Emperor's face, despite the embalming, had turned black and even the features had changed completely."

Only the royal family saw the open coffin. The final farewell took place in the chapel at Tsarskoye Selo after midnight. The priests were told to leave and sentries were placed at the doors. In the dim candle-light, the Romanovs saw the skeleton of the late tsar. Alexander, named for his uncle, was present at this secret farewell. He was seven years old.

Eleven years after the death of Tsar Alexander, a holy man appeared in Siberia called Fedor Kozmich. The austere man seemed to be a peas-ant, but he knew the customs of the court and he spoke foreign lan-guages fluently. It became clear from his stories that he had been in Paris with the victorious Russian army.

The most popular portrait of the mysterious elder showed a startling resemblance to Alexander I, although he never mentioned the tsar. As his popularity and rumors about him grew, the holy man saw his visitors less and less frequently, and the door to his monastic cell was more often locked.

Alexander II's mother noted in her diary that Alexander I had once said to her, in a conversation about his dream of renouncing the throne, "How happy I will be to see you driving past me, and I'll be in the crowd shouting Hurrah! at you and waving my hat."

CHAPTER 2

Heir to the Throne

When little Alexander was seven years old, two terrifying memories entered the consciousness of the impressionable, nervous child: the uncontrollability of nature and of men.

A great flood occurred in the last year of the reign of Alexander I. Alexander and his family were living in the Anichkov Palace, which later became the traditional home of every heir to the throne. It was on a night in November when the worst flooding on record took place in St. Petersburg. At 7:00 P.M. on the seventh, the signal lanterns to warn residents were lit on the Admiralty Spire, opposite the Winter Palace. A violent storm shook the night; wind gusts rattled the enormous windows of the Anichkov Palace. By morning the infuriated Neva River flowed onto the streets. The water roiled like boiling water in a kettle and the wind blew against the current. White foam swirled over the mass of water. Huge waves crashed on the flooded Palace Square.

The square and the Neva formed a giant lake, fed by the Nevsky Prospect, which had turned into a broad river flowing past the Anichkov Palace. The water of that "river" reached the balconies. Rats from the cellars raced up the marble staircases, leaping, squealing, running up toward safety.

A woman with a child floated on a large door past their windows, as soldiers in a boat tried to reach her. People climbed rooftops, clung to lampposts. The contents of a library floated out from a nearby house, the books bobbing in the waves outside their balcony. Sheets of metal, torn from the roofs by the hurricane-force winds, flew through the air.

Several days later, when the waters receded, little Sasha, as Alexander was known, was taken by his father to survey the city. The embankment in front of the Winter Palace was strewn with smashed ships. Sasha was given permission to climb up onto one and touch a real mast. On top of the ship's side was a coffin that had floated from the cemetery.

The unprecedented rebellion of the waters was a harbinger of more violence of the human kind a year later.

When the messenger from Taganrog brought the news of the death of Alexander I, Alexander's father immediately called the military governor of St. Petersburg, Count Mikhail Miloradovich. Nicholas told him of the late emperor's secret manifesto and his last wish, to hand the throne over to him, Nicholas.

But Miloradovich was well aware of the feelings of the guards, who did not like the martinet Nicholas. He also knew about the guards' conspiracy. They were all his friends. They were scions of Russia's greatest aristocratic families, brilliant officers who had fought Napoleon with Miloradovich.

The count warned Nicholas, "Unfortunately, no one knows of the secret manifesto, but everyone knows the law on succession. And everyone knows that according to the law, the throne belongs to Konstantin."

Alexander's father hastily, and apparently with great relief, agreed with Miloradovich. Nicholas hurriedly ordered the guards, the Senate, and the State Council to swear fealty to Konstantin. And he swore his, as well. That is how much he feared the dangerous throne.

But it was all in vain. A messenger galloped from Warsaw with a letter from Konstantin, who refused to be tsar. He wrote: "My previous intention is immutable." And he demanded that the late tsar's will, as expressed in the manifesto, be obeyed. Nicholas must become emperor.

The messenger galloped back to Warsaw from St. Petersburg. Understanding how strange it would seem otherwise, the dowager empress "begged on her knees for Konstantin to come to St. Petersburg and declare his renunciation of the throne openly."

The messenger hurried back from Warsaw to St. Petersburg. Konstantin refused to come to the capital (so worried they would persuade him to accept the throne). He asked his "beloved mother" to announce his renunciation on his behalf.

While messengers on troikas sped back and forth, the guardsmen realized that this moment of confusion over succession was the best time for a revolt.

At last, on December 13, the birthday of the late emperor Alexander, Nicholas decided to accept the will. He agreed to wear the crown. "What a day for me, Lord, determining of my fate," wrote Nicholas in his diary. That same day a sealed envelope was brought to him. "I opened it and learned of a horrible conspiracy. I had to take decisive measures," he recalled later.

The damned guards, who had killed his ancestors, were at it again. He knew what threatened him. Little Sasha was now the official heir to the throne. The next day, December 14, was the day his father was to take the oath. That same day, Nicholas wrote to his sister, "Pray to God for me. . . . Take pity on your wretched brother, victim of the Will of God and his two brothers."

That evening was filled with anxious debates among the conspirators. Some did not want to risk a mutiny, because they doubted its success. One—Count Rostovtsev—decided to take a desperate step. He told his fellow conspirators that he was particularly obliged to Nikolai Pavlovich and now, "foreseeing danger for his benefactor, decided to go to him and beg him not to accept the throne." All arguments to stop him were in vain.

The day after his meeting with the tsar, Rostovtsev brought a paper to the conspirators, entitled "The most beautiful day of my life." It was a description of his meeting with Nicholas, who welcomed him amiably.

Rostovtsev warned the tsar that "accepting the throne was very dangerous to him." He "said nothing more than that." Nicholas did not ask for
details, but thanked him and sent him away.

Rostovtsev had hoped that by revealing the conspiracy he would
force his comrades to give up their plans. He was wrong.

Now Nicholas knew for certain that there would be a mutiny. He
had no choice but to carry on. In the evening Military Governor of St.
Petersburg Miloradovich said to Prince Württemberg, a relative of
Nicholas on his mother's side, "I am anxious, because I do not expect
success from tomorrow. The guards love Konstantin."

"What do the guards have to do with success? There is the legal will
of the late tsar," said the prince.

Little did he know that the law of succession was subject to the will
of the guards.

The conspirators were in the barracks, feverishly preparing their soldiers for the mutiny. They could not speak of a republic, which so many
of them wanted, to the soldiers. When one of the officers told his soldiers that now they would have a republic, the soldiers immediately
wanted to know who would be tsar then.

"No one."

"Sire," they told him, "you know that is just not possible." As a Russian historian has written, "In Russia it was easier to imagine a country
without people than without a tsar."

According to legend, that night Nicholas had trouble sleeping, and
he wandered the corridors of the Winter Palace, tormented by insomnia.
A servant with a candelabra followed him. In the moonlit White Ballroom they saw a figure in a white nightgown. Nicholas froze in terror—
it was his father. In an instant, Paul vanished through the wall.

If this story is true, then that is the moment that imbued Nicholas
with the amazing determination he showed throughout the next terrible
day. That meeting for him was like Hamlet meeting his father's ghost. It
was a call for revenge against the descendants of the officers who had
killed his father and grandfather.

———

December 14 was not just another attack on the palace—it was a fight for a constitution. A great day for Russian liberals, and a watershed in Russian history.

Nicholas described what happened: "On that fateful day I awoke early. All the generals and regimental leaders of the guards were gathered at the Winter Palace." Nicholas read them the will of Tsar Alexander I and the renunciation of the throne by Konstantin Pavlovich. "Receiving from each commander an oath of loyalty and readiness to sacrifice himself, I ordered them to go to their men and have the guards take the oath."

The courtiers were "ordered to gather at the Winter Palace by 11:00 A.M." While they got organized, Nicholas went to his mother's rooms. He waited, on the alert.

It had begun. The conspirators had raised rebellion in the army barracks. They told the soldiers that the lawful emperor, Konstantin, to whom they had pledged their oath, had been forced to abdicate. Without their greatcoats, despite the December cold, warmed by the fiery speeches of their officers (and even more so by vodka), the guards rushed with loaded rifles to Peter (now Senate) Square, to defend the rights of Konstantin.

They lined up on the square near the Senate building, ten minutes' walk from the Winter Palace. The famous statue of Peter the Great on a rearing steed had its back to them. The great emperor seemed to be fleeing from them.

The soldiers shot into the air and shouted: "Long live Konstantin and Constitution!" The Russian word, *konstitutsiya,* takes a feminine ending, and the officers explained the unfamiliar term as the name of Konstantin's wife.

No sooner had Nicholas entered his mother's rooms than (according to Nicholas) "Major General Neigardt, chief of staff of the Guards Corps, appeared and announced that the Moscow Regiment was in complete mutiny."

All the dignitaries had gathered at the Winter Palace. "But I had to keep the true situation from them, especially from Mother [who had already seen the guards at work, murdering her husband, Paul I—E.R.]." But Nicholas did not keep the truth from his wife. "I looked in on my wife and told her, 'There is trouble in the Moscow Regiment; I am going there.'"

He remembered the fate of his father and grandfather; he had no doubt that this was a life or death moment. And not only his death, but that of his entire family. He was enraged. Though he wrote that "Thoughts came to me by inspiration," more likely, he had thought through the situation in those anxious days before he took the oath, when he learned of the conspiracy.

He took action. He sent the regimental commanders gathered at the palace back to the barracks to bring out the regiments of loyal guards. He sent generals to the square to persuade the mutineers to disperse. He gave orders, then tossed his greatcoat over his shoulders and ran out of the palace.

He encountered a huge crowd of gawkers on Palace Square. "The procession toward the palace had begun, and the square was filled with people and carriages."

A crowd that size in front of the palace was dangerous; it could easily be incited to turn into a mob. They could head over to the rebels on Senate Square or (more terribly) attack the defenseless palace. "I had to distract the people with something unusual. . . . I had to win time to allow the troops to gather."

Nicholas began reading the manifesto of his succession to them. The crowd was thrilled to see the tsar addressing them in person. People applauded and roared hurrahs, drowning out the sound of shots from the mutinous square.

After he finished reading the manifesto, Nicholas experienced "the most terrible moment." He saw a troop of guards running toward the Winter Palace. "A crowd of life grenadiers, led by officer Panov, was coming to take over the palace and in case of resistance to destroy our entire family."

But at just that moment, loyal troops appeared in the courtyard—the Sapper Battalion, standing behind the new emperor. Seeing "strangers," as they called guards loyal to Nicholas, the grenadiers turned back and ran to the square. That minute was the salvation of the family. Nicholas writes that he "saw a sign—God's mercy." Then came the battalion of the loyal Preobrazhensky Regiment. Nicholas got on his horse and led the battalion to Senate Square.

One hundred meters along, by the arch of the General Staff Building, he saw the guards of the Grenadier Regiment. They were walking without officers and not in military line. They were a huge crowd with banners.

"As we approached them, I wanted to stop the grenadiers and have them take formation. But in response to my 'Halt!' they shouted at me: 'We are for Konstantin!' I pointed them to Senate Square." He could not engage in battle in front of the palace, to be seen by his unsuspecting mother and dignitaries. "My heart froze so many times during that day . . . and only thanks to God's support I got through it."

Nicholas would never forgive the rebels for his humiliating fear.

He gave orders to move the children from the Anichkov Palace to the Winter Palace. As usual Sasha was at his lessons with the governor, Captain Merder, when the carriage came for him. The boy was quickly dressed and taken to the Winter Palace. Nicholas also had them "ready country equipages for Mother and my wife." He had decided "that if events are still threatening to send them with the children out of the city to Tsarskoye Selo."

In the meantime, Alexander sat in the study of his late uncle, Alexander I, with his mother and grandmother. Hungry, the boy was cranky. They brought him a meat patty. He realized that something was going on, for he could feel the tension of the adults. He ate his patty.

By this time, Nicholas was joined by the generals who had returned from the square. They told him bad news: There were more rebels—added to the Moscow Regiment were the two-meter-tall grenadiers and the Naval Regiment of the guards. The police were frightened into inaction, taking a wait-and-see position. The laborers building St. Isaac's

Cathedral hailed the rebels and threw stones at the tsar's ambassadors, the generals.

Count Miloradovich, the governor of St. Petersburg, went to Senate Square to negotiate. The news came back almost instantly that he had been killed. Miloradovich had fought the entire war against Napoleon, he had been in every battle, without ever being wounded. He was nicknamed "Lucky," only to be killed not by enemy fire, but by his own people. He fought in all the capitals of Europe only to die in his own.

The only good news was that the rebels were staying in Senate Square. That gave Nicholas the time he needed to gather loyal troops around him.

He did not want to begin his reign in bloodshed. He sent his youngest brother, Grand Duke Mikhail, to talk to the rebels, but they would not let him speak, and it was a miracle that they did not kill him. A madman shot at him twice; both times the gun would not fire. Then Nicholas, surrounded by the Preobrazhensky Regiment, headed for the square to persuade them himself, but the rebels would not let him approach. "They shot at me; the bullet flew over my head and fortunately no one was wounded. The laborers of St. Isaac's began tossing lumber at us over the fencing."

It was then that Nicholas sent the Horse Guards to attack the rebels, who easily fought them off with rifle fire.

It was getting dark. "I had to make the decision to put a swift end to this, otherwise the mob might join the rebels and then the troops surrounded by the mob would be in the most difficult circumstances."

Alexander's mother and grandmother were terrified. While Sasha ate his meat patty, they were imagining the worst. His grandmother was now fully informed. Twenty-four years earlier she had seen the mutilated body of her husband, the emperor. Now she might have to look upon the corpse of her son, the emperor. Sitting with her was Nicholas's wife, worried to death, knowing the names of all the Russian tsars killed by the guards. Alexander's mother developed a lifelong nervous tic over that day's events.

Unable to stand the uncertainty, she asked Nikolai Mikhailovich

Karamzin, the famous writer and historian who was inside the palace for the festivities, to go see what was happening.

Nikolai Karamzin was a brilliant writer, the leader of the sentimental vein in Russian literature, who betrayed his muse of fiction at the height of his career. He served a new muse, the divine Clio, and became a historian. This career brought him immortality, as he realized his dream "to animate Russian history." The first edition of his history of Russia sold out in twenty-five days. It was a revelation for the Russian public and became a source of inspiration for future Russian writers, and naturally an object of ruthless criticism for professional historians.

That day the brilliant writer and historian saw with his own eyes a fateful moment in Russian history.

Karamzin returned and told them about the rebel regiments on the square, just a ten-minute walk from the Winter Palace. He told them that the mob around the square hailed their success with delighted cheers and threw stones at him when he tried to reach the rebels. In his haste to get back (perhaps he had been forced to run for his life), Karamzin lost a heel. Now he paced the formal room in his socks. He was in a panic: "Is Peter's city really going to fall into the hands of three thousand half-drunken soldiers, mad officers, and the mob?"

Nicholas made one last attempt to persuade the rebel regiments. He sent to the palace for the metropolitan, who was preparing for a religious service for Nicholas's ascension to the throne. Now, instead, the metropolitan in his formal vestments headed for the square to talk to the rebels. They awaited his return anxiously at the palace. He returned frightened, threatened by gunfire and chased from the square.

A bloody decision was made. "Adjutant General Vasilchikov (commander of the guards) turned to me and said, 'Your Majesty, there is nothing to be done: we need grapeshot!'

"'Do you want me to spill the blood of my subjects on the very first day of my reign?'

"'In order to save your empire,' Vasilchikov replied."

This is how Nicholas remembered it. But this is most likely the version all rulers use to explain bloodshed; they oppose, but their advisors insist.

In fact, Nicholas liked history and knew Bonaparte's reaction when he watched the mob storm the French king's palace. "What an ass the king is! It wouldn't take more than a battery to disperse these scoundrels!" (The vanquished Napoleon remained an idol of the victorious Russian officers.)

Nicholas commanded the cannon himself. He thirsted for revenge for his father and grandfather, and most of all, for his fear.

Inside the Winter Palace, the dignitaries in their ribbons and medals sat along the walls and awaited the results of the battle. Suddenly the palace's tall windows were illuminated, as if by several bolts of lightning at once, followed by distant thunder. The cannon were shooting. The first was a warning shot over the rebels' heads that struck the Senate building. The cannonball stuck in the wall, and Nicholas did not permit its removal for several years, as a reminder to hotheads. The rebels responded with scattered fire and shots of "Hurrah Constitution! Hurrah Konstantin!"

Hearing the cannon fire, Alexander's grandmother exclaimed, "Oh, my God! What will Europe say about us! My son is ascending the throne in blood!" But his youngest brother, Mikhail, soothed their beloved mother.

"It's bad, impure blood!" he assured her.

Everyone happily made the sign of the cross. The dignitaries understood that a real master had appeared: a strict tsar. Sasha was told by his mother to bless himself. Then his father came in, embracing grandmother, mother, and children. They all headed to the Big Church, where they knelt and said thanks for the deliverance.

Then little Alexander was dressed in a tiny parade Hussar uniform, and his grandmother's valet carried him out to the palace courtyard. His father and the guards awaited him in the bonfire light. They were men from the Sapper Battalion that had saved the palace.

Nicholas raised his son in his arms and exclaimed, "Here, boys, this is my heir, serve him faithfully!" And they responded, "Hurrah! Long live Grand Duke Alexander Nikolayevich!" And then Nicholas ordered the first man from each company to step forward to kiss him, which was done. They came up in turn to kiss the boy, scraping him with their rough cheeks and enveloping him in the smell of cheap shag. Little Sasha wept. He did not like it.

The mutineers of that December became known as the Decembrists in Russian history. The Russian intelligentsia has loved them ever since.

But the Decembrists left us a puzzle. Why did they just stand on the square in that strange inactivity? Why didn't they attack the palace before the loyal troops got organized?

The answer lies in the nature of the conspiracy. It was easy for them to dream of liberty over cards and punch, at balls and in salons. But then they saw it in action—the drunken ignorant soldiers who believed that Konstitutsiya was Konstantin's wife and the mob that was on the verge of rioting. The mob was picking up the lumber from the construction site of St. Isaac's in preparation for attacking the city and looting it. That was when the bloody specter of the French Revolution rose above the rebel square, the specter of Terror. The Decembrists felt fear. Not knowing what to do, the guards' intellectuals and handful of civilian intelligentsia shuffled their feet mindlessly until the cannons roared.

Before bedtime, little Alexander was taken to say good night to his papa. The room was brightly lit by candles. An arrested guards officer stood before his father. His hands were tied by the officer's sash (just like the one used to strangle Emperor Paul). On a sofa next to a small table sat an old general, who took down the prisoner's statement. The emperor himself led the interrogation.

All night, while Sasha slept soundly, the leaders of the Decembrist uprising were brought to his father's study.

Later that room became Sasha's schoolroom.

The next morning was their first in the Winter Palace, now home for little Alexander. His governor, Karl Merder, led him through the rooms.

Their private rooms ended at the bronze-covered doors. An enfilade of formal halls followed. Beyond the windows lay the Neva River, constrained by ice. The low, bloody winter sun hovered over the Neva. The ice glittered. The gold and silver plates hung by the doors glistened and so did the brass helmets of the cavalry guards. They stood at attention by the columns, as immobile as the columns themselves.

Only people close to the royal family were permitted to enter past the cavalry guards into the private family rooms. Empress Elizabeth had installed them there. There had been cavalry guards on post for the last half century.

Alexander's grandmother continued to care about Europe's opinion, but Nicholas calmed her. He wrote his own account for Europe: "At the time when the residents of the capital learned to their great joy that Tsar Nikolai Pavlovich had accepted the ancestral crown, on this long-awaited day there was a sad event, which for just a few hours upset the tranquility of the capital. At the time that the new Tsar was met everywhere by expressions of sincere love and loyalty, a handful of vile-looking scoundrels in frock coats . . ." And that was it. There was no rebellion, no shooting, no cannons. There was an unpleasant event, nothing more. It was not the guards who had mutinied, but a few civilian scoundrels.

The situation remained grim, however. In the first round of interrogations, Nicholas learned that the most notable families of Russia were involved in the conspiracy, descendants of the pre-Romanov rulers Rurik and Gedemin—Volkonsky, Trubetskoy, Obolensky and other families that were part of Russian history. They were brought for questioning from flood-damp cells of the Fortress of Peter and Paul to the Winter Palace, where they had so recently attended balls and duty tours, covered in military orders for their exploits in the war with Napoleon.

Nicholas was not yet thirty. He knew that he was unpopular in the capital. Next to him was his terrified, unhappy wife, who spoke Russian poorly. Outside the palace, the short winter days with long, dangerous nights helped St. Petersburg to seethe with hostility. It was filled with the powerful relatives of the men now incarcerated in the fortress. Nicholas expected a strike in response from the arrogant St. Petersburg elite, whose ancestors had killed his grandfather and father. He expected a continuation of the uprising.

But the unexpected occurred. The cannons and rifles had an instant sobering effect on society. "From all sides came cries of delight: 'Victory! Victory!' As if a foreign army had been vanquished instead of a handful of fellow countrymen. There were church services held for the salvation of the Homeland! Former friends, brothers, and lovers were now called 'state criminals,' and fathers readily led their children to their punishment. There was a flood of volunteers to play executioner," wrote a contemporary.

Most zealous of all were the people known as "liberals." It was then that Nicholas learned an important law of Russian life: If the ruler is firm and the retribution is ruthless, those who had been the boldest become the most cowardly. That is why Nicholas decided to bring the main liberals into the uprising inquiry.

As it turned out during the investigation, the conspirators had wanted to make the famous Count Mikhail Speransky the future leader of republican Russia. The late Alexander I had dreamed of great reforms at the start of his reign—he wanted to emancipate the serfs. Count Speransky had been his chief advisor. He had a great mind. Napoleon had jokingly suggested that Tsar Alexander exchange Speransky for a kingdom of his choice. But when Alexander came to hate his youthful infatuations, he sent the count into exile, where he remained for six years, a symbol of liberal ideas.

Nicholas put Speransky in charge of the Supreme Criminal Court to determine the punishment for the Decembrists. Speransky, the great liberal, created such a long list of candidates for the gallows that Nicholas could appear merciful. He shortened the list significantly. But five were still condemned to death. Once again the emperor could show mercy—he replaced the medieval punishment of drawing and quartering, recommended by Speransky, with ordinary hanging.

There had been no executions in Russia since the reign of Elizabeth.

The empress had vowed to God to repeal the death sentence if her uprising was successful. Now the strict tsar revived the practice. But something intolerable had occurred in the interim—they had forgotten how to hang people. The gibbet was made too high, so that school benches had to be brought from the Merchant Marine School, located nearby. The five condemned Decembrists walked up the steps to the gallows and then stood on the benches under the ropes. The nooses were wrapped around their necks, but the second the executioner left the gallows, the bridge collapsed. Two were hanged, but the other three fell down into the gaping hole, hitting the steps and benches.

Despite custom, it was decided to hang them once again. The bridge was repaired and the wretched three were brought up again.

Colonel Muravyev-Apostol, hero of the war against Napoleon, said as he went up the gallows again, "Damned country, where they don't know how to form a conspiracy, hold a trial, or hang people!" To a drum roll, the nooses were placed once more, this time successfully.

The rest of the participants were sentenced to hard labor, reduced in rank, and stripped of nobility. The once-dashing guards officers found themselves in the mines of Siberia in horrible conditions.

Throughout Nicholas's reign, he was begged to pardon the Decembrists. But he was implacable. And when eleven women, the wives and fiancées of the sentenced men, decided to follow them to Siberia, Nicholas did his utmost to punish them, too. They lost not only the privileges of nobility, but also the most ordinary civil rights.

Society zealously distanced itself from the rebels. It even resorted to the saving grace of sarcasm: "In Paris the cobbler revolts to become a landowner—that's understandable. In Russia, when the nobility makes a revolution, is it because they want to be cobblers?" wrote Countess Rostopchina, once an acquaintance of the sufferers.

Having suppressed the uprising, Nicholas learned the lesson of how to rule Russia. He tried to pass the wisdom to his son: "In Europe the ruler must have the art of being sometimes fox, sometimes lion. That is what General Bonaparte taught politicians. In Russia, he must be only the lion."

The rout of the Decembrists proved to be the end of the guards' political role. There were no more attacks on the palace. Now the obedient troops worked assiduously on their training. Nicholas made the guards look like a corps de ballet. And as funny as it may sound, he made the ballet resemble the guards. During a production of *Abduction from the Seraglio,* the corps de ballet had to portray janissaries. Nicholas ordered that the ballerinas be taught to handle sabers. Junior officers were sent to the ballet to give instruction. The ballerinas treated it as a joke, but Nicholas would not put up with insubordination, even from ballerinas. It was a matter of principle. It was in the middle of winter, and the tsar passed word that noncompliant dancers would be sent outdoors to practice in the cold in their ballet slippers. Everyone complied.

During Nicholas's reign, not even a fly dared take to the air without his approval.

In the Summer Garden, a sentry stood in the middle of a meadow. Nicholas once asked why there was an armed guard there and what was he guarding? No one could tell him. They finally found an old adjutant general, who recalled what his father had told him: One day Catherine the Great was strolling in the Summer Garden and saw the first snowdrop poking through the snow. She asked that the flower be protected while she continued her walk. Since the empress did not rescind the order, a sentry stood on the spot for the next half century.

Nicholas enjoyed the story very much. He told it to Bismarck, who was then ambassador to Russia. He added that, during the great floods in St. Petersburg, sentries who had not been ordered to leave their posts had stayed and died as the waters rose.

An order from the Russian sovereign was an order forever. Nicholas wanted this to be understood not only by soldiers but by the entire country.

This was the man who ruled Russia for thirty years. And for those thirty years Alexander was to live as heir to the throne.

CHAPTER 3

His Father's Empire

The new emperor became one of the most awesome tsars in Russian history. Having dealt with the guards, Nicholas came to a sad conclusion: None of the Romanov governments before him had known what was happening in their own capital.

The conspiracy and murder of his grandfather, Peter III, and the conspiracy and murder of his father, Paul I, were the most glaring examples. Numerous people took part, but the poor sovereigns learned about them in their final hour. The Decembrist plot had gone on for several years. Yet the uprising had not been prevented, and it could have been disastrous for the dynasty. The previous secret police force in Russia had "proven its paltriness," in Nicholas's words.

Nicholas decided to create a new, efficient secret police force. All subsequent Russian special agencies came out from beneath Nicholas's greatcoat, to paraphrase Pushkin on Gogol's seminal short story.

The tsar envisioned an agency that would be able to not only discover a developed conspiracy, but signal its conception; that would not only learn the sentiments of the public, but know how to manage them. It would be an institution that could nip sedition in the bud and punish not only actions but thoughts.

And in the bowels of the Imperial Chancellery, the mysterious Third Department was born. Count Alexander Khristoforovich Benkendorf was the guards general who wrote to Alexander I to denounce the Decembrists, some of whom were acquaintances of his. His report, which had been ignored, was found among the papers of the late tsar.

The new emperor read it, and was much more attentive. Nicholas invited Benkendorf to work on the creation of the Third Department and then to be its chief. He was quickly becoming the tsar's new favorite.

Chief Director Count Benkendorf reported to and was subordinate only to the tsar. Moreover, all the ministries were controlled by the Third Department. St. Petersburg did not at first grasp the all-encompassing nature of the new agency. When the tsar explained the aims of the Third Department, he handed Benkendorf a handkerchief and said, "Use this handkerchief to dry the tears of the unjustly injured."

The public applauded. But it soon became apparent that before drying the tears of the innocent, Count Benkendorf would inspire copious tears in the eyes of the guilty. And not only the guilty, but those who might be guilty.

The staff of the Third Department was misleadingly small, just a few dozen people. But it was given an entire army, which came to be called by the French word *gendarme*. The Third Department had its Separate Gendarme Corps, and the chief director was also the chief of this political police force.

It was only the tip of the iceberg. The main force of the Third Department was its invisible secret agents. They enveloped the country; they were everywhere—in the guards, the army, the ministries, in brilliant St. Petersburg salons, in theaters, at masquerade balls, and even in society bordellos. The invisible ears were listening. "They're in my soup," complained a contemporary.

Members of the elite became informers, some as a career move, others, because they found themselves in difficult straits: men who lost at cards and women involved in dangerous adultery.

The kind-looking blue eyes of the chief of the secret police now watched everything. The unheard-of occurred: The tsar permitted Benkendorf to reprimand Grand Duke Mikhail himself, for his dangerous puns. The tsar's youngest brother raged impotently.

Serving in the secret police was considered quite reprehensible, but Nicholas forced men from the best families to work in the Third Department. To make the light blue uniform of the gendarmerie acceptable in society, he kept Count Benkendorf at his side in his carriage when he went out for rides in the city. With every year, "with Germanic tenacity and precision, Nicholas tightened the noose of the Third Department around the neck of Russia," wrote the great Russian essayist Herzen. Literature came under the purview of the secret police, because the tsar knew that sharp words had started rebellions in Europe.

Nicholas banned writers from criticizing the government and even from praising it. As he put it, "I've cut them off once and for all from interfering in my work." Stringent censorship was put in place. Anything with a shade of double meaning or that could weaken the sense of "loyalty and voluntary submission to higher authority and the law" was ruthlessly excised from print. Words crossed out by the censors could not be replaced with ellipses, either, lest the reader "fall into the temptation of thinking about the possible contents of the banned part."

A certain sense of responsibility for the printed word was introduced permanently into the consciousness of Russian writers, yet their responsibility was not before God or conscience, but before Emperor and State. An author's right to a personal opinion that differed from the state's was declared "bizarre and criminal."

Gradually Russian writers stopped imagining a true literature. The great victim of censorship, the liberty-loving Pushkin, wrote in all sincerity:

> I would not wish, by a false idea seduced,
> To disparage censors with offhand abuse
> What's opportune for London is for Moscow oversoon.
>   (Translated by Anya Kucharev.)

The last line took on life as a proverb.

Many writers worked as censors, including the great poet Tyutchev and the novelists Aksakov and Senkovsky. Benkendorf, not known for his love of literature, was now forced to read a lot. The elderly Baltic

German's sad, crumpled, and weary face was bent over manuscripts he hated. The tsar read manuscripts, too. The tsar and the chief of the Third Department became Russia's supreme censors.

Scary stories started spreading about the Third Department. It was said that in the building on Fontanka Canal, "Sheshkovsky's room," with its special floor, was still in use.

In the reign of Catherine the Great, Sheshkovsky was the unofficial chief of the secret police. The empress, who corresponded with Voltaire, had done away with torture, but the whip survived. Sheshkovsky found a handy use for it. A free-thinking nobleman would be called in for a talk. Sheshkovsky would be extremely amiable, offer a comfortable chair, and then give a mild lecture. The person being rebuked would think that he was getting off lightly, when Sheshkovsky would turn to the abundance of icons in his office and pray fervently and loudly. The floor beneath the erring gentleman would suddenly sink down and the chair seat fall away, exposing his nether regions to people armed with switches. Stealthy hands would pull away his trousers and the nobleman would be whipped long and hard, like a slave, until his buttocks bled. The miserable victim would scream in pain and damn Sheshkovsky, who continued at his prayers.

Then the same hands would pull up the victim's trousers, smooth his shirt, and send the chair back up. Sheshkovsky would turn and gently resume the conversation as if nothing had happened.

This would not be the end of the affair. Soon the regiment (thanks to Sheshkovsky) would learn of the incident. A nobleman whipped was a nobleman dishonored, and he would be forced to retire from the army.

Benkendorf played at being Sheshkovsky, gazing kindly at the men he interrogated tenderly yet ruthlessly.

As usual in Russia, when you can't blame the tsar you blame the lackey. Everyone believed that Benkendorf himself had created the unprecedented might of the secret police. Periodically a happy rumor would circulate that the "executioner of thought" Benkendorf had lost the tsar's favor. For instance, after the dueling death of the great poet Pushkin, it was thought that the tsar was wrathful and that because Benkendorf had not been able to prevent the duel that destroyed the genius of Russian literature, he would be forced to retire.

Funnily enough, the chief of the Third Department believed the rumor, too. He did what every official in Russia resorts to in a moment of the tsar's anger—he became "direly ill." People gloated. But the tsar came to visit the patient, which prompted a traffic jam at Benkendorf's house. Everyone who had gleefully awaited his downfall the day before now hastened to show sympathy for his illness. Hundreds of visiting cards were left in the reception room.

It had been yet another test of the public's docility. Benkendorf, like all ministers, was a puppet in Nicholas's hands. Yet when Benkendorf died, the tsar had his bust sculpted and placed in his office as a reminder of how much the tsar valued his police.

Nicholas treated Russia like a teacher with eternally mischievous children. He was very strict and took care that the children not grow up too much. They were easier to handle that way. As his minister of education Uvarov used to say, "If I can extend Russia's childhood another fifty years, I will consider my mission accomplished."

Soon afterward, the tsar summed up in satisfaction, "In Russia everything is silent because it is flourishing."

"At first we feverishly wanted to be heard. But when we saw that they were not fooling with us; that they demanded silence and inaction from us; that our talent and intelligence were doomed to grow torpid and rot at the bottom of our souls, . . . that any bright thought was a crime against the social order, when, in a word, we were told that educated people were pariahs in our society; and that . . . a soldier's discipline was considered the only principle—then our entire young generation became morally depleted." So wrote Alexander Nikitenko in his famous diary. He was a very wise critic who had to work as a censor. Nikitenko was sent to the guardhouse more than once for his attempts, in his words, "to give secret aid to literature," that is, for being insufficiently vigilant. His diary is an eloquent account of how the reign of Nicholas killed talent and energy and made people believe that the "only wisdom was silence and patience."

The emperor's physical appearance embodied the majesty of power. "Nicholas was handsome, but his beauty radiated cold; there is no face that reveals as ruthlessly a man's character as his face. . . . The features expressed implacable will and weak thought, more cruelty than sensitivity. But most important are his eyes," wrote Alexander Herzen.

Nicholas's regal gaze was remembered by his courtiers to their dying day. Alexander, his son, practiced the autocrat's merciless gaze, "which had the quality of a rattlesnake to freeze the blood in your veins."

Alexander's father, while not endowed with a profound mind or education, had monstrous willpower and capacity for work. He labored in his first-floor office at the Winter Palace until late at night. He slept there, too, in spartan quarters, on an iron camp bed, covered by a soldier's greatcoat. That was to stress yet again that Russia was a military state. As he fell asleep in his office on the camp bed, he could see the marble face of his faithful hound Benkendorf.

Besides creating the secret police, Nicholas made one more great contribution to the establishment of a totalitarian state. In his reign a formula was produced that survived the empire: "Autocracy, Orthodoxy, and Nationality were the three pillars on which Russia was to stand." The formula was invented by Minister of Education Uvarov and it became the basic ideology of Nicholas's Russia. Alexander would be reminded of it more than once.

The third mainstay of the formula in Russian is *narodnost'*, traditionally translated as "nationality," which has no equivalent in English. It means being based on the *narod,* the people, and therefore has overtones of the peasantry, as in German, the *Volk.* In the Russian Empire, where the highest levels of society spoke French and the most influential part of the court was made up of German families and where the tsars had 90 percent German blood, it seemed an odd conceit.

But in fact, it was a brilliant invention. The servile, docile, and hounded public was given a necessary toy—great pride. The country of serfs, who could be bought and sold or gambled away, was declared the crown of civilization. Innumerable writings described the imminent collapse of rotten, obsolete Europe, which only Russia could save with an influx of fresh blood. Some of the discourse lapsed into the comical—for instance, Nadezhdin, the editor of the liberal journal *Telescope,* praised "the mightiness of our Russian fist," as compared with the puny European fist. Millions of serfs, suffering daily beatings, would attest to its might.

Naturally, the tsar's beloved creation, the Russian army, supposedly the greatest in the world, was also praised. The army consisted of serf recruits, also with no rights, who were subjected to cruel corporal punishment.

Autocracy was pronounced the main reason for Russia's incomparable greatness. The Russian people were the people of the great tsars, and the Russian tsars were the heirs of the biblical kings. "Only Autocracy corresponds to the spirit of the Russian people," declared Nicholas.

The grandeur of autocracy and nationality was complemented by the idea of the grandeur and immutability of Russian Orthodoxy, inseparable from autocracy. In fact, it was the remnants of paganism remaining in Orthodoxy that were inseparable from autocracy. Just as the Roman Caesar was a religious leader, the Russian tsar, taking the title of Caesar, was head of the church. Like Caesar, the tsar was a pagan god. When Nicholas addressed the troops, the soldiers blessed themselves, as if before an icon. Railroad watchmen who met the train carrying Alexander II knelt and made the sign of the cross. The courtiers were no different from these simple folk, and they too perceived the tsar as a living deity.

"No one was better created for the role of autocrat than [Nicholas I]. His impressive handsomeness, regal bearing, and severe Olympic profile—everything down to his smile of a condescending Jupiter, breathed earthly deity. There was something solemn and reverential in the palace air. People spoke in hushed tones and were slightly bowed . . . in order to appear more obliging . . . everything was imbued with the presence of the lord." So wrote lady-in-waiting Anna Tyutcheva in her diary.

The triad—Autocracy, Orthodoxy, and Nationality—took on immortality in Russia. When Stalin created the Bolshevik empire, he said, "The Russian people need a God and a Tsar." He made himself tsar and god and turned Marxism-Leninism into a new religion. The great paradox was that the Bolshevik empire, created by Russian radicals, had an amazing resemblance to the empire of their hated Nicholas I. The words of Alexander Herzen, pronounced in the middle of the nineteenth century, were indeed horribly prophetic: "Communism is merely Nicholas's barracks transformed."

Such was the world of iron-willed Nicholas, in whose shadow Alexander spent three decades.

CHAPTER 4

How to Bring Up a Caesar

Alexander grew up in a happy family. His parents made a handsome couple: Nicholas, the indomitable giant, and his wife, Empress Alexandra Fedorovna, frail and gentle, with azure eyes. This difference helped create the great harmony of their marriage. They were the first Nicholas and Alexandra on the throne, and they loved each other as tenderly as the last crowned Romanovs, Nicholas II and his Alexandra. However, there was a certain nuance in their love. But more about that later.

Next to the magnificent Peterhof Palace, which rivaled Versailles, Nicholas had built a small cottage, which he called Alexandria, in honor of his wife. There the tsar got away from his cares and the grandiose columns, marble, and gilt of the imperial palaces. Here the children lived. It featured low ceilings, small rooms with many paintings on the walls, and a cozy study for Nicholas on the second floor with a marvelous endless vista of the gulf. Meadows and forests surrounded them.

In 1825, the imperial heir, Sasha, was in his eighth year, and it was time to start the tsarevich's education seriously. A family council decided unanimously to make Vassily Andreyevich Zhukovsky, the famous poet and father of Russian Romanticism, the chief tutor of the heir.

The kindness and sentimentality of Zhukovsky were the subject of jokes. The poet had been seventeen when the eighteenth century ended. But that eternal romantic remained a man of the gallant age. Even his birth was a romantic story.

During the war with the Turks, the Russians took a beautiful Turkish girl prisoner. Some serfs serving in the army gave the Oriental beauty to their master. He had her baptized and naturally made her his concubine. Thus issued the love child Vassily Zhukovsky. As the son of a Turkish woman and a wealthy Russian landowner, he was given a brilliant education at the Moscow University boarding school, which was attended by the children of Moscow nobility. Many of his school friends became the elite of Nicholas's reign—ministers, courtiers, and masters of the minds of the coming age.

Young Zhukovsky suffered over his dubious social position, but his amazing heart not only did not become embittered, it "broke into music." He started writing poetry that immediately received recognition. During the war with Napoleon, the entire country recited his patriotic verses.

Yet it was not his fame as a poet that opened the palace doors to him, but his translations from German into Russian. The dowager empress, widow of Paul I, Maria Fedorovna, and the mother of Alexander, Empress Alexandra Fedorovna, adored Schiller and the German Romantics. They were delighted by Zhukovsky's translations and particularly by conversations with him about their favorite poets.

Zhukovsky was appointed reader to the dowager empress. He also taught Russian to the young empress. Zhukovsky had an "in" at the palace and with the royal family. When the question of the heir's education came up, the answer was obvious. The family council entrusted little Sasha to the Master of Russian Poetry. Society members (trying to forget the days when they called the tsar a martinet) considered this decision desirable and beautiful—the great poet would raise the future great tsar.

Zhukovsky was a bachelor. As a true Romantic poet should, he had fallen in love at an early age and had been rejected; he carried a torch for his first love for years. Sasha was like a son for him. In his later years, Zhukovsky received a reward for his fidelity. At the age of fifty-five, the gray-haired poet fell in love for the second time in his life—with a sixteen-year-old. His love was requited, and he enjoyed a happy marriage, with children.

Later, in his forties, Alexander II would recall his teacher's example when he, too, fell in love with a seventeen-year-old.

When Zhukovsky began his tutoring, Alexander was only seven. Zhukovsky devoted himself totally to the royal scion. The poet wrote to his sister, "My real duty will take up all my time. Farewell forever to poetry with rhyme. A poetry of another sort lies ahead of me." In his hands lay the future of Russia.

Zhukovsky put together a ten-year plan of "Journeys," as the poet called the heir's education. Like everything else in Russia, the plan had to be approved by the tsar. Nicholas supervised its execution closely, often severely correcting the tutor.

Zhukovsky brought up the heir to be a true Christian, with feelings of compassion. Once Nicholas came into their classroom after a history lesson. It was the same room where Nicholas had once interrogated the participants in the Decembrist uprising. It awakened memories. He knew how often kindly Zhukovsky spoke about Christian forgiveness with little Sasha. The tsar asked his son, "What would you have done with the Decembrist rebels?" The boy answered as Zhukovsky had taught him, following Christian doctrine, "I would have forgiven them!"

Nicholas said nothing and left in silence. But later he told the boy, shaking his fist and repeating the words over and over, "This is how you rule. Remember this: Die on the steps to the throne, but do not give up power!"

The heir was unusually handsome, a true prince. His father thought him too feminine, with a too-tender heart. When his mother left on a trip, Sasha sent a bouquet of heliotrope after her, as befits the student of a romantic poet. He adored solitude and daydreaming. Nicholas wanted his son to be manly. The tsar demanded that Zhukovsky arrange for classmates for Alexander. Two boys, the sons of courtiers, were selected—Alexander Patkul and Josef Vilyegorsky.

To Nicholas's relief, Zhukovsky formulated a strict schedule for this trio. Reveille at six. By seven, the heir was in the classroom with his comrades. Lessons continued for five hours, until noon. No one, not even the tsar, could enter the inner sanctum, the classroom, during lessons. A two-hour break began at noon. Zhukovsky and his three pupils would leave the palace and walk around St. Petersburg, where the lessons continued. Dressed in military uniform, the boy was supposed to "attentively observe the public buildings, educational and scientific institutions, industrial establishments and other points of interest along the way," and to discuss them with his tutor. "Learn from childhood to read the book that belongs to you from birth. That book is Russia," Zhukovsky taught him.

During their walks, poetry was read aloud. Like Seneca in his letters, Zhukovsky gave his primary pupil aphoristic guidelines for his life.

"A tsar's power over man comes from God, but do not make that power a mockery of God and man."

"Respect the law. If the tsar neglects the law, it will not be kept by the people."

"Love and disseminate education. A people without education are a people without dignity. They are easily led, but it is easy to turn slaves into furious rebels."

"Revolution is a destructive effort to leap from Monday directly into Wednesday. But the effort to jump from Monday back to Sunday is just as destructive."

The aphorisms were carefully vetted by "the best of fathers" and Nicholas repeated them himself during his rare walks with his son.

After the walks came an hour for lunch and then more lessons from three until five. An hour for rest followed, and then the boys changed for sports. They had gymnastics and athletic games from seven until eight. Dinner was at ten, after an "edifying conversation with his parents." After dinner came prayers and sleep.

The list of subjects that the heir was taught at the age of thirteen is instructive: history, Russian, mathematics, physics, philosophy, geology, law, French, English, German, Polish, drawing, music, gymnastics, swimming, fencing, dancing, military studies, woodworking . . . and on and on.

The best minds of Russia taught the heir. The famous Count Speransky taught him jurisprudence. The tsar did not fear the influence of the former freethinker. Exile had had a good effect on him, as his participation in the trial of the Decembrists had proven. Speransky taught the heir about the permanence of autocracy. "There is no power on earth, either within the borders or outside the borders of the empire, that could put an end to the Supreme power of the Russian monarch. All the laws of the empire serve that power."

On Sundays, with other children of members of the court—Adlerberg, Baranov, Shuvalov—he played the kind of competitive games his militant father so enjoyed. At the upper level of the fountain in the park grounds near the Big Palace at Peterhof, the empress stood next to a marble table holding the children's prizes. She had an excellent view of the watery fireworks—the Grand Cascade of the Peterhof Fountains. Sixty-four fountains sent powerful streams of water up to the sky. The water cascaded down marble steps. The bronze statues of antique gods gleamed in the sunlight.

At the very bottom of the cascade, at a statue of Samson, Nicholas lined up the boys. On his command, they rushed forward and ran up the slippery steps through the icy jets of water. There were a thousand steps through the watery curtain. The empress awarded the happy, wet contestants chocolates and books, but the best prize was Nicholas's benevolent smile. One day it went to Sasha Adlerberg, son of the minister of the court. His father, however, chided him for winning—the emperor's son must always be first.

An ordinary boy can sometimes be lazy, cranky, and disobedient. Alexander's classmates were permitted that, but not Alexander. The enormous and regal emperor kept explaining to his son, "You must always remember that it is only through your whole life that you can repay your God-given birthright."

Alexander had to keep a diary, in which he would record all his transgressions:

"K.K. [his governor, Karl Karlovich Merder] was pleased with me throughout the day," he reported at the age of eight. But shortly after, on Tuesday, January 12: "I did not do very well at my lessons. . . . K.K. is not very pleased: I teased my sister, Maria Nikolayevna, and stopped writing before I was told."

Kindly Zhukovsky loved him and forgave him many things. But Karl Merder, who initiated Sasha into the mysteries of warfare, did not. Merder also loved Sasha, but to the great pleasure of his father, Merder ruthlessly hounded anything that could keep the boy from becoming a real warrior. Merder did not like the boy's hot temper, but even more so, the strange melancholy that sometimes plunged him into absolute inaction. He was also concerned by Sasha's tearfulness, so inappropriate to a military man.

They made the heir add tears to his list of transgressions in his diary, which his father read scrupulously.

"March 30. Wrote badly, and cried for no reason."

"April 1. Studied well. Hit myself with butt-stock and cried."

Alexander really did like to cry. When strict Merder died, sixteen-year-old Sasha buried his head in the couch pillows and no one could stop the flow of tears for a long time. His tears were a gift from his beloved tutor Zhukovsky. The sentimental poet often wept. He wept with joy reading Schiller, he wept over his pupil's disobedience, he wept recalling his unrequited love. The poet's frequent tears came from the previous century. In eighteenth-century Russia it was fashionable to be sensitive. When Alexander's great-grandmother, Catherine the Great, told the Kazan nobility about the work of Peter the Great, the entire room wept over the grandeur of Peter's acts. When Catherine read her new "instruction" to the deputies of the Legislative Commission, the legislators wept out loud over the wisdom of the empress. When Catherine's young lover died, her former lover, the very ruthless Prince Potemkin, wept bitterly with her.

This was the great sensibility of the gallant age, learned by little Alexander. A half century later, signing his final decrees, he would weep with excitement.

Nicholas hated the tears, and the boy was often punished for them.

His father knew the remedy for tears and foolish sensibility. It was the favorite activity of Nicholas I, his father, Paul I, and his grandfather, Peter III—army drill. To Merder's delight, Nicholas demanded more military mustering. Zhukovsky boldly disagreed. "I fear that then His

Imperial Highness will think that the people are a regiment and the country a barracks."

Nicholas benevolently allowed Zhukovsky to grumble, for he knew that his son loved the army, as did all Romanovs. He was put on a horse at the age of six, and he liked it. At eight, he galloped gleefully on the flank of the Life Guards Regiment. And during the coronation of Nicholas, the eight-year-old "Heir on Horseback" stole the show.

"At 7 A.M., Alexander Nikolayevich in full parade uniform of the Life Guards Regiment galloped to the Peter Palace. Here he mounted the Arabian steed prepared for him and flew to the Emperor, past whom the troops were marching ceremonially—67,000 men. All of Moscow ran out to look at the majestic sight," wrote Karl Merder in delight. "The appearance of the heir on a marvelous steed, which he controlled with incredible agility, eclipsed everything else."

The triumph was repeated a few days later. "Everyone was mad about him, especially the ladies," wrote Merder jokingly. Napoleon's marshal Marmont (who had betrayed Bonaparte and opened the road to Paris for the Allies) was impressed by the small rider. His severe father finally expressed his highest approval, out loud. And his maternal grandfather, the Prussian king, was very proud when he read the accounts of the event.

Like all the Romanovs, Sasha loved the order of the guards, the glimmer of the cuirasses, bared sabers, and brass helmets topped with eagles. He even drew a new design for the grenadiers' uniform. The heir to the Russian throne had to be "military in spirit." "Russia is a military state and its destiny is to be the terror of the world." That sentence, uttered by Nicholas, was made part of the textbook for the cadet corps. A civilian "is lost in our age," the tsar explained to his son.

Sasha understood all that. He wanted to be with the troops and found it a bore publishing his own magazine, *The Anthill,* under the auspices of the poet Zhukovsky. As Count Peter Panin once said, "I think the Romanovs will not give up their love of the army until a cripple tsar is born in the family." Over Zhukovsky's protest, Nicholas sent ten-year-old Sasha to study at the Cadet Corps, where he would be taught soldiering and become a junior officer so that he could become a staff captain at thirteen and take part in his father's beloved parades.

Nicholas was willing to forgive Zhukovsky's battle with military training, because the main point of Zhukovsky's teaching, which he inculcated in Sasha daily, was the cult of his father and total obedience.

"Never praise the Grand Duke," he begged the tsar. "Ordinary gentle treatment from Your Majesty is already the highest reward." "His Highness must tremble at the thought of his father's rebuke." "The thought of his father's approval must be His Highness's secret conscience."

Whenever the boy dared to be disobedient, he had to bear his father's wrath, which all of Russia feared. "Begone! You are not worthy of approaching me after such behavior; you have forgotten that obedience is a sacred duty. I can forgive anything except disobedience!"

He would resort to the greatest threat for the little Romanov: "I will deprive you of the right to wear the parade uniform for an entire month if you ever show the least bit of disobedience again."

His father. The fear of his father. Obedience, subordination. His father as role model. An idol in everything. His father slept on a camp bed under an old soldier's greatcoat, on a thin straw-filled mattress. He wore his uniform at breakfast, he despised robes. "Even when he was sick, Nicholas wore an old military coat instead of a robe, and he slept under it," recalled lady-in-waiting Maria Frederiks.

Alexander would try to follow in his father's footsteps. He would keep a camp bed in his study and he would die in it, like his father.

But no matter how hard he tried to emulate his father, he was his mother's son. His father supervised his studies, but he spoke to him very rarely. His father was strict, his mother tender. He came to her with his troubles.

Lady-in-waiting Anna Tyutcheva gives a portrait of Alexander's mother. "The daughter of the King of Prussia, she came from Germany, where everyone was delirious over the sensitive poetry of Schiller. . . .

Her tender nature and shallow mind replaced principles with sensitivity. Nicholas had the passionate adoration for this frail and exquisite creature of a strong nature for a weak thing, who obediently turned him into her sole ruler and legislator. . . . Nicholas placed her in a golden cage of palaces, brilliant balls, and handsome courtiers. . . . In her magical dungeon she did not once think of freedom. She did not allow herself to dream of any life beyond the golden cage. She adored and saw only the beautiful and happy. . . . When once she saw a worn dress on a girl being presented at court, she wept."

The empress was like a charming, constantly chirping, flighty bird. That pleased the emperor. Like Napoleon, Nicholas hated intelligent women who interfered in politics.

Nicholas and Alexandra were a harmonious couple. The court delightedly glorified their undying love out loud. But the whispers spoke differently. The palace was full of rumors, and adolescent boys are nastily observant. Sasha learned that his mother's lady-in-waiting, who lived right in the Winter Palace and was the court's greatest beauty, Varenka Nelidova, was his father's mistress. It was horrible for him to find that his father kept her under the same roof as his adored mother. Every time his father sent for the lovely lady-in-waiting, he imagined them together.

As is to be expected at that sinful age, Sasha watched everyone and saw everything with different eyes, the eyes of Adam after he had tasted the forbidden fruit. He also had to learn about the young ladies who quickly vanished from the palace. They were all given in marriage to officers of the Life Guards, and they all gave birth prematurely. Then they brought a beautiful bourgeoise to the palace with a petition, and the emperor agreed to receive her. She left his study smiling and happy, and never was seen at the palace again. Alexander learned as a teenager what was later described by the marquis de Custine in his famous book about Russia:

"And just as a landowner was in charge of the lives and wishes of his serfs, so the tsar here is in charge of all his subjects. He gave his attention . . . not only to all the young beauties in the court—the ladies-in-waiting but also the young women he met during walks. If someone caught his fancy on a walk or at the theater, he told his adjutant. She would then be checked. If there was nothing against her, the husband (if she was married) or her parents (if a maiden) were informed of the honor that had befallen them. . . . The tsar never met resistance to his lust. . . . In that strange country sleeping with the emperor was considered an honor . . . for the parents and even the husbands."

This was well known in St. Petersburg and it was "the usual order" of things. The young radical, the famous critic Dobrolubov, wrote right after the tsar's death, "The usual order was thus: A girl from a noble family was made a lady-in-waiting and she was used to service our most pious and most autocratic tsar."

Custine traveled around Russia but never did understand who the tsar was for his subjects. "The most autocratic tsar" Nicholas I was not a landowner in charge of his serfs as much as a terrible god come down from Olympus.

"I grew up with a feeling not only of love but also reverence. . . . I regarded the tsar as our earthly god, so it is not surprising that there was also inexplicable fear," wrote the nineteen-year-old beauty Maria Patkul (who married Sasha Patkul, who was educated with the heir). "The door opened of the Empress's formal study, and Their Majesties came out. My God, my heart fluttered so. I felt my knees buckling, so I leaned against the billiard table, lowered my eyes and bowed my head, and made a low bow. When I raised my eyes, I saw that Their Majesties were coming straight toward me. When they approached, I curtsied again, and the Empress, addressing the Tsar, said, 'My friend, I present to you the wife of Patkul.' To which the Tsar, offering me his powerful hand, bowed with the words, 'I ask for your love and pity.' I was so stunned by that unexpected and very gracious greeting that I could not say a single word, blushed, and at first could not tell whether I had dreamed those words of the Tsar or whether I was awake. . . . Could I have ever dreamed that the Tsar, that Colossus of the Russian land, would turn to a nineteen-year-old girl with the words, 'I ask for your love and pity.'"

The tsar's mercurial attention, which once made the beauty happy, was a gift from Zeus.

Zeus's escapades were wrapped in secrecy. "All that," Maria Frederiks later wrote, "was done with such secrecy and such propriety . . . that it never occurred to anyone to pay any attention." As if those court slaves drilled by Nicholas would have dared notice his behavior.

When one of the empress's overly loyal ladies-in-waiting tried to hint subtly about Varenka Nelidova, Nicholas's main mistress, the empress simply would not seem to understand the hint, and the stupid lady-in-waiting would soon vanish from court. The empress, whom Anna Tyutcheva and other ladies considered not very intelligent and blind, was in fact wise and eagle-eyed. She had mastered the difficult art of living with a passionate man from the house of Romanov. She continued chirping insouciantly in her golden cage. The emperor was truly grateful to her and loved her deeply.

When she was ill he stayed by her bedside until very late. She begged him not to do that, for fear that her adored spouse would not get enough sleep. In order not to worry her, Nicholas would pretend to leave, and take off his boots behind the screen. "You had to see this regal giant carefully tiptoe out from behind the screen and tread noiselessly in his socks. He was afraid to leave the patient alone for a minute," wrote Anna Tyutcheva. He was afraid his bird might fly out of her golden cage.

As an adolescent, Alexander began to feel the sensual fire he had inherited. The fire had burned in all the Romanovs: Peter the Great, Elizabeth, Catherine the Great, Paul, Alexander I, and his father. Nicholas I had a collection of antique phalluses that survives today and serves as a reminder of that fire.

The Winter Palace was a fine hearth for that fire from the start. The ghosts of the emperors' lovers and the stories of lustful empresses created an aura of sensuality that lived on in the luxurious apartments.

Peter II was the first resident of the Winter Palace and he started the tradition by moving in his mistress Vorontsova. Catherine, here in the Winter Palace, slept with her lover Grigory Orlov and bore his son while her husband was alive. Once she became empress, she had a series of thirteen official lovers—not counting the brief flings that the palace saw.

When she was in her sixties, her last favorite, number thirteen, Platon Zubov, was only a bit over twenty. In response to cloaked rebukes, she said mockingly, "The homeland should be grateful to me for zealously bringing up brilliant young men for it."

The adoration of feminine beauty made Alexander's grandfather, Paul I, continually "point out some lovely Dulcinea," and his helpful lackeys "took her into account and tried to instantly execute the master's desire," according to cavalry guardsman Yakov Skaryatin.

Like ghosts, the titled descendants of august sins walked through the palace. Count Bobrinsky, the descendant of Catherine's illegitimate son, played with little Sasha. His grandfather had several illegitimate children. Alexandra Vyrobova, the confidante of the last Russian tsaritsa, was descended from Paul. Alexander I had a beloved daughter by Countess Naryshkina. When she died young, the Winter Palace was plunged into mourning. Everyone, including the empress, consoled the grieving emperor.

And now, Varenka Nelidova, of the marble shoulders, high breasts, and wasp waist, was living in the Winter Palace alongside Alexander's mother.

Alexander gave full rein to the Romanov sensuality. He seemed to sense subconsciously that this was the area where he could find freedom and release. Here his father would not dare interfere. Sasha fell in love, seriously. At the age of fourteen he fell in love with his mother's lady-in-waiting Natalya B. He could not hide his attraction. He did not know how to do things "secretly and with propriety." "Every new passion is immediately written on his face," lady-in-waiting Alexandra Tolstaya (a distant relative of the great writer, Leo Tolstoy) recalled.

"He is constantly in love and therefore kindly disposed," said Bismarck, then Prussian ambassador to Russia.

From his adolescence until his death, Alexander was wildly passionate and sensual. When the Bolsheviks took the Winter Palace in 1917, they found a collection of pornographic drawings in his old study. They were made for him by Mikhai Zichi, a famous artist at the time in Russia. Of Hungarian descent, a member of the Academy of the Arts, he was appointed court painter. His duties were quite varied. He created numerous watercolor scenes of court life, and as was later discovered, he also executed more intimate commissions from the passionate tsar.

Nicholas was also crazy about war and knighthood. At Tsarskoye Selo, in the Arsenal, he had a marvelous collection of armor and antique arms. On occasion, fantastic spectacles were organized. The handsome emperor and the handsome heir, in armor, on Arabian steeds, headed a procession followed by all the young grand dukes in page costumes on horseback, and followed by the ladies of the court in dresses of the era of Lorenzo the Magnificent. Natalya B. was dazzling in her attire, and she knew it. Unlike his father, Sasha had trouble bearing the weight of the suit of armor, and was relieved to be allowed to remove it.

On the way back from the Arsenal, he ran into her in a secluded grove. Naturally, the wench had been waiting for him. They were on horseback. They tied up the horses. She lifted her skirts, but could not get the medieval pantaloons off quickly enough. The damned Florentine outfit and his haste ruined everything, that time. The next time was a success.

The very serious circumstances forced his mother to speak to his father, and Natalya B. was sent packing, married off to someone hastily.

At sixteen, Alexander took the oath of the heir to the throne, to serve tsar and country faithfully. The entire court gathered in the Big Church of the Winter Palace. His father led Sasha to the lectern, and Sasha read the text of the lengthy oath. His main concern was not to cry.

"He read the oath in a firm and cheerful voice, but as he started the prayer he had to stop because of his copious tears." He was not the only one to get emotional. "The Tsar and Tsaritsa also wept. When he finished, the heir rushed over to embrace his father. Then his father led him to his mother. All three embraced and wept." Naturally, the moved court also had to weep. "Many wept, and those who did not rubbed their dry eyes, trying to squeeze out a few tears," recorded the poet Pushkin in his diary.

After that day, the heir was treated differently. As his uncle Mikhail put it, "The tsar is not quite a God, but is human only in part." Alexander now had duties as a representative of the crown.

His list of infatuations continued. But at eighteen he once again fell in love seriously, with Olga K, another lady-in-waiting. Later, when Alexander was tsar, he taught his own son, "Remember, we have the right to nothing more than drawing-room intrigues." But he broke that rule. He even told his mother about his pure love for Olga K. His father was informed of everything about his son, and he even read his diary secretly. Nicholas only smirked at the word "pure." He took measures. Olga K. was given in marriage to the Polish magnate Count Oginski. She had a son who always believed that he was son of the Russian tsar.

The empress made a decision. "He needs to have a stronger personality, otherwise he will perish. He falls in love too easily. He must be removed from St. Petersburg for a while," wrote lady-in-waiting Maria Frederiks.

Getting the easily infatuated Don Juan out of the capital was simple. His education (truly outstanding, by the most stringent European standards) was completed. He took his exams, facing the cream of Russian scholars, who had been his teachers. The head of the commission, naturally, was the tsar. The exams went well, and the tsar gave out rewards to the students and teachers.

Now, according to Zhukovsky's plan, the education was to be polished by two very important journeys. First Sasha would travel around his own country. He would travel for over six months around Russia's roadless expanses. Alexander would be the first heir to the throne to have personally seen the vast country he would rule.

Zhukovsky was supposed to accompany him on his travels. Sasha told the eternal child about his pure love (the Romantic poet would not have understood anything else) for Olga, and his suffering. Zhukovsky must have been informed of her pregnancy, but what was pitiful truth in the face of great invention! They wept in each other's arms.

Then, with Zhukovsky present, the emperor read, in his resonant voice, "This voyage, dear Sasha, is an important milestone in your life. Leaving your parents' roof for the first time, you will be placed in a certain way in judgment of your subjects in a trial of your mental abilities."

After which Zhukovsky made a speech. "Russia is a Book, but an animate one. Your Imperial Highness will be reading it, but at the same time, it will be learning about its reader. This mutual comprehension is the true goal of this voyage."

Nicholas's preferred method of communication was sending instructions. That same morning, Alexander was given his first list. Everything was laid out point by point. "Your first goal is to familiarize yourself with the state that you will rule sooner or later. Second. Your judgments during your trip must be extremely cautious. Avoid making remarks, for you are traveling not to judge but to learn. . . . You should rise at five and depart at six."

Sasha traveled throughout the European part of Russia. From each provincial capital he sent a letter to his dear father. Thus, the entire voyage is recorded in detail in his letters to Nicholas.

How happy he was to feel free, and how merry and insouciant he became at a remove from his strict father. In the city of Kostroma he saw the Ipatyev Monastery, where their dynasty had begun. His ancestor, the first Romanov invited to rule the country, had lived in a monastery cell. After the turmoil of the Time of Troubles, following the death of the last Rurik tsar in 1598, after near civil war, after regicides and the invasion of Swedes and Poles, the Zemsky Sobor, or National Assembly, elected in 1613 as the new tsar sixteen-year-old Mikhail Romanov, a relative of the defunct Rurik dynasty of Moscow rulers.

From atop the monastery walls, Alexander saw the Volga River. In that year, across the frozen river, a long procession had come to the monastery. The armor of the soldiers and gold of the boyars' clothing gleamed in the winter sun as they followed the clergy in sparkling vestments and bearing jewel-encrusted icons. They came to the Ipatyev Monastery to ask Mikhail Romanov to rule them. And what was his response? Mikhail wept and cried, "I do not want to be your tsar."

It was as if, there at the monastery, he foresaw how heavy would lie the crown of Monomakh on the heads of his descendants. But he was persuaded to accept the throne, and Russia swore to Alexander's ancestor that the Romanovs would rule as autocrats by divine right, responsible only to God.

The heir to the throne was met reverently by thousands of people wherever he went. As he traveled along the Volga in the Kostroma region, people stood knee-deep in the river for hours to get a glimpse of their earthly god. When he left the cathedral, the crowd of thousands shouted huzzahs and tried to press closer, to touch him. The entourage that protected Sasha from the crowd was severely bruised and battered by his enthusiastic subjects.

Sasha would remember the cities in the Urals and Siberia. In Simbirsk a huge crowd, shouting "Hurrah," ran after their carriage. Teary-eyed Zhukovsky extended his arms to the running crowd and exclaimed, "Run after him, Russia. He is worthy of your love!" Simbirsk would be the hometown of the future leaders of both revolutions of 1917, in February and October—Alexander Kerensky and Vladimir Ulyanov (Lenin).

The tsarevich was the first Romanov heir to visit Siberia, where convicts and exiles were sent. He was also the first to go to Ekaterinburg, where after the revolution, in the cellar of the house belonging to the merchant Ipatyev, Alexander's wretched grandson, Nicholas II, and his great-grandchildren would be murdered.

Thus on this trip he met his glorious past, the Ipatyev Monastery, and the bloody future, the Ipatyev house, where his dynasty would end with the execution of the last tsar and his family.

In a small town in Siberia, during a church service, he saw a sad group of people. They were the exiled Decembrists. When the liturgy's litany reached the priest's petition for prisoners, he turned in their direction and bowed, with tears in his eyes, naturally. Zhukovsky also wept. Everyone in the church wept.

He did not dare promise them anything, on the orders of his father. But he wrote to his august parent, begging him to ease their lot.

Zhukovsky awaited the response anxiously, for "the noble impulse of compassion." Nicholas responded—the exiles were to be transferred from harsh Siberia to be soldiers in the Caucasus, where there was a fierce war with native tribes. From freezing Siberia to face Chechen bullets—that was the extent of the tsar's mercy.

Nicholas would never forgive them. But Alexander was delighted. His father had acceded to his request. Zhukovsky (who understood better) supported the boy's delight, and they wept tears of joy.

Alexander brought back sixteen thousand petitions, which would never be read.

He traveled around Russia for seven months, visiting thirty provinces. It was still not enough to cover the vast country, but at least now he had an idea of the boundless land he was to rule. He was pleased that his father was in his prime and that he would not be ruling in the near future.

On December 10, 1837, he reached St. Petersburg. He was not to enjoy his homecoming for long. A week later fire destroyed the Winter Palace. In early winter, Nicholas ordered the construction of a fireplace in one of the palace rooms. The architect dared to inform him that it could pose a danger. Nicholas merely gave him one of his regal looks, and the architect hastened to obey. The flue began to smoke, the servants tried to plug it with a clay-covered mop, and the palace caught fire. Their Majesties were at the theater, watching *Abduction from the Seraglio.* Nicholas could not stay to see if the ballerinas had mastered the use of sabers. He was informed of the fire during the performance. The royal sleigh had been sent away, so Nicholas took his adjutant's troika. The empress followed in a carriage.

The younger children were instantly taken to Anichkov Palace. As the tsar approached the blazing Winter Palace he was told that the Galerny Port was on fire, too. He sent Alexander to deal with it. Thrilled by his father's unusual trust, Alexander rushed to the port in the royal sleigh, which flipped over at the reckless speed they took. He left his adjutant to deal with the sleigh and mounted the adjutant's horse to gallop to the port. The guards of the Finland Regiment were fighting the fire. He took command, and the fire was extinguished by morning.

In the meantime, his parents were fighting the fire at the Winter Palace. The high winds fanned the blaze. "It seemed like a volcano in the middle of St. Petersburg," wrote Zhukovsky. The empress stayed in the palace until the last minute, helping to pack things. The flames were approaching her rooms when Nicholas sent an adjutant. "Leave now! The fire will be here in a minute."

The empress and her favorite lady-in-waiting, Cecilia Frederiks, were walking quickly past the rotunda, when the doors to the rotunda blew open with a howling screech. The enormous chandelier was sucked out the door by the force of the wind and fire.

Flames blazed in the rotunda as the empress and her lady-in-waiting ran to the Saltykov Entrance, where the carriage awaited them.

The guardsmen rescued the royal valuables. These were soldiers brought up by Nicholas, whose only thought was to please the tsar. Some carried out the regimental banners from the Field Marshal Hall, others saved the imperial regalia and the treasures of the famous Diamond Hall, still others brought out personal family items. The empress's favorite mirror would not come free of the wall. The guardsmen struggled to get it out of the burning bedroom. Nicholas had to break the priceless mirror in order to get the soldiers out of the room to save their lives.

The salvaged items were brought out onto Palace Square and piled up by the Alexander Column. Snow fell on them. In the snow lay the imperial regalia—crown, scepter, and orb—fabled jewels, "sacred icons, vestments from both chapels, paintings, precious ornaments of the palace," wrote Zhukovsky. The army guarded these riches. Beyond the cordon of troops surrounding Palace Square stood the people, "countless crowds in deadly silence." All night long in the snowy square the clocks made by famous craftsmen struck the hour and played soft melodies. The palace burned until sunrise.

By the time Alexander returned from the port, the palace was gone. The homeless royals moved into the Anichkov Palace.

Nicholas gave orders to restore the vast palace, setting an impossible deadline of one year. But it was met. Serfs were brought from all over Russia to work on it. It was minus thirty-five Centigrade, terribly cold, and they kept fires lit inside the palace to dry the walls faster. Hundreds of workers died before the project was completed.

The royal family moved back into the revived palace as Nicholas had ordered. Iron discipline in everything, that was the testament Nicholas left to his heir and to future rulers. Alexander must have thought with longing about his seven months of freedom, traveling without the oppressive, ruthless will of his father. He did not stay long in St. Petersburg.

Zhukovsky's plan had Alexander traveling in Europe after his Russian voyage, not only to complete his education, but to find himself a wife. His mother did not want a repetition of the lady-in-waiting affair. A list was compiled of possible brides, all German princesses, naturally. As the French historian Charles Masson noted in the eighteenth century, the German duchies had long been a harem for Russian tsars from which to select wives. The former provincial princesses left their parents' stingy palaces and were stunned by the barbarous opulence of the Russian court.

So, once again, on the road with instructions from his father. Once again, everything was merry and free as soon as Alexander left St. Petersburg. First came Prussia. His grandfather, Frederick Wilhelm, was very elderly, after forty years on the throne. With his grandfather, he visited the grave of his grandmother, Queen Louise, the most beautiful monarch of Europe. His grandmother's beauty had almost conquered Napoleon. After his defeat by Bonaparte, his poor grandfather lost almost half of Prussia. Queen Louise (then at the height of her loveliness) decided to win back at least a part of the lost territories. At the peace talks, she went off alone with Bonaparte and asked him to leave them several lands. She was so successful that if Frederick had not come in just then, as Bonaparte later related the story, "A little longer and I would have had to give up Magdeburg." Alexander I, who defeated Napoleon, had also been in love with her.

The Prussian cousins were charming. All the temptresses certainly dreamed of becoming the empress of Russia, but Alexander decided to leave Prussia and continue his journey. They had not won his heart. Vienna was next. They stayed at the home of Prince Metternich, who had not only been a clever adversary of the great Napoleon, but also a top-rank Don Juan. His house was complete temptation. Napoleon had advised, "Marry Austrian women. They are as fresh as roses and as fecund as rabbits." But Alexander was drawn to the German principalities, where his ancestors had found their incomparable wives.

In the meantime, there was Italy. In Italy no one forced boring ceremonies on him. They stopped in small towns, where he enjoyed total freedom. He recalled his uncle Alexander, who had wanted to give up the crown. Italy's sky, the marble palaces, the ruins that remembered Julius Caesar made him weep for joy with Zhukovsky under the Italian skies. Things changed in Milan, where he was greeted by cannon fire and long parades in his honor.

Another missive from his father moved them along to the German principalities of Baden and Württemberg. There were princesses there, but his heart was untouched. The voyage continued. They reached Darmstadt, the capital of the tiny duchy of Hesse-Darmstadt. Its princess was not on the list of possible brides, and Sasha stopped there only because it was along the way, for one day. But that evening in the court theater, he saw her, the young princess hiding in the back of the box. He was swept off his feet by "the modest charm of the princess," who was still a child, only fourteen. She was graceful in the style of a Dürer Madonna. Even when she grew up, she remained fragile, spiritual, and girlishly graceful.

Alexander stayed to dine with the boring Duke Ludwig, in the hope of catching another glimpse of her. Princess Maximiliana-Wilhelmina-Augusta-Sophie had a tiny waist, golden hair, and blue eyes. Like his mother.

That night he wrote to his father, "I liked her terribly at first sight. If

you permit it, dear father, I will come back to Darmstadt after England."
He had the messenger deliver the letter to his father on the day of the
Annunciation, nine days later. The messenger raced through Europe to
reach the emperor on that day.

The princess was not in Nicholas's plans. Yes, she came from a German principality, but she was only fourteen. In monarchic Europe all the
kings knew everything about one another. Spicy rumors were passed
around, and the word was that the princess was not the duke's daughter,
but that of his handsome stable master, the Frenchman Baron de
Grancy.

But when his son's dispatch was brought to Nicholas on the day of
the Annunciation, religious Nicholas did not fail to see the good omen
of the day of glad tidings. (Just as clever Sasha had planned.) He gave
permission for Alexander to return to Darmstadt. While Nicholas ques-
tioned the messenger closely on the appearance, education, and moral
qualities of the princess, Sasha headed for England.

It turned out that leaving England would be difficult. It was the fault
of Queen Victoria. She was twenty years old and she, too, had gorgeous
blue eyes. She was flawlessly elegant as only Englishwomen can be. Soon
Victoria wrote in her diary, "I like the Grand Duke extremely; he is so
natural and gay and so easy to get on with."

Alexander's face, as usual, revealed that he was in love again. Victoria
was not only charming, intelligent, and witty. There was something
about her that he found very attractive: She was completely independent
and free in her opinions. He could be free and easy around her, which he
could not be at the court of his father.

The next day Victoria and the Russian heir were at the royal theater,
in separate boxes. In the intermission Alexander entered the queen's box
and spent close to a half hour alone with her behind the velvet curtains.

Dispatches flew to St. Petersburg: "The queen is clearly enjoying the
society of His Imperial Majesty. Everyone is saying they are an ideal couple. Were the Grand Duke to make a proposal to the queen, it would be
accepted without hesitation."

The eternally besotted tsarevich awaited his father's decision. Victoria described the history of their brief romance in her diary: "Monday, 27th May 1839. Windsor. At 1/4 to 8 we dined in St. George's Hall, which looked beautiful. The Grand Duke led me in and I sat between him and Prince Henry of Holland. I really am quite in love with the Grand Duke; he is a dear, delightful young man. . . . I danced 1st a quadrille with the Grand Duke, then followed a Valse, during which time I sat down, then another quadrille . . . this was followed again by a Valse (of course I and also the Grand-Duke sitting down during the Valse) . . . After supper at 12 they danced a Mazurka. . . . The Grand-Duke asked me to take a turn; the Grand-Duke is so very strong, that in running round, you must follow quickly, and after that you are whisked round like in a Valse, which is very pleasant. . . . This concluded our little Ball at near 2 o'clock. I never enjoyed myself more. We were all so merry; I got to bed by a 1/4 to 3, but could not sleep till 5."

But it was in vain. His father's letter was delivered to him. His father's orders were "Back to Darmstadt!" Russia needed an heir to the throne, not a pathetic husband of the English queen. "Don't be a milksop!"

Now Nicholas was willing to accept the Darmstadt match with the dubious German princess. Anything to get him out of perilous England, for the tsar knew his son's dangerous impulsiveness. As the loyal Zhukovsky wrote, "The princess is modest, charming, and even intelligent."

The sight of the grand duke made everything clear to Victoria. After the last dance on May 28, "which was over at 20 m. to 3, I went to the little blue room next to my Dressing-room, where Lord Palmerston brought in the Grand-Duke to take leave. The Grand-Duke took my hand and pressed it warmly; he looked pale and his voice faltered, as he said, 'Les paroles me manquent pour exprimer tout ce que je sens' [I lack the words to express what I feel]; and he mentioned how deeply grateful he felt for all the kindness he met with, that he hoped to return again. . . . He then pressed and kissed my hand, and I kissed his cheek; upon which he kissed mine (cheek) in a very warm affectionate manner, and we again warmly shook hands. I really felt more as if I was taking leave of a relation than of a stranger, I felt so sad to take leave of this dear amiable young man, whom I really think (talking jokingly) I was a little in love with, and certainly attached to; he is so frank, so really young and merry, has such a nice open countenance with a sweet smile, and such a manly fine figure and appearance."

With that "jokingly" she freed herself of regrets and of rejection. She understood the Russian tsar, for Victoria was first and foremost a great queen, as she would prove. She must have expected that a lover would at least try to behave as a lover should, but how could he have disobeyed his father? As if anyone in all of Russia could.

As a farewell gift, Alexander gave the queen his favorite dog, Kazbek. She kept it with her until it died.

From London, Alexander returned to Darmstadt, which he had so easily forgotten. While he was falling in love in London, however, his father had come to terms with the duke, whose daughter would convert to Orthodoxy.

The court welcomed the bride warily. Her "inadequate French" was noted, as was her less-than-perfect nose and her mouth, which was too narrow, "with tight lips and without spiritual sensitivity." But Nicholas liked her, she resembled his beloved wife tremendously—just as fragile and ethereal, with the same delightfully golden hair. Most important, her slightly bulging blue eyes showed the familiar meekness and all-forgiveness that were so necessary for life with Romanov men. Sometimes, however, her thin lips curved into a sarcastic smile that showed that she understood everything even as she forgave. That was just the wife for his son. Nicholas forbade the court from discussing nasty rumors about her, from even thinking about them. The court immediately shut up. Nicholas knew how to rule.

In 1841, in the Winter Palace that had risen from the ashes, the wedding was held in the Big Church. After her conversion to Russian Orthodoxy, the Princess of Hesse-Darmstadt became Grand Duchess Maria Alexandrovna Romanova. She was magnificent that day, her gown embroidered in silver and decorated with diamonds, a mantle of purple velvet trimmed with ermine on her shoulders, and a diamond diadem on her lovely head.

The bride's brother accompanied her to Russia. Tall and handsome, with military bearing and elegance, he knew how to swagger in uniform, which predisposed Nicholas to him immediately. He was a treasure trove of anecdotes and jokes, which set him apart from the cowed and cautious court. The tsar's benevolence and the enormous allowance assigned to the prince gave rise to great hopes for him. But an affair with his sister's pretty lady-in-waiting ended in her pregnancy. The prince felt he was honor-bound to marry her. Nicholas "could not stand misalliances in the imperial Family." He banished the prince and the pregnant lady-in-waiting from Russia.

The tsarevna learned to be careful in her selection of ladies-in-waiting. Anna Tyutcheva, daughter of the great poet Fedor Tyutchev, became her next choice. She was an intelligent young woman of strong morals. More important, she was unattractive.

Anna spent thirteen years at the Winter Palace, in a room pathetic in comparison to the opulence of the royal apartments, with her carriage always ready in case she needed to accompany the tsarevna. She kept a chronicle of court life for those thirteen years. Her "Reminiscences" help us see the tsar's court in the era of Nicholas I and Alexander II, the Russian Atlantis gone forever.

Separation from her favorite brother was a blow for the tsarevna. She got over it with difficulty, but she drew the necessary conclusions. Life in the Russian court demanded "daily heroism," she wrote. "I lived like a volunteer fireman, ready to jump up at the alarm. Of course, I wasn't too sure about where to run or what to do." In fact, after the business with her brother, she realized very well what to do and where to run. Because there was only one thing the court had to do: Please Nicholas. She had to understand the emperor's wishes and execute them.

The coldness of the court no longer frightened her, because Masha (as Alexander called her) quickly learned how to manage it. Nicholas lived on a rigid schedule, which applied to everything. The "volunteer fireman" made sure she kept to the schedule.

She got up early and made sure the children were dressed and fed, because they had to be in the chapel by eleven. At the stroke of eleven, the emperor walked into the chapel. The tsarevna was inside at 10:50, waiting for the emperor, the family around her. The heir was still and respectful, as were all their children. As the clock struck the hour, the emperor entered and the service began. The emperor stood near the choir and sang along in his beautiful voice. The tsarevna's face showed complete concentration. Even their smallest child, not yet three, stood still, and most important, quietly.

The emperor's hearing was excellent, and woe to the courtier or lady who whispered during the service. A few hours later a clerk from the Ministry of the Court would bring an official written rebuke from His Majesty.

Nicholas came to love his daughter-in-law. He considered her intelligent, and sometimes even asked for her advice. Naturally, everyone at court considered her intelligent then, too. That started rumors that Alexander was ruled by his wife. He put up with it, because in the early years of their marriage, he was in love with her. And she was happy with him—a happy wife and a happy mother. She had children one after the other, to the happiness of father and grandfather. Maria Alexandrovna had six sons and two daughters. The first son was named Nicholas, naturally, in honor of the emperor. (Alexander's brother Konstantin and sister Masha named their first-born sons Nicholas, too.)

The next heir, little Nicholas (who was called Niks by the family, like his grandfather), was incredibly talented and willful. He was the only one allowed by his grandfather to display his will. Niks did not want to study French. Alexander scolded him in the presence of the emperor.

"And how will you converse with ambassadors, Your Highness, if you do not learn French?"

"I'll have an interpreter!" the boy countered merrily.

"Bravo, my little friend! But then, Your Highness, all of Europe will laugh at you."

"Then I'll declare war on Europe," Niks replied, to his grandfather's delight.

In fact, the boy studied French and spoke it brilliantly.

The frequent pregnancies and the damp climate of St. Petersburg had a deleterious effect on Maria Alexandrovna's health. The combination led to pulmonary disease, which ate away at the tsarevna, as it had with previous German princesses.

As for the heir, there is little to write, except "His father eclipsed him." The intelligent and sparkling young man turned dull the minute he returned to Russia. His position required him to be a member of the State Council and the Committee of Ministers, but he did not show any particular initiative. He merely attended the meetings. His iron father wanted nothing but obedience and subordination.

Serfdom had become an abnormality in Europe, where it had been long abandoned. Nicholas realized that he had to do something with Russia's serfs. Slave labor was not productive, but that was not the issue. Back in 1839, Benkendorf wrote in a report from the Third Department that "serfs were a gunpowder cellar under the state." The head of the secret police cautiously raised the question: Should not the matter be settled from above before the serfs tried to free themselves from below?

Nicholas formed a Secret Committee on the Agrarian Issue. He always kept secret anything to do with possible change. Society should not be aware of the considerations of authority, he believed. The tsarevich, the future emancipator of the serfs, took an astonishing position on that committee—he held that nothing should be changed; everything was fine as it was. Alexander sensed that was what his father wanted to hear. He never forgot that any contrary opinion was squashed ruthlessly, and followed with his father's favorite rebuke: "Milksop!"

Alexander's rival for his father's attention had grown up in the meantime. Alexander's brother, Konstantin, or Kostya, was a full nine years younger. He was short and unattractive, unlike the rest of the tall, slender, and handsome Romanovs. He was very intelligent, mean, and sarcastic. His uncle, Grand Duke Mikhail Nikolayevich, dubbed him Aesop.

Aesop had a brilliant education, for Nicholas did not want his sons to have a haphazard and careless education like his own. He had Kostya brought up for the throne, just in case the heir "pulls a sudden trick and decides to die," as Maria Frederiks recalled it.

This education and his great successes in school gave rise to little Kostya's unbridled conceit. His amazing theories reached the tsar. "Sasha was born before our father became emperor, and I was born after. I am the son of the emperor and he is the son of a grand duke. It's not fair that Sasha is the heir."

His father punished the boy, repeating, "A divided kingdom falls. Remember that! God told us that. And it applies to the family." Kostya remembered.

Kostya was groomed to head the Naval Department. He formed a plan, remembering that Catherine the Great had named his uncle Konstantin because she dreamed he would become emperor of what had been Byzantium, which she would win back from the Turks. The boy presented his father with a plan for capturing Constantinople from the sea, so that he could then become emperor of Byzantium.

Once again, Nicholas had to temper Little Aesop's conceit, even though he liked it so much.

While smart little Kostya was growing up, the main intellectual force in the Romanov family was a woman, one of the most outstanding women of Nicholas's Russia. The Württemberg princess Fredericka Charlotte Maria was sixteen when Alexander I arranged a marriage between her and his youngest brother, Grand Duke Mikhail Pavlovich.

Elena Pavlovna (as she became known after her conversion to Orthodoxy) was brilliantly talented. She learned Russian during the journey to St. Petersburg, and then managed to read in Russian all three volumes of Karamzin's *History of the Russian State*.

In St. Petersburg she attended lectures at St. Petersburg University, frequented the Academy of Sciences and the Free Economic Society. She studied Orthodoxy and entered into discussions with Russian theologians. She was the only one permitted to argue (very delicately, of course) with the tsar, and he would hear her out, albeit mockingly. He dubbed her "the family scholar."

Her happy marriage to Grand Duke Mikhail mystified St. Petersburg.

Mikhail and the tsar were inseparable as children. They both proudly considered themselves martinets. When he became tsar, Nicholas appointed Mikhail commander of the guards. Mikhail worked assiduously to turn the dangerous guards into the ballet, harassing them with reviews and parades. Someone said of him, "He's got the Romanov disease, 'military parade fever.'"

He played the role of ruthless commander zealously. Brows furrowed and face grim, he watched the behavior of officers even at palace balls; his forbidding gaze did not pass over the ladies, however. Like his brother, he was a womanizer.

"Why look so dour? Everyone knows how good-natured you really are," the beautiful lady-in-waiting Alexandra Patkul once asked.

"I must punish, and the tsar show clemency," he explained gruffly, and then, without changing his somber tone, made her laugh with yet another of his puns. Gloomy-looking martinet Mikhail was brilliantly witty, and it was he who gave everyone in the family a pet name. His witticisms were repeated throughout St. Petersburg, and he was helpless, in turn, in the face of anyone's wit. Despite the cautions from Benkendorf, he often saved witty guardsmen from the wrath of the Third Department. He was mentor to a well-known wastrel in the Horse Guards, Bulgakov, whose dangerous jokes made the rounds. Bulgakov always lost at cards. He would casually drop by Mikhailovsky Palace to see his strict commander. In the presence of the valet (who was accustomed to the procedure), he would slip an envelope marked with the amount of his losses under the study door of the grand duke. In response, the envelope returned by the same path, filled with money.

Grand Duke Mikhail died young, and his forty-year-old widow turned her energies to public service. She built hospitals, created the

Russian Red Cross and the "sisters of mercy" movement. She was also the greatest patron of the arts in Russia. She described her mission as "bandaging the wings of young talents."

Her music secretary was one of the greatest musicians of the era, Anton Rubinstein. When he was a child, Liszt heard Rubinstein play and called him his heir. Later, young Rubinstein performed his famous act for the tsar, which never failed to amuse him. The wicked teenager imitated Liszt, ruthlessly parodying his manner of playing and his celebrated grimaces.

Rubinstein, the son of a converted Jew, stocky and with an enormous head of hair, very similar in appearance to Beethoven, became a close friend of Grand Duchess Elena Pavlovna. It was only with her help that a Jewish pianist could have founded the first conservatory in Russia, where a twenty-two-year-old official would come to study. His name was Peter Ilyich Tchaikovsky.

Elena Pavlovna gave young Rubinstein rooms in her wonderful palace on Kamenny Ostrov. His piano pieces, including "Kamenny Ostrov," capture the brilliant musical evenings in the palace of the middle-aged but still charming duchess.

She was always ahead of the curve, and naturally she was the first (after Nicholas) to manage to read Catherine's "Notes." Copies of the manuscript made during the reign of Paul I circulated in St. Petersburg's higher circles. Paul, stunned by his mother's memoirs, lent them overnight to his then close friend Prince Kurakin. (Overnight, his serf scribes made a copy for him.) Elena Pavlovna did not hide her delight in reading them, after which Nicholas ordered everyone in the court to hand over their copies; he started a real hunt for them.

Young Kostya and the not-young duchess formed the radical wing of the family. The faceless, apathetic heir looked even more gray next to them. No one would have thought then that a couple of decades later he would perform the greatest act in Russian history and that they would become his closest associates.

The question is whether the tsarevich was in fact apathetic or chose to appear that way.

"I don't need smart men, I need loyal ones." Nicholas's phrase was the motto of his empire. Everything in the country was done according to the rules, everything was subordinated once and for all to the established order. The idea of order was best served by the military. A military man, habituated to executing orders without asking questions, and capable of training others to follow orders, became the ideal executive. Real talent, knowledge, and experience stopped mattering. Gradually, the military held all the government positions.

All state officials wore uniforms. Even students wore uniforms. The dream of the assassinated Peter III and Paul I had come to pass: The country was ruled by the Prussian barracks. Reviews and parades became the primary content of state life. Everything was done for show, for the tsar, so that he would come and say, "Good!" hand out awards, and leave.

"What was behind that, in real life, no one bothered to look, that was the back alley," wrote a contemporary.

The military had to correct disorder everywhere. Nicholas was quite worried by the Jews who were unwilling to subordinate themselves to the general order of things, that is, become Christian. They wore the wrong clothing and read the wrong books. The tsar levied a tax on Jews for wearing yarmulkes and long coats. Then he banned Jewish clothing completely. A special committee for the final correction of Jews and converting them to Christianity was created. Naturally, the tsar considered the best medicine for improving Jews to be his beloved army. It used to be possible to pay a tax to avoid army service, but now the Jews were expected to send recruits. The tsar believed that in the course of army service, which was twenty-five years, Jews would become Christian. To speed up the process, Jewish boys at the age of twelve were given military preparation in special canton schools.

One such converted Jew who graduated from a canton school was an ancestor of Vladimir Ulyanov, better known as Lenin.

We will never know what young Alexander thought during those years of the country's silence. But the perceptive Custine, who saw him

then, wrote, "Beyond the external appearance of kindliness, which ye
and beauty and German blood usually give, we must recognize powerful
secretiveness in him, so unpleasant in a very young man." Life with an
all-powerful despot father will do that.

But the talented and sensitive young man had to see the amazing failures that occasionally happened in the iron system. The order that
Nicholas imposed to the point of absurdity began to turn into disorder.
It had begun even in the first decade of his reign. In 1836, in the darkest
hour of brutal censorship, the servile journal *Telescope* printed a daring
article that elicited shock and then a storm.

Its author was Peter Chaadayev, whose name would become a talisman
for all Russian liberals. His life could have been described by the bitter
words of his friend, Alexander Pushkin. "The devil made me born with
spirit and talent in Russia." The poet wrote of Chaadayev, "In Rome, he
would have been Brutus, in Athens, Pericles, but here he is simply a
Hussars officer." Alexander Griboyedov modeled the protagonist of *Woe
From Wit*, one of the most famous plays in Russian literature, on Chaadayev. The original title of the play, *Woe to Wit*, could serve as yet
another epigraph for his life.

A dashing officer who fought courageously in the Napoleonic wars,
and a handsome aristocrat, Chaadayev had a brilliant career under
Alexander I. The idol of St. Petersburg's youth and a celebrated dandy,
Chaadayev always went against the current. Russian higher society was
in the thrall of Francophilia—they dressed, spoke, and even thought in
French. As the diplomat Joseph de Maistre put it, "the French genius has
saddled Russia." So, naturally, Chaadayev became an Anglophile.

He retired in an extraordinary way. On his way to a top position, as
adjutant to the tsar, Chaadayev asked for permission to retire. At the age
of twenty-four, he became a mystic and philosopher. At the start of
Nicholas's reign, Chaadayev appeared frequently in St. Petersburg salons
and balls. His glorious head with perfect profile and cold gray-blue eyes
rose above the crowd. "He stood in silence, with a bitter smile and his

The arms formed the Latin letter V," wrote Alexan-
... it gestured showed his scornful veto to the servile life

... the mystic and philosopher spoke publicly—he printed an
article that blew up the obedient silence of the times. It was titled
"Philosophical Letter." How could it have appeared in the *Telescope*?
Censorship was so pervasive that no one expected anything any longer
from writers. The censors worked on automatic pilot. The dull title mis-
led them, and they read it inattentively.

"There hasn't been such a scandal in all the time since books and literary activity began in Russia." "For an entire month in all of Moscow
there hasn't been a house where they haven't been talking about Chaadayev's article and the 'Chaadayev affair,'" wrote contemporaries.

In his "Letter," Chaadayev attacked everything Alexander's father
held sacred. He blamed Russian Orthodoxy, and said it was a "fatal flaw"
that Russia "took Christianity from hopelessly outdated Byzantium,
which was despised by other nations by then." "This did not only create
a schism in Christianity. This kept us from going hand in hand with
other civilized nations. Isolated in our heresy, we could not absorb anything that went on in Europe. The separation of churches violated the
general course of history toward universal unification of all nations of
the Christian faith, violated "Thy Kingdom come.'"

Chaadayev wrote that "true religiousness sadly differs from the stifling atmosphere in which we always lived and apparently will live. For
we exist between West and East without having mastered the customs of
either one. We are in between. We are alone."

Looking at Russian history, Chaadayev made his terrible diagnosis,
"If we are moving forward, it is strangely: crookedly and sideways. If we
are growing, we never flourish. There is something in our blood that is
an obstacle to any true progress."

This was a challenge to a society accustomed to slavery. With shameful unanimity, it demanded ruthless punishment for the audacious
writer. The tsar responded wisely. If he were to punish Chaadayev, it
would imply that a person could have his own opinion, hostile to the

state, in his empire. Instead, he came up with an amazing punishment: He declared one of the most exceptional thinkers of Russia mad. The tsar mockingly ordered the Moscow governor to protect Chaadayev "with his addled reason" from "the effects of the damp and cold air that could exacerbate his illness." That meant that the philosopher was to be kept under house arrest. Further showing his "concern," the tsar ordered constant medical supervision for Chaadayev. Now he would be visited by a physician who would report monthly to the concerned tsar "on the health of the deranged."

What did eighteen-year-old Alexander think of Chaadayev's work? Most likely, he did not read it. But he had to be aware of the scandal that rocked both capitals, Moscow and St. Petersburg, especially when the tsar himself dealt with Chaadayev.

Certainly Alexander knew about the next literary scandal, which resonated throughout Europe.

When he had traveled abroad, Sasha saw that his father was mocked in Europe. His uncle, Alexander I, the savior of monarchic Europe from revolutionary Bonaparte, felt entitled to interfere in European affairs. Nicholas considered himself the legal heir of his conqueror brother. The tsar believed that Russia's historical mission was to control European affairs—to guard European order.

He gave Europe a lesson early in his reign. Poland rose up, and the army of his field marshal Paskevich stormed Warsaw. Scaffolds, the scorched estates of rebellious aristocrats, and the destruction of the remnants of Polish self-rule was the penalty the insurgent Poles had to pay.

Karl Nesselrode, Nicholas's minister of foreign affairs, formulated the goal this way: "The threat of revolutions in Europe forces Russia to support the regime wherever it exists, bolster it where it is weakening, and defend it where it is attacked."

Thus Nicholas appointed himself the gendarme of Europe. He was also ridiculously high-handed. Never forgetting that after his defeat at the hands of Napoleon, the king of Prussia had only saved his throne thanks to Russia, he treated his father-in-law like a butler. On his trip, Sasha heard people wonder at Nicholas's rudeness in Berlin and openly laugh at his pretensions in London and Vienna. In Europe Sasha read the European press, filled with jokes and insults at his father's expense. His father hated the European newspapers and had them confiscated at the border.

Benkendorf came up with a way to change public opinion. His agents in Paris reported that a famous writer, the marquis de Custine, was hoping to travel in Russia and write about it. The marquis was the grandson of a famous general guillotined during the terror of the French Revolution. His father died on the guillotine as well. He was influential in Paris, had entrée in fashionable salons, and (most important) was a fanatic supporter of absolute monarchy. "His book will change the unfair opinion of Europe," claimed Benkendorf.

Nicholas liked Benkendorf's idea. He decided to invite the marquis and make him welcome in Russia. Nicholas even agreed to receive him. But unfortunately, as the saying goes, "We wanted to do it as well as possible, but instead it turned out as usual."

While the tsar prepared to charm the Frenchman, customs agents at the border roughly searched the marquis and confiscated all his books in French. His pleasures continued in St. Petersburg, where he stayed at the best hotel (today's Hotel Evropa), where he was kept awake all night by hordes of bedbugs.

The emperor received the marquis. Expecting sympathy, Nicholas laid out his principles to Custine, monarchist to monarchist. "Russia has despotism, because only it suits the spirit of the people. As for a constitution, I would sooner retreat to China than permit that kind of government in Russia."

Custine liked Nicholas's appearance: "The most handsome monarch in Europe." Custine's sexual orientation made him particularly sensitive to masculine beauty. But the conversations with the tsar did not inspire the marquis. Custine was a monarchist, yes, but he was a proponent of enlightened monarchy. Police despotism, which he saw at every step, did not please him.

Visiting the place where the emperor's father and grandfather had been killed, Custine noted the Russian paradox: Ruthless despotism in Russia did have limitations, imposed by ruthless murder.

Other Russian paradoxes struck the marquis throughout his journey. For example, at the Kremlin in Moscow he was proudly shown the two greatest points of interest. The Tsar Bell, "the biggest bell in the world, weighing 200 tons, from which unfortunately a piece had broken off and it never rang. And the Tsar Cannon, the world's largest cannon, which had, unfortunately, never been shot."

While in Moscow he met with the period's greatest dissident, Chaadayev. Custine borrowed one of Chaadayev's famous bon mots for his book. Chaadayev said, "What a lovely city Moscow is: They keep showing people historical absurdities, a cannon that was never shot and a bell that fell and does not ring. A bell without a tongue is the perfect symbol for my beloved Russia."

Custine's book *Russia in 1839* was published in 1843. The marquis painted his portrait of Russia in it: "You have to live in that desert called Russia in order to feel all the freedom of life in other European countries." "Here everything is oppressed, cowering in fear, everything is grim, silent, and blindly obedient to the invisible rod." "Stupid and iron army discipline has shackled one and all." "In France you can achieve everything using the orator's tribune. In Paris the ability to speak will elevate you to the heights of power. In Russia, the ability to be silent will elevate you." "The most insignificant person, if he manages to please the tsar, can become the most important one in the state. As one of the emperors said, 'An aristocrat in Russia is someone with whom I am now conversing and for only as long as I converse with him.'" "There are slaves in many countries, but to see so many court slaves you must travel to Russia."

This applied not only to the emperor's court. Custine described the heir's court, where he was struck by the "toadying spirit that united nobles with their own servants" and the astonishing combination in courtiers of "servility and arrogance."

Custine, like many foreigners, had not understood Russian traditions. Ambassador Herberstein, who came to Russia in the reign of the father of Ivan the Terrible, was stunned by the servility of Russian boyars. Even if the tsar meted out the most horrible punishment, impalement, the boyar who sat on the pike continued to praise the tsar.

"We serve our tsars not in your manner," they explained, proud of their slavery.

This was a country where noblemen in petitions called themselves serfs, that is, slaves. Ivan the Terrible formulated those relations: "We are free to pardon and to execute our serfs."

Universal lying came out of the slavery. "Until now I had thought that the truth was as necessary to man as air and sunshine. My travels in Russia have shown me otherwise. Lying here means preserving the throne, telling the truth means shaking the foundations," wrote the marquis.

Custine made a remarkable prediction. Observing the gigantic empire cemented by fear, slavery, lies, the Third Department, church, and autocracy, the Frenchman wrote, "In less than fifty years, Russia will have a revolution." He was off by only a decade. In 1905, in the reign of Nicholas I's great-grandson and namesake, the revolution began.

When Nicholas I read Custine's book, he threw it on the floor. "It's my own fault! Why did I ever speak to that scoundrel!"

The book was banned, carefully confiscated from foreigners at the border, and yet, it was read by everyone in Russia. "The tsar barricaded the country with a fence, but the fence has cracks and the wind blows through them harder than a free wind," wrote Alexander Herzen scornfully. In the country stifled by the Third Department, books smuggled in from the West circulated in great numbers.

Did Alexander read Custine's book? Most likely. There is no better advertising than a ban. "Banned goods are like forbidden fruit: The price doubles with the ban. Custine's book was read by all of educated Russia," wrote Alexander Turgenev.

There was another power in Russia: Along with the power of the emperor, there was the power of the bribe. As a contemporary joked, "I could bring in not only French books but a French guillotine—I just have to settle on how much it will cost."

The military were not good executives, and corruption began to rule. The military became part of it. It took place in the back alley of the regime; along the façade, everything looked good.

Nicholas demanded that the "scoundrel" Custine be paid back. The Third Department organized articles against Custine in Russia and abroad. Zhukovsky wrote to Alexander Turgenev and asked him to reply to Custine. He warned him that "the reply to Custine should be brief; you should not attack the book, for there is a lot of truth in it, but Custine."

"Why attack it, if it's true?" wondered Turgenev.

Alexander Herzen is the greatest figure in the history of liberal Russia. All the famous radicals of Europe—Proudhon, Garibaldi, Owen, Kohut, Hugo—knew and respected that fantastic Russian. He was the illegitimate son of a wealthy Russian landowner and a German woman his father brought back to Moscow from his European trip. The love child was given a surname based on the German word for "heart." At university, Herzen contracted a rare disease in imperial Russia—a love of liberty. It ended with the arrest of the twenty-two-year-old student, exile, and emigration. Once abroad, Herzen did an incredible thing: He declared war on the empire.

In the silent country, oppressed by censorship, the truth resounded only from abroad. Herzen founded the Free Russian Printing Press outside Russia, and with another émigré, his friend the poet Nicholas Ogarev, began publishing the famous newspaper *Kolokol* (The Bell), with its motto, "I toll for the living." Despite the strict ban, *Kolokol* was smuggled into the country, to be read by all of educated Russia. A lone émigré became the mighty empire's greatest foe.

Scandalous financial affairs of influential Russian officials and secret government decrees appeared in the pages of *Kolokol*. Who informed Herzen? Officials. When one wanted to damage another, he wrote a denunciation. Not to the tsar, who might not pay heed, but to a more powerful source—*Kolokol*. That got the tsar's attention right away, because Nicholas read the despised newspaper closely.

Alexander knew this.

The years passed. It was not easy for Nicholas to love Alexander, for their characters were so different. Nicholas's temper erupted frequently. He could not bear tardiness, and the very first time the heir's wife was late for a ceremony, although Nicholas was a true knight who could not scold a woman, Alexander was called a "sluggish cow" publicly. His constant docile apathy irritated Nicholas.

His brother was quite unlike him. Konstantin unfurled furious activity at the Naval Department. He founded the Russian Geographical Society, where he gathered other energetic young men. Many of his ideas seemed foolish and even dangerous to the tsar. Kostya suggested building steamships, but Nicholas did not like newfangled things. Stubborn Kostya then offered to build them with his own money. Nicholas still believed in sails, but he was enchanted by Konstantin's wild energy. He saw himself in him.

To rouse his heir a bit, the tsar sent his son to war in the Caucasus. The Caucasus was a Babylon with dozens of ethnic groups that spoke forty languages. From the cloudy peaks of Ossetia, Kabardia, Chechnya, and Dagestan, militant mountain raiders attacked Russian lands. The Caucasus was in constant turmoil, and the peoples there allied themselves with Russia's ancient foes, the Turkish Empire and the Persians.

In 1828, Nicholas began a war on the Caucasus with the aim of uniting the northern area with the previously annexed Transcaucasus— Georgia, Armenia, and Azerbaijan. But the sons of militant Islam did not want to follow in the footsteps of the Orthodox Georgians and Armenians. Mullah Mohamed declared a jihad against Russia. It was in Dagestan and Chechnya that Muridism, the militant branch of Islam, was born. It provided the prototype for the Islamic warriors of the twentieth century.

The Murids sought salvation in shedding the blood of Christians. They fought fearlessly, a contemporary wrote, because they were filled with "fantasized descriptions of paradise with beautiful houris and other earthly delights. Dead warriors immediately were sent to this picturesque paradise. It was Allah's generous reward for the blood of the infidels. Thus death itself was conquered by these wild beliefs, which helped them kill fearlessly and die joyfully."

The Murids hid in the woods, like animals, and attacked from there. In order to move forward, Nicholas's soldiers had to try a new tactic—chop down the forests and build fortresses in their place. The cruelty of the Murids elicited cruelty in response, in an ever-spiraling escalation of violence. Peaceful villages that had sheltered Murids were burned down.

Things came to a head when the Caucasian tribes found a great leader, the imam Shamil. He managed the impossible: He united the various tribes that spoke different languages and that often fought among themselves under his authoritarian rule. He created a strong state in the wild mountains, a new system of relations in an anarchic milieu.

Shamil created a religious state (imamate) uniting Chechnya, Dagestan, and Avaria, headed by himself as the imam, the military and religious leader. The conflation of spiritual and earthly power is in the tradition of Islam, and it gave Shamil absolute power over the souls and lives of his subjects. He was a typically ruthless eastern dictator. He armed the entire male population between fifteen and fifty. The men now lived in military camps, where they were trained in using rifles.

Throughout the 1840s, Shamil terrorized Nicholas's army. This period revealed the impotence of the huge Russian army in fighting the imamate. Partisan war—the sudden raids by the tribesmen—brought larger casualties to the Russians than ordinary battles. It was impossible to fight in Chechnya in the summer, when the mountains were covered by forests that hid the Murids. In the winter, the Russians could not fight in Dagestan, where the mountain passes became impenetrable. Shamil's troops had much more room for maneuver.

Shamil always led his men into battle. Always in front, he was wounded nineteen times.

The war had dragged on for over twenty years, with no end in sight. In 1850, the tsar sent Alexander to Chechnya, "to smell gunpowder." As usual, away from his father, Alexander was completely transformed. He was full of energy and looked forward to combat.

The first real battle for Alexander took place near the fortress of Achkhoi, where a Chechen company was discovered in the forest. The battle began early in the morning. We can imagine the officers' tent, heated by burning coals. He slept a heavy but restless sleep, as to be expected before battle. It was still dark when his adjutant woke him, with candlelight in his sleepy eyes and the respectful announcement, "Your Imperial Highness, we are attacking."

The mountain range drowned in the sunrise. Smoke rose from the villages on the mountainside, a small river glistened. The Russian army was going up the heavenly mountain when two dozen Chechens burst out of the woods above. One, in a dark *beshmet,* a quilted coat, stood in his stirrups and juggled his whip, then tossed it to his left hand and seemingly plucked his rifle out of the air like a magician. He twirled it, tossed it up, caught it, and shot. This was the first time Alexander heard a bullet whiz by at such close range. A young orderly clutched his chest and slipped from his horse.

Alexander galloped at the Chechens, bringing the convoy and Cossacks after him. The Chechens headed for the woods, where they hid behind fallen trees. All that showed was the glint of their rifles, catching in the sun. Jumping down from their horses, ahead of Alexander, the Cossacks and the retinue attacked the log barriers. They began hand-to-hand combat, while other Chechens shot at them from the trees. Many soldiers were buried after Alexander's bold but irrational attack. They killed all the Chechens and he was given their leader's saber. His father awarded him the Cross of St. George, but recalled him to the capital.

This is all that can be told about his dashing time in the Caucasus. But in the early 1850s Count Leo Tolstoy arrived in the Caucasus. He was twenty-three and of a notable aristocratic family. His celebrated ancestors had been military leaders and had taken part in very bloody events. His great-grandfather, Peter Tolstoy, was a comrade-in-arms of Peter the Great and had been head of the terrible Secret Chancellery, the secret police. He managed to lure the tsarevich Alexei back to Russia. Peter I's son, who had dared to take a stand against his father, had fled abroad. Peter Tolstoy got him back and took part in killing him—killing the tsar's son on the father's orders.

Leo Tolstoy had not come to the Caucasus as a tourist; he was feeling the vapidity of high society and of himself—his gambling and drinking sprees. This flight from his previous life is the start of his great biography, just as another would be its culmination. At the end of his life, the old man tried to flee his previous life, leaving behind his family and his house in Yasnaya Polyana. The great refugee died along the way, in a small railroad station.

In 1852, Tolstoy was an army cadet taking part in the war on Chechens. (Three of his serfs came as cadets with the count.) In combat, Leo Tolstoy earned the rank of officer. Through the eyes of a brave officer and great writer we can see that side of the war in the Caucasus. In the manuscript of "The Raid," Tolstoy describes an ordinary scene: A general cheerfully allows his soldiers to loot a captured village.

> "Well, colonel," said the general, smiling, "let them go burn and pillage, I can see that they really want to do it." Dragoons, Cossacks, and infantry scattered across the village. A roof collapses there, a door is broken in, here a fence burns, a house, a haystack. . . . Here's a Cossack dragging a sack of cornmeal, a soldier a carpet and two chickens, another, a wash basin and a jar of milk, a third has loaded up a donkey with all kinds of goods; others are leading an almost naked, frightened, decrepit old Chechen, who had not managed to run away.

Here is another description, from Tolstoy's *Khadji Murat*. "Returning to the village, Sado found his house looted. His son, a handsome boy with shining eyes, had been brought dead to the mosque. He had been bayoneted in the back. Women wailed in all the houses. Small children wailed with their mothers. The hungry cattle wailed, too, and there was no food for them."

Had Alexander seen that side of the war? How could he not? It was side by side with the romance. It was a bloody and ruthless war. His father left as his legacy a war that dragged on for a quarter century. Alexander would have to bring it to an end, as he would another war, humiliatingly lost by his father, which would become a catastrophe for Russia.

Count Leo Tolstoy would be in that war, too.

Following the traditions of Catherine, whom he disliked, Nicholas regarded his growing grandson with hope. There was someone who could be a true tsar. But the boy was not growing fast enough. Something had changed in Nicholas's health. He was weary and an unconscious anxiety wore away at him. As Herzen put it, "Animals worry this way before an earthquake."

He turned seriously to preparing Alexander for the throne. He spent hours taking walks with him, talking. Later, Alexander would say that "we always used the informal 'Thou' with each other." But how it differed in usage. Alexander addressed his father as a god, and his father treated him like a milksop.

In 1848, Europe was shaken by an earthquake when revolution came. Nicholas said with some exulting that he had foreseen it. When the monarchy fell in France, he appeared at a ball and allegedly said to the officers: "Saddle up, gentlemen, France is a republic!"

He thought his hour of glory had come: Russia would return order to a crazed Europe. He called on Austria, England, and Prussia to recollect the principles of the Holy Alliance that had been created against revolutions. No one heeded his call, yet. Nicholas was lucky. A Hungarian uprising began in the Austro-Hungarian Empire and Nicholas offered his aid to the Austrian emperor. Franz Josef gladly accepted. At last, they really could saddle up. Once again, Nicholas's most talented general, the conqueror of Poland, Field Marshal Paskevich, crushed the revolution. Rebel Hungarians were hanged mercilessly. But for some reason, instead of being grateful, Europe called Nicholas a despot and a cannibal.

After the revolution in Europe, Nicholas instituted total supervision in literature. Almost everything was banned. The great writer Nikolai

Gogol, once a favorite of the tsar, was banned. When another great writer, Ivan Turgenev, wrote a powerful obituary after Gogol's death, he was imprisoned for a month and then banished from the capital. Another celebrity, the playwright Alexander Ostrovsky, was placed under police surveillance for one of his comedies (*It's a Family Affair—We'll Settle It Ourselves*), as was the renowned satirist Mikhail Saltykov-Shchedrin.

Not long before, the Westernizers (writers and pundits who believed in a European path of development for Russia and were therefore particularly enamored of the reformer Peter the Great) and the Slavophiles (who believed in Russia's special, national path and therefore did not like Peter) had debated furiously in literary "holy battles." Now both sides were silent, because both tendencies were banned. Any thought at all was persecuted.

"There is reason to lose one's mind . . . the situation becomes more intolerable with every day. Many decent people have fallen into despair and watch with dull calm to see when this world will fall apart," wrote the famous Westernizer Professor Granovsky.

In that deadly silence, in that dense fog, a very dangerous light exploded.

In the later 1840s a certain M. Butashevich-Petrashevsky served as translator in the Ministry of Foreign Affairs. As Pushkin put it, "He is an original in our country, for he thinks." And in fact, at a time when all the loyalists had fully comprehended that thinking was out of the question, Petrashevsky not only dared to think, he spoke his thoughts aloud. He was an original in everything. When officials tried to appear unremarkable and dressed in uniforms or similar civil dress, this gentleman wore outrageous clothing—a Spanish cloak and top hat. Long hair was banned by the authorities, but Petrashevsky figured out how to get around it. He shaved his head and wore a long-haired wig. He added a beard, which was also not approved. In those extremely serious times, Petrashevsky mocked the rules.

Soon this original, mocking gentleman decided that thinking alone was not enough. On Fridays he invited other young men to come think at his house. They were minor officials, officers, teachers, writers, painters. Gradually the Fridays at Petrashevsky's turned into a club. They discussed fashionable European movements—the socialism of Fourier, Proudhon, and others (whose books were naturally banned in Russia)— and spoke of the necessity for freeing the serfs and for open trials. The most radical even thought about setting up an underground printing press.

Benkendorf's creation worked efficiently. The secret police learned about the thinking young men right away and infiltrated the circle with an agent. The Petrashevsky group was arrested. Among the prisoners was a young but already known writer, Fedor Dostoevsky.

From his youth until his death, terror and revolution, an apocalyptic vision of the future held Dostoevsky in its grip. Blood, suffering, and religion were part of his birthright. He was born in the section for the poor of the Maryinsky Hospital, where his father worked as a doctor. Family legend has it that his father, a temperamental and tormented neurasthenic, was killed by his own serfs. His passionately religious mother took the children annually on a pilgrimage to Russia's main monastery, Trinity–St. Sergius Monastery. She taught them to read using the book *Four Hundred Holy Stories from the Old and New Testaments.* "In our family we knew the Bible from our earliest childhood," wrote Dostoevsky. They read aloud Karamzin's *History of the Russian State* and the poetry of the "demigod" Pushkin.

In January 1838, Dostoevsky, seventeen, entered the Main Engineering School, which trained military engineers. The school was located in Mikhailovsky Castle, where Paul I had been murdered, but now the tragic castle had been renamed the Engineering Castle, and the bedroom where the tsar's blood had been shed was locked forever. (In midcentury, the Chapel of Sts. Peter and Paul would be erected on the spot.)

Painful associations inflamed his morbid imagination. Study there was hard for him. The nervous youth was quick to take injury, conceited, and profoundly resentful of mustering and military discipline.

The meaning of his life, his relief, and his island of tormenting solitude was literature.

He started writing, and dreamed of devoting himself to literary work. As soon as he graduated, he retired from engineering. He had no doubts that glory awaited him as a writer.

His dream came true strangely and marvelously. "Unexpectedly, all of a sudden," Dostoevsky began writing the novel *Poor Folk* and "gave myself up to it wholeheartedly." His friend (subsequently a famous writer himself, Dmitri Grigorovich), who shared a flat with him, gave the manuscript to Nikolai Nekrasov, then already a celebrated poet and, more important, a successful publisher. What happened next is a legend in the history of Russian literature. Nekrasov and Grigorovich stayed up reading *Poor Folk,* unable to put it down. At four in the morning they came to awaken "the great talent and express delight."

Nekrasov published the novel, which was a triumphant, smashing debut. Vissarion Belinsky, the main literary critic of the period, predicted a great future for Dostoevsky. He was accepted in Belinsky's circle, composed of Russia's most famous writers.

Tragedy followed right away. Everyone had expected a new masterpiece from him. Dostoevsky worked feverishly, writing ten novellas before his arrest. He was too hasty. One evening at Belinsky's, he read "The Double." His great admirer and all the members of the circle failed to appreciate or understand it. The split personality and the dark subconscious games of the story were alien to their harmonious and simpler worldview. But young Dostoevsky would not forgive their lapse in recognition. A chill developed in the relationship between the writer and the critic and his circle.

Dostoevsky fell into the typical syndrome of a man ahead of his time—a constant shortage of money, literary hackwork to pay the bills, and a falling-out with the literary establishment. It tormented him. He "suffered from an irritation of the entire nervous system" more and more frequently, and the first symptoms appeared of the epilepsy he had for the rest of his life.

It was in that spring of 1847 that Dostoevsky started attending

Petrashevsky's Fridays. It eased his loneliness. He also joined a secret society formed by Nikolai Speshnev, the most radical member of the Petrashevsky circle. Handsome, a wealthy landowner, cold seducer, and ruthless revolutionary, he dreamed of a bloody revolt. Nikolai Speshnev was the first devil in Dostoevsky's life. This "Mephistopheles" had an enormous influence on the writer, who eventually used him for his character Nikolai Stavrogin in the novel *The Possessed* (also known as *The Devils*).

At dawn on April 23, 1849, the writer who had made a triumphant debut was arrested with the other members of the Petrashevsky circle and incarcerated in the harshest part of the Peter and Paul Fortress, the Alexeyevsky ravelin, where he spent eight months under investigation and interrogation.

When they were brought to the Third Department, "Some walked trying to keep to the wall, afraid to step on the parquet floor in the center of the room, for they believed in the Sheshkovsky trap. They were afraid that the floor would sink and they would be whipped," recalled P. A. Kuzmin, one of the members of the circle.

Things turned out much worse than that. As Petrashevsky put it, they were tried and "found guilty for their intentions." So that no one else would consider being original in the future, that is, to think dangerous thoughts, twenty-one people were condemned to execution.

The inventive tsar came up with a little guignol scenario to play out. The men who had dared to think would be brought to the execution site on Semenovsky Square, and after all the preparations for the execution squad to begin had been made, they would be pardoned. The commander of the guards was to organize the "execution."

The commander, Grand Duke Mikhail Nikolayevich, "martinet and wit," died while Dostoevsky and the others were incarcerated in the fortress. The emperor came to the fortress for the funeral of his favorite brother at the Cathedral of Sts. Peter and Paul. It had been a difficult year for the royal family, and especially for Alexander. His daughter, Grand Duchess Alexandra, died that summer at the age of seven. He marked that day in his diary, outlining the page with a black mourning stripe and placing a dried flower between the pages. It must have come from her funeral.

Upon the death of Mikhail, the tsar made Alexander the new commander of the guards and grenadiers. Now he would have to act out the sham execution. On its eve, the minister of war told Alexander, "The implementation of bringing out the squad and the announcement by Adjutant General Sumarokov of the highest confirmation [clemency], already known to Your Imperial Highness, depends on the orders of Your Imperial Highness."

Alexander got up before dawn on December 22, 1849, to organize the terrible show on Semenovsky Square. Thus it was that Dostoevsky and Alexander virtually met on the scaffold.

Dostoevsky returned to those minutes many times in his work. They were awakened on the black December morning. The cathedral bells struck 6:30. They were placed in carriages and brought to Semenovsky Square to hear the sentence. Still dressed in the April clothes they wore at the time of their arrest, they were brought out into the freezing cold of the square.

They were led up onto the scaffold, which was covered in black cloth, and there each man was read his death sentence. A priest, carrying a cross, rose to the scaffold to hear their last confessions. "The horrible, immeasurably horrible minutes of awaiting death began," recalled Dostoevsky. "It was cold, so terribly cold. They removed not only our coats, but our jackets. And it was minus twenty degrees."

Loose white garments were put on them and the first three condemned men, including Petrashevsky, were brought down from the scaffold to be shot. Stakes had been erected. They were tied to the stakes and hoods were placed over their heads. The execution squad lined up.

"We were taken in threes. I was in the second group. I had no more than a minute left to live," Dostoevsky wrote. He had spent a horrible quarter hour, convinced that he would be dead in a few minutes.

"Aim!" The soldiers raised their rifles.

And then came the reprieve. The tsar's pardon was read out loud.

"I received the news of the termination of the execution dully. There was no joy at returning to the living. People around me were shouting and making noise. But I didn't care, I had already lived through the very worst. Yes, yes, the very worst. Wretched Grigoryev went mad. . . . How did the others survive? I don't know. We didn't even catch cold."

The inexpressible joy of life came to him later, in the cell, when the predeath shock was over and he fully realized what had happened. "I was at the last moment and now I am alive again!" His wife remembered, "He was so happy that day. He would never recall another such time. He walked up and down in his cell and sang loudly, he kept singing. He was so happy to have the gift of life."

Instead of execution, the Petrashevsky group was sent to hard labor, with convicts. Petrashevsky did not stop his mocking, even after the execution farce. As they put on their convicts' uniforms and shackles, he looked around and burst out laughing. "Really, friends, we look so ridiculous in these outfits."

Dostoevsky was sentenced to four years of hard labor, "stripped of all rights and with subsequent service as a soldier."

Having restored order at home, Nicholas went on with restoring order in the world. In 1853, he protected the rights of Orthodox Christians in Palestine with his usual bluntness. He demanded special rights for Orthodox Christians from the Turks—an ultimatum. When the Turks refused, he declared war. His armies quickly occupied the Danube principalities of Moldavia and Walachia. But here, to his surprise, Austria, which he had recently rescued, moved its army to aid Turkey. He gave the order to retreat, but too late. The British and French fleets had arrived in the Black Sea. Turkey's brave refusal was suddenly explained— European powers supported the Turks. Nicholas was caught in a trap. Instead of his being able to dictate the rules to Europe, those states had united against him and were going to dictate to him.

The coalition against him included the hated France, now ruled by Bonaparte's nephew, Napoleon III. England was with him. The Austrian emperor, whom Nicholas had helped end the uprising in Hungary, was behaving in a particularly low manner. He was with his enemies.

This was the start of the Crimean War. The army Nicholas considered the most powerful in Europe was destroyed. It turned out that his army was fighting the army of Napoleon III with weapons of the era of Napoleon I. His navy was hopelessly obsolete. The might of his army existed only in parades and the reports of his yes men. The allies landed sixty thousand French and British soldiers in Crimea and surrounded the Russians in Sevastopol. In a very short time, the enemy navy entered "his" Baltic Sea, and he could observe the ships through binoculars from his study in his favorite little villa, Alexandria. His family could see that shame every day.

It was then, for the first time, that Alexander saw that his father did need him. The guards went off to war and he, commander of the guards, began preparing reserves on his father's orders. The allies might land men onto the shore and try to take St. Petersburg. Alexander and the reserves would have to protect the Baltic coast and the imperial capital.

Losing the war changed Nicholas. The giant grew stoop-shouldered and much gentler. He readily listened to family suggestions. Grand Duchess Elena Pavlovna proposed sending female nurses and the famous surgeon Nikolai Pirogov to the Crimea. Nicholas agreed instantly. The Württemberg princess saved numerous lives: Pirogov operated on hundreds of men, and one-hundred and sixty nurses struggled to help the wounded in terrible circumstances.

Nicholas wanted to show ungrateful Europe that he was a knight despite their betrayal. He sent Alexander to besieged Sevastopol, turned to ruins by allied artillery, to verify that prisoners of war were being treated humanely.

Upon his arrival, the heir saw an amusing scene. There had been a storm the night before and the British ship carrying wages for their troops had sunk. In the breaks between attacks, Russian soldiers dived for British coins.

Then he spoke with French and English prisoners. They were satisfied and said that they were treated well. As he was leaving, one French officer asked for permission to speak to him privately. He said, "Your Majesty, we ask only one thing: Please keep us in separate quarters from those Englishmen!" That was how much love the European allies had for each other. It convinced Alexander that the European unions and friendships were always temporary. He also understood something else on that visit—Sevastopol, the most vital Russian port on the Black Sea, was doomed.

He told his father frankly, and his father's weakness was horrible to behold. His eyes filled with tears. "That giant, so intolerant of men's tears, now often wept," wrote the maid of honor Anna Tyutcheva. The tsar, who had once thrown Marquis de Custine's book on the floor in a rage, now almost repeated the "scoundrel's" words verbatim in his diary: "Ascending on the throne, I passionately wanted to know the truth, but after listening to lies and flattery every day for thirty years, I have lost the ability to tell truth from lie."

Now, as he watched the catastrophe unfold, he wanted it.

Events wore him down. When Nicholas caught an ordinary cold, he refused to treat it. He no longer wanted to live, after the defeat of his army. Rumors spread later that when he despaired of dying of influenza, the tsar demanded poison from his physician, Dr. Mandt, who begged him not to do it. But the tsar, as usual, brooked no argument. He had trained everyone well; no one dared to say no. In any case, Dr. Mandt hastily left Russia after Nicholas's death.

The poison story seems to be just a legend like the one about Alexander I going off to be a hermit in Siberia. Both brothers simply stopped wanting to live. Nicholas, like Alexander before him, gave himself up to death.

On February 14, 1855, Nicholas ordered the court be informed of his illness. The enormous and cold palace vestibule outside his study filled with people—ladies-in-waiting, maids of honor, all ranks of courtiers, ministers, generals. It was as if no one was there, it was so quiet. In the twilight of the poorly lit vestibule, the only sounds were the howling wind and the breathing of the silent crowd. They stood, waiting for the resolution. The ruthless reign was drawing to a close.

In his first-floor study, Nicholas lay on the camp bed, under a military greatcoat. He no longer allowed anyone in besides his wife and children. For the first time, all state papers were brought to the heir. To the court's amazement, apathetic Sasha was transformed. Now he was full of energy. The liberation from the will of his beloved father had taken place. The coming responsibility, the heavy crown of Monomakh to be worn during the coronation, was making him act.

Alexander went into his father's study. The dying emperor no longer asked about business. He had just taken Communion. The empress, his children and grandchildren were gathered around the bed.

"Will it be soon?" the dying man impatiently demanded of the doctor. Mandt promised that his lungs would soon be paralyzed.

Nicholas blessed everyone individually. Despite his increasing weakness, he talked with each family member. He blessed Masha, Alexander's wife, whom he had loved. He took her hand and looked over at his wife, asking her to take care of her. After blessing them all, he said, "Remember what I have so often asked: Remain friends."

The empress was kind to him to the end. She said, "They wish to say good-bye to you—Yulya Baranova, Ekaterina Tizengausen." For the sake of propriety, she listed all her maids of honor. But she ended with: "And Varenka Nelidova."

Nicholas thanked her with his eyes and said, "No, dear, I must not see her anymore, tell her that I beg her forgiveness, that I prayed for her . . . and ask that she pray for me."

It was Alexander's turn. Everyone moved away from the bed. The dying tsar said, "I am passing command to you that is not in desirable order. I am leaving you many disappointments and cares." He paused. And then in his former strong voice he ended, "But hold everything! Hold it like that!" And making a hard fist with his iron hand, he showed Alexander how Russia should be held.

Then the sanctity of his coming death returned to him and he said, "Now I must be alone, to prepare for the final moment."

This solemn parting enriched the lives of his family, and it was also one of the reasons Alexander would fear assassination so much. He wanted to leave with prayer, like his father.

Lady-in-waiting Anna Tyutcheva described how the dying tsar's mistress, not permitted at his bedside, wandered, hair loosened, through the palace filled with silent, waiting courtiers. When she saw Tyutcheva, Varenka Nelidova clutched her hand, feverishly jiggled it, and whispered, *"Une belle nuit, une belle nuit!"* (A beautiful night, a beautiful night!) She did not know what she was saying, she was so distraught.

The tsar had a pronounced death rattle, and he gasped hoarsely to Mandt, *"Wird diese infame Musik noch lange dauern?"* (Will this disgusting music continue much longer?) Mandt assured him it would not be long.

The priest blessed the dying man with his cross. The tsar made a sign for him to bless Alexander and his wife with it. He tried to show his love for the family until his dying breath. After the Communion, the tsar said, "Lord, accept me in peace." He also managed to whisper hoarsely to his wife, "You were always my guardian angel, from the moment I first saw you until this last minute."

He said nothing else. The death agony was brief. He passed away, and the thirty-year reign was over. The family kneeled at his bed.

When Alexander looked at his father, he was amazed: His father looked younger and his features seemed carved in white marble. As Anna Tyutcheva later described it, "The unearthly expression of peace and completion seemed to say, 'I already know everything, see everything.'"

Alexander got up from knees as Emperor Alexander II.

As he came out of the study, he heard people saying, "May the Lord bless you, Your Majesty." He said, "Don't call me that yet: It's still too painful. I have to get used to it."

At the funeral in the Cathedral of Sts. Peter and Paul, the sun shone. The coffin rested on a pedestal covered with red brocade under a canopy of silver brocade and ermine. The cathedral, filled with rays of sunshine, also glowed with thousands of candles. The new empress told Anna Tyutcheva later that at the moment when the coffin was to be closed, the dowager empress put a cross made of the mosaic from the church of Hagia Sofia in Constantinople over his heart. She wanted to believe that the dream of liberating Constantinople and the fellow Slavs from the Turks was what had killed her knight.

His brother Kostya was first to pledge his loyalty to Alexander, in order to quell any rumors of rivalry between them. Before the ceremony, they fell into each other's arms and wept bitterly for their father. Kostya said, "I want everyone to know that I am the first and most loyal of all the emperor's subjects." There had been rivalry, but the death and the final words of their father reconciled them forever. They would be together to the very end.

Then came the ringing of the bells, followed by a gun salute in honor of the new emperor. The celebratory shots somehow echoed the horrible cannon fire that had accompanied his father's ascension to the throne. It reminded Alexander that the guards' attacks on the palace were over, thanks to his father. The guards were forever banished from interfering in the affairs of the Romanov dynasty. For the first time in almost a century and a half, the succession passed in total tranquility.

Tsar Alexander II and his large family came out on the balcony of the Winter Palace above the Saltykov Entrance (that was the entrance to the private apartments of the royal family) to greet his subjects. Nicholas, 13, Alexander, 11, Vladimir, 9, Alexei, 6, and Maria, 3, and their mother surrounded the new emperor.

He would come out on that balcony above the Saltykov Entrance after every assassination attempt. A quarter of a century later, his bloodied body would be carried through those doors.

PART II

Emperor

CHAPTER 5

The Great Time

For almost four decades, Alexander had been waiting in the wings. And now, as his thirty-sixth year drew to an end, he came out to center stage. The time was perfect for the new ruler: Russians understood that they could not go on living the way they were.

Hard as it was for him to admit, a heaviness was lifted from the capital after his father's funeral. The oppression was over, and it was removed from him as well. They had buried not only a tsar, but an entire era.

Anna Tyutcheva recorded this impression. "I feel terribly sorry for him, may he rest in peace. But he reaped what he had sown. For in the last few years he was not concerned with his country but with some 'order in Europe,' and nations considered him a despot."

It was February, but there was unusually sunny weather in St. Petersburg. After the funeral, Alexander sat with his wife and Kostya and summed up the situation. His father had left the affairs of state in disorder. The treasury was empty, the army helpless, its weapons prehistoric, and there was no steam-powered fleet. All of Europe had done away with corporal punishment, but in Russia people were still flogged. Wherever one looked, things were rotten. They had serfdom, forgotten in Europe, and a bizarre feudal court system where officials were judges, often without the presence of the contesting parties, and where bribes decided the outcome.

Direct and fiery Kostya suggested immediately announcing a break with the past and the start of radical reforms. But the empress expressed

Alexander's thought: "Everything is crashing, but we will have to be quiet now," in order to preserve his father's honor and memory. Alexander decided that first they would erect a monument before beginning reforms.

The monument was erected not far from the square where Nicholas routed the rebel Decembrists. Then they began preparation for a great event.

Even though Alexander had shown nothing but wordless obedience to his father, the change in regime elicited great hopes in Russia. Leo Tolstoy, who had transferred from the Caucasus to the Crimean army, wrote from besieged Sevastopol, "Great changes await Russia. We must work and take courage to participate in this important moment in the life of Russia."

But the skeptic Chaadayev did not believe it. He was irritated by the eternal Russian "docile enthusiasm." Chaadayev came up with a very eccentric gesture. He asked a doctor for a prescription for arsenic, to kill rats. Any time anyone started talking about his hopes for the new emperor, he took out the arsenic prescription and silently presented it.

But beneficial steps were taken right away. Alexander had not forgotten his meeting with the Decembrists. After thirty years of imprisonment and exile, the remaining Decembrists were given permission to return. The former brilliant guards officers who came back were now elderly.

There were also the first liberal changes in the censorship system. The immovable, eternally frozen river cracked noisily, its ice broken.

Voices that had been silent for so long spoke up loudly. Everyone criticized the past and everyone demanded reforms. There was public outrage over the embezzlement of state funds, which had reached epic proportions by the end of Nicholas's reign. Petitions with suggestions flooded the palace. "Here, in St. Petersburg, public opinion is spreading its wings. . . . Everyone is talking, discussing matters inside and out, sometimes stupidly, but at least talking. And by doing so, learning. If this continues for five or six years, an informed and powerful public opinion will be created, and the shame of our recent mindlessness will be reduced somewhat," wrote the pundit Konstantin Kavelin to another columnist, Mikhail Pogodin.

The writer Nikolai Melgunov announced his belief that "under the new tsar European glasnost would at last appear." The father of the lady-in-waiting Anna Tyutcheva, the poet and diplomat Fedor Tyutchev, hailed Alexander's first orders with the famous definition, "The Thaw." Glasnost and thaw would be key concepts, and they would be inherited by all later Russian perestroikas—as would the rake, on which Russia always steps during reforms.

A phrase was repeatedly circulated in society, allegedly spoken by the dying Nicholas to his son and heir. "I had two desires—to free the Slavs of the Turkish yoke and to free the peasant from the power of the landowners. The first is impossible to do now. The second, to free the serfs, I will to you to do."

These words were persistently repeated. Apparently, this was the way Alexander and his brother Kostya intended to prepare Russia for the greatest upheaval in Russian life. The conservatives were asked to believe that the coming change was not a new-fangled idea of new people but the legacy of Nicholas I.

First, they had to end the war. The new emperor decided to head to Sevastopol yet again. The empress suggested that they go to the Trinity–St. Sergius Monastery before the trip to the Crimea, to pray before the relics of St. Sergius of Radonezh. In Russia, German princesses gladly and quickly turned into medieval Moscow tsaritsas. The former Lutheran believed in the power of holy relics to win Sevastopol.

Her lady-in-waiting Anna Tyutcheva was part of the retinue. In those days, she had a schoolgirl crush on the empress, but that did not keep sarcasm from creeping into her description of that visit.

The emperor, empress, and retinue came to the monastery. A very long service was held in the magnificent cathedral. The metropolitan's words could barely be heard over the arrogant chatter of the retinue. Then the royals kissed all the ancient icons and relics of saints, of which there turned out to be a great number. The metropolitan was falling off his feet, but the empress was inexhaustible. After the service she asked to be taken to the famous caves. At the caves they were met by a *yurodivy,* or holy fool, who lived as the Christian ideal of a character neither corrupted by the world nor impressed by worldly status or authority. This one had a hangover-puffy face and unfocused gaze.

"Thank God! This is a truly Orthodox Empress," said the Metropolitan, who had accompanied her, barely audibly. He had lost his voice in the speeches and prayers.

"But the Empress did not give up even after that. At midnight she led the Tsar to the ancient church, dimly lit by votive lights. They prayed a long time at the shrine with the relics of St. Sergius."

Nonetheless, Alexander lost Sevastopol.

When he arrived in the port, the new tsar understood the futility of resistance. For more than a year the city had held up under hellish cannon attack. Leo Tolstoy, who fought in Sevastopol, described the daily life of war in the besieged city. "Early morning . . . the doctor is hurrying to the hospital; somewhere a young soldier climbs out of a trench, washes his sunburned face with icy water, and turning to the reddening east, quickly makes the sign of the cross and prays to God; somewhere a tall, heavy wagon creaks its way to the cemetery to bury bloodied corpses, with which it is piled almost to the top. . . . White flags fly from our bastion and the French trench, and between them in the flowering grass mutilated bodies are gathered and loaded into carts. A horrible, heavy smell of dead bodies fills the air. People speak with each other peacefully and kindly, joking, laughing. . . . But the cease-fire is only for picking up the bodies. And the firing resumes."

When Sevastopol fell, the allies got piles of rubble and earth steeped in blood. Tens of thousands of Russian soldiers and their enemies lay in the Sevastopol soil. Alexander's relative the king of Holland "had the despicableness at that time to send two medals," wrote lady-in-waiting Anna Tyutcheva, one to Alexander II to commemorate his ascension to the throne and one to Napoleon III to commemorate the taking of Sevastopol. The king's mother, Alexander II's aunt, left the Netherlands in protest and headed for Russia. His aunt's protest was generous, but unfortunately, his aunt was a very difficult person, and having her near for the rest of her life created many cares.

"Sevastopol is not Moscow, and even after Moscow was taken, we later got to Paris," Alexander told the nation. But he knew then that it was impossible to continue the war. At sea, he did not have contemporary ships; on land, he had no long-distance rifles or rapid-fire artillery. And even the antediluvian weapons did not reach the army. Pavel Annenkov, a celebrated writer, noted in his memoirs, "Robbery had taken on Roman scope by the end of the reign. In order to get appropriations for their units, commanders paid bribes to the treasury—eight percent of the total. A bribe of six percent was considered a courtesy."

The bribe-taking, theft, and corruption were everywhere. During a coronation the entire square in front of the Kremlin is traditionally covered in red cloth. When they began preparations for Alexander's coronation, it was discovered that most of the red broadcloth supplies had been filched from the warehouse.

It was impossible to wage a war with such a rotten system. First, order and might had to be restored. And for that, he needed peace. Alexander made a decision: In 1856, in the Paris his father had hated, Alexander II concluded a peace. He sent Prince Alexei Orlov as head of the Russian delegation. Four decades earlier, as commander of the cavalry guards regiment, Prince Orlov had entered Paris with Alexander I. Now Orlov was meant to remind Napoleon III that Russian weapons had defeated the great Napoleon I.

The prince was a warrior personified. The magnificent cavalryman with big gray mustache, medals for his victories over the French on his chest, astonished Paris. He executed the tsar's mission: He demonstrated the new direction in Russian policy—he embraced French generals, scornfully cold-shouldered the treacherous Austrians, and was very cool toward the British.

In response, Napoleon III was tender in his attitude toward Orlov. But he and his allies forced Russia to accept difficult terms. Russia essentially lost the Black Sea, which had been won by Catherine II, Alexander's great-grandmother. It lost the entire eastern shore (Kars Fortress and part of Bessarabia) and the right to keep a military fleet in the Black Sea or build fortresses on its coast. The Black Sea was of paramount importance for the Russian economy. Four-fifths of Russia's main export, wheat, went through its ports.

Russia also lost Nicholas I's favorite mission—the right to be the protector of the Slavic peoples vanquished by Turkey. Consequently, the old dream of the Russian tsars to revive Byzantium and the Great Slavic Empire was also lost. In signing this treaty, Alexander seemed to betray the cross placed in his father's coffin. He had no choice.

The court criticized the Treaty of Paris (in whispers, naturally) and spoke of the indignation in the army. In her diary, Tyutcheva cites a "modest officer outraged by the peace. 'We would have gladly died for tsar and Russia. The tsar should have said to us in the words of the blessed Alexander I: We'll go to Siberia, but not yield to the enemy.'"

Interestingly, at the same time, her future husband, the Slavophile writer Ivan Aksakov, wrote to his father, "If anyone talks to you indignantly about the shamefulness of the peace, don't believe it. With the exception of a very, very small number of people, everyone else is delighted."

Right after the conclusion of the Treaty of Paris, as if to stress the new turn in Russian policies, Alexander appointed a new minister of foreign affairs, Prince Alexander Gorchakov. Gorchakov was in his fifties, as were the other ministers brought in to reform Russia. All these nobles had been brought up in his father's time. Nicholas had taught them unquestioning obedience, which was what Alexander needed.

Gorchakov, the scion of an ancient line, had studied at the Tsarskoye Selo Lycée with the poet Alexander Pushkin, his friend. "Disciple of fashion, friend of high society, observer of dazzling customs," was how Pushkin described him.

At twenty, Prince Gorchakov began his brilliant career. He was an aide to Count Nesselrode, Russian minister of foreign affairs, and attended all the congresses of the Holy Alliance, the monarchs who had defeated Napoleon. He had knowledge of all the infighting among the allies for the primacy of Europe.

Gorchakov dared to ignore certain rules of Russian life. For example, when the omnipotent chief of the Third Department Count Benkendorf came to Vienna, where Gorchakov was the Russian ambassador, Gorchakov paid him the required call. Benkendorf asked the accomplished diplomat to order lunch for him.

"If you need lunch, the custom here is to call the maître d'hôtel." Gorchakov rang the little bell. Benkendorf was surprised, because it was a society of slaves. Together they were slaves of their emperor, and then, down the ladder, everyone was the slave of his boss.

The incident became known, and Gorchakov got the dangerous reputation of "behaving like a European grandee." His inflexible backbone ended his career.

But Prince Gorchakov continued to scintillate with wit in St. Petersburg salons, being a master of social conversation, reminiscent of the French salons of the gallant age. His too-refined French, like his velvet waistcoat and long jacket, seemed a bit old-fashioned.

Now his career was taking off again. On becoming minister of foreign affairs, Prince Gorchakov vowed that he would see the shameful Treaty of Paris undone. Alexander II made the same promise to his family. In the meantime, his new policies were enough to make his father spin in his grave.

The main policy point was nonintervention in European affairs. "The defense of the interests of the nations subject to the tsar cannot serve as a justification for violating the rights of foreign nations," wrote Gorchakov in the famous letter circulated to embassies and missions on August 21, 1856. The policy of being the gendarme of Europe was jettisoned.

"This does not mean that Russia refuses a voice in European international questions," explained Gorchakov, "but now it is gathering its strength for the future." *"La Russie ne boude pas—elle se recueille"* (Russia is not pouting, it is gathering its strength) became a famous sentiment in Europe.

The tsar and Gorchakov formulated this policy: "For a long time the imperial cabinet was shackled by traditional memories and family ties, which, unfortunately, were sacred only for Russia. The war returned freedom of action to Russia. . . . Everyone who wishes Russia ill is an enemy of Russia, no matter what they are called."

Now, instead of the "traditional union" with Austria (that had sided with his enemies) and "family ties" with "dear uncle and friend," the Prussian king (as the tsar had called his German relative in letters), the new tsar received Charles de Morny, the French ambassador.

Alexander charmed him. The new tsar then decided to meet with Napoleon III, yesterday's sworn enemy so hated by his late father. The king of Württemberg arranged the meeting by inviting both to his seventieth birthday celebration.

The Russian press began printing amusing pro-Bonaparte articles. They said that destroying Napoleon I's empire was an error on the part of Alexander I. Many people had recommended to the tsar that he chase Bonaparte out of Russia and stop at that, so that Bonaparte would have the opportunity to destroy the Germans and the English. Then, they should have concluded an agreement with the weakened Bonaparte to divide the world in two parts, as he had once offered. The entire East, Turkey, the Slavic nations, and Constantinople could have been Russia's.

But Alexander I had dreamed of riding into Paris on a white horse as the liberator of Europe. "And what did Russia get for it?" wrote one columnist. "The day after the victory, Europe forgot everything that Russia did for it. . . . No, Europe will never be grateful to us. For Europe, Russians are always Scythians and barbarians. Russia saw that yet again in the Crimean War."

He turned thirty-seven. The new emperor was at the height of his power and his Romanov good looks. The celebrated French Romantic Théophile Gautier, who saw him in the splendor of a palace ball, described the tsar with a poet's delight: "Amazingly regular features, as if they had been carved by a sculptor. A high, handsome forehead. . . . A tender, gentle expression . . . big blue eyes . . . the line of the mouth is reminiscent of Greek sculpture."

But others drew a completely different portrait. The eyes were "big and blue, but inexpressive." And the facial features were off, too. "His regular features become unpleasant when he feels obliged to look solemn or majestic." So said our constant eyewitness, lady-in-waiting Anna Tyutcheva.

Why such a difference? The courtiers who had known the late tsar had their own concept of handsomeness in tsars. First of all, it was a "regal gaze," Nicholas I's merciless, icy stare that made the courtiers tremble. A Russian tsar always had to strike awe in the beholder. As the great Russian historian Klyuchevsky put it, "Our tsar is not a mechanic with a machine but a scarecrow in a field." To the court's disappointment, the new tsar did not have that regal gaze. When he tried to approximate it, he looked ridiculous. The court kept comparing him to the late emperor, and the new tsar did not live up to the standards. The tsar was "too kind, too pure to understand people and rule them," Tyutcheva wrote.

The tsar's very first steps elicited the hidden disagreement of the court. Its members discussed the rumors that the late emperor had wanted the emancipation of the serfs. They worried that the new tsar would seriously consider that dangerous madness.

But the court was not asked its opinion. His late father had taught Alexander that everything was to be decided in the royal apartment. Nicholas had trained the court well—no one dared to criticize or even discuss the tsar's actions.

The court found someone else to blame: Aesop, Grand Duke Konstantin, the "demon-seducer of our kind Sovereign," as Maria Frederiks called him. Anything the court did not like would be attributed to the bad influence on the kind and pure emperor and empress. That included the shameful peace treaty.

Thus the answer was found right away to the all-important question of the court: Against whom will we be friends? Hatred of Konstantin united them. The court had its enemy.

"Konstantin was angry at those who were unhappy with the peace," wrote Tyutcheva. "As for the Sovereign and his wife, their belief in him is unlimited. And when they say, 'Grand Duke Konstantin says so,' they think they are adding a seal of approval to their decision!"

An invisible and dangerous "retrograde opposition," as Konstantin called it, formed right after Nicholas's death.

In the meantime, the "kind and pure" sovereign took care of military matters. Having finished the Crimean War, Alexander renewed the bloody war in the Caucasus. He wanted revenge for the defeat in the Crimea.

Russian troops expanded military action on a large scale and Shamil's army found itself in a catastrophic position very quickly. Shamil's fall was paradoxical. Islam had once been his greatest source of strength, but now religion was weakening his army. The central idea of a holy war with infidels was being replaced by a new religious movement. Zikrism, a variant of Sufism, was founded by the theologian Kishiev Kunta-Hadji. He called on the fighting Murids to transfer the holy war from an external to an internal struggle. They should fight not the Russians but the sins in their own souls. He called for humility. Of course, there were limits: "If your women are raped or if you are forced to forget your language and customs, rise up and fight to the death." But the most important work was self-perfection.

Exhausted by decades of bloody warfare, the steady loss of their men, and the sense of the futility of fighting a gigantic empire with its ever-replenished army, the mountain tribes listened closely to his strange call. He was undermining discipline and destabilizing Shamil's army.

Shamil punished the adherents of this movement harshly, but he soon had to accept the fact that they were no longer with him, neither the masses nor the elite, which Shamil had in fact created. Over the years of struggle, a wealthy class of officials arose in the imamate. They did not wish to sacrifice their newfound gains to a losing battle. Shamil was interfering with their desire to stay rich.

The Russian army moved on the offensive. The territory controlled by Shamil contracted rapidly. By the summer of 1859, Shamil lost Chechnya for good and almost all of Dagestan. The forces of the Murids melted away. By the end of July, Shamil holed up high in the mountains in the village of Gunib, with only four hundred men. That was all that was left of his enormous army. In the middle of August, the Russians surrounded Gunib.

Commander in chief Prince Baryatinsky understood the cost of storming the village, how many of his soldiers would die in these mountains, right under the sky. The prince offered Shamil the opportunity to lay down his arms in exchange for a guarantee of safety for the imam, his family, and all the Murids with him. He even promised free passage to Mecca, if that was what Shamil wanted.

The imam did not trust the idea of forgiveness. He never forgave his own enemies. He decided to fight to the end, but saw that there was no one on his side. Not his sons, not the Murids, not the villagers—they did not want to die. The wailing of the women, pleading with him not to kill them, let him save face. He surrendered for them. After a chat with Allah, Imam Shamil came out to Prince Baryatinsky. He said briefly, "I recognize the power of the White Tsar and I am prepared to serve him faithfully."

With his harem, the imam was brought to St. Petersburg. The journey stunned Shamil, as he saw the extent of the empire. It was only then that he understood whom he had been fighting.

He was brought to the palace. In his snow white turban, he stood in the middle of the formal palace room. With an athletic body, narrow face, and beaked nose, he seemed younger than his age despite his nineteen wounds. His hair was a reddish brown only lightly touched by gray, and his fair-skinned face was framed by a luxuriant beard dyed dark red. For a quarter century, this man had made Russia bleed. More than a hundred thousand Russian soldiers had died in the war. Despite the promises made him, Shamil expected to be sent to Siberia or thrown into a cell or publicly executed.

Alexander kept his word. He embraced the prisoner, that great warrior. He ordered that he be given money and a coat of black bear. Shamil's wives and children all received gifts. Shamil was conquered by Alexander's generosity, and it was then that he truly became his prisoner.

The emperor had him sent to the small town of Kaluga, along with his relatives, sons, and harem. Among his wives was a Jewish woman of incredible beauty. Alexander was told that Shamil, thunderstruck by her loveliness, stole her from her father's house. At the request of her father and brother, the tsar had someone inquire whether she would want to return home. She replied that she could have left the master of the Caucasus, but she would never leave her vanquished husband.

Shamil was held as an honored prisoner of war. He traveled around Kaluga in an open carriage with four horses. He was an incredible sight in that provincial town in his white turban, bearskin coat, and yellow calfskin boots.

A few years later, Shamil asked permission to go to Mecca. He wrote to Alexander: "Being frail and in weak health, I do not wish to leave my earthly life without performing my sacred duty." He was given permission, but not right away. Death found the old warrior on the way to Mecca.

In the five years after the capture of Shamil, the entire Northern Caucasus was annexed by Russia.

The capture of Shamil sweetened the bitterness of the Crimean defeat. There had been an earlier success, as well. Alexander got back the priceless Ussuria region, which Russia had lost, from China. Now the entire territory between the Pacific Ocean and the borders of Siberia, the age-old taiga with tall cedars and forests full of wildlife, was part of Russia. The newly annexed Caucasus fit very nicely in the empire's underbelly.

A new map of Russia was brought to his office. The endless empire lay spread out before him. It was not enough: He wanted to move farther. As long as his hands were tied in Europe, his path had to lie in Central Asia: He would conquer the khanates, the land of a thousand and one nights, and then move on toward India, Afghanistan, and Persia. Let the British remember in horror how they had dared to defeat his father. Then, after taking Central Asia, he would concentrate on taking back the Black Sea. After that, Turkey and the liberation of the Slavs. Then the mirage of the great Slavic empire, his father's dream, would become reality. The cross placed in his father's coffin lay on his heart as well.

Those were grand dreams. Once upon a time Napoleon had warned Europe about Russia. He coarsely explained how terrible it would be if "a tsar with a big cock was born." Had that victorious time come? A great time first needed great reforms. He started them.

Dostoevsky has a description of how couriers carried the royal mail. The coachman sat on the box, in full song. When the courier hit him on the head from behind, the troika ran faster. The courier, as if beating sense into the coachman, kept bopping him on the head. The docile, subordinate coachman transferred the ferocity of the blows to the miserable horses.

The whipped troika galloped forward, turning into a bird from the constant blows.

Gogol called Russia a flying troika. It was driven forward in exactly that way by the great reformers Ivan the Terrible and Peter the Great. But Alexander lacked the harsh character of those Russian reformers, who killed thousands and exiled the opponents of their innovations. For the time being, he didn't need it. His father had made fear, obedience, and toadying to the tsar the norm. That fear and universal obedience were enough to bring about the most daring transformations—at the start.

Alexander II was a reformer of a new kind for Russia—a two-faced Janus, one head looking forward while the other looked back longingly. Mikhail Gorbachev was this kind of reformer.

Alexander's first reform would be truly incredible—he intended to emancipate the serfs. His great-grandmother, Catherine, had known that serfdom had to be eliminated. But she also knew and said that in Russia "the better is the enemy of the good." She did not eliminate it. His uncle, Alexander I, also knew it had to go. It was his favorite project. He thanked the great poet Pushkin for his poem "The Village," for the line, "And slavery, fallen by the tsar's will." He thanked him, but did not do away with slavery. Because he believed not the fiery poet but the very wise diplomat Joseph de Maistre. The ambassador from Piedmont, who spent many years in Russia, said, "Giving the Russian peasant freedom is like giving wine to a man who had never had alcohol. He will go mad."

Alexander's father, Nicholas I, also knew that the serfs had to be emancipated, but he went no further than the banning the sale of individuals without their families, and he did not do away with serfdom.

They all understood the economic benefit of emancipation, but they worried about the political damage. An autocratic empire needed harmony. The last tsar, Nicholas II, correctly described the role of the Russian tsars: "Master of Russia." Everyone was a slave of the master. At bottom, the slavery of serfs, and above them was the slavery of courtiers and officials. As the philosopher and writer Nikolai Chernyshevsky, a contemporary of Alexander II, said, "Everyone's a slave from bottom to top."

Alexander II decided to blow up this thousand-year harmony. He wanted to get rid of the slavery, the backbone of Russian life. The enlightened Russian landowners, those admirers of Voltaire and Rousseau, who collected priceless libraries in their country homes, bought, sold, and gambled away their serfs, sometimes even trading them for hunting dogs, and whipped them mercilessly in the stables.

As a poet, the Hussar Denis Davydov, wrote:

> Old Gavrila [the serf] is struck by our Mirabeau
> For not ironing the master's wrinkled jabot.

The laws of religion and marriage were flouted every day. Sex with peasant beauties and harems of serf girls were quite usual. The children of these relationships were rarely adopted. As a rule, the illegitimate children became the slaves of their legitimate siblings.

But at least the state did not need courts or a large police force to handle the peasants. The landowner was judge and policeman—he took care of his own serfs. The peasants were the source of the million-strong army. It had beaten Napoleon, but now it was a vanquished army.

Alexander was going to blow up Russian life that had been blessed by the ages and the Russian Orthodox Church. He knew he would have to create everything anew—a new way of managing the peasants, a new court system, and a new army. Dangerous uncertainty lay ahead. But 23 million serfs awaited his decision hopefully. Rumors were circulating, even though all royal deliberations were surrounded by strict secrecy.

He even got a letter on the subject from Alexander Herzen, his father's bête noire. The new emperor had already had a taste of Herzen's power. When he became tsar, he had Catherine the Great's "Notes" brought to him. His father had not allowed him to read them, and now Alexander and his wife were bursting with curiosity about the scandalous work that had delighted the "family scholar," Grand Duchess Elena Pavlovna.

The manuscript was kept in a secret vault in Moscow. It was delivered to St. Petersburg. Alexander read it and understood his father's rage. He sealed it again, with his own seal, and gave orders to keep it locked up. But soon after his own reading of it, Herzen published the carefully guarded manuscript. (Later it was learned that while the manuscript was being transported to St. Petersburg and then back to Moscow, the young archivist Bartenev had made a copy, which he took to London, to Herzen. He wanted the work to be accessible to historians.)

Now Herzen, the enemy of his empire, called on the tsar to act. "Wash away the shameful spot from Russia. Heal the scars from the whip on the backs of your brothers. Spare the peasants from the blood they will inexorably have to spill." This was no empty threat. Nothing had started yet, but the peasants, awakened by the rumors, had become agitated and demanded their freedom. The Third Department reported that the nobility was agitated, too. He made his decision. He began to speak.

In March 1856 in Moscow at the Assembly of the Nobility the tsar spoke to a full house. "I've decided to do it, gentlemen. If we don't give the peasants freedom from above, they will take it from below." Thus the emperor of all of Russia repeated the thought of the most hated of émi-grés and the words once written to his father by the chief of the secret police. Alexander added that it would happen "not at all today."

He was vacillating.

This was one of his main personality traits. Once he decided on something of extreme importance, he indulged himself in vacillation. He needed people around him to beg him to do what he had already decided to do. This relieved him of the responsibility for the conse-quences. He transferred it to the shoulders of those who persuaded him and, thereby could, if needed, blame them for the failure of his decision.

The trio of his advisors and allies tried to persuade him. This holy trinity were his brother Kostya-Aesop, Grand Duchess Elena Pavlovna, and naturally, the empress, who knew his character very well after fifteen years of marriage.

The empress was charming. Despite the onset of her lung disease and dire warnings from Dr. Botkin, she laughed and prayed. She was a mass of contradictions: laughter and tears, rationality and extravagance, Ger-man penny-pinching and prodigality, kindness and a constant need to mock, prayers, fasts, and spiritualist séances. And through it all, there was her indomitable German willpower. She passionately executed everything that was expected of her in Russia, and she would not let Sasha, as she called the tsar, retreat. She insisted that he had to end serfdom.

The tsar's brother, Kostya, would not let up, either. He saw him daily. Alexander could not find respite even in Germany, in the quiet spa of Bad Ems, where he took the waters. Grand Duchess Elena Pavlovna went there, too. She offered to set an example and free her fifteen thou-sand serfs before the law was passed.

At last, in late 1856, he announced that he had been persuaded. Now the "vacillating" Alexander could become as firm as a rock. Now he was an implacable as his father.

Kostya was to run all the work on the reform. But who would help him? All the dignitaries of his father were retrogrades. He called them the "lost generation," because nothing could be expected of them without an order from the tsar. Yet now, a circle of "liberal bureaucrats" appeared, ready to implement reforms. Many of Nicholas's dignitaries made it seem as if they had dreamed of becoming liberals, but the old tsar would not permit it. The new one did, and they immediately changed.

This was exactly what happened under Gorbachev.

The old grandee Lanskoy, appointed minister of internal affairs, and Count Rostovtsev, who had hated the idea of emancipation, and governor-general of St. Petersburg Prince Suvorov, and even the chief of the Third Department Prince Vassily Dolgorukov were all suddenly liberal bureaucrats. It was fashionable to be liberal, for that was what the tsar wanted.

But along with the liberals by command there were liberals by principle. The Milyutin brothers frequented the salon of Grand Duchess Elena Pavlovna. Their ancestor had been a stoker in the palace. Courtiers maliciously recounted that his duties included feeding the fireplace in the bedroom of the empress so that it would burn all night and then scratching the soles of the feet of Empress Anna Ivanovna (who liked that before sleep) and her lover, Ernst Biron, who often spent the night with her. And now, in the middle of the nineteenth century, the descendants of the stoker, important dignitaries, were the main figures of the imminent reforms.

The dashing bureaucrat from the Ministry of Internal Affairs, Nikolai Milyutin, felt the blood of his ancestor and made fiery speeches at the grand duchess's salon about the greedy nobility that did not wish to comprehend the needs of its country.

Not all talk was of reform, and not all speakers were among the living. Salons were very fashionable in St. Petersburg. The salon of Elena Pavlovna heard a lot of music and a lot of talk about politics. The salon of Empress Maria Alexandrovna also had a lot of music and even more talk about politics. But there was one more topic in all the St. Petersburg salons that was discussed continually and left no one indifferent. Spirits.

In the 1860s the Romanov palaces were all in the thrall of spiritualist séances. Communing with spirits was appropriate in the palaces, where the ghosts of murdered emperors wandered. The greatest enthusiast was Kostya's wife, Grand Duchess Alexandra Iosifovna. The beauty who resembled Mary Stuart was very often visited by visions (before Nicholas's death, a mysterious white specter came to her twice). Even her husband, a well-known skeptic, gave its due to the entertaining and hard-to-explain pastime.

But for the new emperor, it was not merely a nod to fashion. Having decided to embark on great reforms, he thought it would not be amiss to chat with his late father. A famous "table-turner" was brought from Paris. At the very first séance, the late emperor made an appearance.

The séance took place in the Big Hall of Peterhof. Present were the emperor and empress; the dowager empress; Kostya; his wife, of course; Grand Duchess Elena Pavlovna's brother, the Prince of Württemberg (the grand duchess herself, as a learned lady, scoffed at spiritualism); and the emperor's childhood friend Sasha Adlerberg (son of the minister of the court Count Vladimir Adlerberg). Also the ladies-in-waiting Alexandra Dolgorukaya and Anna Tyutcheva.

Once Anna Tyutchev returned to her room, she wrote everything down.

"Everyone was seated at a round table, with hands on the table; the medium sat between the empress and Grand Duke Konstantin. . . . When the séance began, everyone was amazed by his appearance. Ordinarily, his face is rather insignificant, he looks almost stupid. . . . But during the séance an inner fire seems to radiate from him. A deathly pallor covers his features; his eyes are wide open and fixed on one spot . . . the hair, as the revelations of the spirits develop, . . . slowly rises and stands on his head, forming an aureole of horror. Soon knocking, done by the spirits, came from various corners of the room. Questions followed, which were answered by knocking, corresponding to the letters of the alphabet. The table rose to the height of half an *arshin* (about 35 cm) from the floor. The dowager empress felt a hand touch the ruffles of her dress, grab her hand, and take her wedding ring off. Then that hand grabbed, shook, and pinched everyone present. . . . It took a bell out of the Sovereign's hands. . . . This elicited cries of fear, terror, and surprise."

The spirit of the emperor's father appeared in the room together with his deceased seven-year-old daughter, Alexandra, whom they had called Sashenka. Nicholas and Sashenka came another time, in the Winter Palace, to Alexander's rooms. The empress had refused to attend this time (the Russian Orthodox Church did not approve). In her stead, Minister of Foreign Affairs Gorchakov met with the late tsar.

"The table rose, spun, and knocked the anthem God Save the Tsar! [As if to herald the emperor's appearance.] Everyone present, even the skeptic Gorchakov, felt the touch of mysterious hands and saw them quickly run under the tablecloth. The Sovereign says that he saw fingers, translucent and glowing. . . . But most importantly, the Sovereign received a revelation from the present spirits. As during the first séance in Peterhof these were the spirit of Emperor Nicholas and the young Grand Duchess. They both responded to questions from the Sovereign, answering by knocking the letters of the alphabet. The Sovereign noted them with pencil on paper that lay before him. But the answers were inapposite and empty," wrote Tyutcheva.

The conversation between Hamlet and his father's ghost did not take place. The disappointed lady-in-waiting asked a question in her diary that must have occurred to everyone at the séance. "Why were the spirits interested in such trivial pranks? Their strange playfulness and empty responses to questions astonish me." She added what the empress had apparently said to her, refusing to come to this séance. "These are all pranks of the Evil One. Those who commune with us are not all the spirits we call on but the ones St. Augustine called 'spirits of lies.' Those spirits of the air are dangerous and false . . . Apostle Paul spoke of them, too. Dealing with them is a sin."

The dangerous séances had their effect. The Winter Palace had a clock with three monkeys, which played their instruments. It had not been wound in a long time. In the middle of the night, they began playing and woke up a terrified Anna Tyutcheva.

———

The following year, the coronation was held in Moscow. Representatives of the nobility came from all over the country. During the coronation, much became clear to the emperor.

The court and the royal family traveled to the ancient capital, for the first time, by modern railroad instead of carriages (like his father and earlier tsars). But, just as in the olden days, the emperor was greeted by the thunder of gun salutes and the ringing of innumerable church bells. They came from the train station along Tverskaya Street to the din and music: he, on horseback, the empress in a golden carriage. Thousands of startled doves and sparrows filled the sky.

August 26 was Coronation Day, time for the mystical union of emperor and Russia. Things began well. Grandstands stuffed with festive people filled Cathedral Square in the Kremlin, the site of the history of Moscow's tsars. The parade uniforms of the guards glittered with braiding. To the joyous pealing of church bells, the emperor and the empress came out arm in arm onto the Red Porch. Alexander wore a general's uniform with the Order of St. Andrew on a golden chain. His wife was ornamented with the sky blue Catherine ribbon. Her head, onto which he would be placing a crown, was bare, and her hair combed back with two long curls down to the shoulders. The empress had a sad and con-centrated look.

From the Red Porch, Alexander bowed deeply to the people, follow-ing the tradition from the Muscovite reign. This was how Peter the Great and Ivan the Terrible had bowed to the people. The crowd shouted greetings, military bands struck up, and the cannon salute resounded.

Alexander came down the stairs and stood under the canopy held by high dignitaries. The procession moved toward the cathedral, and Alexander looked extremely concerned. His dignitaries were aged, but the walk went without a hitch.

Inside the stuffy ancient Cathedral of the Assumption, he and the empress revered the icons and relics. At the steps of the thrones, the dowager empress, wearing a crown, awaited them. They sat on the thrones. His mother was also pale with agitation. Everyone seemed to be expecting a disaster. It happened.

Adjutant general Prince Mikhail Gorchakov had fought in all of Alexander's father's wars and led the defense of Sevastopol. The honored general held the raspberry pillow on which lay the most important imperial attribute—the Golden Orb. In the stifling heat, the old man fainted and fell, dropping the pillow. The round golden orb clattered down the stone floor of the cathedral. People rushed to catch the orb and help Gorchakov. The poor man regained consciousness quickly, and the old general could have died of shame. But Alexander was quick. He said loudly, "It's all right to fall here. The important thing is that you stood firm on the battlefield."

It got worse. The metropolitan placed the imperial mantle on the sovereign. The tsar kneeled and the metropolitan blessed him. He rose, accepted the crown from the metropolitan, and placed it on his own head. Now he was supposed to crown the empress. Frightfully pale, she rose from the throne and kneeled before him. He placed the Small Crown on her, and an attendant fastened it with diamond clips. When the empress stood up, the crown fell from her head. The horror on the empress's face suggested that she was about to fall as well.

Once again, with great calm, as if nothing had happened, Alexander put the crown on her head, and four attendants, sweating with the effort, pinned it in her hair.

They sat on their thrones to the salute and church bells. He held the scepter and orb. On the steps at attention stood chamberlains in golden uniforms and cavalry guards officers with glittering helmets and bared sabers. On the emperor's right stood his mother, in her crown, and the entire Romanov family. There were so many grand dukes, innumerable Nicholases, named for his father, and Konstantins named for his older brother, and a sprinkling of Alexeis and Georges.

The poor empress clearly showed the strain she was under.

Lady-in-waiting Tyutcheva indignantly wrote in her diary about the new attitude people had toward a coronation. No one prayed. They laughed and joked, and some had brought food and munched away during the sacred ceremony.

Alexander left the cathedral in crown and mantle, wearing many kilograms of orders and medals and regalia. The empress walked next to him. Her face was bloodless. He, too, was pale. Once again they walked through the screaming crowd to the roar of cannon and the ringing of bells along a wooden bridge covered with red cloth. This part went smoothly.

Anna Tyutcheva's father, the poet, wrote with overt irony, "When I saw our poor, dear emperor walking under the canopy with a huge crown on his head—weary, pale, bowing with difficulty to the welcoming crowd, tears just welled up in my eyes."

That evening, before dinner, they walked through the Terem Palace. Here, under the ceiling murals, Ivan the Terrible had sat on his golden throne.

They came out on the terrace right under the roof of the palace. Below lay the wooden capital of the Muscovite tsars. It was lit up by fireworks—the crenellations of the ancient towers, the belfry of Ivan the Great, the cathedrals. That fiery magnificence was reflected in the river. But the empress was cheerless, unsettled by the fallen crown.

Only the very first few rows in church had seen the mishaps of the ceremony. The rest of the court had not seen, much less heard, anything over the din in the cathedral. Nonetheless, the Third Department soon reported that rumors were being spread about the evil omens during the coronation. Obviously the rumors had to come from those who had seen what happened—the chief dignitaries, who were in the first few rows. They were the ones who hated the planned reforms, his father's high officials, descendants of the murderers of former emperors. Alexander had to know that they were starting to move. They were frightened by "the actions of madmen and Jacobins in the palace," wrote lady-in-waiting Sofia Uvarova.

The carelessly attached crown, the chatter during the coronation, and the stories of bad omens would have been impossible under his father. The most dangerous change in an autocratic system was taking place—fear was vanishing, following the death of the last emperor.

The fear was only beginning to recede. It was still strong enough for the liberation. Alexander chose the path most familiar to everyone in a land of toadies, the basic law of autocratic rule: This is my command, this is what I want! The nobility as a whole was against the repeal of serfdom, but it was the tsar's wish.

In general, it was best to anger the nobility to the utmost. He knew how to play cat and mouse with them. First he formed the Secret Committee on Peasant Reform. Opponents (Kostya always called them "the retrogrades") were pleased—it was a familiar name. There had been a committee by that name under his father, and nothing came of it. He let them rejoice for a bit, and then saddened them. He appointed his brother, Kostya, with his boundless energy and his brusque intolerance of opposition, to the committee.

For his father's officials, Kostya was a Jacobin, but his regal rudeness reminded them of Nicholas. The reflex kicked in, and they obeyed. Editorial commissions were formed to elaborate the conditions of the emancipation.

Alexander made Count Rostovtsev chairman of the editorial commissions. He was the one who had warned his father of the Decembrist plot. Nicholas had made Count Rostovtsev a director of the military schools. He had never dealt with agrarian questions and, more to the point, was an opponent of emancipation. The retrogrades were happy, yet the tsar wanted emancipation, and Rostovtsev instantly saw the light. As he put it, "I thought about History and dreamed of an honorable page in its scrolls." Now Rostovtsev was a liberal bureaucrat. Nicholas's training still worked.

The meetings and arguments lasted till dawn. The majority of noblemen wanted the peasants emancipated without any land. Alexander understood that you could not free impoverished people. It was a formula for a future insurrection. Rostovtsev fought for giving emancipated peasants land. In fact, the zeal of his swift conversion to liberalism occasionally frightened Alexander.

A group of liberal bureaucrats worked with Rostovtsev. Most came from the Naval Department, brought up through the ranks by Kostya. The discussions in the commissions were furious and hostile. The liberals and retrogrades argued in the Russian manner, that is, without hearing each other.

Nikolai Milyutin (Kostya's favorite, whom the sovereign considered "red") shouted, "You nobles are hard to budge. You just scratch, roll over, and go back to sleep. You have to be jabbed hard to make you jump up!"

The commission members would leave their meetings in early morning, to the twitter and chatter of birdsong. Old Rostovtsev was the first of the liberals to feel the strain of the negotiations. His name had become anathema to his former friends in Nicholas's administration. The stress of the arguments and hostility was too much for him in the end. On his deathbed, the count told Alexander, "Sire, do not fear *them*."

"Poor Sasha is in mourning and wept bitterly," the empress recorded. He was sensitive, as always. But he understood the concern of his faithful servant. *They* had to be watched. The closer the end of the commissions' work, the more dangerously were the retrogrades uniting and the louder were they grumbling. They wrote petitions and warnings: If the peasants were freed, the army would be needed to protect the nobles. Insurrections would start the very first day. Yesterday's slaves would certainly seek revenge for centuries of humiliation.

Kostya told him to pay no attention, but Alexander was a worthy scion of clever, Asiatic tsars. He made a move that astonished the capital. He replaced Rostovtsev as head of the commissions with Count Nikita Panin, his father's minister of justice.

Count Panin was a supporter of the institution of serfdom, a thickheaded old campaigner, whose tough stance made him a symbol of officialdom. He had long been forgotten.

A shock went through the ranks of the liberal bureaucracy. Joy reigned supreme in the land of the retrogrades. The regime was backing down.

Kostya rushed to the palace. Alexander merely smiled and said mysteriously that nothing was changing. Grand Duchess Elena Pavlovna came to the Winter Palace to beg the tsar to reconsider. She made an impassioned speech about Panin's convictions. But Alexander responded briefly and mockingly, "His conviction is my command."

Soon afterward, Panin made an immortal statement of a Russian toady to Grand Duke Konstantin: "I have convictions, Your Highness, strong convictions. Some people think otherwise incorrectly. . . . But I feel obliged first of all to learn the view of the Sovereign Emperor. And if I discover that the Sovereign looks at things differently than I, I consider it my duty to immediately step back from my convictions and act even totally against them!"

That was the result of Nicholas's training. And that was how Alexander pushed through the reforms hated by most of the nobility.

At the final decision level, the State Council—made up of the pillars of Russian nobility—the leaders of the retrograde party held up the reform, swamping it in debates. Alexander saw that they were resisting again. So on January 28, 1861, he addressed a meeting of the State Council.

"I consider the issue of emancipation of the serfs to be a vital question for Russia, on which the development of its strength and might will depend. I demand of the State Council that the peasant question be completed in the first half of February."

The tsar ended on a threatening note: "Any further delay is pernicious for the state. . . . I hope that God will not abandon you and will bless the completion of this affair for the future benefit of our beloved Homeland."

Hearing the familiar intonations of Nicholas I, they made haste. However, they reduced the land allocation in favor of the landowners. The State Council signed the bill ending serfdom.

Thus, the serfs were freed and received arable land. The allotments were disappointingly small, and they were expected to pay a ruinous price for it. The deadline for the buyout was two years.

The important part was done. Centuries-old human slavery no

longer existed in Russia. The law was sent by courier to the Winter
Palace for the tsar's signature.

On February 19, 1861, he was to sign the manifesto repealing serfdom.
The greatest day of his life had come. A great day in the history of Russia. Alexander II became the Tsar Liberator of the Russian peasants.

He awoke as usual at eight. His valet brought his favorite cherry robe
with tasseled belt. He stood at the window. It was still twilight in the
February morning, but the candelabra on the table lit up his face. He
would be forty-three in a few months. Tall, with the bearing of a guards
officer, he had thick mutton chopside-whiskers with a touch of gray and
a threateningly bristling mustache—his uncle Willy, the king of Prussia,
and many other monarchs had such side-whiskers and mustaches. Naturally, all his ministers followed suit.

Despite the threatening mustache, his gaze betrayed his kindness and
gentleness. His eyes bulged a bit, which caused his late uncle, Grand
Duke Mikhail Pavlovich, to call him "Lambkin." His eyes rolled helplessly from their orbit when he tried to imitate his father's intimidating
gaze. But they were divinely radiant when he was being charming. He
was a typical charmer of the gallant era of French kings. Like many others at court who had studied French too assiduously as children, Alexander rolled his *R*s in Russian.

With his mistresses, he naturally spoke French. But his wife, Masha,
was not fluent in French (alas). So with his German wife he spoke Russian. His brother Kostya, on the contrary, spoke only Russian to everyone and liked to show off folk expressions, for instance, calling his wife
zhinka, instead of *zhena.*

The servant brought coffee. Alexander stood at the window. His
apartment on the second floor of the Winter Palace opened on the
Admiralty and Palace Square. When Alexander married, these rooms
were allotted to him by his father. One of them had been his classroom,
where he studied with Zhukovsky. When he became emperor, he

decided to remain in them. The apartment opened to a large reception room, which was the former classroom where his stern father liked to come to inquire after his progress. He had shivered there often, trying to gauge his father's mood.

Then came the library, then the room for the orderlies. And then, the main room, the study that served as both study and bedroom. From here he ruled Russia, from behind a big desk with family photographs, the dear faces watching him while he worked. They looked down from the walls as well, but they were unrecognizable in formal family portraits. By the window stood a secretary desk, always covered with paperwork. He decided it all, the autocrat. Today there were mountains of documents, part of the agrarian reforms. On top lay the manifesto and the historic pen with which he would sign.

Marble columns with a cherry curtain set apart an alcove with the simple iron bed on which he slept. His father had slept and died on a similar bed. On that bed, in this room, he would die.

Like his father, he liked to take a walk before breakfast around the palace, before starting work. He breakfasted with the empress in the lettuce-green room, after which he returned to the study and started work. Every morning the tsar saw the war minister (Count Dmitri Milyutin, Nikolai Milyutin's brother) and the chief of the Third Department (Prince Dolgorukov), and every other day, Kostya and the minister of foreign affairs (Prince Gorchakov).

After lunch he took a second walk, a long one, just like his father. He walked with his setter in the Summer Garden. Past the gilded fence and the marble statues of goddesses of antiquity, bashfully covered by thick foliage. He returned to the palace in an open carriage.

This was his routine year after year, a continuation of his father's daily schedule. He would eventually have to face the incredible: He, the Autocrat of Russia, would be forced to stop his walks in his own capital.

But that morning, his schedule was violated by history. Instead of his morning walk, he went to the Small Church in the palace, so beloved by his father. The huge man had a touching preference for everything tiny and informal. He preferred the chapel to the magnificent cathedral.

Alexander asked everyone to leave, including the priest, and he prayed alone.

In the meantime Kostya arrived at the palace with his wife and son, the handsome Nicholas. Kostya called him Nikola. The heir, also Nicholas, was called Niks, like the late emperor. Their sister Masha also came to the palace. Their mother had died at the end of the previous year. The three siblings, now orphaned, were even more tender toward one another.

The Grand Procession to the Cathedral was opened by masters of ceremony wearing gold-shot camisoles and holding staves. High marshals and the senior high-marshal walked with gilt warders. Behind them came Alexander with the empress and children and other members of the imperial family. Then came a very long human train—members of the State Council, senators, ministers, his retinue, her ladies-in-waiting. This procession, sparkling with gold, medals, and jewels, slowly and solemnly crawled through the enfilade of formal rooms. Its participants did not yet understand that they, like serfdom, belonged to the medieval life that the emperor was about to destroy.

The procession stopped in the antechamber at the doors of the cathedral. The doors were flung open, but only the imperial family and the most important state officials could enter. The rest of the dressed-up masses would wait outside the cathedral doors for the very long service to end. He knew that they would not be silent for long. Many young men were slipping out the back stairs to have a smoke. No one would have dared such a thing in his father's time! He was sure that one of them would be Nikola, a young ne'er-do-well, whose pranks amused the whole family.

Alexander prayed fervently and at length. Next to him prayed the heir, Niks, and the second-eldest son, Sasha. Niks was magnificent, handsome, athletic, and smart. Sasha was a failure—hugely fat and therefore shy and awkward.

A festive breakfast was held in the green salon. Afterward, Alexander, Kostya, and their sister Masha went to his study. Niks was brought in.

The moment that changed Russia took place. With the stroke of a pen, he freed 23 million slaves.

From the diary of Grand Duke Konstantin Nikolayevich:

> 19 February 1861. We gathered for the mass at the Winter Palace, followed by a special service with marvelous prayers. . . . After breakfast, I remained to watch Sasha sign the Manifesto. . . . First he read it aloud and, after crossing himself, he signed. I poured sand on the ink. He gave the pen with which he signed the manifesto to Niks. From this day forth a new history, a new era has begun. They had predicted revolution and other nonsense for today, but the people were as quiet and calm as ever. We had a family lunch at Sasha's.

During the family lunch everyone shuddered at a loud noise outside the window, but it was only snow falling from the palace roof in the thaw.

Alexander did not wish to make the great event public yet. In the best traditions of his father, it was decided to keep it secret. The manifesto was promulgated only on March 5, "Forgiveness Sunday," the day when Orthodox Christians forgive one another. Lent began on the following day, a period of humility, quiet, and peace—not for agitation but for repentance.

In the meantime, Janus Alexander prepared for the promulgation of the manifesto, still in his father's tradition. Troops were put on alert all over Russia. The press wrote that the rumors about decisions made on the agrarian issue were false and nothing in that area was foreseen in the near future. At the same time, printing houses were publishing the manifesto, and messengers on troikas sped to the provinces with copies. They were followed by adjutants who would explicate the manifesto in the provinces.

The stirring Sunday of March 5 arrived, the day to proclaim the manifesto. The retrogrades kept up their warning of rebellion.

"I don't know why P. N. Ignatyev [governor-general of St. Petersburg] and many other high-placed persons feared that disruptions would occur at the announcement of the Manifesto. Only Sasha [Alexander Patkul, who had studied alongside the emperor with Zhukovsky and was now police chief of St. Petersburg] was completely certain that the people would sooner go to church than riot in the streets," recalled his wife, the former lady-in-waiting Alexandra Patkul.

The phlegmatic Patkul was right. The manifesto was read out in churches in both capitals, and everything remained calm.

As usual on Sundays, the tsar was present at the changing of the guards at the Mikhailovsky Manege. He spoke to the officers afterward.

Kostya recorded in his diary: "Sasha gathered officers around him in the Manege and told them that he had declared freedom that day. The response was such a loud 'Hurrah!' that my heart leaped and tears came to my eyes. That 'Hurrah!' accompanied Sasha out onto the street, where it was picked up by the people. It was a miracle!"

That "hurrah!" followed him farther. From the Mikhailovsky Manege, the tsar returned to the Winter Palace. "At Tsaritsynsky Meadow he was hailed with a 'hurrah!' that shook the earth," wrote a contemporary.

Exactly twenty years later in March he would be returning from the Mikhailovsky Manege, from the changing of the guards, when he was assassinated.

So age-old slavery was repealed, repealed a bit earlier than in the United States of America, and without a civil war. But both emancipators would be killed.

The honeymoon between tsar and nation would last only a very brief month. At the Saltykov Entrance of the palace, which he usually used for his walk, an elated crowd awaited him every day. To avoid them, he took to using a different door. "I prayed to portraits of the tsar then," wrote the literary critic Alexander Nikitenko in his diary.

Alexander's foreign foe, Herzen, praised the tsar exultantly. "Neither the Russian people nor history will forget him for this. From the distance of our exile we hail him with a name rarely encountered in autocracy without eliciting a bitter smile—we hail him with the name 'Liberator.'"

Another famous Russian radical, Prince Kropotkin, was a youth then, studying at the most prestigious Page Corps. The future leader of Russian anarchism recalled, "My feeling then was that if in my presence someone had made an attempt on the tsar's life, I would have shielded Alexander II with my chest."

The honeymoon ended when Alexander took a shocking step. The manifesto was a gift to the liberals, so Januslike, he quickly looked the other way, in the direction of the retrogrades. He decided to unite society as his great-grandmother Catherine had taught him: "Work must be started by people of genius and implemented by people who are efficient."

Thanking the main reformers who had beaten the party of retrogrades, he awarded them medals and sent them into retirement. Nikolai Milyutin, the main executive of the reform, who had been called "Jacobin" and "red," Minister of Internal Affairs Lanskoy, who was seriously accused by the retrogrades of leading Russia toward civil war, and other "liberal bureaucrats hateful to conservatives" were removed from their posts.

The only one left was Minister of War Dmitri Milyutin, because military reform was next.

The removals caused a shock. From the diary of Dmitri Milyutin:

> As soon as the goal was achieved and the resolution went into effect, the Sovereign, as befits his character, decided it was necessary to reduce dissatisfaction which the Great Reform had caused in the landowning estate. For that the implementation of the new law was torn out of the hands of those who had attracted the hatred of the landowning estate and entrusted to such people who could not in any case be suspected of hostility toward the nobility.

Having gotten rid of the liberal bureaucrats, Alexander appointed a "conciliatory person" to head the government, who would suit everyone.

Fifty-year-old Peter Alexandrovich Valuyev, a typical bureaucrat of the new era, became the minister of internal affairs.

Valuyev mastered the concept of Griboyedov's comedy at an early age. He managed to hide his intelligence. He allowed himself to shine only in his diary, where the members of the government and its work are described ruthlessly. In his work, Valuyev resorted to "Russian wisdom," that is, knowing which way the wind is blowing. The walking weather vane embarked on his career early.

During Nicholas I's visit to Moscow, he so appealed to him with his retrograde views that the tsar called him "a model young man." After Nicholas's death, he immediately turned liberal and sent a note to Grand Duke Konstantin that boldly declared: "We have glitter on top, rot on the bottom. . . . Everywhere there is scorn and hatred of thought and supervision, as if we were minors."

His boss now was the famous retrograde Muravyev, but he managed to please him, too, without losing his good relations with the liberals.

Valuyev was impressive looking, tall with good features, and he could be eloquent. In the spirit of the times, he made sure to demonstrate true European manners, which the sovereign particularly liked. Alexander believed that Valuyev could reconcile the victorious liberals and the vanquished retrogrades.

It was then that Alexander, who had grown accustomed to the adoration of society, began to realize that no one liked his reform. The landowners were unhappy—some mourned the age-old patriarchal lifestyle destroyed by the emancipation of the serfs, others feared a peasant revolt, when "a million soldiers will not be able to hold back the peasants in their fury."

The peasants were unhappy with their minuscule land allotment. A very Russian rumor arose in the villages: The tsar had given the peasants "true freedom" but the masters hid it from the people. "Wise men" in the remote, illiterate villages began to explain the manifesto in their own way. In the village of Bezdna (Kazan Province), Anton Petrov read in the manifesto that all land, except for inconvenient places, must belong to the peasants. Men from other villages came to Bezdna "for true freedom." Thousands of peasants gathered in the small village. Troops were sent to arrest Petrov, but the peasants would not give up their literate neighbor. They formed a ring around his hut. The army acted as it was taught in Nicholas's time, that is, ruthlessly. On the command of Count Apraksin (son of an adjutant general at the court), the soldiers shot into the peasant crowd, and found and killed the poor literate peasant. Almost four hundred bodies lay on the ground when they were done.

The local landowners, who had braced themselves for another Pugachev Rebellion, a bloody peasant revolt, hailed the count for ably mowing down unarmed peasants. Peasant unrest continued, and it continued to be answered with bullets. Only the advent of spring, sowing time, dampened the explosion.

Young people were not happy, either. Alexander was stunned. They hadn't dared utter a sound under his father. He had eased censorship, allowed people to talk, enlarged the rights of universities, permitted young people to go abroad! Now he learned that students were meeting to discuss the reprisals against the peasants in Bezdna. They dared to criticize his manifesto, quoting a line from the poet Nikolai Nekrasov.

"Enough rejoicing!" the Muse whispered to me. "It's time to move forward. The people are free, but are they happy?"

The Third Department reported worrisome information on the sentiments of youth. By April 13, 1861, Grand Duke Konstantin Nikolayevich would write in his diary: "I am always terribly afraid when they touch on such questions, because this opens a wide field for the retrograde party." Wise Kostya was first to understand that the youth would be the main trump card in the retrograde party's game.

The insulted emperor decided to teach the students a lesson with a reminder of his father's methods. He appointed an admiral (Count Putyatin) as minister of education, a general (G. Filipson) as warden of the St. Petersburg University, and a retired colonel (A. Fittsum von Eksted) as the university's rector. These sixtyish military men were given a task: to use strong measures to kill off any desire the students might have "to stick their noses where they don't belong."

The military men decided that the problem lay in a lack of discipline and an influx of the poor to the universities. Poverty was the hothouse of free-thinking. They decided to do away with scholarships for poor students and to force everyone to pay for their education (65 percent of the students had subsidies).

The remaining students were put under military control. Special booklets called matriculas, for registration lists, were instituted. They served as both a pass to get into the university and a record of all information on the student (grades, behavior, and so on). To avoid discussion of these measures, Putyatin banned all student meetings.

The students left for summer vacation electrified by the rumors of new rules. When they returned in September, the poor students (that is, the majority) discovered that they were locked out. But these were new young people: The new tsar had reigned for six years, more than a quarter of a lifetime for these young men. They had grown up without Nicholas's oppression, so they were completely free of the fear that the emperor's generation knew. They were the children of "perestroika" and they did not want to submit.

In the meantime, the tsar went to the Crimea in the autumn, as usual. After his hectic Days of Creation, he rested at the glorious Livadia Palace. While he rested, students formed a huge crowd in the courtyard of the university in the capital.

"Let's talk to the warden!" shouted the orators. "We'll force them to give back our subsidies!" cried others. The gendarmes made their way to the university. The stunned governor general Ignatyev and the chief of police of St. Petersburg, Alexander Patkul, galloped there, too.

"Bear in mind that they don't dare shoot at us!" shouted the orators. And so the city witnessed a sight a never before seen in St. Petersburg. A long column of students moved down Nevsky Prospect toward the apartment of Warden Filipson. They wanted to complain to the warden, a general, about the minister, an admiral. Police on foot and on horseback moved on both sides of the students, in rhythm with their march. A platoon of gendarmes was behind them, and the rear was brought up by Governor General Ignatyev and Chief of Police Patkul on horseback.

Frightened, Filipson refused to speak with the students at home and agreed to hear them out only at the university. So the procession of students, with the completely confused Filipson at the head, moved back through the center of the city to the university. There were several hair salons along the way. Seeing the procession, the French hairdressers and barbers recognized a familiar picture. They ran out of their establishments, shook their fists, and shouted joyfully: *"La révolution! La révolution!"*

Minister of Education Admiral Putyatin sent panicked telegrams to Livadia—What was he to do? The tsar, enjoying sea and sun, replied kindly, "Deal with them like a father." The old admiral remembered that in Nicholas's day, being fatherly meant giving a whipping. Fortunately, Grand Duke Konstantin Nikolayevich managed to stop the punishment and saved them all from great shame.

Lectures were postponed until the matriculas were handed out. The university was closed and it was announced that only students with booklets would be allowed to take classes. The unrest continued.

October began with clashes between students and police. Crowds of onlookers gawked at the unusual spectacle. In the tsar's absence, the Senate held a session. On October 12 a crowd of students gathered in the university courtyard. More fiery speeches were heard. The students who had agreed to the matriculas got caught up in the enthusiasm, and to the applause of their comrades, tore the booklets up and threw them on the ground. A carpet of paper stretched out in front of the university's main entrance.

Then came the turn of the retrogrades. The Senate and the Holy Synod made a decision. Guardsmen—a half platoon of the Preobrazhensky Regiment and a platoon of the Finland regiment—were sent to the university. They surrounded and arrested the students in the courtyard. The soldiers formed a corridor through which the prisoners were brought out. Students out on the street attacked the soldiers with sticks. Then came the command the soldiers wanted to hear: "Butt stocks!"

As Minister of War Milyutin wrote, "The enraged soldiers went at it seriously."

Soon, 270 beaten students were led to the Fortress of Peter and Paul. They cursed the regime as they went. "The fortress was overcrowded," wrote Milyutin. Six of the wounded were sent to the hospital. Student unrest traveled to Moscow and the provinces. Everywhere, it was put down by gendarmes and policemen.

That was the tsar's first step toward the Catherine Canal. During the student riots in Moscow a certain Peter Zaichnevsky was arrested. A student of Moscow University, he was soon to play a fateful role in Alexander's life.

When the tsar returned to St. Petersburg, Kostya persuaded him to correct the situation. Janus agreed and once again looked forward: Putyatin was removed, and he appointed a young liberal from Kostya's circle as the new education minister. Forty-year-old Alexander Golovnin reopened the closed departments in St. Petersburg and allowed expelled students to sit for exams. The universities were given the autonomy they wanted.

But it was too late. The students had tasted the intoxication of rebellion.

It did not end here. The next spring, in 1862, the "fantastically bloody" proclamation of a group named Young Russia was found by the secret police. The tsar read in astonishment: "We need not a divinely anointed tsar, not an ermine mantle that hides hereditary inability, but an elected elder who receives a salary for his service. If Alexander II does not understand this and is not willing to voluntarily cede to the people, the worse for him."

Then came the bloody call: "There is only one way out of the oppressive situation—revolution, revolution bloody and inexorable, revolution that must radically change everything, everything without exception, all the foundations of contemporary society, and destroy the adherents of today's order. We are not afraid of it, even though we know that rivers of blood will flow, that there might be innocent victims. We will have just one cry: 'To the hatchets!' and then attack the imperial party, without pity, the way it does not pity us now. We will attack in the squares, if the vile blackguards dare to come out, attack them in their houses, attack in crowded city alleys, attack on the broad avenues of the capitals, attack in the villages and towns! Remember that those who are not with us are against us, and those who are against us are our enemy, and enemies must be obliterated by every means."

It was signed: "Central Revolutionary Committee."

Another bloody proclamation was laid on his desk. "A Bow to the Masters' Peasants from Their Well-Wishers." It was aimed at the peasants, calling on peasant Russia to take to their axes, to more bloodshed.

Now Alexander could see what the retrogrades had warned him about, the consequences of the "thaw" on young minds.

Kostya had been right to worry. Alexander was furious. His entourage sensed the imminent wind of change. Count Peter Shuvalov, close to the tsar, left the circle of liberal bureaucrats. He spoke to the tsar about the inability of another friend of the tsar, Prince Dolgorukov, to lead the Third Department effectively.

Within the Third Department, they began to talk of "the need for a harsh course." Denunciations began appearing on the tsar's desk about how the rebellious International, formed by the German professor Marx, had penetrated into Russia. A secret international alliance of revolutionaries was behind those proclamations. They were in Russia!

It would become clear later who was behind those mad proclamations.

In a Moscow cell, Peter Zaichnevsky and some other students arrested during the student riots awaited trial. They were given surprisingly comfortable accommodations. Actually, suspiciously comfortable ones, considering the habits of Russian policemen trained in Nicholas's harsh times.

On Sundays the prisoners were taken to an ordinary city bath house. Their friends awaited them along the way. A small group would gather and the police guard would wait patiently and tactfully to one side while the gentlemen chatted. It would end with an invitation for the friends to come talk in the cell.

"The small, low-ceilinged solitary cell was full; people sat on the bed, the window ledge, the floor, and the table. Most were young people, including several friends of Zaichnevsky from university. There were heated arguments," wrote one of the participants. It was bizarre, to say the least, for the police to permit a political meeting for students who had been arrested for attending such meetings.

Peter Zaichnevsky with a few incarcerated others had written the proclamation that so disturbed Alexander. Naturally, they made it harsh—it included a call for killing the entire royal family and landowners and other quotations from the Parisian Jacobins of 1793. The title "Young Russia" was a paraphrase of Young Italy, an organization of the Italian Carbonari revolutionaries.

For a small reward, a guard had agreed to take the proclamation in an envelope to the prisoners' friends. The text was published by an underground press and distributed in many copies, and thereby reached the Third Department. When it was brought to the tsar, the department branded it the fruit of international revolutionaries.

Immediately, as if to continue the momentum, mysterious fires broke out in St. Petersburg. Beginning on May 16, the capital burned every day. The nauseating odor of smoldering filled the air. The white nights had a red glow. The worst catastrophe occurred on May 28, 1862, when a monstrous fire broke out in Apraksin Yard. The fire leaped along the rotting wooden sheds filled with rubbish. The flames covered an enormous territory, jumping across the Fontanka River to the woodpiles in the backyards of magnificent palaces. Fire bells rang in vain, as all the efforts of the fire brigades were useless. The army was called in. Minister of War Milyutin came on horseback.

He recalled, "When I got to the fire, around 7:00 P.M., I saw a sea of flames the entire length of Gostiny Dvor (which fortunately was unharmed) to Sagorodny Prospect and from the Page Corps to Apraksin Yard. The Ministry of Foreign Affairs was engulfed in flames; they were throwing packets of files out the windows."

Alexander immediately came from Tsarskoye Selo to the inferno. He headed the fire fighting, for this was a real battle. By 2:00 A.M., the fire was stopped. Gostiny Dvor and the Page Corps were saved. But the center of the city had been turned into black, smoking ruins. The victims of the fire were settled on Semenovsky Square, where once Dostoevsky and the Petrashevsky group awaited execution.

Milyutin recalled, "Fires are a habitual catastrophe for us in Russia in the summer . . . and the people bear their bad luck docilely. But in 1862 the 'red rooster' took on such scope and character that there could be no doubt of intentional arson."

This was just what the secret police reported to Alexander. They fingered young people, students, as the arsonists. Rumors about student activity were constantly circulated during the huge fire.

Milyutin wrote, "The people who had gathered made a strong impression on me, I was astonished by their rage. It became dangerous for students to appear in the streets in uniform. ('Rebel student' is a common phrase among the simple people now.)"

Minister of Internal Affairs Valuyev made a strange notation in his diary, that the fires and proclamations had "the desired effect."

On May 21 an Investigation Commission was formed. In consisted of St. Petersburg's chief of police Alexander Patkul and delegates from the ministries of Internal Affairs, Justice, and War, and of course, the Third Department. They started an investigation of the fires, but they could not find the arsonists. There was one poor Jew in Odessa who was hanged for arson, but he was the only one. The question remains—did they fail as detectives? Or was there no one to be found, because the fires were a police provocation to frighten the tsar?

"The retrogrades" had been the pillars of Nicholas's reign, his military figures and officials. Tellingly, the court *camarilla*, a Spanish word for "intriguers at court," was used in Russia to refer to the court elite.

They all sensed that society had awakened dangerously after the hibernation under Nicholas. They wondered whether a major earthquake was coming. Would autocracy survive? Their banner was Great Russian chauvinism—the old triad of Autocracy, Orthodoxy, and Nationalism—with a hatred of the new reforms that might lead Russia down the Western path toward an end to autocracy.

At the beginning of the tsar's reign, they preferred to be anonymous, while he was wrapped up in his transformations. But with time, they became well known and they had a dangerous leader. The summer of fires marked their first victory. In expectation of the commission's conclusions, the tsar agreed to numerous arrests of "suspicious persons."

On June 8, he ordered the Department of Engineering "to prepare with all possible haste rooms for 26 political prisoners in the prison of the Fortress of Peter and Paul." He approved a resolution on the supervision of printing presses. By his decree the publication of the journal *Sovremennik* (The Contemporary) was suspended for eight months.

The journal was a symbol of glasnost. Its editor, the poet Nikolai Nekrasov, had become the idol of liberals in the early years of the new reign. *Sovremennik* "printed all the famous living writers. At its traditional lunches, the cream of literature gathered. As a contemporary joked, 'If the ceiling were to fall during one of those lunches, the great Russian literature would vanish.'"

The main authors of the essays in the journal were the very young Nikolai Dobrolubov and Nikolai Chernyshevsky. The former's satirical essays and articles and the latter's articles were quoted by young people everywhere. "If Chernyshevsky is a viper, then Dobrolubov is a cobra," wrote an author offended by their criticism. Dobrolubov died very young, leaving the criticism and punditry to Chernyshevsky, who became the intellectual trendsetter for youth. The ban on the journal affected him most of all.

Chernyshevsky was everything: philosopher, economist, pundit, literary critic, and writer. Paradoxically, the level of his philosophical and economic works is pathetic and he was a mediocre writer, yet he wielded enormous influence on all of Russian life. In an age of the titans Tolstoy and Dostoevsky, he would write the novel that was most popular among progressive young people in Russia, *What Is To Be Done?*

His father was a Russian Orthodox priest, who was a true pastor of his flock. In Nicholas's time, when "people were to be treated severely for their own good," people heard only words of kindness and welcome from him. The father's kindness, spiritual purity, and renunciation of the petty and vulgar were passed on to him. Nikolai Gavrilovich Chernyshevsky was a luminous man; even his greatest foes admitted that. They called him a fallen angel.

He was a follower of the humanist Mill, and he called for enlightened self-interest. "In acting nobly, we act for the exclusive benefit of ourselves." But this kindhearted man would be the ideological teacher of future terrorists and young Lenin.

When Alexander began work on peasant reform, Chernyshevsky had been thrilled. But the final result of the reforms elicited his determined protest. Overt political activity was out of the question, so with other disillusioned radicals he created the secret organization called Land and Freedom. It was secretly and closely bound to Herzen. It wanted true freedom for the peasants with a just allotment of land. It felt that the miserable allotment given by Alexander would lead to shock waves and a bloody rebellion, meaningless and ruthless.

In his "Letters Without an Address," Chernyshevsky wrote of the coming threat: "Our people are ignorant, filled with crude superstition, and blind hatred for those who have rejected their wild habits. Therefore we are equally against the anticipated attempt by the people to rid themselves of all supervision and care and to take on ordering their own affairs. In order to avert this horrifying denouement, we are prepared to forget everything—our love of freedom and our love of the people."

After the fires, Chernyshevsky was arrested and charged with inciting the very peasant revolt that he so feared. The proclamation "A Bow to the Masters' Peasants from Their Well-Wishers" was attributed to him. On June 12, 1862, he was brought to one of the prepared cells at the

Fortress of Peter and Paul, where he would spend close to two years, admitting nothing.

The investigation, prison, and the unfairness of the regime changed him. He became an implacable opponent of the regime. Sitting in the damp solitary cell, where he would occasionally go on a hunger strike to protest his conditions, he started writing *What Is To Be Done?* His hatred for the regime illuminated his work with a secret fire.

From his prison cell, Chernyshevsky would dictate to an entire generation what it was to do. The novel's hero would have an unprecedented, fantastic influence on Russia's youth.

Alexander, by now, was caught between retrogrades in his regime and radicals in the universities. Once he filled up the cells of the Fortress of Peter and Paul, he surprised the retrogrades by looking in the opposite direction. Very far.

In that hot summer filled with smoke in the capital, turbulent peasant unrest, and student riots, Alexander called in his chief of cabinet Valuyev. He commanded the minister to prepare in total secrecy a new draft project. The State Council, appointed by the tsar, was to be reorganized into a bicameral legislative advisory institution with elected deputies.

Valuyev was stunned. It would be the first higher elected institution in Russia. Was the autocrat heading toward a parliament and constitution? The ever-helpful Valuyev did not discuss the tsar's orders and asked questions only in his diary. The human weather vane instantly started work with great enthusiasm.

While his assiduous minister wrote a draft of the decree, Alexander decided to test the constitutional idea on the empire's borders. His brother, Kostya, and Grand Duchess Elena Pavlovna were by his side again.

He selected the Polish Kingdom and the Grand Duchy of Finland as his constitutional testing grounds. Before they were annexed by Russia, both states had had a much more progressive form of government than the empire. They had constitutions. The tsar began with Poland. He decided to expand Polish self-government significantly, which his father had always been against, hating the continually rebellious Poles.

In late June 1862, the family's chief liberal, Grand Duke Konstantin Nikolayevich, went off to Poland as viceroy to implement the reform of self-government. But the Poles rejected "miserable hand-outs." They felt the winds of change and wanted everything right away. They demanded independence and did not want a Russian viceroy.

They shot at brother Kostya at the theater. Fortunately, it was a slight shoulder wound that did more damage to his gold epaulet than to his arm. The grand duke remembered his father's tradition: The would-be assassin was hanged as an example to others.

But the shot was only a prelude.

Alexander was at a ball when he learned that an uprising had begun throughout Poland. The rebels had formed a national government and declared their independence. Kostya, not very good in the role of gendarme pacifier, was having trouble putting down the rebellion.

Alexander was furious. He decided to give the "ingrate rebels" a taste of his father's medicine. He sent General Mikhail Muravyev to Poland. Muravyev was a huge man, short of breath, with the face of a bulldog and the eyes of a tiger. He was a leader of the retrograde party. When he had served as governor in western provinces, he was ruthless in implementing the policy of Russification. He was one of the few to openly criticize the reforms of the new emperor. After serfdom was abolished, Muravyev retired demonstratively.

A distant relative had been hanged with the Decembrists. But as he used to say, "I'm not one of the Muravyevs who get hanged, I'm one of those who do the hanging."

Muravyev set conditions: Grand Duke Konstantin was to be recalled and he was to have dictatorial rights in Poland. Alexander did not argue. When Muravyev set out for Poland, he joked, "The only good Pole is a hanged Pole." He came to be known by the name of Muravyev the Hangman.

A hundred-thousand-strong Russian army shattered the poorly

armed Polish rebels. Then Muravyev began a vicious "purge" of Poland. Estates were taken away, entire families were sent to Siberia, monasteries were closed, and monks and nuns who had helped the rebels were driven out of their cells. Twenty-two thousand Poles were sent to hard labor, shot, or hanged. Several thousand rebels escaped to Europe.

It was the end of Polish self-government, not the beginning. Poland was now ruled from St. Petersburg and Russian was the mandatory language for all officials.

After these atrocities, Alexander once again felt the approval of society. "What a man that Muravyev! What a fist! He executes and hangs. Hangs and executes! God grant him health," wrote the Slavophile Alexander Koshelev.

This was an expression of Orthodox Russia's age-old dislike and distrust of Catholic Poland. In the Time of Troubles, the Poles almost conquered Russia and put pretenders on the throne, and quite recently they had fought with Napoleon against Russia. Russians never forgot nor forgave that.

Pushkin called it "Family enmity among Slavs." But Europe was not about to accept the atrocities of the family affair.

Muravyev's bloody exploits outraged European public opinion. The refugee Poles spoke eloquently of the horror. When France, England, and Austria, who had recently put Russia on its knees in the Crimean War, protested against the violence in Poland, it made pacification of Poland even more popular in Russia. The Russian press called Muravyev the "Russian knight" who was "fighting Europe, which wanted to use the Poles for a new humiliation of Russia."

Herzen called this reaction "patriotic syphilis."

The pressure from England, France, and Austria continued, and those governments began to issue ultimatums. They demanded amnesty for the rebels, autonomy for Poland, and so on from the "bloody barbarians" (as the French newspapers called the Russians). Gorchakov brushed them off with clever envoys, offering assurances of friendship

and fiery promises for the future. Not without some mockery he promised England that Poland would eventually have a constitutional government similar to England's.

Reading the memoranda from his former enemies, Alexander just
sighed. He couldn't fight. Once again, he had to embrace a Prussia that
understood him so well. His "dear uncle and friend" King Wilhelm also
held conquered Polish territory and was a willing ally. Soon the tone in
Europe changed. No one wanted to fight a Russian-Prussian alliance
over Poland. Alexander was relieved by Europe's betrayal of Poland.

The tsar sternly lectured the French ambassador. "I had wanted to
offer Poland autonomy. And what came of it? The Poles wanted to create
their own state again. But that would have meant the collapse of Russia."
He chided France for giving refuge to thousands of Polish émigrés.

Privately, while giving lip service to Muravyev's action, the European
Alexander was revolted by his reprisals. He kept trying to rein in the gen-
eral. Muravyev wrote, "Not only did I receive no approval from St.
Petersburg, they used all measures to counter me."

The tsar's inner circle—Kostya in the Marble Palace, Elena Pavlovna
in the Mikhailovsky Palace, Prince Dolgorukov, chief of the Third
Department, Prince Suvorov, governor general of the capital—all felt
scornful hatred for the Hangman.

When Prince Suvorov was invited to sign a proclamation for
Muravyev's birthday, he replied, "I don't honor cannibals."

Once Poland was back in line, the tsar fastidiously put Muravyev at a
distance. He awarded him the title of count and sent him into retirement. The general went back to his estate, where he sat on the balcony
in his white uniform, puffing his pipe, putting on weight, and writing
his memoirs. It seemed that the fat bulldog with tiger eyes had plunged
forever into the political Lethe. But in Russia, one needs to live a long
life to get revenge.

In revenge for Poland's constant rebelliousness, tranquil Finland was
allowed a representative institution. The tsar called on the Finnish Seim
to write a constitution. The Seim had not met since 1809; the country
was run by a Senate under the Russian governor general. Alexander

decreed: "If the work of the Seim is successful, this will be the basis for expansion of the experiment." After 1869, the Seim in Finland met regularly, but Alexander did not need to expand the experiment.

Having squashed sedition (as he considered it) and feeling public approval, the tsar decided that he did not need any new reforms. When Valuyev brought his carefully formulated project for a constitution, the papers were sent to the archives. Valuyev was happy, for he did not want to be seen as a "red" in the eyes of the powerful camarilla.

But the tsar would have occasion to recall the project.

The first year after the emancipation of the serfs was the celebration of the most important jubilee in the nineteenth century—Russia's millennium. The tsar and his family went to Novgorod. It was there a thousand years earlier that the Varangian princes founded the Russian state. Weary of internecine warfare, the Slavs sent messengers to the militant Varangian princes with an amazing invitation: "Our land is rich and abundant, but we have no order. Come rule over us."

There are not many parallels to be found in history. But the foreign princes did not become autocrats in Novgorod. "Master Great Novgorod" remained a free republic for almost four hundred years. The Novgorod Veche (assembly of urban dwellers) hired and fired its princes and passed laws. The Great Novgorod Republic was finally destroyed by the willful Moscow tsars, who left only one path for Russia—autocracy.

That is why in a year of upsets—student riots, fires, and proclamations—Alexander preferred to celebrate the millennium quietly in the land that retained the memory of the once mighty Russian republic.

Alexander was hostage to his achievements. He was bound to the wheel of reform. After all, the emancipated peasants had to be managed by someone. The landowners were not an option. The reforms that had caused him so much anxiety had to be continued. A new local authority had to be created—the zemstvo institutions.

The very word *zemstvo,* from the word for land, *zemlya,* was imbued with liberty. Back in Muscovite Russia, important decisions were made by meetings of all the estates, the Zemskoe Assembly, which were assemblies of all Russian landowners. It was appropriate to use the word for land in the name of local organs of self-government, because for the first time the entire land, the whole population, was involved. There were representatives of the nobility, the peasantry, and the urbanites in the assemblies. But the chairmen of the zemstvos were the heads of the local nobility associations, and the zemstvos could deal only with local affairs. State politics were strictly out of bounds.

For the first time in Russia, the state budget was published. Alexander wanted the public to see what money was spent on in the state, formerly a deep secret of the tsars. Now the budget was discussed in the newspapers. The court camarilla kept repeating, "If only the emperor could see this!" They meant Nicholas, of course.

He had to create a new court system. Under serfdom, the landowners were the judges of 20 million serfs. Even the free people did not have much better courts. Bribery was part of the judicial system. There was an almost official joke, "We accept money and we accept your case." A judge could make a ruling in the absence of both plaintiff and defendant.

In 1864, Alexander signed new judicial bylaws. Russia suddenly had what it had never had: equality of all citizens under the law. In a land of yesterday's slaves, a jury system was instituted to create a court that was "swift, just, and compassionate," and equal for all citizens. The independence and glasnost of the judicial system and the competitive trial process stunned contemporaries. The new profession of defense attorney gave rise to famous orators, whose speeches were printed in the newspapers and who were quoted by the whole country. The new Russia was learning democracy in the courtrooms. And the courtroom orators would do a lot to promote the fall of Alexander's dynasty. Just fifty-three years later, the leader of the victorious revolution would be the advocate Alexander Kerensky.

There was one last reform, perhaps the most important: of the army.

There were no more serf recruits, the foundation of the army of Alexander's ancestors. On January 1, 1874, the universal draft was introduced. It put an end to the burden of military service being on the tax-paying classes, or estates (that is, the peasants and the bourgeoisie). Equality was introduced: Now all the estates had to serve in the army.

Nicholas's anti-Jewish laws were significantly softened. The tsar repealed his father's secret instruction barring Jews from government posts. Alexander did not dare do away with the pale of settlement for all Jews. But Jewish merchants of the first guild and craftsmen, Jews with scholarly degrees, and Jewish soldiers who had served the required twenty-five years in Nicholas's army were given permission to live beyond the pale.

The military reform included a ban on corporal punishment. Whipping was a Russian tradition, a remnant of the good old days. Serfs were whipped, high school students were whipped, wives were whipped. The famous sixteenth-century book *Domostroi,* on how to run a Russian household, had a long list of rules on how to beat a wife so as to teach her a lesson but not cripple "living property belonging to the husband."

Criminals were flogged, of course. But soldiers were most viciously treated. They were flogged for misbehavior, for sloppiness in uniform (up to 500 blows), for attempting desertion (1,500 blows and 3,000 for a second attempt).

Nicholas, to toughen up his sissy son, had once forced Alexander to watch a whipping. A soldier was being punished for attempted desertion. Nicholas tried to be merciful and commanded that he be struck only 500 times instead of 1,500. The small soldier with high cheekbones sniveled and muttered, "Have pity on me, brothers." But he knew that they would not, because if they held back, they would be flogged.

The men were lined up in two rows, to form a gauntlet. They called it the green street. The soldier was bare to the waist. The drummer set a beat; the soldier was led down the gauntlet, his hands tied to two rifles. Two soldiers led him, and they led him slowly, so that each man could strike him with a rod as hard as he could. Screaming louder than the drum, the wretch begged for mercy, but the blows fell. His skin hung in strips. He staggered and collapsed. They lifted him up. He had no back, only naked, bloody flesh. He fell once again and could not get up. He no longer begged. It was over. His bloody corpse was laid on a cart and two soldiers dragged it through the rest of the line, so that the prescribed number of blows could be struck on the slurping, bloody mess that had been the soldier.

The new tsar remembered Bonaparte's popular phrase, "A whipped soldier loses the most important thing—his honor!" Along with corporal punishment, he also banned branding.

Now, in the newly liberated country, the only anomalous feature was autocracy itself.

CHAPTER 6

An Awakened Russia

The first fifteen years of Alexander II's reign saw an unprecedented stirring in Russia's spiritual life. It was a Russian Renaissance—a feast of spirit and intellect, the birth of great literature and a time of turbulence and success in science. In the 1860s, Mendeleyev published his Periodic Table of the Elements, and science became fashionable. Materialism and scientific thought were de rigueur. Darwin was the idol of the young generation, which was delighted by the concept of man's descent from the apes. The fury of the clergy only added to their delight. All of Darwin's major works were instantly translated.

It was in the 1860s that Petr Boborykin coined the term *intelligentsia* (modeled on the Western *intellectuals*). The great Russian intelligentsia was born in the days of Alexander's great reforms and great hopes. At first it was called the *raznochinnaya intelligentsia,* meaning that the intellectuals came from all estates and strata of society. It was a roiling mixture of people from every walk of life (clergy, merchants, bourgeoisie, minor officials), primarily those in "white-collar" positions, who became writers, journalists, teachers, and scientists.

They proudly hailed a new era, and they replaced the nobility as the avant-garde of Russian society. A required characteristic of the intelligentsia was opposition to the regime. The Russian intelligentsia would be the hotbed of all the Russian revolutions to come, and of international anarchism, and the modern use of terror.

Russian literature played an enormous role in developing the revolutionary fervor of the intelligentsia. After the Revolution of 1917, the literary critic Semyon Vengerov would write, "The revolution must thank our literature, which constantly called for revolution."

"If you write, don't be afraid, if you are afraid, don't write." That was the slogan of the new Russian literature. It would remain the call in Russia for more than a century, right up until Gorbachev's perestroika, yet the period of Alexander's reforms saw a flourishing of literature that was never to be repeated.

When the dam of Nicholas's taboos was broken, great literature ruthlessly criticizing society was unleashed on a society that was unaccustomed to hearing criticism. Coupled with writers came the equally celebrated literary and social critics, who explained the stern condemnation of the books. Literary heroes seemed to step from the pages into life, becoming "realer than real" and role models for readers.

Ivan Goncharov wrote the novel *Oblomov*, in 1859, when he was middle-aged. It was slightly autobiographical and a bit of a grotesque parody of himself. He was a typical landowner, heavyset, well groomed, always rather sleepy and with lethargic gestures. The novel's plot is simple: The landowner Oblomov, a bachelor (like the author), spends his entire life on his favorite couch. He sleeps, eats, and dreams there. Handsome, intelligent, refined, Oblomov is totally incapable of action. His entire life is apathy, fear of action, enjoyment of indolence. His estate, Oblomovka, is the perfect match for its owner. The main activity its residents start preparing for in the morning is the afternoon nap. The main event is the midday meal. The only loud sounds interrupting the tranquility of Oblomovka come from the kitchen. Oblomov's life is the apotheosis and poetry of indolence that devours talents, love, and life itself.

As soon as the book was published, the young critic Nikolai Dobrolubov wrote "What Is Oblomovism?" The novel became more than famous; its eponymous hero was turned into a symbol. The critic explained that Oblomov and Oblomovism were the curse of Russian life. Russia was the den of a somnolent bear, where all change ended with the bear rolling over and going back to sleep. Oblomovs were everywhere. Inactivity and well-meaning chatter were the hallmarks of

Russian life. "If I see a landowner expounding on human rights and the need to develop personally, I know from his first words that he is Oblomov. And when I am in a circle of educated people hotly sympathizing with the needs of humanity and for many years telling the same stories about bribery and all kinds of illegal acts—I find myself thinking that I have been transported to old Oblomovka. . . . Who will at last move them from their spots with the all-powerful word 'Forward!'?" wrote Dobrolubov.

Aesopian language, euphemism, and writing in code were required by Alexander's censorship. Young people, who had quickly learned to read between the lines, understood the real meaning of the article: The absence of political life, that is, autocracy, was turning Russia into a land of Oblomovism. Enough chatter, enough bold speeches; now was the time for bold actions, new people, people of action to lead us forward into the new life.

The young men of action appeared soon enough. Unlike their fathers, who were satisfied with Alexander's reforms, the sons demanded new, radical reforms and violently rejected all the values of the past. In 1862, Ivan Turgenev published his novel *Fathers and Sons*. The novel's hero, Bazarov, was the new type, a man of action. He was a doctor. He served science, which, unlike art, was useful. He was obsessed with utility. Gleefully, to the dismay of the "fathers," he denounced "useless art," "useless great poetry," he rejected all the previously accepted concepts, ideals, and even norms of behavior. He was a *nihilist*. The critics quickly picked up the term, making it a byword in Russian society, which immediately turned into two camps, pro and contra the nihilist Bazarov.

In the mouths of the retrogrades, nihilist became more than a pejorative, it was another word for revolutionary. The court whispered that Grand Duke Konstantin Nikolayevich was a nihilist. But the new young men bore the title proudly. One in particular, the critic and essayist Dmitri Pisarev, adored Bazarov and considered himself a nihilist.

Pisarev was a seminal figure of those turbulent times. A wunderkind who could read and write at the age of four and speak foreign languages, he became maniacally obsessed with negation. As sometimes happens with thinking young people, he pushed the idea to its ultimate point, that is, to the negation of his own existence and to madness.

He was hospitalized in a mental institution, where he attempted suicide twice before escaping. He was taken to his family estate, where his health was eventually restored, but his tendency toward the most determined negation remained.

What was once considered illness now made Pisarev famous. The thirst for renunciation was mighty in the new era, a time of general criticism and angry young men. Pisarev became the bard of nihilism. Like the fictional Bazarov, Pisarev harped on "utility." He formulated the basic dilemma facing humanity: "feed the hungry" or "enjoy the marvels of art—and spend money on it." He compared a "society that has hungry and poor people in its milieu and yet develops the arts" to a hungry savage who ornaments himself with precious stones. He concluded that only that which is useful has the right to exist. He denounced the sacred cows of Russia, the great Pushkin and Lermontov, for their "useless poetry," and praised scientific tomes.

In an essay on Darwin's *On the Origin of Species,* Pisarev painted his own picture of the world. "The vast majority of organic creatures enter the world as if it were a giant kitchen where cooks are constantly chopping, eviscerating, and roasting each other. Finding itself in such strange society, the young creature goes directly from its mother's womb into a pot and is eaten by one of the cooks. But before the cook can swallow his dinner, he himself is already in a pot, with the unchewed food still in his mouth."

The young understood the message of their favorite essayist: The world in which they lived was irrational and cruel, and it had to be changed immediately.

Yet another child of Alexander's perestroika was Russian satire. Dostoevsky described it in his diary. "Russian satire seems to be afraid of good deeds in Russian society. Upon encountering such a deed, it becomes anxious and does not calm down until it finds somewhere deep in that deed a scoundrel. Then it rejoices and shouts: 'It's not a good deed at all, there's nothing to be happy about, see for yourselves, there's a scoundrel in it!'"

That is exactly why satire was so successful among the intelligentsia. Constant criticism is what the new social class demanded and welcomed. Their idol, Saltykov-Shchedrin, wrote an immortal satire, a sacred book for Russian liberals, *The Story of the Town of Glupovo*. The miserable inhabitants of the town are whipped and robbed by the rulers, the city officials, who compete in viciousness, greed, and idiocy. The townspeople compete in docility. One of the city officials turns out to have an artificial head. It does not keep him from ruling the docile residents of Glupovo, or keep the people from fearing and obeying him. Young readers easily recognized Russian tsars in the town officials and the history of Russian fear and servility in the history of the townspeople. The moral of the book, the thread through the entire narrative, is to put an end to the docility and our stupid history.

Alexander's reign produced many literary gems. Leo Tolstoy and Fedor Dostoevsky wrote their greatest novels in that period. They were the first Russian writers to win world fame. Of all contemporary writers, only they had points in common. Both studied the cosmos of the human soul, the disharmony of the world, the relationship of man and God. And yet these geniuses, who were jealously interested in each other, never met. They both knew every other well-known writer. Once they were both present at a public lecture by the philosopher Vladimir Solovyov, whom they both esteemed. Yet even though they were in the same hall, they did not meet. It was as if they were avoiding each other.

Why? The scope of their personalities did not permit it. They would have found it too crowded. They would have immediately plunged into an ideological battle, which in Russia always ends with hatred. That is why both Tolstoy and Dostoevsky feuded with Turgenev, a writer beneath them, whom they both knew well. As a Russian grandee in the eighteenth century once said, "We Russians don't need bread, instead we eat each other up and feel satisfied."

Death changed everything. After Dostoevsky's death, Tolstoy immediately wrote, "I never saw the man . . But suddenly, when he died, I understood that he was the closest, most necessary, dearest man to me." *The Brothers Karamazov* was Tolstoy's last reading before his own death in 1910.

The end brought our two greatest writers together. But this was only the beginning. Count Leo Tolstoy retired to his estate in Yasnaya Polyana, where in the 1860s he wrote *War and Peace,* a novel with resounding success.

When Alexander II ascended the throne, Dostoevsky had served his sentence of hard labor and was serving as an ordinary soldier in Semipalatinsk, a distant Siberian town. The new regime restored his rights and his noble rank. Like Tolstoy, he retired from the army with the rank of officer and went back to literature. Dostoevsky began using the terrible capital he accrued at hard labor, which no other Russian writer had at that time. It was the "black, ill-starred life," the world of social outcasts and prison camps. Dostoevsky was the first to reveal it to Russian readers in *Notes from the House of the Dead.*

The book was not only about the hell of hard-labor prison camps, but also about freeing oneself from a personal hell. In the camp where "suffering was inexpressible, endless, and every minute weighed you down like a stone on your soul," Dostoevsky went through a spiritual cataclysm—a "trial of myself" and a "severe examination of my former life." He became an enemy of the ideas for which he had paid with years of suffering, the best years of his life. He came to think that the idea of revolution was innately sinful—it was wrong to think that happiness could be won violently, through blood. He returned from hard labor a new man.

Dostoevsky was tormented in his ideological seekings and in his personal life. He was passionately in love with Maria Isaeyva, wife of the warden. He married her when she became a widow and their happy union ended only when Masha, as he called her, died of tuberculosis. But even as she lay dying, Dostoevsky embarked on a new passion, love for the "tormenting woman," Apolinaria Suslova. He felt "tormenting guilt" before the dying Masha. The day after his wife's death (April 16, 1864), he wrote in his notebook, "Masha is laid out. Will I see Masha again?" He pondered life beyond the grave and expressed his fear of meeting her there, his fear of his sin.

The image of Apolinaria Suslova pursued him to his deathbed, appearing in novel after novel: Polina (*The Gambler*), Nastasya Filippovna (*The Idiot*), and Grushenka (*The Brothers Karamazov*). His passion for her was combined at that time with another "tormenting passion," gambling. His mad gambling forced him to work madly. The 1860s saw a fertile flow of his works: "Uncle's Dream," "The Village of Stepanchikovo and Its Inhabitants," *The Insulted and Injured,* among others. The money he earned was instantly consumed by the roulette table. He was continually in debt and his creditors hounded him.

So Dostoevsky decided to embark on two novels at the same time, *Crime and Punishment* and *The Gambler.* On the brink of debtor's prison and pressed by creditors, he sold the rights to all his works to the publisher Stellovsky, with the obligation to add a new work to the previous ones. The contract was stringent: If he did not turn in *The Gambler* on time, the publisher could publish all of Dostoevsky's work for free for nine years.

Time flew and he had less than a month before his deadline, yet he had not written a line of it. He decided to dictate the novel to a stenographer in three weeks. Thus the young secretary Anya Snitkina entered his life. Working feverishly, Dostoevsky completed *The Gambler* in three weeks.

By the end of the dictation, the kind, pure, and naïve Anya had replaced his old love. Now Apolinaria Suslova lived in the novel he had dictated to Anya, and Anya entered his real life.

The writer, who feared he would be rejected, proposed in a literary way. He told Anya the plot of a new novel. The hero was "a man prematurely aged, sick with an incurable disease, grim and suspicious, albeit with a tender heart but unable to express his feelings . . . an artist, perhaps talented, but a failure who has never been able to shape his ideas into the forms he dreamed of." This was Dostoevsky's pitiless self-portrait.

"And this unsuccessful artist," he continued, "has fallen in love with a girl, not a beauty, but very pretty. . . . The more he saw her, the more he was attracted to her, especially since he was convinced that he could find happiness with her. Is it possible that a young woman, so different in personality and age, could fall in love with my artist? Would this be psychologically inaccurate?"

Only toward the end of this monologue did Anya Snitkina realize, looking at his suffering face, what he was talking about. The twenty-year-old told the forty-five-year-old writer, "I love you and I will love you all my life."

They were married in February 1867. His insight was correct, and he finally "found the happiness I had so desired." *Crime and Punishment,* which was published then, was the first of his novels to have "huge success with readers." The novel's protagonist, the student Rodion Raskolnikov, was a "theoretical killer" who "dreamed of making humanity happy and saving the poor through murder." He ends up collapsing and discovering revelation and repentance in prison camp.

The novel was the new Dostoevsky's dire warning to society after his return from Siberia and seeing the revolutionary mood among the young. The fashionable radical critics attacked *Crime and Punishment,* condemning it for slandering the young and playing into the hands of the retrogrades. But they could not keep it from being a popular success.

While the novel was in press, a murder took place in Moscow. A student named Danilov, who had killed someone during a robbery, explained his crime with a chilling similarity to the fictional (and as yet unpublished) Raskolnikov. Dostoevsky was very proud of his foresight.

His foresight would become even more dangerous. Very soon, under that sorrowful St. Petersburg sky, the young terrorists would appear. The "theoretical murderers" would be tormented by Raskolnikov's questions: Can you cross the line? Can you kill a man for the sake of an idea? For the sake of the future happiness of humanity? Like Dostoevsky's character, they would overcome their doubts and go out to kill.

Chapters of both *Crime and Punishment* and *War and Peace* were printed in the same issues of the journal *Russkii Vestnik* (Russian Herald). And even though both works were hugely successful, the most progressive young people were lining up for a different magazine. They wanted the issue of *Sovremennik* with Chernyshevsky's novel *What Is To Be Done?*

Impossible under Nicholas I, it happened in Alexander II's reign: a novel written by a prisoner was published. The copies of *Sovremennik* were quickly confiscated, but too late. The novel took on a life of its own. There wasn't a thinking young person in Russia who had not read *What Is To Be Done?*

The book is a mystery of Russian literature. Without a trace of great talent, it nevertheless influenced people for half a century. The terrorist Alexander Ulyanov considered it his revolutionary bible. When his younger brother, Vladimir Ulyanov (Lenin) read it, he claimed, "This book plowed me up." *What Is To Be Done?* made the future leader of Bolshevik Russia a revolutionary.

The book is ideological, offering up every radical and progressive idea of the period—happy collective labor, the emancipation of women, free love higher than the bounds of bourgeois marriage—to its young readers. Its biggest attraction, however, was the character of Rakhmetov. He appeared in the chapter "A Special Man." Reading the chapter, young people habitually filled in the blanks in the narrative of the author, sitting in a cell in the Fortress of Peter and Paul.

The "special man" Rakhmetov prepares himself to serve the people (read, "foment revolution"), hardens himself for future deprivation (naturally, prison and hard labor), eats raw meat, and sleeps on a bed of nails. To share the labor of the people and to understand them, the aristocrat Rakhmetov periodically works as a laborer, even as a Volga boatman. (Soon, a whole movement of "going to the people" would spring up among the intelligentsia.) He rejects personal happiness, wife, children, anything that could distract him from serving the happiness of people (again, revolution). He spends his money not on his own needs, but to help needy students (rebellious students, naturally).

Readers took the author's word as a testament and appeal: "Here is a real man, who is particularly needed by Russia today. Make him your model and whoever can and has the strength, follow his path, for it is the only path for you that can lead us to the desired goal."

Revolution and Rakhmetov was the answer to the question in the title. For decades the iron ascetic Rakhmetov captured the imagination of Russian youth. He was a symbol for revolutionaries, a Che Guevara for his time.

Rakhmetov offers a key to the behavior of future Russian terrorists. Heading off to revolution, young people would enthusiastically submit to Rakhmetov's deprivations, repeating Chernyshevsky's admonition, "Whoever can and has the strength, follow his path, for it is the only path for you that can lead us to the desired goal."

Leon Trotsky would later write, "We read *What Is To Be Done?* with ecstatic love and tried to imitate Rakhmetov in every way." He added, "He was the future member of People's Will."

Indeed, the future terrorist member of People's Will. Chernyshevsky threw his bomb into the future from his cell.

He handled himself regally at his trial. The Senate sentenced him to fourteen years at hard labor (reduced to seven), followed by exile.

It drizzled in St. Petersburg on the day of Chernyshevsky's banishment, a ceremony known as "civil execution." A black pillory with chains topped the scaffold. A thousand admirers had gathered by eight in the morning: writers, editors, medical students, and officers. He was brought in a carriage, surrounded by mounted gendarmes. On the scaffold platform the executioner removed his hat and the sentence was read. "For criminal intent to overthrow the existing order," he was stripped of "all rights of his estate" and sent "to hard labor" and then was "to be settled in Siberia forever."

The rain increased. Chernyshevsky wiped his wet faced and myopically wiped his fogged glasses. After reading the sentence, the executioner made Chernyshevsky kneel, broke a sword over his head, and put chains on his hands. It was pouring, and the executioner put Chernyshevsky's hat on his head, for which Chernyshevsky thanked him politely and adjusted the brim, chains clanking.

On his knees in the lashing rain, the creator of the iron Rakhmetov patiently waited for the end of the pillorying. The crowd waited silently with him. At the end, people rushed toward the carriage, but the mounted guards kept them away. The crowd threw flowers into the carriage.

Chernyshevsky was sent to Siberia in leg irons, under an armed guard, and he spent almost twenty years there. The leaders of Land and Freedom were also arrested. Its main organizers, the Serno-Solovyovich brothers, were sentenced: Nikolai, thirty years old, philosopher and sociologist, was sent to eternal exile in Siberia, and his brother, Alexander, twenty-four, who had managed to leave Russia, was sentenced in absentia to eternal expulsion from Russia. Abroad, Alexander headed the young Russian community, while Nikolai soon died in Siberia.

While myopic Chernyshevsky did his time, students remembered their favorite author in a popular drinking song:

> *Let's drink to the author of*
> What Is To Be Done?
> *To his heroes and his ideals.*

Ideals and *ideas* were favorite words among the young intelligentsia. They valued literature only if it was ideological. Even poetry had to be ideological for them.

The leader of the new civic poetry, the idol of the nihilists, was the poet Nikolai Nekrasov, editor of the journal *Sovremennik.* "Muse of revenge and sorrow" is what Nekrasov called his poetry. His young followers, adept at deciphering Aesopian language, read the line as follows: "Revenge for the pitiless regime and sorrow for the impoverished people without rights." "No Russian can look without love at that pale Muse, bloodied, lashed by the knout," the poet wrote. His readers added "by the knout of the tsarist censors."

Nekrasov had some powerful and direct poems, which became proverbs and slogans. All the future terrorists knew these lines: "No heart can learn to love if it wearies of hatred," and, "You will not die in vain, the act is solid when blood streams beneath it."

He formulated a new concept of poetry: "You don't have to be a poet, but you must be a citizen." The willful, imperious Muse of Pushkin, the Muse of Apollo, was declared an anachronistic, useless toy. She was replaced by Nekrasov's Muse, who served society, who criticized power, the Muse of the new intelligentsia. Only that kind of poetry had the right to exist, because it was useful. "Useful" was the highest word of praise of the new youth and the new times.

Nekrasov's journal, *Sovremennik,* attacked everything that did not correspond to that civic approach. However, the great civic poet himself was not always the most luminous of men. He was a celebrated cardplayer and, rumor had it, a clever cardsharp. When he played in aristocratic clubs he had an enviable record of beating wealthy cardplayers, but managed to lose to "necessary people," for example, the card-mad Count Alexander Adlerberg, son of the minister of the court. The count (who had been a childhood friend of the tsar) was very close to the emperor at that point.

The "demon of self-security" (as Dostoevsky put it elegantly) or "greed for enrichment" (as Alexei Suvorin described it less elegantly) was always present for Nekrasov, who had known true poverty in his youth. The civic poet was a smart and ruthless businessman, a quality that was new among Russian writers.

He had founded his journal with the writer Ivan Panayev. Soon after, as a contemporary wag put it, "I saw Nekrasov in Panayev's carriage with Panayev's wife." Nekrasov took over the journal and made Panayev's wife his mistress.

One of his favorite poetic images was that of the mother. But when his own mother died, he did not go to her funeral. And when Panayeva, who had loved him faithfully, grew old and needed money, he did not help her. "You once dedicated your lyre to her, now give her a few rubles for rent," a contemporary wrote angrily. He didn't.

Nekrasov's chief devil was not greed. It was fear. While truly fearless in his poetry, in real life Nekrasov was a coward. Fearful for the continued existence of *Sovremennik* (and more important of himself), he sometimes denounced his own journal. In conversation with authorities, he complained about his unruly coworkers. This constant fear would make him shameful to all of reading Russia. But which of us who lived in the USSR would throw a stone at him?

In a conversation Turgenev described the last pathetic cry of a hare chased (and caught) by borzoi hunting dogs. That image is always unconsciously present in everyone born in Russia. Nekrasov's younger contemporary, Gleb Uspensky, wrote, "You must continually be afraid—that is the point of life in Russia. Fear, the sense of guilt for your very existence, have permeated all our thoughts, all our days and nights."

The epigraph to Nekrasov's life could have come from Pushkin, the great poet he did not particularly care for. "But as soon as the Divine Word touches sensitive hearing, the poet's soul starts to tremble."

The minute he started writing, he was transformed—there was his fiery hatred for injustice, his enormous love of Russia, and his constant repentance in his poetry. No Russian poet ever repented with such power and lyricism as Nekrasov. The Rasputin formulas of "If you don't sin, you can't repent" and "Where it's vile, it's also holy" accompanied Nekrasov throughout his life. It was an acrobatics of the soul: sin turned into an unusual repentance, and repentance poured out in immortal lines, the poetry becoming his confession, his plea for forgiveness. Dostoevsky protected his epilepsy, which sometimes gave rise to incredible insights, and Nekrasov protected his sins. Reading Dostoevsky, one understands a lot about Nekrasov.

Nekrasov's definition of Russia—"You are squalid, you are abundant, you are mighty, and you are impotent"—applies to himself, the great and miserable, very Russian man.

In this new society with a literature that ruled minds, the emperor managed to live as if none of it were happening. Even his father, who had muzzled Russian literature, charmed the most famous writer of his time, inviting Pushkin to the palace. Nicholas went to the theater to watch Gogol's dangerous comedy, *The Inspector General,* which exposed the state embezzlement of his officials. At the end, he uttered his famous phrase, "Everyone got lambasted, but none more than me." The august self-criticism tamed the harsh comedy into a well-meaning call for ending embezzlement.

Even that mighty despot cared about having contact with influential writers. But Alexander II, the reformer, the student of the poet Zhukovsky, had no interest in writers. He did not wish to understand the power of the word in the society he had himself awakened. He did not understand that literature and the press were painting a portrait of his rule and shaping the minds of the youth. While reforming Russia, the two-faced Janus continued to live in the prereform period of his father's reign, when the portrait of the regime was created by the Third Department, which also handled the minds of the youth.

He had aroused Russia irreversibly. The reprisals against Chernyshevsky and the Land and Freedom group did not stop the great ice flow in the thaw after his father's severe winter. Everything was public now. There were political dinners where the Slavophiles and Westernizers argued furiously about Russia's future. In fighting each other, they demanded further and almost instant changes from the government. "We want the newborn [that is, the society freed of serfdom] to have teeth on the first day and be able to walk on the second [this in a country where more than 80 percent of the country was illiterate]—we do not need administrative nannies with diapers and swaddling clothes." That was the manifesto of the new era.

Passionate debates in the zemstvos, thunderous speeches by celebrated lawyers in overfilled courtrooms, charity balls with lectures by orators, public readings of their new works by great writers—disputes, meetings, and speeches were everywhere. They even managed to turn a funeral into a discussion. At Nekrasov's burial, Dostoevsky put Nekrasov, with a few reservations, on a par with Lermontov and Pushkin. A few youthful voices interrupted him with shouts of "Nekrasov is higher! Higher!" Followed by applause.

The discussion of Nekrasov at his grave site moved to the press, where it continued to be argued.

CHAPTER 7

Anni Horibiles

Alexander not only had no interest in literature, he had no time for it. In 1865, he suffered a personal tragedy that became a tragedy for the country. He and his wife adored their son Niks, the heir to the throne. The handsome and incredibly gifted young man was a true European in his convictions and was to continue his father's reforms. His teachers called him "Russia's hope," "a brilliant young man," "a flexible and subtle intelligence fervently responding to everything new." Everyone loved him. "The crown of perfection" was what Grand Duke Konstantin Nikolayevich called him. His huge and clumsy brother, Sasha, loved him with touching fidelity.

Sasha was next in line. Aware of the rivalry between Alexander and Konstantin, the empress (who never could overcome her dislike of her younger son) did not give Sasha the education that Niks received. Sasha was intentionally not groomed to be Niks's understudy.

This did not bother sweet Sasha, who was not interested in scholarship. Like all the Romanovs, he loved military affairs. He called himself "the parfait regimental commander," although unlike the real guardsmen in his family, Sasha wasn't very good at it.

He never danced at the balls, because he was ashamed of his clumsiness. He sat with the old men in a corner, a good vantage point for watching his beloved brother dance. Sasha was immensely strong; he could bend a horseshoe as a child, after which he would look to his brother for approval.

His constantly kind gaze, fat face, and canine loyalty prompted

Grand Duke Mikhail Nikolayevich (Uncle Misha) to call him Pug. The court called him Little Bulldog.

It was an accident. Alexander's nephew, young Duke Nicholas of Leichtenberg, was a guest in the palace. Niks enjoyed gymnastics and wrestling, and so did his cousin. Niks suggested a wrestling match. The two Nicholases met, with Sasha looking on. During the match Niks hurt himself, right on the spine. "He hit himself so hard on the corner of the marble table, that if he had not been helped, he would have fallen," recalled Alexandra Patkul. "My husband, the officer on duty at the Winter Palace under the tsar just then entered the room where Their Highnesses were playing in order to greet them. Seeing the heir pale and unable even to rise, my husband ran to fetch a glass of water, as no one had thought to do so. Then he inquired as to what had occurred and learned the details from Grand Duke Alexander Alexandrovich [Sasha]. He told Count Stroganov [Count Sergei Stroganov was Niks's governor] to send for a doctor immediately, that a serious blow to the spine needed attention . . . but no energetic measures were taken."

Princess Dagmar, Niks's Danish fiancée, arrived soon afterward. The petite and charming Dagmar was madly in love with him. She rode very well, so a fox hunt was organized in Peterhof. When Niks leaped up into the saddle, his face contorted in pain. His father asked what was wrong, but instead of an answer Niks spurred the horse and, with a cry of pain, almost fell from the saddle. No one treated this incident seriously, but in a short time the tsarevich began to change. He lost a lot of weight and he began to hunch over when he walked. His father did not understand and angrily chided him for "walking like an old man." Niks tried to overlook the pain, thereby doing greater damage to himself.

Eventually, he was given a thorough physical. The court physician, Dr. Botkin, went into the tsar's study with his report. The emperor came out, pale with shock. The blow to the spine had led to the development of a horrible disease, tuberculosis of the bone.

Niks was sent to Nice for treatment. He grew worse, and Sasha was granted permission to join him. In April 1865 the tsar received a telegram with more bad news: The illness had spread to the brain. The heir's days were numbered. They sent word to Copenhagen, and Dagmar and her mother headed for Nice.

The tsar and his entire family set out to see Niks for the last time. They held a service at the Kazan Cathedral before departing. The family prayed. "We traveled with one thought—would God allow us to find him still alive. . . . The train flew at terrifying speeds," wrote the heir's governor.

In Berlin they were met by King Wilhelm, the heir's uncle Willy. The monarchs embraced in silence. In the Prussian station, a car with Dagmar and her mother was added to the imperial train. The women wept. In Paris, the train was met by Napoleon III. The tsar "was grateful for the look of grief on his face."

With unprecedented speed for those days—three days and nights—they reached Nice. No one had ever traveled that fast from St. Petersburg. The train platform in Nice was filled with weeping Russians. Everyone loved Niks.

He was dying in the Villa Bermont, which Alexander later bought. The whole family came in. Niks lay in bed with a cheerful face, or rather, a cheerful smile on his waxy, emaciated face. Dagmar and mother stood at the bed, with the giant Sasha behind the petite Danish women.

The empress rushed to Niks. He kissed them all; he was alert and awake. But that night he had a wonderful delirium, addressing deputations with speeches, commanding regiments, explaining his father's achievements, quoting Latin, and speaking of the needs of the Slavs oppressed by the Turks. "We all blamed ourselves for not having it written down," Lieutenant General Litvinov, his governor, later recalled.

In his confession, Niks said he felt guilty for being impatient and sinfully wanting to die soon. The family and Dagmar came back into the room. Niks joked, "Isn't she wonderfully sweet, Father?"

April 12 was his last day. The tsar's family was staying across the street in the Villa Verdie, purchased for their arrival. At six, the governor rushed in to awaken them. He was dying. His medication was making him vomit. Dagmar kneeled at his bed and wiped his chin. He held her hand and then said, "Papa, take care of Sasha, he is such an honest, good man."

"After two, he raised his hand and caught Sasha's head in his right, and he seemed to be reaching for Princess Dagmar's head with his left . . . his tongue weakened and he said his last words. Holding the empress by the hand and indicating her to Dr. Harman, he said in French, 'Take good care of her,'" recalled Litvinov.

The family legend tells the story a little differently: On his deathbed Niks allegedly embraced his brother's head with one hand and with the other took his fiancée's hand. He placed her hand in his brother's hand. This justified what happened later.

Dagmar wrote to her father in Copenhagen: "I thank God that I reached him in time, my darling treasure, and that he recognized me in his final minute. I will never ever forget the look he gave me when I approached him. No, never! The poor Emperor and Empress! They were so attentive to me in my, and their, sorrow; his poor brothers, especially the oldest, Sasha, who loved him so nobly—not only as a brother but as his only and best friend. It is very difficult for him, poor thing, because now he must take his beloved brother's place."

Now Sasha was the heir. His teachers were saddened, for they knew his limited capabilities. Grand Duchess Elena Pavlovna begged the tsar to make the next son in line, Vladimir, the heir. He was no great star, either, but he was not as stubborn and dim as Sasha, or rather, as it was put more gently, he was not burdened by such "static thought."

Alexander was too depressed by his loss to think about making changes.

The heir was given many new teachers. Famous historians, jurists, and economists who had been teaching Niks now tried to fill in the gaps in Sasha's education. As one of them, the legal historian Boris Checherin, said, "We took on a hopeless task."

Everything the older brother had, the younger brother liked enormously. The new heir liked Dagmar, too. Sasha was very monogamous in his love. As a youth he had fallen in love with Princess Meshcherskaya and touchingly kept her slipper, which a servant stole for him. The princess had to be given away in marriage, and his father sternly lectured him.

He never had another infatuation until now. As Sasha dreamed of Dagmar, he wrote in his diary, "I keep thinking of Dagmar and pray every day that He arrange what will be my happiness for all my life."

He spoke to his father, told him that he loved Dagmar and wanted to marry her. It had seemed to him in Nice that she would not mind. His somewhat stupefied father wrote to Copenhagen, inviting Dagmar to St. Petersburg. The emperor soon learned that Sasha's perception had been correct.

From Sasha's diary: "Her mother wrote that she would not like to send Dagmar to us now, because she needed peace and she must bathe in the sea." That meant that they agreed to the marriage, but it had to be postponed, otherwise Europe would think that she was in a hurry to marry Dagmar off to the new heir. "As for me, that's all I think about. I pray to God for Him to arrange this and bless it," the heir wrote simply.

The proprieties were observed, several months were allowed to pass. Autumn came and Dagmar was ready to travel. The engagement was announced.

She arrived in September, to glorious weather, clear and sunny. The obligatory festivities began—balls, illuminations, fireworks. This was torture for the clumsy heir, who hated to dance. He declared his refusal to dance, and kept his word, to the consternation of court and family.

Count Sergei Sheremetyev, who played with Sasha when they were children and was later appointed his adjutant, recalled in his memoirs, "In general, the tsarevich was impossible in the role of fiancé. He showed himself in public only because it was his duty, he felt a revulsion for illuminations and fireworks. Everyone pitied the bride, deprived of the graceful and gifted bridegroom and forced to join another without love, a crude, unpolished man with bad French. That was the reigning assessment in court circles."

But she was not the one to be pitied. Russia was.

The bride conquered everyone. Dagmar regarded life with radiant eyes, and her simplicity and charm boded well for family life, although Sheremetyev wrote the truth: Not everyone in court accepted this hasty switch from the dead brother to the live one.

They did not understand that her small and graceful body belonged not to Niks or Sasha but had been intended from birth for the heir to the throne. That is why her mother bore her. Her mother married off her daughters and sons with great cleverness. Dagmar's sisters and brothers were related to all the royal houses from England to Greece. Dagmar's mother was called "the mother-in-law of Europe." Through her numerous offspring, the Danish queen amusingly created a united Europe.

From the day their engagement was announced, petite Dagmar was in charge of enormous Sasha. Once they were married, he never left her side. When she went to visit Denmark, he sat lost in her rooms, like a big hound that had lost his master.

Sasha always had to be a sidekick, always in love. First it was Niks, now it was Dagmar, yet he was the new heir to the throne of the Russian Empire. Dagmar, whose new Orthodox name was Tsarevna Maria Fedorovna, "Minny" in the family, was very happy in her new country.

If only she had known then what awaited her in Russia. She would see the death of her husband, Alexander III, and of her four sons. The first two of her children died early: Alexander in infancy, followed by Georgy, who died of tuberculosis. In 1917, she survived the revolution and the abdication from the throne by her sons Nicholas and Mikhail, and their deaths. Mikhail was executed in Perm. The last Russian tsar, Nicholas II, was executed in Ekaterinburg and, with him, her grandson, the tsarevich, and her four granddaughters. She would also outlive her favorite brother, King George of Greece, killed by a shot in Thessalonica. She would see the end of the great empire and the three-hundred-year-old Romanov dynasty and live out her days in a foreign land.

But during the engagement festivities she was so happy that it made people glad just to look at her. The poet Tyutchev called it "Dagmar's happy week."

Her mother-in-law, Empress Maria Alexandrovna, was more restrained in her attitude toward her. Everyone noticed. "She cooled the outbursts of her kindness, as if to stress the betrayal of her favorite son," wrote Count Sergei Sheremetyev. It was painful to look at her young daughter-in-law, who reminded her of her youth and young love. Now her relations with her husband were very different. She had given birth to their last child five years earlier. Tuberculosis—the result of the damp climate of St. Petersburg—and frequent childbirth had shattered her.

The empress retained her sense of humor. Every morning, her husband, Alexander, whom she called Sasha, maintained their ritual: He came to her rooms for their coffee, to give her a kiss, ask about the children, and remark that she "looked wonderful today." One day, she responded angrily. "The only thing I'm wonderful for is the anatomical theater—a teaching skeleton, covered with a thick layer of rouge and powder." She laughed bitterly. But that was just for a moment.

The group around the empress grew smaller. Her salon, once the top attraction, emptied. The death of the heir seemed to draw a line summing up her life. Dr. Botkin explained to the tsar that her lung disease made it impossible for her to fulfill her matrimonial duties. She and Alexander sighed in relief. Those "duties" had not been fulfilled for many years, anyway, but now the falseness of the situation disappeared. That part of life was closed to them and therefore, he was not really cheating on her any more.

They had a different relationship now. She became fervently devoted to religion and good works. Her office was filled with icons and she constantly spoke to him of newfound undecayed saints' relics.

The court began calling the empress a saint. The court, which had not liked her, now did not like the young beauties who went through the revolving door of the emperor's bedroom.

The emperor's amusements were becoming more exotic. He invited a French troupe of actors, who performed dialogues from the banned works of the Marquis de Sade for a select audience. Court rumors had them showing more than dialogues.

He also had a chief mistress. From the diary of Grand Duke Konstantin Nikolayevich: "22 November 1861. For lunch with wife to

Tsarskoye Selo. At the Orlov Gates met Sasha on horseback and behind him Alexandra Sergeyevna Dolgorukova, also on horseback and completely alone. The conclusion is not difficult. Painful."

Kostya wrote "painful" not because he was so moralistic, but because lady-in-waiting Princess Alexandra Dolgorukaya was an extremely predatory lady.

She was considered a true beauty. "However, if no one is looking at her, you will see to your astonishment that she is not beautiful!" Anna Tyutcheva wrote. "Long-limbed, flat chest, bony shoulders, zinc-white face." But no sooner did the princess notice "an interesting man's gaze" than her lithe body straightened, a blush appeared on her cheeks, and all her movements took on a dangerous grace. She acquired a feline friendliness.

The pussycat should have been called a tigress. Her body and sly and ingratiating smile ensnared her quarry. She was incomparable and yet a typical court beauty. Her interests were limited to the court, intrigue, and gossip. She had mastered the school for scandal, she knew how to give left-handed compliments that would please the devil himself.

As befits a master of court intrigue, she was a brilliant actress. Once she had slept with the tsar, she found a clever way to announce her relationship. The empress was reading the *Dictionary of History and Geography* in her sitting room, surrounded by her ladies-in-waiting. The tsar came in and Alexandra Dolgorukaya prompted fainted. The tsar hurried to her side. She was pale, her pulse was weak. The tsar, flustered, held her in his arms too long. The empress remained calm and dignified, continuing to leaf through her book.

The empress tolerated the liaison stoically. As had happened before, Alexander's passion faded, and the lady-in-waiting was retired. He arranged a marriage to his adjutant general and wrote her a gallant letter. "My spiritual wound will not soon heal, and my poor heart, which you read like a children's book, will suffer for a long time. Farewell forever."

Our experienced Don Juan obeyed the trite rule: If you want to leave a dangerous woman without consequences, allow her to think that she left you.

In 1865, the empress grew concerned, sensing that something unusual was happening. He had the look of a new love, but no one knew who she was. There were strange rumors of some schoolgirl from the Smolny Institute for Girls of the Nobility with whom he took walks in the Summer Garden. But that was ridiculous, for platonic love was not for the Romanovs. Moreover, she could see from the windows of her Golden Parlor that an unknown lady was often brought to the palace by carriage, and that lights would go on in the memorial study of Nicholas I, where he had died. Apparently that was where they carried on, shaming his father's memory. She would not learn the identity of her rival for some time.

By 1866, eleven years into Alexander's reign, the new leaders of the young generation were young themselves, high school and university students who had not completed their degrees. They were caught up in the intoxicating scent of liberty and they thirsted for political activity. "Whatever the last book read told him is what will be on his mind," wrote Nikolai Nekrasov, idol of Russia's youth, about the youth of Russia.

Banned books and mad ideas circulated. The hardest young people despised the previous generation of liberals and even the former hero of radical Russia, Alexander Herzen. With the hatred of youth for the old, they called them "conciliators, important gentlemen, who for all their erudition and revolutionary phrases, were impotent to break with the old order." They believed revolution would inevitably come to Russia, and soon. All it needed was a strong external push. That push was to be the assassination of the tsar.

This belief would persist through all the revolutionary movements of the second half of the nineteenth century. The meager intellect of these Russian Jacobins was a product of the country's history. As Dostoevsky would sorrowfully write, "The French Revolution happened after Corneille and Voltaire, on the shoulders of Mirabeau, Bonaparte, Danton, and the Encyclopedists. All we have is the Brockhaus and Efron Encyclopedia. Our expropriators, killers, and bomb throwers are mediocre writers, students who did not finish their degree, lawyers without trials, actors without talent, scholars without science. People with enormous ambition and tiny talent. A lot of ambition, not enough ammunition."

N. A. Ishutin, who failed to graduate from high school in Penza, came to Moscow and became an auditor at Moscow University. The son of a poor merchant (with only one blue shirt and worn trousers tucked into swamp boots to his name), he was morbidly ambitious. He wanted to lead his peers. He may have had a miserable wardrobe, but he had a wealth of new ideas, which he brought from the provinces. The main one was about imminent revolution. Ishutin had read about it in banned books, and the wretch wanted to lead it.

"He tried to look grim and angry, as a brutal revolutionary should," wrote a female contemporary. "But in fact he was an envious mediocre man . . . who passionately dreamed of popularity."

In 1863, after the fires in St. Petersburg, most of the Moscow rebel students, led by Zaichnevsky, were sent to hard labor, and Ishutin picked up the baton. There was a large apartment building in Sytinsky Cul de Sac in Moscow. It consisted of tiny cell-like apartments that were rented to students. It turned into a huge dormitory for poor students. Here Ishutin easily found candidates for future Robespierres, and his circle grew.

First the Ishutinites decided to implement the socialist ideas of Fourier, to create a working commune together with workers. They would start a book bindery, without blood-sucking middlemen so that they could divide up the earnings equally. But the bindery unfortunately required them to do actual work. And as Dostoevsky once put it, "Who in Russia wants to work?" So they moved on to more attractive plans.

Inside his circle, Ishutin created a narrower circle called "The Organization," made up primarily of provincials. The goal of this underground circle was no more and no less than building socialism in Russia. Ishutin told the members that their little Organization was part of a

"European Revolutionary Committee" preparing revolution throughout the world. Just as he had thought, the myth made the participants quiver with delight—and with fear and obedience to him. Ishutin was the first to make falsehood an integral part of revolutionary work.

Then, within The Organization, Ishutin created a top-secret nucleus called Hell, of his most trusted students. Their purpose was to kill the tsar, which was to be the signal for the great social uprising. The peasants would rise up instantly, followed by a general rebellion that would destroy the regime. It was discussed over endless cups of tea with chunks of sugar and cheap sausage sandwiches.

Each member of Hell had to see himself as a doomed man, cut off from ordinary society and totally dedicated to the revolution. They were from Hell because they could not fear the most terrible and dirty methods, so long as they served the revolution. To impress new members, Ishutin would tell them how one of the circle poisoned his own father for the inheritance that he gave to the revolutionary work.

These methods would later be used by the uncompromising Russian revolutionary, the precursor of the Bolsheviks, Sergei Nechaev.

The same conundrum comes up again and again. The journalist Elena Kozlinina wrote in her memoirs, *Over a Half Century,* that at the time "many knew of the existence of Hell, but treated it as no more than empty chatter of young people." But if many knew of it, why didn't the omniscient Third Department know about Hell? After the student riots, which were particularly violent in St. Petersburg and Moscow, they watched students closely. They must have had agents in that dangerous student anthill. And of course, they should have been extremely alert to "chatter" about regicide. But no action against them was taken.

A highly mysterious young man, Ishutin's cousin Dmitri Karakozov, was accepted in Hell. The son of an impoverished aristocrat, the always silent Karakozov was a dangerous and very Russian type. He said nothing while others argued. But he listened attentively. And while his comrades made noise and amused themselves with dangerous fantasies, the religious young man came up with the idea of self-sacrifice. If the tsar was in the way of socialism, which would bring happiness to his country, then the tsar did in fact need to be killed. He understood that his comrades were all talk. He saw that he would have to do it himself.

Saying nothing to his comrades, Karakozov left for St. Petersburg.

It happened on April 4, 1866. That day the tsar took a walk as usual in the Summer Garden. This time he was with his sister's children, Nikolai (Kolya) and Masha Leichtenberg. His sister, Masha, beloved daughter of their late father, Nicholas I, found herself in a piquant situation. She was widowed very young. Her husband had been the cheerful drinker and gambler duke of Leichtenberg, son of Napoleon's stepson, and grandson of Napoleon's wife, Josephine.

Masha embarked on a stormy affair with Count Grigory Stroganov, and they married secretly. As Anna Tyutcheva put it, "The former tsar would have sent Masha to a convent and exiled the count to the Caucasus." But the gentle Alexander, who was now head of the dynasty and was supposed to keep order in the family, preferred not to let on that he knew about the secret marriage. Count Stroganov grumbled that he was too old (at forty-two) to sneak into his own wife's bed at night. Once they had children, they were forced to live in Italy.

Masha begged the tsar to recognize her new marriage and permit them to live in Russia, in the marvelous palace their father had built for her. It had a glass conservatory like none other in Europe, with peacocks and parrots among the palms, orchids, fountains, and waterfalls. It was a mirage of the South in the midst of the St. Petersburg winter.

He did not dare permit it. He suggested that his sister continue living abroad and he continued to pretend not to know about it. He was very sorry for Masha, especially when he himself, at almost fifty, had fallen in love, as if for the first time. (You have to live long to become young.)

Since the emperor could not permit his sister's misalliance, he paid special attention to her children by her first marriage, who lived in St. Petersburg without their mother.

The tsar came out of the Summer Garden after three; the Leichten-

bergs stayed to walk some more. On the Neva embankment by the garden's marvelous wrought-iron fence, the usual crowd had gathered to see
the tsar. This happened every day. The policeman pacing by the crowd
stood at attention. The gendarme junior officer waiting by the carriage
came to attention when he finally noticed the tsar. Alexander lifted the
long tails of his military coat and prepared to get in.

At that moment came the deafening bang of a shot. Someone tall
and young ran out of the crowd, racing down the embankment toward
the bridge. The policeman and the gendarme ran after him. The policeman knocked him down and disarmed him; the gendarme punched him
in the face. The man tried to block the blows and kept shouting, "Fellows, I shot for you!" He was brought to the tsar.

Minister Valuyev wrote an account in his diary. "The tsar asked him
whether he was Russian [hoping he was Polish] and why he shot at him.
The killer replied that he was Russian and that the tsar had allegedly
been deceiving us too long. Others say that he said that the tsar had
cheated the peasants of land. Still others, that he turned to the crowd
and said, 'Fellows, I was shooting for you.'"

After the assassination attempt the tsar went to the Kazan Cathedral
and held a thanksgiving service. When he returned to the Winter Palace,
Prince Dolgorukov, chief of the Third Department, recounted the amazing circumstances that would be written up in all the newspapers the
next day.

It turned out that "the man standing next to the villain pushed his
hand at the moment of the shot. God Himself used his hand to push the
villain's hand. This ordinary Russian man named Komissarov was from
Kostroma.

"Long ago in the Time of Troubles, Ivan Susanin was from Kostroma,
and he saved our tsar's august ancestor, founder of the dynasty Mikhail
Romanov, from a troop of Poles and paid for it with his life."

The emperor commanded that Komissarov be brought to him.

The guards lined up in the great White Hall. They greeted him with
a thunderous "Hurrah!" They brought in the savior—a short, pale, and
shabby-looking man. Alexander embraced him, kissed him, and elevated

him to the nobility. Now he was the aristocrat Komissarov-Kostromsky. Another shout of "Hurrah!"

In his notebook, Alexander wrote a very brief account, as usual. "Was walking with Marusya and Kolya in the Summer Garden. Shot from a pistol, missed. Killer caught. General sympathy. I went home and to Kazan Cathedral. Hurrah! The entire guards in the White Hall. Name is Osip Komissarov."

The heir, Sasha, wrote much more: "You can say without mistake that all of St. Petersburg came spilling out onto the street. Traffic, agitation was unimaginable. Running in all directions, primarily toward the Winter Palace, shouts, most of them with the words 'Karakozov!' 'Komissarov!' threats and curses for the former, delighted exclamations for the latter. Groups of people, singing 'God Save the Tsar.' General delight and thunderous 'Hurrahs.' Then they brought in the man who saved him. Papa kissed him and made him a nobleman. Another terrific 'Hurrah.'"

The Third Department had acted with great efficiency, which it had lacked before. Everyone involved in the attempt was quickly discovered and arrested. The tsar was told all the circumstances: The assassin was the nobleman Dmitri Karakozov, age twenty-six. He had been a student at Moscow University, but was expelled for not paying his tuition. He came from the provinces. In Moscow he met his relative, Ishutin, an auditor at Moscow University. That young man with criminal aims had created an underground group, and so on.

"The capital is mad with joy," wrote a contemporary. "They've remembered their love for the tsar, remembered everything he has done for Russia! You hear 'God Save the Tsar' everywhere." Naturally, there was a special performance of Glinka's *Life for the Tsar,* about Ivan Susanin's heroism (dying to protect the tsar from Poles). The two bassos in the company who alternately sang the role of Kostroma native Ivan Susanin fought to sing that night. Susanin's aria was accompanied by constant applause. The other Kostroma native, the savior (as Komissarov was called by the press), sat in the box next to the royal box.

Dispatches and telegrams came from all over Russia. Cities, ethnic groups, and social estates competed in expressions of patriotic feelings. Workers in the provinces rallied in honor of the tsar. In Moscow (from where Karakozov had come) students, in expiation of their mutinous recent past, organized a procession to the Icon of the Iversk Mother of God, singing "God Save the Tsar," and then prayed in Red Square by the Church of Vassily the Blessed.

The exultation began developing a tinge of pogrom. Drunken "patriots" roamed the streets, knocking off the hats of passersby who did not seem sufficiently thrilled and dragging all "long-haired bespectacled types" (students) to police precincts.

While the populace rejoiced that the tsar was saved, a completely different version of the assassination attempt was told in whispers in the capital. In this version, Komissarov was just one of the crowd of gawkers waiting to see the tsar come out of the park. After the shot, he was rounded up along with the others and first sent to the governor general's house and then to the Third Department. He thought he was doomed. But when the authorities learned that he was originally from Kostroma, they decided to turn him into a new Ivan Susanin.

That was the start of the "savior's" path to glory. Russians rushed to heap him with gratitude. Priests called him a guardian angel in their sermons, poets called him "the humble weapon of God's providence." He was given a multistory house and his wife wandered through the stores in the Gostiny Dvor complex, buying up silks and diamonds and presenting herself curtly as "the wife of the savior," embarrassing the merchants.

Komissarov-Kostromsky eventually ended up forgotten in the provinces and died of delirium tremens.

The day of the assassination attempt, Dostoevsky burst into the apartment of the poet Appolon Maikov, shouting, "They shot at the tsar!"

Maikov responded "in an unnatural voice: 'Did they kill him?' 'No . . . saved him . . . he's fine . . . But they shot, they shot, they shot!' Dostoevsky kept repeating in despair and shock."

The writer understood that, despite the miss, the shot had in fact been a hit. Before, the tsars had been killed in the palace, secretly, and they were said to have died peacefully of hemorrhoidal colic or stroke or something. Now, someone had taken a shot at the tsar in public, shattering the inviolable aura of the sacred person that is the tsar.

Alexander understood this, too.

While the country rejoiced, the tsar was in a fury. Kostya rushed from the Pavlovsky Palace to St. Petersburg to be with Alexander. He remembered from childhood how dangerous and uncontrollable Alexander's wrath could be. He begged him not to be hasty and to keep their slogan in mind: "No weakness, no reaction," but in vain. Alexander demanded revenge. He gave the ingrates freedom and what did he get? Bloody proclamations, arson, and now a bullet. The tsar must have recalled his father's tight fist, his testament on his deathbed.

Disappointing Kostya, Alexander signed a decree creating an Investigation Commission headed by General Muravyev the Hangman, who had suppressed the Polish uprising. The nihilists had to see that the authorities were not going to mollycoddle them.

This was the end of the chain of strange events: the incomprehensible conditions of incarceration for the rebellious students that led to their mad proclamations, the terrible fires and their unknown arsonists, the underground organization about which so many people knew except for the police, and the shooting. The result was the tsar's readiness to fulfill the dream of the retrograde party—to start serious reprisals.

The tsar commanded that Mikhail Muravyev be brought to the palace. The stunned and pleased general appeared and asked for the heads of his former enemies, the liberal bureaucrats. "They are all cosmopolites, adherents of European ideas. Now real Russians must come to power!"

In just a few days, Muravyev shattered the liberal party. His sworn enemy, Prince Suvorov, lost the governor generalship of the St. Petersburg region, and Prince Dolgorukov, a friend of the tsar, lost his position as chief of the Third Department. Ministry of Education Golovnin,

Kostya's man, was fired for "letting young people get out of hand." The famous retrograde Count Dmitri Tolstoy was appointed minister of education. He was soon to be called "the damnation of the Russian school."

Among the liberals forced out was Lev Perovsky, governor of St. Petersburg. His daughter, Sofia, was twelve. Fifteen years later the terrorist Sofia Perovskaya would be standing on the Catherine Canal, where we left the tsar. The bombers would be following her plan.

The news of Muravyev's appointment brought a chill to the capital. Everyone remembered how he burned villages in Poland, hanged Catholic priests, and exiled entire families to Siberia. They knew he would show no mercy. Interrogations of suspects began. Saltykov-Shchedrin wrote, "St. Petersburg was dying. What horrible people had risen from their graves. Everything was remembered and avenged. A herd of 'well-meaning' people hurried to let loose the grudges they had been nursing."

The Muravyev Commission brought in everyone for questioning—writers, officials, officers, teachers and pupils, students, peasants, princes, merchants. The investigators were allowed to insult female "nihilists." They asked the college girls how many men they had slept with and threatened to give them a yellow identification (which meant they were prostitutes) unless they answered the question.

Panic and fear ruled the capital. People remembered the reprisals of Nicholas I after the Decembrist uprising. The most unstable (just as they had been then) were some of the liberals. Nekrasov was frightened, too. The great poet worried for himself and for his journal, *Sovremennik*. He first turned for help to his card partner Count Adlerberg, who could do nothing. The zealot Muravyev had everything in his power. So Nekrasov decided on an action he thought would help.

The English Club gave Muravyev an honorary membership, which was cause for a celebratory dinner. Nekrasov attended. After the lavish dinner, Muravyev, a ton of wheezing blubber, rested in an armchair. The civic poet Nekrasov asked for permission to read his new poem dedicated to the man all decent people had just recently called the Hangman. But Muravyev did not bother with a response, continuing to smoke his pipe. He seemed not to have noticed Nekrasov. The poet, not waiting for gracious agreement, started reading his panegyric to the Hangman.

But that didn't seem like enough to Nekrasov. When he finished, he said beseechingly, "Your Excellency, will you permit me to publish this poem?"

Muravyev replied dryly, "It's your property and you can do what you wish with it." He turned his back on the poet. One of the people in the room said very loudly, "He thinks he can bribe justice by reading verse! You just wait, you won't get away!"

The poet left, mortified.

His *Sovremennik* was shut down. Neither Russian youth nor high society could forgive Nekrasov. Students took his picture down from their walls and threw it away, or, scribbling "scoundrel" across it, mailed it to him. He suffered terribly.

Nine years later, Nekrasov grew severely ill, his life turning into protracted death throes. "You asked for an easy life from God, when you should have asked for an easy death," he wrote. Lying in bed, tormented, he continued trying to explain that act and repenting: "Beloved Homeland, bless your downed son, instead of beating him."

News of his mortal illness spread across Russia and it reconciled people to him. Letters, telegrams, greetings, and notes came from all over the empire. On the eve of his death, he was the idol of youth once more.

He died on December 27, 1877. It was extremely cold, but for the first time in the history of Russian literature, several thousand people came to a writer's funeral. They followed his body to its final resting place at the Novodevichy Monastery in Moscow.

The first plan proposed to Alexander was to declare Karakozov insane, the way Nicholas I had handled Chaadayev. This would make it clear that no sane person would ever attempt to kill the tsar. But Alexander did not want that: He wanted to teach villains a lesson, or else others might try to shoot at the tsar if they thought it could be done with impunity, which would be the end of the state. Karakozov and Ishutin were sentenced to die by hanging.

Karakozov spent the entire time in prison praying. He wrote a letter to Alexander begging for forgiveness. "I beg your pardon as a Christian of a Christian and man of a man." The tsar "spread his hands in regret." Karakozov was told, "His Majesty forgives you as a Christian, but as the Sovereign he cannot forgive you. You must prepare yourself for death."

He did forgive Ishutin and commuted his sentence to hard labor for life. The gift of life was not to be announced until the last second, when he was on the gallows. He punished him with the anticipation of death, remembering how his father had treated the Petrashevsky circle members.

The first execution on Semenovsky Square took place. Karakozov was hanged. He had passed out and had to be dragged up to the gibbet. Ishutin was dressed and then told about the change in his sentence.

Alexander had needed to bring in Muravyev to scare the country, but the tsar could not stand the monster for long. The Hangman was soon retired. He died in sadness in 1866. However, the tsar did not return the liberal bureaucrats to power nor did he wish to hear anything else about liberal reform. Let the public digest what was given to them first.

Thus, while the country was moving forward in the late 1860s, Alexander decided to stop the reforms and the country's dangerous motion. Only military reform, because of the immensity of the problems, continued into the 1870s. He needed the army to get his revenge for the Crimean War.

Alexander did not know the rule: Starting reforms is dangerous, but it is much more dangerous to stop them.

Alexander realized that he had to think about fighting sedition, which meant a new chief for the Third Department who would be able to control society's new friskiness. He appointed Peter Shuvalov, son of his late mother's high marshal.

The Shuvalovs rose to power in the reign of Empress Elizabeth, in the mid-eighteenth century. One Shuvalov had been her lover. His uncle was a major financier and also the requisite embezzler and devious states-man. When Elizabeth became infatuated with a new young cadet named Beketov, dropping the older Shuvalov's nephew, he took measures to return his relative to favor. He became the best friend of the young and simple lover and gave Beketov a cream "to whiten the face." The poor fellow broke out in a pus-filled rash. Someone whispered into the empress's ear the words "venereal disease," which the cadet allegedly picked up from someone else, and the infuriated Elizabeth cast him aside and returned Shuvalov to her favors.

The son of this enterprising bastard had a subtle mind, nobility, and good education. His French was so good that he published poems in Paris. Catherine the Great, who wrote fluently in French, sent her famous letters to Grimm and Voltaire to this Shuvalov first for editing, which he did with determination. Catherine called him "my wise washerwoman."

This was the line from which Peter Shuvalov came. He was ten years younger than the tsar and a companion in some of his merry adventures. Using his friendship with the tsar, he dared to court the daughter of Maria Leichtenberg, the tsar's sister. The tsar was forced to reprimand him severely. Count Peter wised up immediately, becoming what was needed—"loyal but smart" (as Alexander described him) and "a dog on a chain" (as Kostya did). Count Peter combined many qualities of his ancestors. He was lively, witty, absolutely *comme il faut* and at the same time ruthless and a cruel superior.

He was liberal when necessary but a retrograde at heart. The retro-grades rejoiced at his appointment. They quoted Shuvalov as saying that he would soon "wring the necks" of the liberals and "the tsar himself would toe the line."

Shuvalov ruled Russia for eight years, a period of counter-reform, when the regime undercut its own good deeds. Alexander was happy: The reforms were in place, and he hoped the country would quiet down. He intended to relax, because he was in love. But a leader can never rest, for his time off is always severely punished.

While he was away from active ruling, an extremely dangerous change took place. The new head of the Third Department reinstated the broad powers of the secret police. Using them, Shuvalov began to take over the Committee of Ministers. Minister of War Dmitri Milyutin was astonished to find that he had been "completely removed from military affairs."

"It is all being done under the exceptional influence of Shuvalov, who has frightened the Sovereign with daily reports on terrible dangers," he wrote in his diary. "Under the guise of protecting the person of the tsar, the count interferes in affairs. He has surrounded the Sovereign with his own people. . . . In the Committee of Ministers, the majority acts as one with the count, like an orchestra directed by the conductor."

For eight years, Count Peter Shuvalov, chief of the secret police, was the de facto prime minister. This brought about a most dangerous situation for Alexander: the unification of the retrograde party with the secret police.

The court referred to Shuvalov as Peter IV. In order to become him truly, Shuvalov had to get rid of the chief liberal, Grand Duke Konstantin Nikolayevich. The camarilla relished the anticipation.

CHAPTER 8

Love

The year following the assassination attempt in the Summer Garden, 1867, began with an event for which Russia still had not forgiven Alexander II. Negotiations to sell Alaska had begun under his father and continued for fifteen years. The great monarchist Nicholas was prepared to befriend even republican America against royal England.

Guests from the New World were taken to visit Peterhof, where a young oak now grew on Tsaritsyn Island, A bronze plaque next to it read: "This acorn planted in the ground came from the oak shading the grave of the unforgettable Washington and was given as a sign of extreme respect for the Emperor of All Russia."

Nicholas I had planted the acorn personally. The sale of Alaska was a nod in the direction of the young state. But immeasurable Russia has a paradoxically heightened sense of its "own territory," and even Nicholas I preferred that the negotiations be held in great secrecy and that they never come to an end.

The warm relations between the two countries continued under Alexander II, as did the negotiations over the sale of Alaska. The tsar sensed that it was time to move things along, because Russian holdings in Alaska could become an apple of discord between the countries.

The Russian-American Trading Company that owned Alaska "with the right to monopoly use of all game and minerals" had long been losing money. Only a few hundred people worked for the company. If the Americans had decided to take Alaska, Russia would not have been able to defend it. It would only spoil the good relations between the countries. St. Petersburg had little doubt that it could happen sooner or later, especially after rumors of gold in Alaska circulated. Gold could provoke an attack. Fighting so far from home was unrealistic, and the tsar could not permit another Sevastopol.

He decided to complete the negotiations on March 18, 1867. The agreement that Russia would cede its North American colonies was ratified in Washington. On March 23 the editors of St. Petersburg newspapers received news of this by Atlantic telegraph.

The emperor learned quickly that irritating discussions were taking place in Russia. There were articles about the error of the sale, pointing out that they sold for a mere $7.2 million islands of 31,204 square kilometers and part of the North Atlantic mainland of 548,902 square kilometers with everything built on those lands, fortifications, barracks, and other buildings, and that with the appearance of the Atlantic Telegraph connecting the continents, Alaska had taken on a new significance, and so on.

Sankt-Peterburgskie Vedomosti printed a description of the ceremony that had to embitter its Russian readers. "Russian and American troops stood at the flagpole. Two Russian junior officers began lowering the Russian flag. The audience and officers took off their hats, the soldiers were at attention. The drum roll continued. But the Russian flag did not want to come down. It was tangled at the top of the staff. On the commander's orders, several Russian sailors climbed up to untangle the flag that hung in tatters. One of the sailors finally reached it and threw it down. The flag fell right on the Russian bayonets."

Alexander still did not wish to speak in public. He did not explain why he sold Alaska, and he did not explain that he could not get more from America, because the news of the sale to the United States did not please the American public. The newspapers were filled with headlines like "Seward's Folly" (Seward was secretary of state), "Polar Bear Zoo," and "Seward's Ice Chest." The influential *New York Herald* was sarcastic about Seward's Napoleonic plan, buying "fifty thousand Eskimo inhabitants, each of whom was capable of drinking half a bucket of fish oil for breakfast."

Another mistake was added to Alexander's list: more territorial losses after the Peace of Paris. It might have been far away, but it was still lost. Once more people called him "Unlucky Tsar," a dangerous reputation to have in Russia.

May 1867 brought a new disaster. The situation in Europe, as Grand Duke Konstantin Nikolayevich wrote in his diary, "was threatening the world with a bloody commotion." King of Prussia Wilhelm "has decided to eat up France." Ever since Alexander I had persuaded Napoleon to preserve the crown of his Prussian grandfather, the Russian tsars had been very high-handed with their Prussian relatives. Nicholas I was the worst offender. But things had changed dramatically, all due to a single man, Bismarck.

Prussia's position as poor European relation did not suit the young Prussian bourgeoisie and the militant rich landowners. Barons and capitalists dreamed of uniting the German lands around Prussia. Once ambassador to Russia and now head of the conservative party, Bismarck demanded enormous sums from the Prussian parliament to fund a powerful army. The liberal majority was outraged. The situation in Berlin was turning revolutionary, with a parliamentary delegation threatening King Wilhelm, reminding him of the fate of Louis XVI. His queen begged him to relent: After all, Europe had just undergone terrible revolutions. The aging king was about to acquiesce when Bismarck came to see the king and made an inspired speech.

As Bismarck later told it, he said, "Your Majesty must not think about Louis XVI—he was weak in spirit. Better recall Charles I—won't he always be one of the most noble monarchs for fearlessly unsheathing his sword in defense of the rights of the monarch? Yes, he lost the battle, but he proudly strengthened his royal convictions with his own blood! Your task is to create a great army in order to gather all Germans under the wing of your dynasty. You cannot yield to Parliament, even if it endangers your life. Your Majesty is facing the necessity to fight for the divine right of the Prussian monarch to decide everything himself."

The more he spoke, the more animated Wilhelm grew. Bismarck understood him well. He wrote, "Wilhelm is the ideal type of Prussian officer who in the line of duty will fearlessly go to certain death with the single word: command. But when such an officer is supposed to act on his own, he fears more than death the condemnation of his superiors, and that fear keeps him from taking decisions."

After the conversation with Bismarck, to the horror of the terrified court, King Wilhelm understood his role, "The role of a Prussian officer who is grabbed by the sword belt even as he is commanded to hold a certain position at the cost of his life."

Wilhelm began playing the role with daunting success. With his huge army, the king, in alliance with Austria, shamelessly took Schleswig and Holstein away from Denmark. Then the Prussians destroyed their former ally, Austria. Bismarck created his Northern German Union, headed by Prussia, and became its chancellor.

Alexander II's old friend Bismarck and his uncle Willy placated the tsar with sweet talk while they gobbled up all the independent German lands around Prussia. Alexander saw that he had allowed a new Prussia to form, with 11 million subjects. The specter of a new aggressive empire rose on Russia's borders. Bismarck did not intend to stop there. His next victim was France. Germany had superior artillery and the famous French forts were not prepared for modern warfare. The Russian military analysts predicted that France would be crushed and that the Prussians would take Alsace and Lotharingia and become the most powerful state in Europe. Alexander could not permit this alarming breach of European equilibrium.

The tsar decided to go to Paris for the opening of the World's Fair, which all the European monarchs would attend. There he would show Uncle Willy Russia's support of France. He had long discussions with War Minister Milyutin before coming to this decision. They were in accord: France should be supported.

But at afternoon tea, the empress made a scene. She begged him not to go to Paris, which was teeming with Polish émigrés. They were the children of the people suppressed by his father and the ones who had recently risen up against him. They were filled with ideas of revenge. Maria Alexandrovna pleaded with him to send Prince Gorchakov to Paris instead. Yet he was determined to go.

She knew him well, and naturally, she guessed the real reasons for his passionate desire to go to Paris and why he was implacable.

On May 20 at the Gare du Nord in Paris, Emperor Napoleon III, military mustache bristling, met Emperor Alexander II. The French emperor extended every courtesy to the tsar. He needed an alliance with Russia. The tsar was given the Elysée Palace, where some forty-five years earlier, his uncle, Alexander I, had lived after conquering Napoleon Bonaparte, uncle of the French emperor.

But while Alexander's retinue proceeded from the train station to the palace, some of the people lining the streets shouted, "Long live Poland!"

That evening the emperor went to the Opéra Comique for a show that had been highly praised by the newspaper critics. It turned out to be a rather ribald story about his great-grandmother, Catherine the Great. He had to leave during the second act.

The rest of the night was later recounted by Count Peter Shuvalov, chief of the secret police, to lady-in-waiting Countess Alexandra Tolstaya. He would remember the events to the end of his days.

Coming back to the Elysée Palace, the retinue gladly went to bed. But close to midnight, the emperor knocked on the door of the soundly sleeping and elderly minister of the court Adlerberg. To the minister's complete surprise (and fear) the emperor announced that he was going to take a walk through Paris at night.

"But I don't need anyone to accompany me, I'll manage on my own. But, my dear man, give me a little money."

"How much does His Majesty require?"

"I have no idea, how about a hundred thousand francs?"

The minister turned pale at the sum, but one does not question an autocrat. Adlerberg brought the money. The tsar headed out into the Parisian night, alone with an enormous sum of cash.

Adlerberg immediately awoke Shuvalov. The chief was not particularly worried because his agents (as well as the French police) would be
following the sovereign unseen, wherever he might go.

Everyone awaited the tsar's speedy return. Hours passed, and he was
still gone. No one slept in the palace—the court waited in terror to find
out the conclusion of the mysterious walk. The most incredible theories
were invented about where the tsar could have gone with one hundred
thousand francs.

The tsar came back at dawn. The Elysée Palace was completely lit up;
everyone was awake. Count Shuvalov greeted him in tears. They had
written him off as dead and were dying of fear themselves, and he
seemed simply to have forgotten their existence.

By the next day, Shuvalov knew everything from his agents. The tsar
hailed a fiacre outside the palace and drove to rue Bas-du-ramparts, near
the palace. He let the cab go and consulted a piece of paper, apparently
with an address, under the lamppost. At last he entered the courtyard of
the nearest house.

He quickly realized he had the wrong address, but he couldn't figure
out how to get out of the courtyard. The gates had swung shut and
would not budge. Tossing the portfolio with the cash on the ground, the
emperor vainly struggled with the door to the street. He was trapped.
The agent (who was supposed to guard the tsar unobtrusively) finally
came over and pointed to the rope hanging by the gate. A pull on the
rope opened it.

The happy emperor was freed. He vanished next door, where a certain someone lived. It was the start of his happiest week in Paris. It
turned out that the omniscient Third Department knew very little about
her. The secret police primarily watched the tsar and were required to
know everything about him; the careers of many people depended on it.
But Shuvalov, like the court, had underestimated the tsar. They thought
he was open and simple. The "strong secretiveness" remarked upon by
the perceptive de Custine allowed him to keep his affair private for a
long time.

His mystery woman would outlive Alexander by many years. She would see his death and then learn of the death of the tsar's family. She died in 1922 in a villa in Nice, the heroine of one of the most dramatic affairs in the history of the lusty Romanov men, an affair that was one of the factors in the demise of the empire. After the revolution, the Bolsheviks found very frank erotic drawings of a female nude, of her body, which drove the emperor wild until his dying day.

Alexander II was forty years old when he first saw her. He was observing military maneuvers near Poltava on the 150th anniversary of Peter the Great's victory over the Swedish king Charles XII. Alexander was staying at the estate of retired guards captain Prince Mikhail Dolgoruky. The Dolgoruky line went back to the Rurik princes and even had a saint, Prince Mikhail Chernigovsky, a legendary warrior who was a prince in Novgorod and grand prince of Kiev in the thirteenth century, tortured to death by the Tatars of the Golden Horde.

Prince Dolgoruky was well-married to a wealthy landowner. After a marvelous lunch, the emperor went for a walk in their vast park. He met a walking doll, in a pink cape and with a thick chestnut braid.

"And who are you , my child?"

The doll answered seriously, "I am Ekaterina Mikhailovna." Despite the adult use of name and patronymic, she was twelve.

"And what are you doing here?"

"Looking for the emperor," she replied just as seriously.

She never forgot that first meeting, although he probably never gave it a second thought.

Four years later, old Adlerberg, his minister of the court, brought him a letter from the girl's mother. Prince Mikhail had died, having managed to go through one of the major fortunes in Russia. He left the family penniless, but he did pass along one thing: good looks. Four handsome sons and two beautiful daughters were now impoverished.

Alexander did not leave the noble family in misery; he took them under his wing. The double-mortgaged estate where he had met "Ekaterina Mikhailovna" was taken under royal care. He paid for the children's education: The boys were sent to the prestigious Page Corps and military schools, and Ekaterina and her sister went to the Smolny Institute for Noble Young Ladies. Their mother, Princess Vera, moved to St. Petersburg and rented a small apartment with her remaining funds.

The Smolny Institute, "that lovely hothouse," as Karamzin called it, was a type of convent, a finishing school where the future wives of Russian aristocrats were brought up. "An excess of education" (that is, natural sciences and literature) was considered not only unnecessary, but dangerous. Music, sewing, domestic management, dancing, etiquette, choral singing, and cooking were the subjects of the institute. Classes spent hours on court ceremonies, such as "the ceremony of kissing the hands of August Persons on holidays."

That ceremony, developed by Paul I himself, called for "a deep bow, then bending one knee, make a precise kiss on the hand of the Emperor. Then it is proper to do the same to the Empress. And depart, backing up."

There was also "Reception of August Persons." "You must make a deep bow and curtsy from the waist, and afterward pleasantly say a phrase of greeting in French."

These things were rehearsed for hours.

On an autumn day in 1864, Katya needed all that knowledge. The August Persons came to Smolny and the emperor saw her again.

The petite young woman (she was of average height, but she always seemed small to the very tall Alexander) with thick chestnut hair looked up at him with her enormous eyes, made her bow and curtsy, and spoke her French greeting in a trembling voice.

He was smitten. Since every new love showed on his face, everyone noticed, including the empress. But they did not pay particular attention. He was continually falling in love. The mistresses changed so quickly that even the Third Department stopped watching the women. They saw that the beauties had no influence on state affairs. Their sole function was to end up in the tsar's bed and vanish soon afterward.

Interestingly, the last dangerous mistress, Alexandra Dolgorukaya, was also from the same line and was a distant relative of Katya's.

The director of Smolny knew her job. Katya was given a hint of her good fortune, but for some reason she did not appreciate her luck and was in no hurry to fall into Alexander's arms, as a good, and more important, poor subject should do. The tsar took steps. A relative of the director, a Mme Vera Shebeko, a "very pleasant and charming lady," went into action.

Mme Shebeko called on Katya's mother in her poor apartment and told her that fortune smiled upon them. In view of the family's hopeless finances, Katya had the opportunity to assure her own situation and that of the whole family. And really, what else did the future hold for her? Rich men in St. Petersburg did not marry beauties as a rule. They married money. Poor graduates of Smolny usually stayed on to become teachers there, and usually became old maids.

Shebeko warned Princess Vera: Katya was very pretty, but so many young beauties dreamed of finding a place in the tsar's heart that she had better act swiftly. She became a friend of the family and soon received permission from Katya's mother to give the girl advice. Quite delicately (as befitted the age and the family) she pushed Katya toward the tsar's bed. But Katya remained oddly slow to understand. She clearly liked the tsar and she was thrilled when he visited her in Smolny Institute hospital during her illness. (The tsar had come incognito, and the hospital was guarded like a military outpost.)

But still, nothing. And then, to the total surprise of Shebeko and Princess Vera, the tsar became even more enamored of the girl. He began taking walks with her in the Summer Garden. Girls were allowed to leave Smolny only on the weekend, but the tsar wanted daily walks. So her mother and Mme Shebeko asked Katya to leave the institute.

She did it gladly, because she needed the walks with the tsar, too. But they did not go beyond taking walks. She and the tsar walked next to each other, the dog ran in front, and behind them followed his adjutant. The other park visitors began whispering, "The tsar is taking his mademoiselle out for an airing."

They had to change the venue for their meetings. Now they walked in the parks on the islands. The Don Juan's platonic affair continued. They walked and they kissed under the trees. The tsar's carriage would bring her home. The lovers looked happy—the seventeen-year-old girl and the forty-eight-year-old tsar. He was approaching fifty and behaving like a schoolboy.

Katya was appointed lady-in-waiting to the empress. This was the usual spot for the tsar's mistresses. But even when she became a lady-in-waiting, she did not become his lover. The tsar was burning with desire, but for some reason did not make demands. Once again, it was up to Vera Shebeko to explain things to Katya delicately—to no avail.

The young woman also did not appear in court. That was not because the tsar was protecting the empress, who had long grown accustomed to having ladies-in-waiting who were his mistresses. No, it was Katya who did not want to be presented to the court. It was the secret of the affair that neither her mother nor Vera Shebeko could understand. She was different.

Alexander's reforms affected the Smolny Institute as they did the entire country. The winds of change burst into that conservative institution, bringing with it the well-known pedagogue Ushinsky, who reformed the curriculum. Literature and mathematics were now taught, and young ladies were given a real education. And even though Ushinsky was eventually forced out of the institute, his spirit, as well as the instructors he had hired, remained. Celebrated works of literature and well-known characters from them, once banned, were now taught and discussed. During their walks, the little beauty from the institute told the tsar about the world he himself had helped create and of which he knew almost nothing. It was the world of the new Russia. Katya was the product of his perestroika, and that is why she was not interested in being in the court.

Social position, wealth, intrigues—the main values of the tsar's mistresses—were a waste of time for her. She saw the court with the same unforgiving eyes as that other intelligent young woman, Anna Tyutcheva. "This is an empty world . . . it comes alive only in evening light. . . . Only evening gives it a mysterious beauty. Only one word rules this world—toilette. In that vain sea of lace and precious stones you can be only one more dressed-up doll. You have to be dressed up continually—for the tsar, going to a ball, or for God, going to the palace chapel. . . . Here even God is treated like a boring host who is giving a ball. They visit him . . . and immediately forget about him."

Like the rest of her generation, Katya dreamed of devoting herself to something very important. The tsar fell in love with her completely, totally, forever. But like all the girls in St. Petersburg society, she had heard much about his love affairs, and she feared becoming one in a long series.

The eventual consummation came out of pity for him, so powerful in young women like her. Hadn't he been through two terrible years, starting at the beginning of 1865 when his beloved son had died, and later there was the assassination attempt in the Summer Garden—making her realize what it would be to lose him. Her own mother had died in May 1866, and she was all alone.

It happened in July 1866, on the day of the anniversary of his late parents' wedding. There is a small hunting palace with columns and a classical portico on the road between Peterhof and St. Petersburg, on a small hill called Babigon. It stands to this day. Its windows open on the domes of a distant church, a pond, and green expanses.

It is said that his uncle, Alexander I, used this romantic spot for his assignations. The building had a surprise like the palaces of Louis XVI: When a small pedal in the dining room was pressed, a table set for two rose through the floor to the strains of a minuet.

The tsar settled her in the small palace with Vera Shebeko. To the end, Katya considered Vera a selfless patron of their affair. She had trusted her. The anniversary was being celebrated in Peterhof, in the Big Palace. The parade, which Nicholas I had so enjoyed in his day, was followed by a formal dinner and fireworks. That night, the emperor galloped to Katya in Babigon.

What happened that night is hidden from us, except for the words he spoke in the dark bedroom, where her naked, youthful body lay. "Now you are my secret wife. I swear that if I am ever free, I will marry you." She knew he was telling the truth and that was why he had chosen his father's wedding day to be their first time.

The very next day the court knew she had been deflowered. Apparently Vera Shebeko had spread the word, so that her own important position would be known as the friend of the tsar's favorite. The tsar was amazed to see how much Katya suffered from the gossip. What she feared had come to pass. Not allowed to be his secret wife, she was his recognized mistress.

In order to spare her the intrusive gossip, he decided to send her out of St. Petersburg. This was done delicately. His brother, Mikhail, was married to a cheerful and beautiful Italian marquise, whom Katya liked very much. The marquise invited Katya on a trip to Naples to see her family.

Once Katya left, the court and the Third Department had their own explanation. They decided that it was the usual story. The inexperienced girl had bored the tsar immediately, and the affair was over. Vera Shebeko interpreted it that way, too. Soon after Ekaterina's departure, she told the tsar about the difficult position of her younger sister, Maria Dolgorukaya. She asked him to help her, too. The tsar agreed to see her. Maria was also a beauty, and Shebeko expected the usual result. But to her great surprise, the tsar gave the beauty money, and asked for nothing.

An even greater surprise for Vera Shebeko followed. The tsar wrote to Naples almost daily. He summoned Mme Shebeko and sent her to Paris to rent a house not far from the Elysée Palace. The lovers had decided to meet in Paris.

The affair with Dolgorukaya was a blow for Shuvalov. He had missed a very important part of the tsar's life. He now demanded total surveillance on the tsar and his mistress. In a brief time, the chief of the secret police would be able to assess the young woman's influence on the tsar and the danger of that influence—for Shuvalov himself and for the throne.

In the meantime, Alexander's visit to Paris went according to plan: The next day a reception and dinner in his honor were held in Versailles. Bismarck has described similar dinners at Versailles with Napoleon III's pathetic court. Once the VIPs had eaten and began leaving the dining room, they were met by hungry second-rate guests, who showed an appalling lack of manners. Gentlemen in gold-trimmed uniforms and lovelies in lavish Parisian gowns pushed and shoved, cursing and even fighting to get to the food. Alexander could have quoted Bismarck's comment, "Gone are the days of the Louises, when the French court was the school of politeness and manners for all of Europe."

Every night the hired fiacre brought her to the Elysée Palace.

In Paris, Alexander became very youthful. Passion is the magical elixir of Mephistopheles, and it worked on the tsar. But during a happy walk in the Tuileries, so the memoirs of contemporaries recount, he had his palm read by a gypsy, who saw seven attempts on his life—six times his life would hang by a thread; the seventh attempt would be the last.

The prediction of so many assassination attempts (if in fact, there was a prediction) had to seem crazy to Alexander. But a second attempt on his life occurred right in Paris. He had attended a military show at Longchamp with Napoleon and Wilhelm. On the way back, as a demonstration of his friendship, Alexander got into the carriage with Napoleon. It was not needed: Uncle Willy understood on whose side Russian neutrality lay. Bismarck even permitted himself a threat, saying that Prussia was a powerful friend of its friends and a powerful enemy of its enemies. When this was related to Alexander, he merely smiled.

They were traveling in an open carriage. Napoleon sat next to Alexander, behind them the tsarevich and Vladimir. The carriage was crawling along in the Bois de Boulogne through a heavy crowd. When they reached the Grand Cascade, a man came out of the crowd on the side where the French emperor was sitting. The man quickly raised his pistol and Alexander heard a bullet whiz by. And then a second shot. The coachman struck the horses and the carriage dashed forward, the crowd leaping back.

Alexander thanked God and wondered how the man could have missed at that range. He was told that Napoleon's riding master had reacted quickly when he saw the man and pushed aside his arm.

That evening, Alexander received Empress Eugenie. She wept and begged him not to shorten his visit. Next came the French emperor with the details. The criminal was a Pole, of course—an émigré named Anton Berezovski, twenty years old. He had been seeking an opportunity for the last few days. Fortunately, he was a bad shot. His double-barreled pistol exploded from too much gunpowder, changing the bullets' trajectories. The riding master had done nothing. The next day, they brought him the prisoner's statement. The Pole made a full confession. He said that he had always wanted to kill the tsar, but had never spoken of it and had acted alone.

The French newspapers commiserated with the assassin. Alexander was furious. Why had he come to protect them if those senseless people hated Russia so much? No wonder his father detested the eternally rebellious French. Now he no longer loved beautiful France. He applauded his son's sentiment, "I hope we'll be leaving this den soon?"

The tsar was determined to complete the scheduled visit, so that no one would dare think that the tsar of all Russia could be scared off by one Pole's pistol. Empress Eugenie sweetly tried to sit next to him on the street side of the carriage, but he, naturally, asked her never to do that.

Back in St. Petersburg he learned the results of the trial. The tsar had been sure that his would-be assassin would be condemned to death and then he would be required to make the obligatory gesture of mercy, asking for a pardon. But the French spared him this hypocritical gesture. Berezovski's lawyer, to the courtroom's applause, abused Russia, and helped his client. The Pole was given a life sentence, and the newspapers gleefully guessed that he would soon be released.

Alexander had returned to St. Petersburg with the firm conviction that Russia would be better off having a union with Germany. The

French and Sevastopol were one of the reasons for his father's death. He should have never forgotten that. He was punished for it by the Pole. In what now would inexorably happen to France he saw the hand of providence, punishing the French emperor for his past injustice. He was sure that Napoleon III's days were numbered.

He was right. Prussia attacked France and destroyed it. His father's old enemy, Napoleon III, surrendered at Sedan. But the results would have dire effects for the Romanov dynasty. The mighty German Empire would now arise on Russia's borders, with its motivating idea of "marching on the East."

The empress met him with tear-filled eyes. She reminded him that she had begged him not to go to Paris. They chatted. It was only as he was leaving that she said, "I ask you to respect the woman in me, even if you will not be able to respect the empress."

He could no longer live without Katya. He wrote her passionate love letters in a mix of Russian and French.

His letters of 1866 (in the private collection of S. Baturin) are filled with rapture:

> August 14: "When I saw you at a distance in the allée, my heart beat so hard that I trembled all over and my knees grew weak, and I kept wanting to simply squeal with joy."

> November 12: "Don't forget that you are my whole life, angel of my soul, and its only goal is to see you happy, as happy as one can only be in this world."

He underlined those words.

The court had aligned itself against Katya, secretly of course. Alexander's great-grandmother Catherine had been right—the heartfelt hatred for one another was the main trait of the Russian court. Now they all pitied "our saint," the empress, because they hated and envied Katya.

Shuvalov was particularly worried. As chief of the Third Department, he had to think of the future, and it was problematic. Instead of the revolving door of endless ladies-in-waiting, there was the strange young woman with whom the tsar was clearly besotted. He saw her every day. And when he wasn't with her, he wrote her letters. What if she had a child by him? The empress was failing visibly. The tsar might marry her. And then, instead of the dull-witted heir, who had enjoyed listening to the late Muravyev the Hangman and to Shuvalov's ideas of reviving his grandfather's autocracy, there could be another heir.

Shuvalov hurried into battle. Trying to poison the large Romanov family against the new favorite, he dared to say, "It turns out we went to Paris because of her! We risked the sovereign's precious life over her!"

The tsar was informed. But the chief of the Third Department handled his duties in an exemplary manner, so the tsar put up with him. For the time being.

PART III

Underground Russia

CHAPTER 9

The Birth of Terror

Fair is foul, and foul is fair.
—*MACBETH*, ACT I SCENE 1

It seemed to him that the entire world was doomed to be sacrificed to some terrible, unknown and unseen . . . pestilent ulcer. Now there were these trichnines, microscopic creatures that moved into people's bodies . . . people who hosted them immediately became possessed and mad, but never had anyone felt as smart and unshakeable in the truth as did the diseased. People were killing one another in the grip of some meaningless anger.
—FEDOR DOSTOEVSKY, *CRIME AND PUNISHMENT*

After the assassination attempt in 1866, many young people involved in the student riots had been expelled and went abroad to study. Most of them were not poor and could afford it.

On the platform seeing them off had been heartbroken parents and servants. They sighed for the times when people traveled by coach to Paris with none of these terrible crashes that were in the newspapers nowadays. The engine came into view. Shining black steel, menacingly large wheels, loud whistling and wheezing, steam belching from its tall chimney, the steam engine pulled into the station. A gendarme in a long coat walked along the platform. The second bell rang, followed by the alarming ringing of the station bell and the conductor's piercing whistle. The train smoothly pulled out of the station. The parents stood still, wiping away their tears, while the servants ran along the platform, bowing their farewells.

It had become easy to move around Europe in the second half of the nineteenth century. The railroads were a great help to people with police problems, and they would do much (as did all technical advances) to aid insurgents all over the world.

Before settling down in the university of their choice, the young Russians, intoxicated by freedom, traveled around Europe. They did not rush to sinful Paris like their fathers, grandfathers, and great-grandfathers did. Paris remained a city of conspirators, poets, pamphleteers, courtesans, salons, and secret societies—"the nerve center of European history, regularly sending dangerous impulses to Europe." Napoleon III was wrong in thinking that he had brought order to the city.

But to discover the disorder one needed to get deep into the secret life of Paris, which was inaccessible to the Russian students. Another capital was much more attractive for the young nihilists, because the men who held sway over the minds of progressive youth lived there.

It was London, of course. Herzen lived there, a cult figure, considered so dangerous that corresponding with him was punishable by hard labor in Russia. He was a living symbol. Back in the eighteenth century, travelers in Europe felt bound to pay their respects to Voltaire. A hundred years later, a freethinking Russian abroad wanted to see the dangerous exile in secret.

Young Leo Tolstoy went abroad, and naturally met with Herzen. Tolstoy described how he approached the two-story building at the back of a small courtyard. Behind the house were trees with thin spring foliage. He heard rapid steps on the stone paving, overgrown with grass. Herzen was a small, fat man, full of energy and with quick movements.

Tolstoy saw Herzen every day he was in London. Later, the writer quoted Herzen's bitter words, with which he agreed completely. "If people wanted to save themselves instead of saving the world and to free themselves instead of freeing humanity, they would do so much for saving the world and freeing humanity."

But unlike Tolstoy, the young people coming from Russia did intend to save the world and free humanity. They found like-minded people in London. These were the young émigrés who left Russia after the fires of 1862 and the routing of Land and Freedom. The new arrivals were surprised to learn that Herzen was not highly regarded in these circles. He was not tough enough, and it was unfashionable to meet with the old man. Radical Europe had other idols. For instance, one of the fathers of European communism, the latest fad, often came to London. The illegitimate son of a laundress, Wilhelm Weitling was a former tailor. He gave up his trade and rushed by train from country to country, to share with the working classes his recipe for creating heaven on earth—communism. Raising a well-tailored trouser leg, he would show the marks of prison shackles, his payment for discovering that recipe.

According to Weitling, the construction of communism would begin in a very bloody manner. An army of criminals would have to lay the path to the coming paradise, by destroying the existing order. "Criminals are merely the product of the present social order, and under communism they will cease being criminals."

After a general uprising, the united workers and criminals would start building a radiant future without private property. Society, the commune, would be the only capitalist in the communist state. "People freed from the shackles of property will be as free as birds in the sky." All relationships would change. Since marriage was an exclusive form of private property, "women will leave marriage and become common property." A new era of peace and joy would begin.

A much more serious proponent of communism also lived in London. He was the new star of European radicals, exiled from Prussia and many other European countries, the German genius Karl Marx. He had already warned, "A Specter is haunting Europe, the specter of communism." Marx naturally scoffed at the "vulgar communist," the tailor Weitling. But he was kind to him, seeing in his speeches a childish "manifestation of the proletariat's attraction to communism." Weitling was a welcome guest in Marx's house. Not for serious conversation, but for cards. Marx loved playing at night and the miserable "vulgar communist," dying for sleep, had to hold up until morning playing with the indefatigable philosopher.

In Russia the nihilists knew that Marx had founded the mysterious Communist International, which was to bring a new messiah, the proletariat, to power. "Workers of the world, unite!" The world proletariat would create a happy classless society. But first there would be great bloodshed, the ruthless dictatorship of the proletariat. "Violence is the midwife of History," Marx taught.

The new arrivals from Russia liked Marx's grim thoughts. Marx was very popular among Russian émigrés, and a Russian section was formed in his International.

We can only imagine how, after long negotiations and consultation with other Russian émigrés (for he was suspicious), Marx agreed to receive the expelled students. They arrived at 9, Grafton Terrace, Maitland Park, an expensive town house in the center of London.

He came out to greet them. He was short, stocky, and covered with thickets of hair—blue-black with a handsome streak of gray—a mane of hair on a leonine head, proudly held, with his chin hidden under an enormous beard (you can't have a prophet without a beard). Even his stubby fingers were covered in black hairs. He held himself monumentally in an elegant jacket, buttoned wrong.

The group was invited into his legendary study, the place where the downfall of capitalism was to be directed and where the future happiness of humanity was being forged. It was a very cozy room, and despite the noon hour, a lamp with a green shade was lit, for the usual London fog had turned day into night.

The anticipated conversation began. It can't be called a conversation, because Marx turned it into a monologue. He lisped, but that was quickly forgotten because his masterful tone was hypnotic—his absolute faith in his predestined role as master of men's minds was clear.

A marble bust of Zeus, whom the host called Prometheus in conversation, looked down at the young men from the mantelpiece. Prometheus was a favorite image. His words in the ancient Greek drama, "In truth, I hate all gods," formed the credo of Marx's philosophy, directed against all gods, heavenly and earthly. Thus the severe question at the end of monologue directed at his guests: "Do you believe in God?"

The quick-witted young men denied God. They were praised and told that "communism makes all existing religions unnecessary and replaces them."

Next to Prometheus on the mantle was a portrait of Chernyshevsky, which delighted the Russian guests. Marx explained that it had been a gift from a "Russian steppe landowner," who had promised to give funds for the International but had not sent anything yet. Marx gave the young people a searching look, but they were silent. Their families did not give them extra money. Marx, who had heard they were wealthy, lost interest in them. Instead of giving money, the young people asked about the Communist International.

Marx readily told them the basics: Before him, philosophers merely explained the world, while his philosophy would change the world. That was the goal of the International, to overthrow the bourgeoisie, assure the victory of the proletariat, and found a society without classes or private property. "It is too soon to do it in Russia," Marx warned them, "because there is no proletariat there yet."

The young people sighed sadly, and they were instantly forgotten, because a conversation among great men had begun.

The great men had arrived while Marx was entertaining his Russian guests. One sat on the couch. His name was Friedrich Engels. The other stood by the window—Mikhail Bakunin, the father of Russian anarchism. He was an old giant with thick, unkempt hair and a child's eyes. He had sent the young people to see Marx.

The scion of a wealthy aristocratic family, Bakunin graduated from the brilliant Mikhailovsky military school. Since the very thought of serving in the guards "brought on melancholy," Bakunin quit his military career and left for Europe without telling his father. There, "like a savage thirsty for culture, he threw himself into the study of philosophy." Young

Bakunin quickly came to prefer the pistol to the pen. The admirer of great philosophers turned into a fearless revolutionary. Unlike Marx, who performed his exploits at his desk, Bakunin fought on all the barricades of European revolutions and spent time in the most horrible prisons.

In Prussia the Russian rebel was sentenced to death, but then the Prussians turned him over to the Austrians, who also condemned him to death. He tried to escape, so he was chained to the wall. He spent several months in chains. Then the Austrians turned him over to Nicholas I. The tsar personally interrogated him. Praising him for his courage on the revolutionary barricades, Nicholas sent him to the stone sack, solitary confinement in the Alexeyevsky ravelin in the Fortress of Peter and Paul. His influential relatives persuaded the tsar to commute the sentence to exile in Siberia. The giant escaped and soon after took part in the Polish uprising against Nicholas I.

After the Poles were quelled, Bakunin moved to Geneva. From there, this aficionado of Chopin's music and of philosophy, tender and loving in person, called on Russia to start a bloody revolution. Naturally he was a member of every secret society and naturally he joined the International. But every visit to Marx turned into a verbal battle.

Tin mugs of porter and long clay pipes were laid out on the table. The old giant, quaffing mug after mug, smoked continually and talked continually. "The state of the proletariat is nonsense, for the state itself is an evil that must be destroyed. A communist state would be no better than a capitalist one, and leadership would still be concentrated in the hands of a few. And even if the country is led by workers, they would soon become just as corrupt and despotic as the tyrants they overthrew. Only anarchy can save the world, with power so diffused that no one could abuse it. That will be done in Russia. Everything will be determined by the Russian peasant revolution and the uprising of the Russian criminal world."

Bakunin pinned his hopes for revolution in Russia on the national character, and on the hatred peasants felt for the nobility.

"The Russian people have an either childish or demonic love of fire . . . no wonder we burned down our capital during Napoleon's invasion. It is easy to convince peasants that setting fire to the estate and their masters with all their riches is a just and God-pleasing act."

Bakunin, himself a landowner and descendant of landowners, gleefully recalled the rebellions of Stepan Razin and of Pugachev, when landowners were hanged and estates burned. "The time is drawing nigh for the rebellions of Stenka Razin and Pugachev. We will prepare for the festivities," Bakunin declared. Bandits were the main resource for the future Russian revolution, according to Bakunin. "Bandits are respected in Russia."

Bakunin went on revealing the joyful horizons of the coming apocalypse. "Engulfing Russia, the fire will spread to the whole world. Everything will be destroyed that is deemed holy from the heights of modern European civilization, because it is the source of inequality, the source of all of man's misery. Bringing into motion a destructive force is the only goal worthy of a rational man."

His monologue was interrupted by Marx, first with sarcastic remarks, then with furious ones. Bakunin's monologue was followed by another uninterrupted monologue by Marx. As he spoke, Marx paced back and forth in his small study.

Marx's usual pacing while he waxed political was described by his friend, the great poet Heine:

> *He gallops, he jumps, he bounces,*
> *As if to catch and pull down to earth*
> *The enormous cover of the sky.*
> *He shakes his monstrous fists, and screams*
> *As if thousands of devils pull at his hair.*

The big hair, small body, and the badly buttoned jacket rushed back and forth before the frightened young Russians standing by the fireplace. They heard the words, rather, the furious cries of Marx: "A peasant revolution in Russia is adventurism! Any child knows that! The bourgeois revolution must conquer first! Only the bourgeoisie will give birth to its gravedigger, the working class! And only the working class can solve all the problems of humanity. This is as simple as the alphabet. . . . While you and those like you waste time on projects of world revolution, day by day and night after night fooling yourselves with the motto: 'It will begin tomorrow!' we are spending our time in the British Museum, trying to gain knowledge and prepare weapons and material for the coming battle of the proletariat!"

Then the Russian students learned that their country was the greatest evil of Europe. "I began one of my articles with this story: Two Persian wise men argued over whether bears give birth to live cubs or lay eggs. One of them, apparently more educated, said, 'That animal is capable of anything.' That is the point, the Russian bear is capable of anything except revolution. The Eastern world in the image of Russia has not simply left the historical stage, but in some way is stuck in place and is keeping the rest of the world from moving forward!" shouted Marx.

Now he was not running around the room alone. His alter ego, Friedrich Engels, jumped up from the couch to join him. They made a ridiculous-looking couple. Marx was a small, dark-haired Jew with an enormous head, and Engels was a tall fair-haired Aryan with a very small head. But they had one thing in common. Both Engels and Marx were besotted by Marx.

The wealthy capitalist Engels supported the genius Marx in his fight against capitalism. A successful entrepreneur and fashion plate, member of elite clubs, who filled his cellars with expensive champagne and hunted during the annual Cheshire races, Engels supplied Marx with economic data for his books, which were going to destroy capitalism. He regularly sent Marx money secretly taken from the bank accounts of his company. He handled it so exquisitely that neither his father nor his partner ever noticed the losses. His money paid the rent on the London house.

Now all three men were shouting simultaneously—Marx, Engels, and Bakunin—gradually disappearing in the swirls of tobacco smoke, for they could not open a window: The strident argument would attract crowds outside.

Their faces disappeared, and words flew from the smoke. Gradually the words became unclear, too, as the trinity switched to their famous macaronic language. This was their great polyglots' conspiracy language, a mix of Latin, German, French, Spanish, Italian, and English.

The hungry students sadly watched the last meat pie enter Bakunin's mouth. Tobacco smoke covered everything. The appearance of the "family dictator," Helen Demuth, the small, neat servant, stopped the argument. Helen Demuth had lived in the Marx household for many years. She had an illegitimate son, fifteen-year-old Freddy, who bore a frightening resemblance to the great teacher of the world proletariat. (In 1962, Engels's account was published explaining the reason for the resemblance: The father of revolution was, of course, Freddy's father.)

At last, Bakunin remembered the young people he had sent to Marx, and they decided to move the conversation to a London pub, where they could be fed. In a Piccadilly pub, the company grew larger, with comrades from the International joining them. Marx decided to end the argument. The comrades must believe that no one dare argue with him except those he permitted to argue.

The conversation moved to frivolous topics, which meant that the main speaker was Friedrich Engels, the Casanova of scientific communism.

They came out of the pub after two in the morning. When Marx was tipsy and shamelessly merry, his exits from pubs could be rather turbulent. In his memoirs, Karl Liebknecht described a similar scene. "With quick steps we walked away from the pub, until one of Marx's fellow drinkers tripped on a pile of stones being used for the roadway. He picked up a stone and—bang!—the gas lamp was shattered. Marx kept up and broke four or five lamps. It was around two in the morning and the streets were empty. But the noise attracted a policeman. We ran with three or four policemen chasing us. Marx demonstrated an alacrity I had not expected from him."

After London, the young nihilists naturally headed for Geneva. In 1867 the city was lovely, with flower-covered balconies, and crying gulls flying low over the shore. A warm rain had fallen over night, but the morning fog was lifting as they arrived. The sun's rays burst through, revealing boundless Lake Geneva and the spectral Savoy Mountains in the distance. It was the view seen by every famous revolutionary of Europe, for Geneva did not give up political criminals. Geneva was a Noah's Ark, where all the participants of suppressed European revolutions had gathered.

The atmosphere stunned the young Russians. There was no permanent army, and very few uniforms, which were the main color effects seen on the streets of St. Petersburg. You could walk into a café and see the president of the canton having coffee. It wasn't easy to notice him, for he sat like any ordinary citizen, waiting for the slow-moving waiters. No Cossack bodyguards surrounded him. There was no censorship and no struggle against any ideas. Yet for some reason, the revolution that had rocked Europe's countries with their great armies and great bureaucracies had bypassed Geneva.

Whom could the young nihilists have seen in Geneva in 1867? The Congress of the League of Peace and Freedom was meeting there. All of Europe's liberals had gathered to discuss how to prevent war. Despite their fiery speeches and wise resolutions, war would break soon between France and Prussia. But at the moment, the streets were lined with people waiting to see the chairman of the Congress. He arrived in an open carriage, the idol of liberal Europe, Giuseppe Garibaldi. He looked extremely colorful in a red shirt and Mexican poncho, standing and waving his hat to the applauding crowd. One of the most ardent applauders was a young woman, Anya, wife of the writer Dostoevsky.

They were on their honeymoon. The trip was the only way the writer could escape his creditors. Dostoevsky got an advance from his publisher for a new book, *The Idiot*. On that long, four-year trip, the simple and innocent girl experienced her husband's intoxicating "Karamazov voluptuousness" and the genius's epileptic fits and his gambling passion. He sometimes lost not only all their money, but even his suit and her dresses. They would have to stay put, penniless, waiting for help from his publisher in Russia.

Anya put up with all of it. Often, as he would go out to gamble, he would ask for her permission. She knew there was no point in refusing; he was possessed. "I told him I agreed to everything," she wrote in her diary. "He must appreciate that agreement, and that I never argue with him about anything, but always try to agree as quickly as possible, so that we do not quarrel."

For those four years his main interlocutors were his notebooks, where he held a conversation with himself, and kind Anya. "Last night we talked about the Gospels and Christ, we talked for a long time," she wrote. "At night, when he came to say good night, he kissed me a lot, tenderly, and said, 'I can't live without you, look how we've grown into one person, Anya, you couldn't separate us with a knife.' . . . Later, in bed, he said, 'It's for people like you that Christ came.'"

Throughout the entire journey he suffered from epileptic seizures, and he noted them carefully. "A half hour before the fit I took opii benzoedi: 40 drops in water. After total unconsciousness, i.e., already up from the floor, I sat and filled *papirosy* [rolled cigarettes with a cardboard tube filter], and I counted 4 that I filled, but not neatly, and I felt a terrible headache but could not figure out what was wrong with me."

It was impossible to get used to the disease; the fits were terrible. He could die in a few minutes, in convulsions and—for him, most terribly—unconscious. He worked furiously under that sword of Damocles, without losing his sense of humor.

As he joked to Anya, "When we leave [this pension], they will start telling their friends, 'Ah, we had Russians staying here, she was young, so pretty, always so cheerful . . . and an old idiot. He was so mean that he fell out of bed at night, and he did it on purpose!'"

By the fall of 1867, they had reached Geneva. Dostoevsky, completely unknown in Europe, worked on *The Idiot* in their small room in a cheap pension, while Anya took walks to be out of his way.

The next book after *The Idiot* would be based on another Russian visiting Geneva. Just eighteen months later, on the same shore in that city, the forerunner of the bloody Russian revolution and the hero of Dostoevsky's next novel would appear—Sergei Gennadyevich Nechaev.

———

Dostoevsky would depict Nechaev in the novel *The Devils* under the name of Verkhovensky. But the real Nechaev was to the fictional character as the real devil was to a petty demon.

Sergei Nechaev, a young man of short stature and an ordinary round peasant face, had an amazing gaze. A contemporary woman (a relative of Herzen's) wrote that she could never forget that subjugating, hypnotic stare. The descriptions of his stare are very similar to descriptions of Grigory Rasputin's gaze. When Nechaev was incarcerated, the chief of gendarmes himself, head of the Third Department A. Potapov, came to his cell. He came to humiliate him and demand he become a stoolie. Nechaev responded by slapping Potapov in the face. And beneath his gaze, the chief of gendarmes, with slapped face, sank to his knees! Later, Potapov left, came to his senses, and got his revenge. But he had knelt— such was Nechaev's power.

Nechaev created many legends about himself. In actuality, he was the son of a man who worked as a servant in inns. His profession served him badly. The "nouveaux gentlemen," rich industrialists in Russia's textile capital, Ivanovo, often hired him to serve tables at family weddings and parties. They paid very well. The easy money and constant drinking at weddings turned Nechaev's father into an alcoholic.

Sergei Nechaev came to Moscow to attend the university. But something made him change his mind, and instead he moved to St. Petersburg and passed the exam to become a village schoolteacher. The atheist started teaching catechism in a small school.

He started going to the university as an auditor. From his first day there, he spoke of the inevitability of the revolution. The young religion teacher dreamed of serving it. Skinny, nervous, nail-biting, the youth attended all student gatherings. Like every young radical, he adored Chernyshevsky's fictional hero, Rakhmetov. Nechaev had no property, and he slept in friends' apartments, often on the floor. "Every one of us had something, he had nothing. He had only one idea, one passion—the revolution," recounted one of his female adherents. His passion was accompanied by morbid hatred for life as it was.

Even back then he proclaimed the right of the revolutionary to use any means—blackmail, murder, lies, and constant provocation. Everything that Ishutin used to say before losing his mind in prison, Nechaev now repeated. He accepted the baton of Russian Jacobinism from Ishutin.

"The government does not scorn anything in its struggle with revolutionaries, particularly their Jesuitical methods of provocation, and what about us? It's Jesuitism that we've lacked until now!" he said.

Provocation and lies became his companions, along with the idea of regicide on a mass scale. When asked which of the royal family should be killed, he laughed and replied, the whole *ektinya* (the prayer for the tsar's family listing all the members). Young Ulyanov-Lenin would later be particularly fond of this phrase, and able to execute Nechaev's dream.

Nechaev had furious energy and scary charisma. From the very beginning to the very end, he was surrounded by people ready to serve him unquestioningly. There were real leaders among them.

In 1868 he met a well-known radical, the writer Petr Tkachev. The son of a wealthy landowner, brilliantly educated, a follower of Blanqui and Machiavelli, Tkachev had served time in tsarist prisons but continued to dream of the revolution that would destroy his own class. This short and shy young man, slender and easily embarrassed, with a smiling cupid's face, resembled a pretty girl ("pretty maiden" is what his friends called him). He hailed a centralized party dictatorship that would seize power and crush resistance through terror.

> No, not humility, not love
> Will save us from our shackles.
> Now we need the axe,
> We need the knife.

That was the pretty maiden's poetry. Released yet again from the fortress, the pretty maiden, smiling shyly, told his astonished sister his new discovery: "Only people under twenty-five are capable of self-sacrifice, and therefore everyone over that age should be killed for the good of society."

When asked how many would have to be killed in the revolution, he replied with the same shy smile, "We should be thinking about how many can be left."

But when they met, the not very educated and unknown teacher Nechaev absolutely dominated the celebrated intellectual Tkachev, who subsequently never forgave him for it.

A new wave of student unrest exploded in the capital in 1868–69. It began at the Medical-Surgical Academy, which was under the auspices of the military ministry. Dmitri Milyutin, the minister of war, was one of the last remaining liberals in the government. Ignoring the ban of Minister of Education Dmitri Tolstoy, he permitted the students to have their own mutual aid credit union and to have meetings. This destroyed him. At their first meetings, the students announced that they didn't like being part of the military ministry because "discipline is too harsh at the academy." The rallies began. The academy was shut down, but the unrest moved to St. Petersburg University and from there to the Technological Institute. Those students didn't like not having credit unions and the right to meetings. They demanded an end "to all confining and humiliating supervision from the university."

The nervous little man with terrifying eyes, Nechaev, was behind the turmoil in St. Petersburg. He happily rushed from house to house, from club to club, from meeting to meeting. He frightened student leaders and instigated rebellion. Yet for all his activity, the police did not touch him. Some people began to wonder whether he was a provocateur. He was not a provocateur, but he obviously suited the needs of someone in the police, who could use Nechaev as a reason for more power and funding.

Nechaev actually wanted to be arrested. It was only after serving time that he could wield authority as a revolutionary leader. Fortune smiled upon him: He was called in for questioning. He went off, certain that he would be arrested. Soon afterward, the young revolutionary Vera Zasulich received an amazing letter.

The anonymous sender wrote: "When I was walking on Vasilyevsky

Island today, I saw a carriage transporting prisoners. A hand reached out and threw a note from the window. A bit later I heard the following words: 'If you are a student, deliver this to the address indicated.' I am a student and consider it my duty to execute the request. Destroy my letter." There was an enclosed note in Nechaev's handwriting, asking Zasulich to inform their friends that he was arrested and being held in the Fortress of Peter and Paul.

A rumor followed that he had managed the incredible and escaped from the fortress and was headed for the West. He quickly became famous.

In fact, he had not been arrested. He was released the same day as his interrogation. He made up the story of his arrest and escape. He hid in his sister's apartment while the rumors traveled through student circles.

The invented arrest was only the first step of his daring plan. Nechaev intended to start a national mutiny and burn Russia in the flames of rebellion. For that, he needed a powerful organization and money. He headed for Europe to find them.

On March 4, 1869, Nechaev illegally crossed the Russian border and made his way to Geneva. Back in Russia he had calculated who the most likely candidate was to become his faithful benefactor in the West. Naturally, it was the bloody dreamer and gentle, trusting man, Mikhail Bakunin.

Nachev went to see him, and that evening a sweet mirage arose in Bakunin's Geneva dwelling. Nechaev told the old revolutionary about his incarceration in the Fortress of Peter and Paul, where Bakunin had been imprisoned, and about his "escape." Then he revealed to Bakunin that a very secret and powerful community existed in Russia. A network of secret circles had spread throughout the empire. The All-Russian Committee was at the head of the revolutionary network and controlled the mighty revolutionary forces. The committee consisted of Nechaev and other determined young people. They lacked serious experience in the political struggle, and they lacked funds. That's why his comrades had sent him to Geneva, to see Bakunin and Herzen.

Bakunin was happy; his prophecy, which Marx mocked, seemed true, that a revolutionary fire was coming to Russia. His life had not been wasted. Nechaev's ideas of the right to lie, to murder, and to create provocations in the name of the revolution intoxicated kindly Bakunin. Here was a true Jacobin. Bakunin fell in love with that uneducated, cruel Marat, just as later the intellectual Vladimir Ilyich Lenin would be enthralled by the wild revolutionary Dzhugashvili, known to history as Stalin.

Bakunin elatedly recommended "Tiger Cub" (as he tenderly called Nechaev) to the main figure of the Russian émigré community, Herzen, and then to Marx himself. The noble Herzen had an instinctual aversion to the Tiger Cub. "He's fibbing," Herzen said fastidiously of Nechaev's tales. "I do not believe in the seriousness of people who prefer violence and crude force over development and deals. . . . We need apostles before swashbuckling sapper officers of destruction. Apostles who preach not only to their own, but to the foe. Preaching to the enemy is a great act of love," wrote Herzen wisely.

Hating everyone who did not submit to him, Nechaev got his revenge on Herzen, by seducing his beloved daughter.

Marx did not believe the Tiger Cub, either. But in fact, Nechaev was fibbing only in part. There was no organization, but he had come to Europe in order to return with money and recommendations and to create it. He told the truth about his only dream and goal in life.

Bakunin sensed this and wrote, "He is one of those young fanatics who know no doubts, who fear nothing. They are believers without God, heroes without rhetoric."

With Nechaev, Bakunin wrote incendiary proclamations addressed to the new revolutionary Russia. The proclamations, Bakunin's letters, and revolutionary literature were sent into Russia to addresses Nechaev gave him. Those banned parcels were to be received throughout the European part of Russia.

Naturally, they were intercepted by the police. In St. Petersburg alone, letters addressed to 380 young people were seized. Bakunin had been fooled. Nechaev knew that the mail would be intercepted; in fact, he sent it so that all those recipients would end up in prison.

He had explained it very clearly back in Russia in a speech: "In the first two years, students rebel gleefully and enthusiastically. Then they get caught up in their studies, and by the fourth or fifth year, you see that yesterday's rebel is house-trained, and upon graduation from university or academy, yesterday's fighters for the people are turned into completely reliable physicians, teachers, and other officials. They become paterfamiliases. And looking at one of them, it is hard to believe that he is the same person who just three or four years ago had spoken with such fire about the suffering of the people, who thirsted for exploits and seemed ready to die for the people! Instead of a revolutionary fighter we see spineless scum. Very soon many of them turn into prosecutors, judges, investigators and together with the government they start to stifle the very people for whom they had intended to give their lives. What should be done? Here I have only one hope, but a very strong one, in the government. Do you know what I expect from it? That it put away more people, that students be kicked out of universities forever, sent into exile, knocked out of their usual rut, stunned by persecution, cruelty, injustice, and stupidity. Only that will forge their hatred for the vile government and the society that looks on indifferently at the brutality of the regime."

His plan was to use the Third Department to forge future revolutionaries, to train cadres for the future militant party he dreamed of creating in Russia. For that party, a work was written in Geneva that all Russian revolutionaries damned publicly but followed in secret. It is one of the few truly revolutionary works. Historians still argue about the authorship, whether Bakunin or Nechaev wrote it, since there are elements of each man's style and thought. Most likely, it was written by both in the month of their passionate friendship.

Catechism for the Revolutionary is the title of this revolutionary bible filled with demonic poetry. "The revolutionary is a doomed man. He has no interests of his own, no work, no feelings, no ties, no property, not even a name. Everything is subsumed by a single, exclusive interest, a single thought, a single passion—revolution. . . . He has torn all ties with the general order, with the educated world, and with common morality. . . . He is for anything that promotes the triumph of revolution. Anything that hinders it is immoral and criminal.

"All tender feelings of family, friendship, love, gratitude, and even honor must be squashed in him by the sole passion for revolutionary work. For him there is only one solace, reward, and satisfaction—the success of the revolution. Day and night, he must have only one thought, one goal—ruthless destruction. Moving cold-bloodedly and indefatigably toward that goal, he must be prepared to perish himself and to kill with his own hands everything that is an obstacle. . . . The revolutionary organization must compile a list of people to be destroyed . . . first of all they must destroy people particularly harmful for the revolutionary organization.

"The revolutionary must lure people with money and influence into his nets and make them his slaves. . . . As for liberals, the revolutionary must pretend to follow them blindly while actually getting them in his power, mastering their secrets and compromising them so that there is no way back for them."

Nechaev's favorite refrain repeats throughout the work: "Our work is destruction, terrible, complete, pervasive, and ruthless." Bakunin's favorite thought is repeated as well: "We must join with the swashbuckling robber world, the true and only revolutionary in Russia."

In *The Rebel,* Albert Camus wrote, "He elevated revolutionary expediency to the level of absolute good which would force all considerations of morality to retreat. In the interests of the revolution, for the definition of which he considered himself sole judge, any action was justified, any crime was legal, no matter how disgusting."

The *Catechism* laid out the principles for creating a small organization that could take over a country. This was the organization Nechaev would start upon his return to Russia. Its foundation was the truly Russian principle of subordination, subordination, and more subordination— unquestioning obedience. The obedience that was in the blood of the people, inculcated over the millennia, would guarantee this subordination and ruthless discipline.

The organization would have revolutionaries of the first and second rank. The first rank could use the second rank as its capital to be spent on the needs of the revolution. If a revolutionary of the first rank decided to sacrifice the freedom or even the life of a revolutionary of the second rank, that was his right.

The time had come. The Tiger Cub announced he had to go back to Russia. Under Bakunin's pressure, Herzen gave Nechaev money from a special revolutionary fund (the money had been given to Herzen to spend at his discretion by Bakhmetyev, a mad Russian landowner who went off to create a commune in the Azores).

Before leaving, Nechaev asked Bakunin to give him a letter of authorization from the nonexistent European Revolutionary Alliance. He explained that the idea of joining the mysterious European organization would push the Russian revolutionaries to greater levels of action. Bakunin, who would soon after abuse Nechaev for his shameless lies, readily acceded to this one. Nechaev was authorized as a "Plenipotentiary Representative of the Russian Section of the World Revolutionary Alliance." The mandate signed by Bakunin had a very impressive seal, with two crossed menacing axes.

In August 1869 the "plenipotentiary" returned to Russia and went to Moscow. At the Peter Agricultural Academy, where most of the students were trusting provincials, the awesome plenipotentiary created his organization. At a meeting of the candidates he had selected, Nechaev explained to the vacillating students that there was no going back. They were now part of the mighty European Revolutionary Alliance. Their large organization consisted of "fighting fives," which would know nothing about each other (as demanded by the alliance). Only he, as their leader and member of the alliance's mighty Central Committee, would know them all.

Now the members of the groups of five began to imagine others everywhere, which made them bold. That is how Nechaev created a secret society with the promising name of People's Reprisal. He demanded absolute, blind obedience. He made them spy on one another. They all prepared for the uprising that would sweep away the existing regime. It was set for February 19, 1870, the ninth anniversary of the emancipation of the serfs.

Very quickly, Nechaev's speeches and methods grew repulsive to one of the most talented members of the organization. He was an academy student with the amusing name Ivan Ivanovich Ivanov. Ivanov spoke out openly against Nechaev, casting doubt on the existence of the foreign Central Committee.

Nechaev saw this as an opportunity. He could show the members of the five what insubordinates could expect as punishment. He also needed to bind them in blood. He called a meeting and explained that Ivanov was "muddying the waters" because he intended to renounce them. "The time has come to prove to the Central Committee and to ourselves that we can be ruthless revolutionaries, bringing into practice what is written in the *Catechism*, that the blood of impure revolutionaries binds the organization."

In the name of the committee, Nechaev ordered the "liquidation of Ivanov." Sensing their hesitation and confusion, Nechaev reminded them that "anyone disobeying the decision of the European Committee must understand what that threatens him with." Subjugated by his burning, hypnotic eyes, the students agreed.

The academy was located in the mansion of Count Razumovsky, nephew of the lover of Empress Elizabeth. The large grounds, preserved to this day, had ponds and an old grotto.

On the night of November 20, 1869, the wretched Ivanov was lured to the grotto. Members of the militant five attacked. The student Kuznetsov knocked Ivanov to the ground. The scrawny Nechaev and two others attacked him. Nechaev sat on Ivanov's chest and choked him. Ivanov had stopped screaming, but he was still moving. Then Nechaev took out a revolver and put a bullet through Ivanov's head. They drowned the body in a pond.

The killers were nervous, and they didn't dispose of the body successfully. It floated up soon afterward, and an investigation was begun. Eighty-four "Nechaevites" were tried. Nechaev had worked hard, and had created an organization. But the work of the People's Reprisal was limited to the murderous attack against one unarmed student.

Dostoevsky learned about this incident from the newspaper *Moskovskie Novosti* (*Moscow News*). He greedily read the Russian press while abroad. Not long before the killing, Anya's brother came to see them in Dresden. He was a student at the Peter Agricultural Academy, and was a friend of the murdered Ivanov. Dostoevsky was stunned—the past had been resurrected. A former member of the Petrashevsky circle, he remembered the secret society, the bloodthirsty talk of the handsome Nikolai Speshnev, and the power that "Mephistopheles" had over him.

Dostoevsky wrote in horror, "No, I could never have become a Nechaev, but I can't promise that I might not have become a Nechaevite in the days of my youth." He was pursued by that vision of himself among killers, believing a devil. He began a new novel. It would be called *The Devils*.

While the members of Nechaev's organization, the simple provincials he had turned into zombies, were on trial, Nechaev fled from Moscow to St. Petersburg. There he got a passport and in December 1869 he crossed the border, leaving his arrested comrades to perish. Apparently, according to his *Catechism,* they had been merely second-rate revolutionaries.

According to Nechaev, when Bakunin learned he was back, he jumped for joy "such that he almost cracked the ceiling with his old head." But the joy did not last, because Bakunin learned the truth. He heard it from Petr Lavrov, another person who played a great role in the fate of Russia.

Lavrov was a tsarist colonel, professor of mathematics, and editor of the *Encyclopedic Dictionary.* He had been court-martialed for following "the dangerous direction of Chernyshevsky." He was exiled from St. Petersburg and then escaped abroad. Lavrov lived in Paris, went through the Paris Commune, and befriended the communards. After the fall of the commune, he hurried to London, where, naturally, he met Marx and joined the International.

He told Bakunin and the other émigrés the truth about Nechaev. Bakunin learned that there was no underground organization covering all of Russia, only an organization that had killed one student. He also heard about the scar on Nechaev's hand, the shameful mark made by the teeth of the struggling unarmed student, shot by the Tiger Cub.

Bakunin was stunned. He wrote to Nechaev, "Believing in you unconditionally while you were deceiving me systematically, made me a complete fool—this is bitter and shameful for a man of my experience and my age, and even worse I have ruined my position in the Russian and international cause." Still, knowing the worst, Bakunin continued to love him. Yes, he lied, but it had been in the name of the revolution. As Lenin said, "You don't make revolution in white gloves." Yes, Nechaev had murdered, but he was dedicated to the revolution more than anyone. So Bakunin wrote, "You are a passionately devoted man; there are few like you; that is your power, your glory, your right. . . . If you change your methods, I would like to remain not only connected to you but to join you even more closely and strongly."

Learning that the Russian government had demanded Nechaev's extradition on criminal charges, Bakunin tried to get support from the émigrés for Nechaev. "The most important business at this moment is to preserve our lost and confused friend. Hating everyone, he remains a valuable person, and there are few valuable people in the world."

The "valuable person," finding himself without money, decided to turn to expropriation, robbing the bourgeoisie on the high road, that is, to become a bandit. Russian agents came to Geneva and found him. He was arrested in a small café and brought back to Russia in handcuffs.

Bakunin wrote, "I am deeply sorry for him. No one has ever done me as much intentional harm as he has. But I still pity him. . . . His outward behavior was disgusting enough, but his inner 'I' was not dirty. . . . An inner voice tells me that Nechaev, who is lost for the ages and certainly knows that he is lost . . . will now be calling from the abyss in which he now finds himself, reviled and despised, but not at all vile or ordinary, with all his primitive energy and valor. He will perish like a hero and will not betray anyone or anything. That is my conviction. We will see whether I am right."

Bakunin was right. The trial was open to the public, and people were appalled by the details that emerged. Nechaev was sentenced to twenty years at hard labor, but Alexander crossed out the sentence, and wrote instead: "the fortress forever," underlining "forever."

The story Nechaev had made up about himself was now reality. He was in the Fortress of Peter and Paul, in the most terrible part, the Alexeyevsky ravelin, where Bakunin had once served his time. He would rot in his cell.

First he was given a civil execution. When he was moved to the square, he shouted furiously from the cart: "There will be a guillotine here soon. . . . Here all those gentlemen who brought me here will lose their heads." And he laughed triumphantly. "I'll bet your hearts are beating! Just wait two or three years, you'll all be here! All! All!"

He was tied to the pillar and he continued to shout: "Long live liberty! Long live the free Russian people!" They took him to his cell. The Nechaev story seemed over "forever."

Dostoevsky published *The Devils* in 1873, when he had returned to Russia. In explaining the novel, Dostoevsky wrote that *The Devils* was not specifically about the Nechaev case, but much wider. "My view is that these phenomena are not random, not isolated, and therefore my novel does not have copied events or copied persons."

The Devils was a warning. The trouble sown in a single city by a pathetic group of five conspirators could turn up on a greater scale and affect all of Russia. The "pure of heart" who become tempted by the Nechaev devils pose a great threat. The ideas of universal equality (the eternal Russian dream) as interpreted by devils will end in universal slavery and could become Russia's terrible future. He saw apocalyptic visions.

Dostoevsky's novel elicited a storm of protest. The educated reading public was primarily liberal, and it saw the Nechaev case as an exception, a tragic episode. *The Devils* was universally panned. "The Nechaev case is a monster to such a degree that it cannot serve as a theme for a novel," wrote one of the main critics, Nikolai Mikhailovsky. The novel marks a lapse in the author's talent; it is a horrible caricature and slander on revolutionary youth. Russia rejected *The Devils*.

Dostoevsky himself, as he completed the novel, tried to persuade himself that the Nechaev case had been a horrible but now finished episode in the life of young Russia. After Nechaev's sentencing and incarceration, the writer tried to believe that it was the end. The devil was captured, shackled, and was gone "forever." This is why he chose as epigraph to the novel the biblical parable of the devils who on the command of Jesus fled a man they had possessed and settled into pigs. Dostoevsky wrote in a letter to the poet Maikov, "The devils have left the Russian man and went into a herd of pigs, that is, the Nechaevs, the Serno-Solovyoviches, and so on. They have drowned or will drown, probably, while the healed man whom the devils have left sits at the feet of Jesus. That is as it should be."

But that is not how it was. The great prophet was mistaken. Everything would happen in exactly the opposite way—as he had predicted in the novel rather than in the epigraph. The future history of the Russian revolutionary movement would be imbued with Nechaevism. A few years would pass and the indignant readers of *The Devils* would see Russian terror born of the "pure of heart."

The twentieth century would belong to the devil Nechaev, and the victory of Bolshevism would be his victory. In Bolshevik Russia, people were appalled when they read *The Devils* and the monologue of the book's hero, Petr Verkhovensky (Nechaev), on the society he would create after the revolution: "Every member of society looks after the other and must inform on them. All are slaves and are equal in their slavery. . . . First of all, the level of education, science, and talent is lowered. A high level of science and talent can be achieved only by people with higher abilities, and we don't need higher abilities! People with higher abilities have always seized power and were despots. . . . They are cast out or executed. Cicero's tongue is cut out, Copernicus's eyes are gouged out, and Shakespeare is stoned to death."

The Bolsheviks implemented it all: Nikolai Bukharin, the main Bolshevik theoretician, called for "organized reduction of culture"; celebrated philosophers were forced to leave the country; there was equality in slavery; and universal informing was enforced. In the 1920s, a popular joke in Russia said that the Bolsheviks erected a monument to Dostoevsky with a plaque reading: "To Fedor Dostoevsky from the Grateful Devils."

For a period, young Russians at home and abroad turned away from Nechaev, and took up different and astounding ideas. The serfs were free after 1861, but capitalism, so hated by Herzen, Chernyshevsky, Lavrov, Bakunin, and other Russian radicals, did not come to agriculture. The freed serf did not have the right to sell his land. All land was communal property, held by the *obshchina,* an ancient form of land owning destroyed in Western Europe. It remained in Russia: The land in Russian villages was owned by the "society," *obshchestvo,* that is, by all the peasants together. All decisions were made collectively. Collective property, collective decisions: In this primitive collectivism Russian radicals saw embryonic socialism. These socialist instincts would allow Russia to bypass heartless capitalism and move directly into socialism, they hoped. All that was needed was to revolutionize the illiterate Russian *muzhik,* the peasant, awaken his consciousness, and then lead Russia to socialism.

This required agitators, the new apostles. Herzen's magazine, *The Bell,* called "To the people! Be with the people!" The response was vast. Petr Lavrov wrote, "Every comfort in life that I use . . . is bought with the blood, suffering, and labor of millions. . . . Every 'developed person,' every 'critically thinking personality' must return the debt and take up enlightening the people and awakening them, so that the Russian people will be able to recognize their slavery, refuse to live in that slavery, and prepare themselves for a conscious rebellion against such a life."

The young Russians who had been sent abroad picked up the idea. The Christian mission of serving the needy and returning its debt to the people captivated youth much more than the ideas of Bakunin and Marx.

The Russian government, in the meantime, worried by information on the influence of radical ideas on Russian youths abroad, ordered all students in the West to return to Russia. The hazardous boomerang sent to the West now came back. The young radicals were returning with the bizarre idea of going out to the people, to be with them and awaken them.

CHAPTER 10

The Lonely Palace Cliff

On September 1, 1870, Emperor Napoleon III and his large army suffered a defeat at Sedan and surrendered to Bismarck's Prussian forces. Another Napoleon was brought down. Alexander II could have called it retribution and said that his father had been avenged. The German Empire was recognized in the Mirror Gallery of Versailles. Uncle Wilhelm was now emperor of Germany.

Alexander and Gorchakov had prepared for this outcome. Since the victor of the Crimean War no longer existed, the Treaty of Paris could be declared null and void. Gorchakov sent a circular about this to the Russian ambassadors.

England called this a violation of international agreements, but Russia was supported by the new superpower, the German Empire. Russia and England signed the Treaty of London, which rescinded the humiliating limitations on the Black Sea. Alexander had gotten back Russia's main sea, and without bloodshed. He was exultant and Gorchakov was made a Serene Prince.

The newspapers praised only Gorchakov. It had become unfashionable to praise the tsar, for he had become unpopular.

Alexander seemed oblivious, the years passing by as they do for fifty-year-olds. While the youth prepared for an unprecedented movement, with society in its usual ferment, the tsar lived tranquilly in his palace redoubt. Medieval ceremonies continued, with solemn big and small entrances by the tsar, endless celebrations of birthdays and shared saint's days, anniversaries of the founding of regiments, important dates in the life of the tsar and his parents, and numerous church feast days. Basically, they celebrated everything, even the first time the enemy bombed Sevastopol, "although there wouldn't seem to be anything to celebrate" (Nikolai Milyutin).

Loyal Shuvalov took on all the cares of government. The reforms were not just dead; it was the time of counter-reform. Alexander the two-faced Janus was looking only back. On June 7, 1872, he approved a project of the new minister of internal affairs, Count Palen, to create a "Special Presence of the Governing Senate," a new institution to oversee all serious political cases. These cases would be taken out of the normal course of jurisprudence and tried by the newly created body.

The censor Nikitenko, who had recently hailed the tsar, wrote in his diary: "For some reason everything good in Russia is fated to begin but not reach an end. With one hand we make improvements, and with the other, we undermine them; with one hand we give, with the other we take away. . . . We want innovation in particulars but for the main things to remain as they were."

The tsar retreated into his personal life, unconsciously seeking salvation in love from the growing waves of problems rolling toward the palace cliff. Lost in love, he merely watched his appointee Shuvalov try to push back the water Alexander had agitated.

He still followed his daily schedule. After his walk, the tsar went to the apartments of the empress, with the ritual kiss and the same conversation about her health and the children. They had coffee. The empress was always cold then and wrapped herself in a black shawl. She had become wraithlike. The disease was consuming her. He was desperately sorry for Masha and her dried-up body. He asked her to follow Dr. Botkin's advice and go to Nice, where the climate was better for her lungs. She knew that he wanted to be rid of her. He continued to see the other woman in the late emperor's study, where the dying Nicholas I had blessed her. But now when Alexander brought the other woman there, she was no longer alone.

On April 30, 1872, the tsar noted the birth of his son. It took place in his late father's study. Katya had a difficult birth and the doctors feared she would have puerperal fever. Alexander's orders were: If there is a choice, sacrifice the child. She must live. Near morning, Katya gave birth to a boy. Alexander wrote, "The Lord is so generous. I praised God, in tears I thank Him." The son was called Georgy.

What Shuvalov had foreseen had come to pass. Tsars had always had illegitimate children, but it was done "covertly and decorously." Alexander was no longer interested in hiding. He was spending more and more time in the luxurious house that he rented for her. When she was brought to the Winter Palace, the boy came with her.

The extended Romanov family was concerned, because the newborn child was a threat to the heir. But they did not dare speak to the emperor. They did it through their august relations. Alexander, tired of these messages from relatives, wrote a letter to his sister Olga (the queen of Württemberg). "She [Princess Dolgorukaya] preferred to renounce all social amusements and pleasures so desired by young ladies of her age . . . and has devoted her entire life to loving and caring for me." Then came the part that was intended to calm down the royal houses: "Without interfering in any affairs, despite the many attempts by those who would dishonestly use her name, she lives only for me, dedicated to bringing up our children."

That was all. No one had any pretensions to anything.

But that was not enough for Shuvalov. He knew the tsar and he knew that the tsar was mad about the princess. Even worse, Grand Duke Konstantin Nikolayevich, who hated Shuvalov, had made the acquaintance of the favorite, which boded for a very dangerous alliance.

The chief of the secret police decided to enter into open warfare against the woman. Shuvalov had come up with a unique tone in dealing with the tsar. It was often gruff, the manner of an honest servant who did not fear the tsar's wrath when it came to telling him the truth. To the relief of the family and the camarilla, Shuvalov spoke openly about the threat of the "situation" to the tsar's prestige, "which should be so carefully protected in these difficult times." He made sure the word got back to the tsar. The count felt that managing the Committee of Ministers and the secret police was not enough, he needed to direct the tsar's life, as well. He tried to become a true Peter IV.

The scandal erupted in Ems. Katya had given birth to a second child, a daughter, in 1873, a year after the birth of their son, and now they all went to Ems for the water. They were an elegant couple, a middle-aged and striking gentleman with a very young lady and two charming tots. He was incognito, naturally, but everyone in Ems knew who they were.

Photography had taken Europe by storm. At first (as usual) many were against it. For instance, in Paris the poets declared photography a "humiliation of art." Gradually they grew used to it. Even the king of the poets, Baudelaire, gave in and was photographed. Victor Hugo had a daguerreotype made as well. Even Pope Leo XIII not only was photographed but wrote a poem about his positive impressions. In Russia the Church was not pleased with photography. The tsar's spiritual advisor Bazhenov said, "God created man in his image, and no human apparatus dares capture the image of God." But gradually, the clergy accepted it, too.

In Ems, Alexander wanted to have a group photograph, so that he could see her face before him all the time. They went to an ordinary studio, anonymously. To keep the photo from being dangerous (that is, too intimate), her friends, Countess Gendrikova and Vera Shebeko, posed with them. It was charming, and he ordered more copies. He was informed, however, that it could not be done, because Count Shuvalov had gone to the photographer, bought up the prints and the plates, and destroyed them all. Alexander was furious and commanded that Shuvalov be informed that he had no right to do that.

As Minister Valuyev wrote in his memoirs, Shuvalov replied, "And I ask you to tell the tsar that he, as the Russian Tsar, had no right to make such a portrait!"

This put an end to their good relations. The emperor began looking for a replacement. This pleased Kostya, who nagged him to do it soon. He kept hoping that if Shuvalov left, this horrible period would be over.

Shuvalov understood the grand duke's intentions and probably started preparing his responsive strike then.

Politically, the emperor concerned himself with only foreign affairs. Emperor Wilhelm came to visit, accompanied by his elderly commander in chief, Field Marshal Moltke, the conqueror of Austria, Denmark, and France. The two old men with large gray sideburns had come to make an alliance with Alexander.

They agreed that in case of attack, each side was to furnish twenty thousand soldiers to help the other. That would deter war in Europe, or, rather, war that was inconvenient for them. Austria was supposed to join them. Chancellor Gorchakov, who helped create this Triple Alliance, would only later understand what a far-reaching game the cunning Bismarck was playing. Bismarck knew that as soon as Russia completed its military reform and created a strong army, Alexander would continue his father's work. A Russo-Turkish war was on the political horizon. Germany had no interests in the East, and Bismarck could not contain the Russian ally's appetites here. But Austria had interests in the East, so when Russia and Turkey went to war, Austria would keep Russia from having too great a success.

There was yet another question the emperors needed to discuss. Almost a quarter century earlier, during the revolution of 1848, Emperor Wilhelm saw the maddened crowds of Berlin. They killed soldiers and they forced his brother, the king of Prussia, to bare his head and beg forgiveness before the corpses of the dead mutineers. The king went mad from the humiliation. He was the first victim of revolution in the Hohenzollern family.

Now both emperors felt that ahead lay great disturbances that would make all previous ones seem like nothing. They decided that the chiefs of police of their countries would instantly warn each other of all potential threats. They had to act together. Europe was turning into one big ship, and revolutions could turn into a general wave that would sink their familiar world.

———

The modest Prussian kings were always stunned by the Byzantine opulence of the Russian court. Even though Uncle Willy was now a mighty
emperor, he was still impressed. He was in fine form for a man in his
seventies, dressed in his gold-trimmed uniform decorated with walls of
medals. While he visited, the days were filled with continual military
parades, concerts, and performances, culminating in a magnificent ball
in the Winter Palace.

The formal rooms of the Winter Palace were usually decorated with
palm trees and orchids for balls. Eight hundred people worked for two
weeks on the decorations. The chefs and pastry chefs competed to create
the most sumptuous dishes.

The day of the ball came. In the white marble hall, footmen in liver-
ies with the state coat of arms and white stockings and patent leather
shoes received the guests' fur coats. The guests went up the formal Jor-
dan Staircase: marble walls with gilt decorative plasterwork, mirrors
reflecting thousands of candles, and a ceiling with Greek gods above
their heads. Between the lines of Cossacks in black hats and "Moors,"
actually black servants in turbans, the guests made their way up the
stairs. The men were in blindingly white and bright red uniforms, their
helmets bearing gold and silver eagles. The fashion called for tight-fitting
dresses with trains, and with their bared alabaster shoulders, the ladies
looked like marble statues. Diamonds cascaded everywhere—diadems in
two rows of large diamonds on the head, diamond necklaces, rings and
bracelets on the hands. Smaller diamonds circled the neckline and fell
down the back in sparkling ropes to meet at a diamond flower attached
at the waist. The ladies-in-waiting wore a diamond-outlined monogram
of the empress or her portrait in a frame of diamonds.

At the last landing the guests saw the splendor of the formal rooms:
the Field Marshal Hall with gold portraits of military leaders, the Peter
Room with the throne, the marble thousand-meter White Hall, where
on Epiphany the guards held their parades—an entire regiment fit in
that room.

Among the glittering guests masters of ceremony silently passed, bearing ivory staffs topped with eagles, waiting for the moment. At 8:30, after three blows of the ivory staffs, to the sound of the polonaise, the turbaned Arabs opened the door of the Malachite Room. The tsar and tsaritsa and Uncle Willy and the big Romanov family made their entrance. The guests froze in the required bow. The ball began.

The emperor and the painfully fragile empress opened the ball with the polonaise. The court polonaise was not a dance in the usual sense of the word. It was a formal procession of the Romanov family with their august guest. Several chamberlains, masters of ceremony, and hofmarshals preceded them, announcing the family's walk through the formal rooms of the Winter Palace. The long line of "dancers" included the heir with Tsarevna Maria Fedorovna and the grand dukes and grand duchesses in order of seniority. The grand duchesses wore the family jewels. The stones matched the dress: Pink gowns called for rubies with diamonds, blue ones for sapphires with diamonds, but pearls and diamonds could be worn with any color.

There were not enough young grand duchesses to make up all the couples. There were noticeably more men in the Romanov family. So some of the young dukes escorted "important court ladies," who were not very young and remembered the childhood of the dukes' fathers and often fell asleep in their chairs between dances.

The only dances permitted by etiquette were the quadrille, waltz, and mazurka. The empress left immediately after the opening polonaise. The court always pitied her, knowing that she left the ball not only because she was ill. As they passed through one of the formal rooms, the members of the court surreptitiously looked up at the marble balcony. She was there, the young beauty with blond hair and cameo profile. The tsar made a point of being in that room often and would stop and unabashedly look up with a gentle smile.

The palace gossips had a name for Princess Ekaterina Dolgorukaya—Odalisque—and everyone knew who it meant.

Bismarck put up with the pageantry and got what he wanted at the negotiating table. The tsar's circle continued to shrink. Alexander II's daughter had married Queen Victoria's youngest son, the duke of Edinburgh, in 1874. In January 1873 the "family scholar," Grand Duchess Elena Pavlovna, had died. Now it was up to Kostya to torment the tsar with reminders of the great period of reforms. Every meeting with Kostya turned into a small dispute. Kostya stubbornly tried to reawaken the reformer in the tsar. A new life pulsed outside the windows of the Winter Palace, a life created by his reforms, and now Alexander seemed to be trying to freeze that life.

Kostya and Minister of War Dmitri Milyutin were the only holdovers from the reform period. At that time Milyutin wrote bitterly in his diary, "What an astonishing and distressing comparison to the atmosphere when I entered high government thirteen years ago! Then everything was surging forward; now it is dragging backward. Then the tsar sympathized with progress and moved things forward; now he has lost his faith in everything he had created, everything that surrounds him, including himself."

In 1874, Kostya could no longer be involved in the reforms. The unthinkable, improbable, and horrible had happened. His son, Nikola, the playboy of the Romanov family of playboys, turned out to be a thief.

CHAPTER II

A Hollywood Story

Alexander was head of the extended Romanov family. But he was not able to maintain the discipline his father had. His sister Masha secretly wed Count Stroganov and had children by him.

It was difficult for the emperor to be the moral guardian, since he was living quite openly with Ekaterina Dolgorukaya—and they had children, which everyone knew about. The other Romanovs followed his example. His brother Kostya, who had condemned the emperor's romantic intrigues in his diary, now lived openly with the ballerina Kuznetsova. His younger brother, Grand Duke Nikolai Nikolayevich, also lived with a ballerina. In fact, the Imperial Ballet was more like a bordello for the palace. The carriages of the young grand dukes parked on Rossi Street where the ballet school was located, to pick out their prey. Affairs with ballerinas became their norm. So at the ballet, the audiences watched the imperial box. If one of the numerous Romanovs frequented the performances of a particular young ballerina, the public drew the right conclusion.

Many of the grand dukes (and the last tsar, Nicholas II, when he was heir) traditionally began their sex lives having an affair with a ballerina. In the evenings, the crowd saw the bared body of the woman the tsar's brother caressed at night.

A sign of the dissolution of the Romanov family is the scandal that shocked the court and society, involving Grand Duke Nicholas, Nikola, the tsar's favorite nephew.

Both Alexander and Konstantin had named their firstborn sons

Nicholas in honor of their father. Both young namesakes met tragic ends. After the premature death of the heir, Niks, it was Nikola's turn.

The annual St. Petersburg masquerades were held at the Maryinsky Theater. Nocturnal revelry took place in the opulent imperial theater with its gilt, mirrors, and velvet. Masks hid identities, and the queens of society mixed with the queens of the demimonde. Nikola was a frequent and welcome guest, tall, "the ornament of the right wing," and a trend-setter for the capital's golden youth. One night a petite little cat in a Venetian mask slipped through the dancers to approach him. This was a meeting that can truly be called fateful.

Fanny Lear, an American with a dangerous fire in her French blood, was born in the New World. She was born too late: The golden age of adventure, of Casanova and Cagliostro, the eighteenth century, was over. And her place of birth was not the best milieu for her talents: provincial puritanical America. Her thirst for adventure sent her from the New World to the Old.

She quickly found a place among the charming creatures that flittered from European capital to capital, breaking hearts and acquiring fortunes. She called herself a dancer to avoid the term "courtesan," but she was a brilliant courtesan. Naturally, she ended up in the Babylon of the times, Paris.

In the early fall, the glittering ladies of the demimonde left France's stuffy capital and moved to the promising shores of the Côte d'Azur, where very wealthy Russians congregated. Here, as the poet put it, "the Russian beluga went to lay its golden caviar." The "newest Russians" (as they were called then in Russia), the newly rich merchants and manufacturers, came to the Riviera to party. The heir Niks died here; the empress with her entourage came here for her health; and here rich Russian aristocrats played and wasted their lives.

Fanny soon developed close relationships with very elderly and very rich Russians. She dubbed them the "club of the silvery aged," and they were quite unlike the cautious French. They easily spent and gambled

The Romanov heritage: Alexander I, Russian Emperor
(1801–1825), eldest son of Paul I.

The Decembrist Revolt against Nicholas I, father of Alexander II, December 15, 1825,
Senate Square, St. Petersburg.

Three views of the capital city, St. Petersburg

1. Nevsky Prospect.

2. Winter Palace.

3. Anichkov Palace.

Nicholas I with his son (the future Alexander II)
and his wife, Alexandra Fedorovna.

Alexander Nikolayevich in the Caucasus.

Vassily Andreyevich Zhukovsky, poet and
translator, tutor of Alexander II.

Alexander Nikolayevich (right) with his
father, Nicholas I (front and center).

Emperor Alexander II and Empress Maria
Alexandrovna in a photograph taken on
the 25th anniversary of their wedding.

Coronation of Emperor Alexander II,
August 26, 1856, Cathedral of the
Assumption, Moscow.

Three Views of Empress Maria Alexandrovna

1. 1840s–1850s.

2. Portrait by F. X. Winterhalter, 1857.

3. At the end of her life.

Tsarevich Nikolai Alexandrovich,
eldest son of Alexander II.

Grand Duke Konstantin Nikolayevich,
brother of Alexander II, commander of
the navy and the naval department.

Grand Duke Nikolai Konstantinovich,
during his "oriental period."

Grand Duchess Elena Pavlovna
(Frekerika-Charlotte-Maria, 1806–1873),
daughter of Prince Paul-Karl of Wurtemberg,
wife of Grand Duke Mikhail Pavlovich,
fourth son of Paul I.

Erotica from the collection of Alexander II, by Mikhail Alexandrovich Zichi
(1829–1906): The Witch and the Devil.

Family portrait: Alexander II with his children, his daughter-in-law, and his grandson, the future Emperor Nicholas II.

Alexander II in his study at the Winter Palace, St. Petersburg, 1880s.

Serene Princess Ekaterina Mikhailovna Yuryevskaya, née Ekaterina Dolgorukaya (1847–1922), Morganatic wife of Alexander II.

Prince Alexander Mikhailovich Gorchakov
(1798–1883), chancellor (1867), member of the
State Council (1862), minister of foreign affairs.

Mikhail Tarielovich Loris-Melikov (1825–1888),
count (from 1878), Russian political figure,
author of the Loris-Melikov constitution.
In the last years of the reign of Alexander II,
almost all power was in his hands.

Dmitri Alexeyevich Milyutin (1816–1912),
count (1878), military minister, liberal.

Konstantin Petrovich Pobedonostsev,
high procurator of the Holy Synod,
tutor of Alexander III.

Alexander II during the Crimean War.

Alexander II and his general staff during the Balkan War, 1878.

Fyodor Dostoyevsky, 1861.

The study of Fyodor Dostoevsky.

Alexander Herzen

Nikolai Nekrasov

Five attempts on the life of the tsar

1.May 25, 1867 (by A. Berezovsky).

2. April 2, 1879 (by A. Solovyov).

3. Bombing of the train carrying the baggage of the imperial retinue, December 1879.

4. At the Winter Palace in St. Petersburg, February 5, 1880 (by S. Khalturin).

5. March 1, 1881.

A gallery of nihilists
and terrorists.

Left to right, from top, are:
Nechaev, Kibalchich,
Karakozov, Perovskaya,
Rysakov, Zhelyabov,
Khalturin, Mikhailov,
Grivenitsky, Zasulich,
and Figner.

The fatal attempt of March 1, 1881:
Two views from contemporary sources.

The carriage of Alexander II after the explosion.

Execution of the regicides. The scaffold, April 3, 1881.
The condemned wear signs saying "regicide."

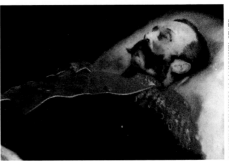

Alexander II on bier.

The end of reform: "Portrait of
Emperor Alexander III."

away entire fortunes. Fanny helped them wholeheartedly. She became entranced with the vision of the distant and equally rich northern capital. She made her way there, impelled to search for new adventures.

In St. Petersburg, Fanny Lear kept to "silvery embraces" at first. Then the queen of St. Petersburg courtesans (and of course an agent of the Third Department), the British Mabel Grey, told her about the tireless seeker of amorous escapades, Grand Duke Nikola. Fanny realized that her silver age was over and it was time for gold. A plan was set in motion. Fanny was noticed, and Nikola's adjutant was sent to her. The grand duke was soon boasting of his conquest to other rascals.

Nikola's father now usually spent the night with his dancer, and his mother lived sadly in the lavish palace in Pavlovsk. On their first night, Nikola brought Fanny to the Marble Palace, where Fanny saw the opulence of the palace in private.

They went up the marble staircase to the second floor. A servant with a candelabra lit the way. Passing through an enfilade of empty formal rooms they came to a white marble room, a thousand square meters in size, illuminated by gigantic crystal chandeliers. We can imagine her delight as she danced alone in that ballroom.

They were together all the time. Nikola's games ended unexpectedly this time: The prey turned into the hunter. When his mother was in St. Petersburg, Nikola took Fanny to Pavlovsk. The halls were decorated with formal portraits of emperors, Nikola's ancestors, the slain Peter III and the slain Paul I, and with furniture and bronzes in the style of yet another slain king, Louis XVI. During military exercises with the emperor in Krasnoe, all the young Romanovs knew and envied the fact that Fanny was there with Nikola, tucked away in his charming cottage. When they took romantic walks, as soon as she saw the tsar or some other family member, Fanny immediately went away, "protecting his reputation," but actually reveling in the knowledge of how much the other young Romanovs lusted after her gorgeous body as they watched her. She was skillfully obedient to Nikola, who was essentially a milksop who considered himself a debaucher.

He wrote an extremely naïve note that he demanded she sign: "I swear by all that is holy for me in this world, to never talk to anyone or see anyone without permission of my august Master. I promise faithfully, like an honorable American, to keep this vow and declare myself body and soul the slave of the Russian Grand Duke. Fanny Lear."

She laughed and signed. She could laugh because she knew which of them was the slave. He showed it off to his friends. But in exchange for "body and soul," Fanny asked for a trifling hundred thousand rubles and a will made out in her favor, so that she, poor thing, would have at least something of her own. The grand duke owned nothing, he lived with his parents, but she knew his allowance was a million francs a year, so he would be able to pay.

Storm clouds began gathering in their sunny skies. Nikola's father learned of the relationship—belatedly, because for some reason the Third Department had not reported it to him, even though many people knew of the connection.

Konstantin consulted with the tsar. Neither man was in a position to lecture Nikola on morality. They decided to send the "love-crazed boy" to war.

Alexander had begun the conquest of Central Asia. In his time, Prince Potemkin, lover and comrade-in-arms of Catherine the Great, had persuaded the empress to look to the south, which is how Russia got the Crimea and the Black Sea. Its temporary loss in the Crimean War was now restored, but for Alexander that was only the beginning. The cross made of mosaic pieces from Hagia Sophia in Constantinople lay in his father's grave, and he dreamed of continuing the war with Turkey. It was for this that he had introduced military reform and was creating a new army.

In the meantime, the emperor continued expansion to the south. The Caucasus was conquered, and it was time to move on to Central Asia. The khanates of Bukhara, Khiva, and Kokand were weak and ready for picking. The British considered it their region because it protected their territories in India. The tsar had to hurry. His official excuse was that Russia's militant neighbors were continually raiding the outskirts of the country. They used robbery as their livelihood, and they could not be taught to change their behavior. Therefore, they had to be conquered.

To begin with, Alexander commanded General Chernyaev to take several fortresses belonging to the emir of Bukhara. Mikhail Chernyaev was a good-looking, sturdy man with narrow Mongol eyes and a thundering voice, a favorite with the soldiers, and had been through the Crimean and Caucasus wars.

In Central Asia, the general was inventive. During the siege of Chimkent, in the deep of night, his soldiers crawled through the ancient and abandoned water channel in the fortress wall. They appeared inside the fortress in the moonlight like ghosts from underground and easily crushed the resistance, after which, Chernyaev took two thousand bayonets toward Tashkent. They moved through a sandstorm: The sand was everywhere, in their hair, their clothes, their food. The general was traveling light, with only twelve cannon, and the storm did not stop his push toward Tashkent. He found a city of one hundred thousand people with an army of thirty thousand.

The emir was furious. The British threatened international complications. Chernyaev was ordered to move swiftly. The first storming of Tashkent was unsuccessful, and the city was filled with whoops and cries of victory, music, and dance. The emir promised to display the heads of Russian officers in the square. But after a second day of fierce attack, the general's small army took the legendary city, sixty-three cannon, and large quantities of gunpowder and arms.

The general had a good sense of Asiatic psychology. The day after he took Tashkent, he rode around the city triumphantly, accompanied by only two Cossacks. That evening, he calmly went to the local steam baths, where, naked, he chatted peaceably and respectfully with naked residents, as if he were among his own people. The city understood that the Russians were there to stay. Soon after, the emir became the tsar's docile vassal.

Samarkand fell next. It was the ancient capital of the great Tamerlane, and where his black coffin with a worn golden cover lay under a seven-thousand-pound marble sarcophagus, beneath the light-blue cupola of the mausoleum.

To soothe the mighty British, the southern advance was halted in the late 1860s. Even the brave General Chernyaev, who was military governor of the region he had conquered, was recalled. But when passions had subsided in the early 1870s, Alexander unexpectedly decided to continue his incursion into Central Asia. The subjugation of the Khiva Khanate began. The entire ancient region had to be part of his empire. This was where the tsar and Kostya decided to send Nikola to fight.

Even though it was an arduous expedition, Nikola was happy, for like all the Romanovs, he adored the army. The advancing Russian troops were met with water shortages and other delights of the desert. Soldiers and officers often slept on the sand with saddles for pillows, chilled by the sudden plunge in temperatures in the night. The Khivans destroyed wells by shoveling in dirt and pollutants. People died of thirst. They found a well at last, from which the soldiers hauled a semirotted dog carcass. Nonetheless, suffering from thirst, they all drank that water. Nikola put up with all the privations easily and described their adventures in long letters to his beloved Fanny.

The Russians took Khiva. The ancient city was a real-life story from *A Thousand and One Nights*—the moon over the minarets and mosques. Long negotiations ensued. The khan, in the manner of the Orient, spoke only of tangential things; a warm-up, like tuning instruments before a concert.

Nikola and his adjutant Vernovsky planned to visit the sultan's harem, going up a rope ladder. But their escapade was stopped. The commander explained to impulsive Nikola that the harem was inviolate, as the khan had accepted Russia's protectorate and would become the faithful supervisor of his people for Russia.

The grand duke returned to St. Petersburg as a colonel with medals. The emperor gave him a captured cannon from Khiva, which was placed in the courtyard of the Marble Palace.

They decided to marry off Nikola quickly, and even bought him a small palace. He moved Fanny into it and continued his affair. His spending was getting out of control. When Nikola's mother returned to the Marble Palace from Pavlovsk, she discovered a theft, an impossible, sacrilegious theft. Precious stones, diamond rays, were dug out of the setting of her wedding icon.

The servants were suspected, and St. Petersburg city governor Trepov led the investigation. Count Peter Shuvalov, chief of the Third Department, who openly hated Grand Duke Konstantin, also took part. His investigation was exceptionally brief. On April 12, 1874, Trepov came to the Marble Palace and in great sorrow informed Konstantin of circumstances that could occur only in a nightmare.

Konstantin recorded them in his diary: "Trepov reported that the diamonds from the icon were found in a pawnshop!!!! And that they were pawned by my son's adjutant. The arrested adjutant testified that Nikola gave him the diamonds and Nikola ordered him to pawn them. . . .

"15 April, the horrible scene of Nikola's interrogation by P. A. Shuvalov and myself. No repentance. Obduracy and not a single tear.

"16 April. Nikola displays obduracy, swagger, and nonrepentance."

They arranged for Nikola and his adjutant Vernovsky to confront each other. "Vernovsky's pure-hearted testimony made it possible to reconstruct the picture." The theft was related to Nikola's expenditures on Fanny Lear. The business with the promissory note signed by Nikola was revealed then, as well.

Trepov had a frightened Fanny brought to his office. As she wrote in her memoirs, it was "a grim building where people sometimes vanished without a trace." She was ordered to leave Russia instantly after returning the promissory note for one-hundred thousand rubles. The thought of that loss emboldened Fanny. She threatened to turn to Mr. Jewel, the American ambassador, for help. But they told her that if the ambassador were to learn only a part of what she had been doing, he would not help her. So she gave up the note.

Someone informed the court of the incident. And the tsar had to tell

War Minister Dmitri Milyutin the story during their daily meeting. Milyutin wrote in his diary: "The tsar told me everything that happened; the details are outrageous. It turns out that Nikolai Konstantinovich after various filthy escapades over several years finally stooped to gouging out the icon at his mother's bedside."

Now the court anticipated the fall of Konstantin. The tsar would have to punish his nephew mercilessly for sacrilegiously attacking a holy icon, one doubly sacred for being the icon in the marriage ceremony of his own parents. How could the father who brought up his son to be a criminal take part in political life?

Alexander and Kostya came up with the only way out of a hopeless situation. From Kostya's diary: "18 April. What to do with Nikola? After long vacillation, we decided to wait for the doctor's evaluation and no matter what it says, publicly to declare him spiritually ill and lock him away. That will be enough for the public. But for Nikola, he will be locked away in strict solitary confinement with a punitive and correctional regime. Yesterday the necessary medical findings came. . . . At the end of the conference, I told myself: 'No matter how painful and hard, I can be the father of a sick and mad son, but being the father of a criminal, publicly stunned by the blow, would make my future impossible.'"

They preferred to declare Nikola mad.

Alexander and Konstantin understood who had been working backstage and who had done everything to make the scandal public instead of hushing it up. The omnipotent Shuvalov lost his position.

How was it done? We can only make suppositions. All the foreign courtesans were under surveillance by, and some actually worked for, the Third Department. Fanny was probably told to inform Nikola of the usual, banal result of an affair: She was pregnant and needed money. She needed a lot, right away, otherwise she'd have to get into the bed of some old rich man.

He asked his parents for money, and they (as Shuvalov knew they would) refused, knowing for whom it was intended. And then, infuriated, Nikola got money by using their icon in revenge. Nikola had been lured into a trap to put an end to his father.

The tsar decided to get rid of the father of the intrigue. Count Shuvalov's eight-year rule ended. The powerful "Peter IV" was removed from his post as chief of the Third Department and made ambassador to England.

But Shuvalov was only the tip of the iceberg. He left a dangerous legacy—the union he created between the retrograde party and the secret police. Shuvalov had given the tsar a chance to remove Grand Duke Konstantin, who was considered the real initiator of the "disastrous liberal direction." The tsar preferred to remove Shuvalov.

That made things worse for the tsar.

The tsar sentenced Nikola: The grand duke was sent "for treatment" thousands of miles away from the capital to Orenburg, in the Urals, stripped of all his medals and rank as colonel. Nikola continued his scandalous escapades in Orenburg. The royal prince married Nadezhda von Dreer, the local police chief's daughter. That was his revenge on the family that had betrayed him. The marriage cost him his royal title and he was sent even farther away, to Tashkent in Central Asia, where he had fought.

Nikola lived in Tashkent like a little tsar. He still received his allowance from St. Petersburg and he spent it generously. He funded numerous scientific expeditions, digging up ancient burial mounds and finding weapons and gold ornaments. He had a canal dug to irrigate part of the hungry steppe. On a cliff by the confluence of the river and the canal, he had carved a huge letter *N* topped with a crown. He built a magnificent palace in Tashkent and filled it with paintings by Russian and European artists that were purchased for him abroad. This collection formed the core of today's State Museum of Art in Tashkent.

He was not permitted to wear a military uniform, so he had a

Parisian tailor make him black suits. He continued to fall madly in love to the end of his days. He abducted a fifteen-year-old high school student and tried to marry her. The wedding ceremony was stopped by the arrival of her parents. Another woman he loved made him jealous, so he had her tied up in a sack and thrown into the canal. She was rescued in time.

With his wife still living, he married a young Cossack woman. Nikola survived the revolution and died on January 14, 1918, in the house of his new wife, peacefully, unlike most of the Romanovs. Like his uncle Alexander I and his grandfather Nicholas I, the grand duke died because he did not want to continue living after the revolution. He is buried at the Cathedral of the Transfiguration in Tashkent.

One other survivor of the Bolsheviks bears note. Her name was Natalya Androsova, and she was the most beautiful woman in post–World War II Moscow. She lived in the neighborhood called the Arbat and everyone called her the Queen of the Arbat. Every evening in a huge wooden barrel built in the Central Park of Culture and Rest, she rode her motorcycle on the inside wall, gradually rising to the very top of the sloping sides. That was her profession. She did fifteen or twenty shows a night.

"It was terrifying and beautiful, the rumble of the motorcycle, her face turned pale, her eyes widened, and her long reddish curls floated behind her, leaving a golden trail. She was a goddess, motorcycle racer and Amazon," wrote Yuri Nagibin. "All the kids from the Arbat and the lanes knew her red-and-chrome Indian Scout bike, in every heart, like a radiant image, burned her eyes, her inhumanly beautiful face, and the flying figure in a man's checked shirt of jacket, her lovely legs in breeches and leggings, tenderly squeezing the roaring, beast-like Indian Scout."

Some of our great poets—Alexander Galich, Andrei Voznesensky, and Yevgeny Yevtushenko—wrote poems about her. The beauty Natalya Androsova was the grandchild of that mad grand duke Nikolai Konstantinovich. She was the only Romanov to live on in the Soviet Union after the revolution. She was born in the Tashkent palace. Her mother was the daughter of the grand duke by his marriage to the police chief's daughter. Her father was a tsarist officer, who fled from Russia after the revolution of 1917. Her mother remarried, hiding herself and her daughter under the name of the new husband, Androsov.

When I met Natalya Androsova in the late 1980s, she was an old woman. But her sad one-room apartment was filled with photographs of her in her youth, a gorgeous woman who brought glamor and Romanov breeding to a bleak time in Moscow. She told me her story. As I was leaving, I asked, "Do you remember him?"

"Very vaguely. For some reason, his hands . . . and his kiss. I remember the palace better. I see the paintings in my dreams. And sometimes him, a clean-shaved handsome man."

She died in 1999, as if refusing to leave the century in which their dynasty was buried. I often recall her eyes, the blue eyes of the great-granddaughter of Nicholas I.

CHAPTER 12

Unprecedented in History

The second half of the nineteenth century saw the development of capitalism in autocratic Russia. But it was a thieving, crony kind of capitalism. After the death of Nicholas I, the boundless country was in last place among European countries in number of railroad lines. Energetic construction began. The emancipated serfs abandoned their tiny allotments and sought wages in the city, becoming workers. Russian capitalism had the cheapest workforce, illiterate and without rights. When Karamzin was asked to give a short definition of the Russian Empire, the writer and historian defined the county in one word: "Theft."

Enormous fortunes were made through dirty deals. The very rich Russian capitalists were called "the newest gentlemen." The poet Nekrasov wrote in 1875:

> *Money's the thing with the very new rich,*
> *Above the law, unchecked by shame.*
> *Sad are they who grabbed and lost*
> *Their claim in the million-dollar game.*
> *Russia raves about America of late:*
> *Her attraction is in earnest—real.*
> *"Our transatlantic kin," she says, "is our ideal.*
> *And their dollar is their God as well."*
> *How true! But here we must discern—*
> *The dollar bill for which you yearn*

Isn't one you simply steal—
A dollar there is one you earn.
(Translation by Anya Kucharev)

Russian capitalism strengthened the faith of the Russian radicals in the need to avoid the capitalist path. Scorn and hatred for capitalism was the unifying characteristic of the young intelligentsia. "We despised the filth of material lust, banks, concessions, we suffocated in the pollution of shares, dividends, and legalized embezzlement," wrote a young contemporary.

The Russian dream was to share fairly, that is, equally. The Russian mentality is anticapitalist. "In Russia, the interests of distribution and equalizing always prevailed over the interests of production and creativity," wrote the great philosopher Nikolai Berdyaev. The idea of a special Russian path to prosperity, to socialism, completely swayed the minds of young educated people. They wanted to go to the people, enlighten them, and rouse them for the struggle. They would bring the country to "new shores where lives the truth." From city to city and mouth to mouth, the unprecedented call traveled—to go to the people.

The young people back from abroad were in the front ranks of the powerful movement, the unprecedented collective exodus of young urbanites into the dark corners of the Russian countryside. "Nothing comparable existed before or after. It seemed as if some kind of revelation was at work. As if a mighty call coming out of nowhere had passed over the land. And everyone with a living soul responded and followed that call, imbued with longing and anger at their former lives. They left their home, wealth, honors, family, gave themselves up to the movement with the thrilled enthusiasm, with the fiery faith that knows no obstacles, measures no sacrifices, and for which suffering and doom are the most burning, insurmountable stimulus to action," wrote the young nobleman Sergei Kravchinsky. He graduated from the Mikhailov Artillery School (as had Bakunin), served a year as an officer in the provinces, retired, and went to serve the cause.

"Listen—from all parts of our enormous homeland, from the Don and the Urals, from the Volga and Dnepr, rises the call: 'To the people! To the people!,'" wrote Herzen elatedly.

The Third Department had information on the strange burgeoning movement. The new chief at the time was Adjutant General Alexander Potapov, formerly chief of staff of the Gendarmes Corps. He was totally devoted to his fired predecessor Shuvalov. He had no other qualities to speak of and was a totally useless leader. (Shuvalov had no need of power-loving men.) Potapov floundered as he read his agents' reports. There didn't seem to be an organization, yet something organized and massive was ripening. There seemed to be the need to arrest people, but it wasn't very clear whom to arrest and for what. There were no obvious ringleaders and the goals, which the agents of the Third Department had so much trouble formulating, were not clear.

And in fact, the *narodniki* (as the members of the crusade to the people, the *narod,* were called) had very different goals. Some wanted to open the people's eyes to the tsar and to the oppression in which they lived, dreaming of creating an uprising. Others simply wanted to teach people to read, to move up out the darkness and poverty; still others wanted to learn from the people, to learn their ideal of a better life.

Young girls from the best families took courses to be rural teachers, paramedics, and midwives. "Our 'plans' and 'dreams' were extremely vague," wrote the narodnik M. Tikhomirov. "We went 'to see,' 'to look around,' 'to test the waters' . . . and then? Maybe to cause a mutiny, many to propagandize. . . . But most importantly, in going to the people there was something so new, tempting, and interesting, it demanded so many minor duties that did not overburden the mind (like studying the costumes and manners of peasants, forging passports, and so on), demanded so much physical deprivation (which was satisfying morally, making everyone feel that he was performing an act of self-sacrifice). And that fulfilled a person's entire being."

But as has happened so often in Russian history, heroism immediately combined with farce and ended in blood.

To be as closely entwined with the people, some of the narodniki decided to wear peasant clothing and pretend to be the people. They falsified documents and bought used clothing, worn boots, and other items of "people's clothing." "Let's throw off our pathetic suits and change into the holy homespun coats of the people," mocked the major historian Vassily Klyuchevsky, writing at the time.

Preparations began. Sergei Kravchinsky and a friend changed into dirty coats bought from a used-clothes dealer, and headed to study the people's habits in one of the poorest inns on the edge of the capital. They reached the impoverished inn by carriage.

The customers were mostly coachmen in neat coats, and the nihilists in filthy rags looked out of place. The owner demanded that they pay in advance. "We were served boiling hot soup in a common wooden bowl with two big wooden spoons. Bits of pickled beef cheeks floated in it."

Starting on the soup, not without some revulsion, the young men tried to get the coachmen to talk about the difficult lot of the people. But the coachmen wanted to finish their meal and get back to work, so they responded curtly. The future narodniki hurried home to get rid of the stinking clothes and head to a decent inn for a good meal.

But they were undeterred and they continued preparations. They decided to learn an itinerant trade that would give them an excuse for moving around the villages, enlightening the people. At a general meeting, they voted to become cobblers. "The people don't demand fancy boot sewing—as long as it's sturdy, so we can learn it quickly."

A grim, taciturn Finn agreed to teach them the trade. He believed that if there was a revolution in Russia, his homeland would be freed as well.

The hour came and the first narodniki set out. They had copies of local maps. Dressed in rough sheepskin jackets, with knapsacks on their backs, they went out two at a time, carefully looking around for agents of the omnipotent Third Department. They reached the Nikolayevsky Station. Their friends shouted, "Bon voyage!" to the avant-garde of the great movement. The next day the friends who had seen them off would head out to the people, followed by more and more ranks of young intelligentsia. This "going to the people" began in March 1874.

The road to the people was not easy. The maps they used were inaccurate. It was only along the way that the young idealists realized that instead of using maps they needed to talk to people who knew. They recalled the proverb, "Your tongue can get you to Kiev." But once they reached their first village, the kindly peasants refused them lodgings for the night. It turned out that there were plenty of cobblers in the villages, so that they had to come up with another occupation. It was proving very difficult pretending to be of the people, that is, lying at every step. They spent most of the summer of 1874 doing casual labor. As a rule, the narodniki lost their jobs because they weren't any good at them. They hired on to plow without knowing how to harness a horse, and they were fired. They worked as fishermen, but didn't know how to set the nets, and they were fired. "But still, this was a happy time for me . . . I breathed so easily," wrote one of them. "Though we were always being caught out. I remember I found some white fleas in my shirt . . . and I mentioned to the men working with us. They almost died laughing—what fleas? Are you a fool, boy, those are lice!"

Thus the children of aristocrats met the people's most important insect. But they continued in their work, doing propaganda and agitation among the peasants. Banned literature awaited them in agreed-upon places, brought by comrades in hay wagons. It had been published by émigrés in the West and smuggled into Russia with great difficulty. Alas, their audiences were unreceptive. The peasants were illiterate. The narodniki tried to read aloud to them, but the peasants did not like that either. At best, they slept through it, at worst they denounced to the police the strange "peasants" who couldn't plow but could read. Only once did the narodnik N. Morozov see unfeigned interest on the face of a peasant as he read some antigovernment verses. The man looked quite concerned, so Morozov interrupted his reading.

"I think you want to ask me something?" he asked hopefully.

"You have good boots," the peasant said. "Where did you buy them, how much did they cost?"

Conversations among the radicals often went like this: "What are we doing here? Wasting time. You see the people . . . they've been turned into animals, even worse. Animals at least dream of freedom, but they're like seaweed. Maybe they'll wake up in a hundred years."

"Oh, no! I'm not willing to wait more than three or four years for the revolution."

Many of them decided to go back to the city and work on their dream: revolution. But some, who worked as teachers and paramedics, held on longer. Vera Figner, a gray-eyed noblewoman, had studied medicine in Lausanne. She took paramedic courses upon her return to Russia and went off to a remote village with her sister. The district authorities were stunned by her beauty and aristocratic mien.

"I soon ended up in Studentsy, a huge village. . . . Before that I knew of peasant poverty from books, magazine articles, and statistical materials. Now, I spent eighteen days a month traveling to villages. . . . I usually stayed in a hut for 'visitors,' where patients immediately appeared, 30–40 people filling the hut; they were old and young, mostly women, and even more children of all ages, who filled the air with shouts and squeals. Dirty, emaciated . . . the diseases were all chronic, all the adults had rheumatism, almost everyone had skin diseases, incurable catarrh of the stomach and intestines, chest coughs you could hear many steps away, syphilis that did not spare any age, scabs and ulcers, and all this with such unimaginable filth of housing and clothing, with food that was so unhealthful and meager, that you stop stunned at the question: is this the life of an animal or a human? Often tears rolled down my cheeks into the mixtures and drops I prepared for these wretches; and when work was over, I fell on a pile of straw on the floor for my bed; and I would give in to despair: where was the end of this poverty, truly horrifying; how hypocritical was it to give these medicines in these conditions; wasn't it ironic to speak to people completely oppressed by their physical deprivations about resistance and struggle? Were not the people in a period of their total degeneration?"

She gave up and left.

The city beckoned, and the narodniki returned. "I can't live in the country anymore, you know, I'm going crazy. Sometimes I'm so lonely I could weep. I want to talk with my kind, I want to read a book—I've become a savage. Once—can you believe this?—I wanted to speak 'our' language, and I turned to the stove and talked to it, pretending that I was having a conversation with one of us!" one narodnik wrote.

The impatient revolutionaries wanted a clash between the people they were enlightening and the government as soon as possible. They wanted a fight.

As the celebrated radical Georgi Plekhanov wrote, "The revolutionary narodnik movement was dying not from blows of the police . . . but because of the mood of those revolutionaries, who wanted at any cost to 'pay back' the government for its persecution and generally enter into 'direct combat' with it."

The government helped. The new chief of the Third Department Potapov decided to teach those young people a tough lesson. The police began putting them away, implementing Nechaev's dream. Four thousand narodniki were arrested in thirty-seven provinces. For the entire three years of the investigation, they were kept in solitary confinement. Thirty-eight went mad, forty-four died in prison, twelve by suicide.

The so-called Trial of the 193 began in October 1877. One hundred ninety-three narodniki were on trial, charged with organizing to overthrow the existing order. It was the largest political trial in the history of the Russian courts. The defense team was the best the country had to offer: V. D. Spasovich, P. A. Alexandrov, N. P. Karabchevsky, among others. Thirty-five lawyers known to all educated Russians defended the narodniki—the regime was growing less popular all the time. The defendants and their advocates seemed to vie with each other in exposing the regime.

Alexandrov said this about the prosecutors: "The history of Russian thought and liberty will recall them and as a lesson to our descendants will consign them to immortality, pilloried in shame."

More than half the defendants boycotted the trial. In their name,

Ippolit Myshkin, a narodnik, spoke to the court. It made him famous. He praised the narodniki and mocked the government (read, the tsar). The chairman of the court had to interrupt him, but Myshkin would not listen. The gendarmes were instructed to bring order and they tried to lead Myshkin from the courtroom. The other defendants began rattling the bars and cursing, the public rushed around the room, several women fainted. The chairman closed the session and the other judges followed him out. Gendarmes with drawn sabers escorted the defendants and the public out of the courtroom. The defense lawyers tried to bring round the fainted ladies with smelling salts. Prosecuting attorney V. Zhalekhovsky cried, "It's revolution!"

One hundred three defendants were sentenced to various forms of punishment, twenty-eight of them to hard labor. Ninety were acquitted. But the tsar wanted them taught a lesson, too. On his command, eighty of the acquitted were exiled.

During this persecution, the idea of "going to the people" died away. A dangerous transformation took place in the well-meaning narodniki, just as the "devil" Sergei Nechaev, serving time in the fortress, had wanted.

"The propagandist of 1872–1875 had too much idealism. A new type of revolutionary was developing, ready to take his place. On the horizon appeared a dark figure, illuminated by a hellish flame, who with proudly raised head and gaze blazing challenge and revenge made his way through the cowed crowd, in order to step with firm tread onto the arena of history. That was the terrorist!" wrote narodnik and future terrorist Sergei Kravchinsky.

In 1876, the narodniki met in St. Petersburg to discuss the results and lessons of the experience. They formed a party that later came to be called Land and Freedom, as it's usually translated, although the Russian word *volya* felicitously for this context means both liberty and will. It was named for Chernyshevsky's underground society. Rakhmetov's followers did not forget their idol.

The bylaws of Land and Freedom contained the favorite ideas of the Russian radicals: All land must be given to the peasants, tsarism must be destroyed, Russia must move toward socialism in its own way, bypassing capitalism, through the native commune, the *obshchina*. But there was something totally new in the bylaws as well: the right to political assassination. It was limited at that point to political murder in "special circumstances," as an act of vengeance for injustice or as a response in self-defense.

All the key narodniki became members of the organization, Kravchinsky, Figner, Morozov, and Tikhomirov among them—all future major terrorists.

They held a demonstration on December 6, 1876, in front of the Kazan Cathedral where the tsar had prayed ten years earlier after the assassination attempt on him. At the tsar's favorite church, the demonstrators flew the red flag for the first time. The police broke up the demonstration and arrested two dozen members, none of them ringleaders.

The central figure arrested was a rank-and-file Land and Freedom member, A. Emelyanov, who was tried under his revolutionary alias Bogolyubov. He would soon enter Russian history.

Thus the tsar took another big step toward the Catherine Canal. He had to have sensed that the times were troubled. He began reacting in unfocused ways. He replaced Potapov with Adjutant General Mezentsov. The new chief of the Third Department lacked initiative and was on the lazy side, just like Potapov. Mezentsov was dubbed "Sleepy Tiger."

So Alexander resorted to the time-honored way out of social conflict: a popular war.

Alexander's military reforms had transformed the army. The navy now had steam-powered ships. Russia was ready for conflict—and Turkey generously provided an excuse for war. In 1875, Bosnia and Herzegovina revolted, exhausted by Turkish oppression. The response was ruthless slaughter. The Slavs were killed brutally, the women raped, infants impaled on stakes, villages burned, heads chopped off. Outrage over Turkish atrocities spread through the Russian public.

In 1876 the Serbian prince Milan Obrenovic started an uprising and Serbia declared war on Turkey. It was a unique event in the history of the Ottoman Empire for a vassal principality to declare war on its sovereign state. The Montenegrins joined Prince Milan, and the Slavs in Bulgaria rose up as well.

In both Russian capitals, Moscow and St. Petersburg, demonstrators called for aid to their brother Slavs. The public demanded war, and even the nihilists in their underground proclamations called for war and accused the government of betraying their brothers.

Alexander saw that he could become one with the public once again. A victorious war would unite the country. The great idealism that led young people to the countryside could find an outlet in this war.

"The great eastern eagle has soared above the world. Not to conquer or expand its borders, but to free and restore the oppressed and down-trodden, to give them a life for the good of mankind . . . and this Europe does not want to believe," wrote Dostoevsky at the time.

Alexander's ministers were against the war. The minister of finance told the tsar that Russia's economy, shaken by the reforms, could not afford it. The war minister was against it because his military reforms were not completed. The minister of foreign affairs, the hypercautious Gorchakov, spoke of the inevitable conflict with the West if Russia won and of the possibility of Britain aiding the Turks.

The tsar allowed Gorchakov the opportunity to seek a compromise. There were conferences of European ambassadors in London and in Istanbul. The ambassadors demanded that the sultan put an end to the atrocities and immediately implement reforms in the Slavic provinces. But as the tsar had expected, England played a double game. Prime Minister Disraeli secretly supported Porte and advised the Turks to be intransigent. Porte proudly rejected the ambassadors' demands. Thus, Disraeli advanced the war the tsar wanted.

Still, Britain had to be appeased. Through his daughter, the duchess of Edinburgh, Alexander informed Queen Victoria: "We cannot and do not wish to quarrel with England. On our part it would be madness to think of Constantinople and of India." All they wanted was to defend their fellow Slavs.

He was truthful about India, less so Constantinople. It was the age-old dream of the Russian tsars, not only to free Slavic nations from the Turks but to create a great Slavic empire. The many Romanovs named Konstantin were a reminder of that dream. The cross with the mosaics from the city's great cathedral lay in his father's coffin.

Alexander decided to fight. But for the time being he pretended to join his ministers in opposing the war. As usual, he wanted to pretend to be persuaded to make the predetermined decision. Milyutin, the war minister, recorded the tsar's antiwar speeches. "I have no less sympathy for the wretched Christians of Turkey than anyone else, but I hold higher the interests of our country. We cannot be drawn into a European war." The tsar added a phrase that the war minister set down in his diary, showing that he understood the secret message: "But if we are forced to fight, we will fight."

In the fall of 1876, the tsar convened his ministers in Livadia. They listened in surprise to the determined speech of the heir, who called on them to start the war. Under previous tsars, the heirs were silent. Elizabeth, Catherine II, Paul I, Alexander I, and certainly Nicholas I were not interested in the opinion of their heirs. Even "bulldog" Sasha, who took part in all the meetings of the Committee of Ministers and the State Council, always held his tongue. Yet now he spoke out decisively. Alexander reprimanded him with surprising mildness, and did not fail to mention that the empress felt the same way as the tsarevich, and so did the public. Therefore he would probably have to accede, against his wishes.

The ministers finally understood: It was war.

The tsar used the eastern tactic of plausible deniability. The old warhorse general Chernyaev appeared in Serbia and formed the Serbian home guards ("naturally, totally unexpectedly for St. Petersburg and of his own doing," was how the emperor explained it). The tsar ordered his ambassadors to declare that public opinion did not allow him to control

the flow of Russian volunteers to the Balkans and that he must permit
his officers to resign their commissions and go to Serbia.

It was then that War Minister Milyutin became certain "that the tsar
is acting dually."

Volunteer committees sprang up all over the country, as did collec-
tions for the suffering Slavs. In St. Petersburg, volunteer fighters were
seen off to war in nightclubs with gypsy dancing and vodka. Bands
played at the train stations, and lovely girls waved good-bye to the
heroes. Idealists and patriots, adventurers, failures in business or love, or
simply madmen who, as Tolstoy wrote, would "join Pugachev's gang or
go to Khiva or to Serbia," went to war. In Tolstoy's novel *Anna Karenina,*
the hero Vronsky, crushed by Anna's suicide, resigns from the army and
goes to fight in Serbia. Many of the narodniki went to shed their blood
for their fellow Slavs.

Thirty-five hundred Russian volunteers crossed the border. Seven
hundred Russian officers and two thousand soldiers joined Chernyaev's
home guard.

Dostoevsky, who was in favor of the war, received a letter. "And now
the false divide between the people and the intelligentsia is over. . . .
Amidst the preparations for war to free our brother Slavs, the holy sacra-
ment of conciliation took place." His correspondent was a young
woman, the narodnik Alexandra Korba, who would later participate in
assassination attempts on the tsar. She wrote as she headed for Serbia to
be a nurse.

The Turks were very strong, and General Chernyaev's troops were
beaten. Now the tsar had to step in; Minister Milyutin noted "the tsar's
impatience to take up arms" in his diary.

On April 12, 1877, Alexander declared war on the Ottoman Empire.
The country was elated. When he came to the Kremlin to the Cathedral
of the Assumption, Moscow's main streets were filled with roaring
crowds shouting huzzahs and ovations. On Cathedral Square people
applauded hysterically and wept on one another's shoulders. It was the
second and last honeymoon for the tsar and his people. Alexander
should have remembered how quickly popular love fades.

In a crowd-pleasing move, Alexander went to war himself. He acted as his uncle, Alexander I, had done against Bonaparte. The tsar was to be judge and arbiter, but not commander-in-chief. The responsibility for military action and for bloodshed must be borne by another. The tsar had to be blameless.

At the front he would visit hospitals, participate in discussions of operations, and settle disputes. He made Grand Duke Nikolai Nikolayevich commander of the two-hundred-thousand-strong Danube Army.

"The men in the dynasty were all tall, six feet. But he was six foot five inches without his boots, so all the tall Romanovs and the tsar himself seemed much shorter," wrote his nephew Grand Duke Alexander Mikhailovich. The gigantic Nikolai Nikolayevich was warlike. "Even at the table he sat tall, as if he expected them to play the national anthem at any moment."

Kostya was in charge of the navy. Another brother, Misha (Grand Duke Mikhail Nikolayevich, the governor general of the Caucasus), was in charge of the Caucasus Army. The heir and his younger brother commanded army units. Nikolai and Yevgeny Leichtenberg were given cavalry brigades.

All the military leaders were Romanovs. That was the tsar's way: Without officially taking part in the management of the army, he could get his decisions implemented through them.

Foreign correspondents covering the tsar's army poked fun at the arrival of his entourage and the general staff. Numerous train cars unloaded magnificent horses and carriages with stately coachmen who looked like generals. The breeze ruffled the peacock plumes on the horses' bridles.

The army officers regarded this splendor bleakly, for they knew that some of these fancily dressed gentlemen would never return to Russia. No one in the army doubted that the war would be bloody; the Turks had an excellent army trained by outstanding European instructors.

The Russian plan was to conclude the war in a few months so that Europe would not have time to interfere. The campaign began successfully, and the emperor's troops easily crossed the Danube, with the Turks retreating. The tsar sent an envoy to the Bulgarian people: "Bulgarians, my troops have crossed the Danube, where they have already fought more than once to ease the misery of the Christians of the Balkan Peninsula. Russia's goal is to build, not to destroy. She is called by Providence to reconcile and pacify all peoples and all confessions in those parts of Bulgaria where people of various ethnicity and various faiths coexist."

General Gurko's units went ahead. Gurko was supposed to take Shipka Pass, which led to southern Bulgaria and the road to Istanbul. A ferocious battle in the foothills ensued, in which General Gurko learned a lesson about fighting wily Asiatic armies. The Turks sent a man with a white flag to meet two of Gurko's advancing artillery battalions. The Russians believed that the Turks were giving up and came close to the Turkish positions. They were met with a squall of fire that brought down 140 soldiers. The battalions retreated, leaving behind dead and wounded.

But soon afterward the tsar was reading a telegram with good news: "Shipka, attacked from north and south, abandoned by Turks, leaving cannon, banners, and camp." The Russians saw the way the barbarous East fought: Arms, noses, and ears were cut off the dead, in some cases, even their heads. Gurko's army continued into the mountains and took Shipka Pass. The road to Bulgaria and Istanbul was open.

The Russian troops and Bulgarian volunteers went down into the Valley of Roses, met by elated residents. It proved to be the end of Gurko's advance. Suleiman-pasha's army of 20,000 met the general and chased him back to Shipka Pass. The main Russian army (the Danube Army) could not move forward. The Russian army's flank faced the fort at Plevna, where Osman-pasha stood with a garrison of 15,000 men. Alexander could not leave this constant threat of a strike from the flank.

He decided to attack Plevna and take the fort. The first attack failed, with 3,000 Russian soldiers dead. Better preparations were made for the second storm, by both the Russians and Osman-pasha. The latter brought in reinforcements, so 24,000 Turks now defended the fort. In a short time Osman-pasha had turned Plevna into an impregnable site, surrounded by fortifications and redoubts. The second storm was also repulsed, with another 7,000 Russian bodies at the walls of Plevna.

The guards were sent to the Balkans from St. Petersburg.

The war was dragging on. Grand Duke Mikhail was unsuccessful on the Caucasus front.

By the time of the third storm of Plevna, there were 34,000 Turks in the garrison. Both sides understood that the outcome of the war could be decided there.

Grand Duke Nikolai Nikolayevich began the decisive third storm on August 30, St. Alexander's feast, the tsar's saint's day. The Russian troops numbered 50,000, joined by 32,000 Romanians. Alexander, who had seen enough of Nikolai Nikolayevich's military leadership, suggested that he turn over the general command of the storm to Romanian king Carol I.

Alexander watched from a high vantage point through a scope as the little figures ran forward. Things were going well. The Romanians advanced from the east and took the Grivits redoubts. On his white horse and in his white uniform (he was called the White General), General Skobelev led the attack that followed. His troops were met with punitive fire, but he captured the two redoubts protecting the city. The way to the fort was open. Osman-pasha threw his last reserves into the fray. The fighting at the gates of Plevna was fierce. It was Grand Duke Nikolai Nikolayevich who doomed the Russians to failure: At the decisive moment he didn't send in the reserves (even though less than half the Russian battalions were in the battle).

Skobelev's troops had to abandon what they had conquered, and the Turks won back the redoubts. Twelve thousand Russian soldiers and 4,000 Romanians fell in the battle. The Turks lost only 3,000 men. It was the bloodiest battle of all the Russo-Turkish wars.

Now Alexander feared that Providence "was giving him a second Sevastopol." He feared a catastrophic loss like his father's. It didn't stop him from writing to Katya every day.

Suleiman-pasha's troops were ordered to break through to help Plevna. They had to take the Shipka Pass, which was being guarded by the Orlov Regiment and 5,000 Bulgarians. Suleiman-pasha concentrated 25,000 men against them.

The defenders were suffering from the terrible heat and lack of food, but they continued to hold the pass. On August 9, the Turks went on a decisive attack that launched a famous six-day battle. The Turks attacked the strongest part of the Russian positions at the Eagle's Nest cliff. Out of ammunition, the defenders fought off the Turks climbing toward them with rocks and rifle stocks. General Radetsky led his men into hand-to-hand combat.

After three days of fighting, Suleiman-pasha prepared to finish off the last handful of resisting heroes by the evening of August 11, but help arrived. General Dragomirov had brought 12,000 soldiers in quick march, 70 kilometers a day in the heat. They attacked the Turks and pushed them back from the pass. After six days, the pass was still in Russian hands, with 4,000 dead Russians and Bulgarians.

Snow blanketed the pass and temperatures plummeted. It was in this period that the Russians suffered their greatest losses—not from bullets, but from the cold. The pervasive theft and corruption in the army were partly to blame—they did not have warm clothing. Hundreds died in battle, thousands died from illness and frostbite.

Winter was coming to the plains as well. Alexander's army was facing two choices. One was to retreat over the Danube and winter there. That was proposed by commander Grand Duke Nikolai Nikolayevich. It would mean stopping the siege of Plevna, leaving the Shipka Pass, giving back everything paid for by the blood of his soldiers. The other choice was to continue the siege of Plevna and try to finish off the enemy. That was very risky, after all their failures.

Alexander wrote Katya an anguished letter: "Oh, God, come to aid us and end this damned war in Russia's glory and the benefit of Christians. That is the cry of my heart, which belongs to you . . . my idol, my treasure, my life!"

———

The next morning he went to the hospital to visit the men. He saw his wounded adjutant and a Hussar colonel dying in the next bed. A shell had torn off his leg, which had been amputated and lay by the bed in a blood-filled basin.

The adjutant was horrified by the way Alexander looked. The lady-in-waiting Tolstaya would write about it later: "A hearty man left for war, and a worn-out old man returned. His hands had gotten so thin that the rings fell from his fingers."

He suffered from asthma and he was continually ill with something like dysentery. It was all from nerves. But as ever, when it came to the final moment, this deceptively indecisive man turned to steel. Alexander made the difficult decision to continue the siege of Plevna and to take it. It meant thousands more dead. He did not want to be the one to rescind the commander-in-chief's order, so he pretended to be vacillating. Apparently he commanded his war minister to play the usual game. At a staff meeting, Milyutin dared to attack Grand Duke Nikolai Niko-layevich's decision. He said that leaving Plevna would cause irreparable harm to the army's prestige and he spoke of all the blood already shed by Russian soldiers.

The infuriated grand duke suggested the minister take charge.

Now the tsar could be the arbiter. He tried not to hurt anyone's feelings. He supported the minister's suggestion but asked the grand duke to remain in charge. But to help him (on the minister's advice) he brought in the military engineer General Totleben, who became famous in the defense of Sevastopol. The "help" expected from him was to run the siege of Plevna.

Totleben rejected new attacks. He wanted a total blockade of the fort first. That meant cutting off the road that brought supplies to the garrison. There were Turkish redoubts defending the road, but a Russian army of 20,000 people, headed by the brave General Gurko, conquered them. Plevna was now in a blockade. By mid-November 100,000 troops attacked the fort, where food had run out. When Osman-pasha tried to escape from doomed Plevna, the Russians forced him back inside. Six thousand Turks died that day in the bloody field of Plevna. Osman-pasha, with the tatters of his 40,000-man army, surrendered.

Osman-pasha stood before the tsar and offered him his sword. Alexander thought of the mutilated bodies, the prisoners who were killed, and the 32,000 Russian dead in battle at Plevna. Alexander showed him how a knight behaves, as he had once done with Shamil. He took the sword, held it, and then returned it to Osman-pasha, who had expected to be executed. He said it was "a sign of respect for the warrior's courage."

A thanksgiving service was held in the captive fort. To keep up the morale of his younger brother, Alexander awarded Nikolai Nikolayevich the St. George Cross.

The road to Istanbul was clear. Joy, like trouble, does not come in ones. General Loris-Melikov came to help brother Mikhail on the Caucasus front. The "splendid Armenian," as he was known, stormed the Turkish forts of Ardagan and Kars and then Erzerum.

Great victories had come. Blizzards had come to the mountains by then. But waist-deep in snow, Russian soldiers fought off Turkish units in the mountain passes and came down from the Balkans. On December 23, without a battle, they took Sofia, the capital of Bulgaria.

As Count P. A. Valuyev wrote in his diary, "The political horizon is getting dark seeing our victories." Britain's diplomacy got tougher, which invigorated Turkey. In order to halt the advance of Russian troops and win time (in hopes that Britain would enter the war), the Turks offered to start negotiation of a truce. Instead, Russian troops marched toward Istanbul. The great dream of Constantinople was coming true.

The Russian army moved through abandoned regions. The populace, frightened by tales of vengeful Slavs, fled in panic. Roads were filled with carts and wagons. The wretches made their way pushing their pathetic belongings, some dying in the crush or run over by carriages of the wealthy. The sides of the roads were littered with corpses of people and horses and overturned wagons.

General Skobelev's unit was moving swiftly toward Adrianople, Turkey's second capital. They fought for and won Turkish positions, bridges, and railroad stations. Along the way, Skobelev routed the troops of Egyptian prince Hassan, who came to protect Adrianople. He captured a big wagon train and a hundred camels. Skobelev handed out the camels among the regiments. Soon Russian soldiers were riding them, and the camels quickly learned to respond to Russian swear words.

On January 8, Skobelev took Adrianople without a battle. Nine days later he was within 80 kilometers of Istanbul. The Turkish government asked for a truce. On January 19 it was signed in Adrianople, where the staff headquarters of the Danube Army were moved. Military actions had ceased, yet Russian troops kept marching toward Istanbul. General Skobelev came closest, taking the town of San Stefano and reaching the shores of the Aegean Sea. Now the White General was only 12 kilometers from the capital of Turkey and the great capital of Ancient Byzantium.

This was the key moment in the war—the Russians were at the walls of Istanbul, or Tsarygrad as it was called in ancient Russia. The proud formula was devised in the sixteenth century: "Moscow was the Third Rome. The first, the Rome of the Caesars, had perished. Then came Byzantium, the heir of the first Rome. It perished, too. Moscow, the Russian kingdom, was the third and last Rome. There would be no fourth Rome." Orthodox Christianity had come to Russia from Byzantium. Now Russia would liberate the cradle of Orthodoxy, the Second Rome.

"Constantinople sooner or later must be ours!" vowed Dostoevsky (*Diary of a Writer*, 1877). Many Russians believed that the chance to take Constantinople was a gift from God. It was a personal dream of Alexander's. It would have been the triumphant conclusion of his work—the serfs were freed of slavery and now the cradle of Orthodoxy would be freed of Muslim slavery. He would be the true Emancipator.

Great-power politics intervened. Britain threatened war if the Russian army took Istanbul. To make its position clear, the British government sent a fleet to the Dardanelles and the sultan allowed them to enter the Sea of Marmara. Simultaneously, the main naval forces began gathering near Malta. Queen Victoria declared that "she would sooner abdicate than allow the Russians to enter Istanbul."

The entire Russian army demanded to free the city sacred to Russians. Grand Duke Nikolai Nikolayevich and all the generals begged to take Constantinople, maintaining that England's threats were empty, that England preferred fighting with cat's paws, and that there was no one there willing to start a war with Russia. But old Gorchakov felt differently. England would start a war because Russia was exhausted by the Crimean War. Others would join London—first and foremost, Austria. Gorchakov implored the tsar to stop and not take the dangerous capital.

Alexander understood that Gorchakov was right. When it came to decisive moments, England fought with its own hands. The valor of its soldiers was seen by Napoleon at Waterloo and by Alexander's father in the Crimea.

Gorchakov's most vociferous opponent was the heir, who had fought alongside his father. For the first time Sasha was truly independent, for the first time he dared to insist even against his father's wishes. As is the case with busy parents, Alexander suddenly realized that his son was in his thirties and was approaching the age at which he himself had begun his reign.

The emperor knew that the retrogrades had been grouping around his son. Muravyev, who had suppressed the Polish uprising (and whom Alexander called on when there was dirty work to be done), had a powerful influence on the heir. Sasha enjoyed his anti-West speeches. Fortunately, the Hangman died before long. Alexander also knew that the heir openly longed for the good old days of serfdom. He knew how easily his stubborn Sasha fell sway to outside influences. And he knew that his main advisor now was his own former tutor, Konstantin Pobedonostsev, now inseparable from the heir.

Pobedonostsev would have a major influence on Russian history. The son of a university professor and himself a professor of law, Pobedonostsev was an enthusiastic participant in judicial reform and one of the cre-

ators of the Law Regulations of 1864. But the events that followed—
fires, proclamation, student riots, and the assassination attempt on the
tsar—changed him completely. "The fear is gone and that is why Russia
is perishing," Nikitenko noted in his diary, and this was Pobedonostsev's
basic thought as well. The former reformer became an implacable foe of
reform. The man's energy and erudition were focused on suppressing
everything new.

Alexander was weary of war. The specter of more blood, on a European
scale, frightened him. He did not have the strength for a new war, and
the country did not have the funds. He told the heir that peace would be
made because that was his decision. "This is what I command, this is
what I want." Sasha obeyed.

To keep face, the emperor commanded: If the British land at Constantinople, take the city immediately, but if the Turks offer a beneficial
treaty, immediately conclude it. He knew that the British would not
land and that the Turks would offer peace, which they did. Now he
could return to St. Petersburg.

He could not be without Katya anymore. No wonder the wise old
men of the East took young beauties to their beds. She was his life, and
her youth gave him strength. He left, to the great relief of the entourage
that had accompanied him.

The small town of San Stefano, so near Constantinople/Istanbul, was
the site of the treaty signing. The town's quiet life was disrupted by the
appearance of VIPs, military and civilian, soon followed by actors and
singers with a multilingual repertoire. Fancy carriages drove through its
streets. In a short period, San Stefano turned into a miniature Paris.

The Treaty of San Stefano was signed on March 3, 1878. Serbia, Montenegro, and Romania became independent states. Prince Milan's
dynasty, the Obrenovic, took power in Serbia. Bosnia and Herzegovina
received autonomy. Bulgaria, after five centuries of Turkish rule, became
an autonomous state, though it had to pay a tribute to Turkey. The Russian Empire was paid an indemnity of 310 million rubles and received

the southern part of Bessarabia, lost during the Crimean War, and the forts of Ardagan, Kars, Batum, and Bayazet in the Caucasus.

The Treaty of San Stefano infuriated Britain and Austria. Devious Bismarck offered to reconcile everyone. A congress of the great European powers was convened in Berlin.

Chancellor Gorchakov went to Berlin. The old hound wanted to show his master that he still had strong teeth. It ended catastrophically. Gorchakov was ill, and on the opening day, the eighty-year-old minister was carried in to the ceremonies in a chair. Fate played a mean trick on the weak prince. He had brought a secret map with him that showed the maximum concessions that were acceptable if the enemies united against Russia. Confused and ill, he inadvertently showed the secret map to British prime minister Disraeli, who instantly understood the situation. Britain and Austria-Hungary made no concessions. Then Bismarck, unhappily, demanded that his Russian friends accept that bad map. The Treaty of Berlin was signed.

The result left only the north of Bulgaria autonomous. The Bulgarian principality was divided by a third. Of the acquisitions received in the San Stefano treaty, Russia returned Bayazet. Austria, which had not fought in the war, received Bosnia and Herzegovina to administer until order was restored. (In the early twentieth century Austria would establish order by annexing the territories.) Serbia's territorial acquisitions were reduced.

After the Congress of Berlin, Minister Gorchakov wrote to Alexander: "This is the blackest page in my biography."

"Mine, too," replied Alexander to the old minister.

Even though the war gave independence to Slavic states and to Greece, even though he had achieved (albeit not completely) his father's dreams, even though he had gotten back the land lost in the Paris Peace (except for the mouth of the Danube), no one acknowledged it. Everyone seemed to forget what he had done and mentioned only what was lost. People in Moscow were particularly bitter about the results of the war. The ones who called themselves Slavophiles had pictured Russia at the head of the emancipated Slavic people with the Orthodox cross and

Russian flag over Constantinople. Better there had been no victory march on Istanbul, better none of the achievements of San Stefano, no dashed hopes.

Protests and speeches started again. Ivan Sergeyevich Aksakov, son and brother of equally famous Slavophiles, and leader of Moscow's Slavophiles (who married Anna Tyutcheva, the lady-in-waiting), spoke at a meeting of the Slavic Committee.

> Is this you, Russia the Conqueror, who voluntarily demoted herself to vanquished? Barely containing their laughter, the Western powers are brazenly stripping you of your laurels of victory and offering you instead a fool's cap with bells, while you obediently, almost with an expression of sincere gratitude, bow your long-suffering head under it. If just reading the papers makes your blood boil, what must the Tsar of Russia feel, bearing responsibility for the country before History? Did he not call our war 'holy'? . . . Russia does not want war, but even less does it want a shameful peace. Ask any Russian in the street if he would not prefer to struggle to the end of his blood and strength! The duty of loyal subjects orders everyone to hope and believe—and the duty of loyal subjects orders us not to be silent in these days of illegality and lies that erect a barrier between tsar and country, between the tsar's thoughts and the country, between the tsar's thoughts and the people's thinking.

The tsar, irritated by the ingratitude, ordered the committee shut down and its Cicero exiled from Moscow to the countryside. When the governor general of Moscow reported that the "enfant terrible is being quiet," the tsar permitted Aksakov to return.

But it was not only the voice of the Slavophiles, it was the voice of the public. The war that was supposed to unite the country brought instead another disillusionment in the tsar. Simultaneously, there was an economic downturn, typical of wartime, and the ruble fell 40 percent on world markets.

The war provoked the attack both of retrogrades unhappy with its result and with reformers and liberals unhappy with its result and the lack of reforms.

One of the leaders of the retrograde party, Prince Meshchersky, wrote: "If not for this sad result of the war, the anarchist movements would have remained a chronic illness in Russia's mental life and would not have found the soil to move into an acute condition and to a daring attack on state order."

The Berlin Treaty was a powder keg for Russia. Tragic events followed quickly.

They began in circumstances that seemed ordinary for the times. Alexander preferred to have people in his service who resembled the yesmen of his father's day. Adjutant General Fedor Fedorovich Trepov, the city governor of St. Petersburg, was such a man. The tsar knew that Trepov was not liked in society. But he also knew that whomever he appointed became disliked automatically. Alexander noted irritably that whatever he did was wrong now.

Trepov, the same age as Alexander, sixty, was of the old school. On a summer day, July 13, 1877, Trepov arrived at 10:00 A.M. on business in the House of Preliminary Detention on Shpalernaya Street. He found three prisoners walking together in the courtyard.

One of them was Bogolyubov, a member of Land and Freedom arrested for demonstrating at the Kazan Cathedral and sentenced to fifteen years of hard labor. Bogolyubov was awaiting deportation to hard labor.

The rest was banal. Trepov was in a bad mood, and he didn't like the way Bogolyubov spoke to him and didn't take off his hat. The city governor vented his anger in the usual way: "Into the isolation cell with him! Take off that hat!" and he flung out his arm to knock the prisoner's hat off his head. Bogolyubov, thinking that the general wanted to hit him, jumped aside. The hat fell off, but Bogolyubov lost his balance and almost fell. The scene was observed by the inmates through the windows, almost all of them political prisoners. They thought that Trepov had struck Bogolyubov. The prisoners were young and free of the fear of

Nicholas's day. Moreover, they were thirsting to show their attitude toward the regime.

They flung curses and everything that fit through the bars at Trepov: mugs, books, toothbrushes. Completely infuriated, Trepov ordered Bogolyubov to be whipped. Thinking the incident finished, Trepov left.

But it was only the beginning. The guards hated the political prisoners. So, to tease them, they made a show of slowly dragging the rods across the courtyard to the isolation cell where Bogolyubov was taken. The political prisoners were a nervous lot, and some of the women went into hysterics. The inmates shouted curses at the regime and threatened to riot. Things were heating up. The incident had to be reported to Minister of Justice Count Palen.

Palen was cut from the same cloth as Trepov, and he declared that the city governor had acted properly. "If disturbances begin, we'll send firefighters to douse them with cold water, and if the disturbances continue, we'll shoot at the whole lot of that trash."

There were no disturbances, and once again, the incident seemed to be over. But the government had not understood that these were different times: The new era of glasnost did not suit the actions of the yesmen. The newspapers learned all the details of the incident. The journalists were not distinguished by sympathy for the city governor, and their articles reflected that.

On January 28, 1878, Trepov was receiving petitions in his office. One of the petitioners was a young woman of medium height, with a long, colorless, and somehow unhealthy face, and smooth, pulled-back hair. She was wearing a gray hooded cloak with incongruous festoons along the hem. She held her petition in one hand, and the other was under the cloak. She offered the petition to Trepov, only to fling open the cloak and shoot at him with a revolver.

She was nervous. The shot was wild. "The prisoner wounded Adjutant-General Trepov in the nether pelvis with a large-caliber bullet," as one report put it. In other words, she got him in the buttock.

She did not flee and permitted herself to be detained. A witness said, "She sat on a chair, staring at the ceiling nearsightedly with her gray eyes

and indifferently responded to the investigator's questions." She stated
that she had never met Trepov before. She shot at him because she had
read newspaper accounts of his brutal treatment of the helpless prisoner.
"It was very difficult to raise your hand against a person, but my conscience forced me."

In the next room, they were having trouble removing the bullet from
the city governor's rear end. The tsar saw it all, for he had come to visit
the wounded Trepov.

Alexander was recently back from the front and had not yet recovered
from the war. Going up the stairs, he "stopped on almost every step,
breathing hard," recalled the celebrated lawyer Anatoly Koni, chairman of
the St. Petersburg District Court. Koni was a liberal. There were still a few
liberals, reminders of past reforms, working with hardliner retrogrades.

Vera Zasulich was the name of the twenty-eight-year-old woman
who had shot at Trepov. Her story was typical. Born to an aristocratic
family (as were most of the revolutionaries then), she graduated from a
German-French boarding school in Moscow, where she came in contact
with the ideas of the narodniki. At seventeen, she decided to devote her
life to the revolution. She moved to St. Petersburg, where she worked in
a bindery, to be with the laborers, and she taught in a factory school.
During the student riots of 1869 she met Nechaev, who failed to get
Zasulich into his organization. But she ended up in the Fortress of Peter
and Paul for dealing with him. That was followed by exile and a transition to an unlawful situation. When she read the newspaper accounts of
the treatment of narodnik Bogolyubov, she began planning her assassination of Trepov.

As was later learned, Zasulich's shot was supposed to have a continuation. There was to have been a public vengeance against another perse-
cutor of the narodniki, prosecutor V. Zhelekhovsky (a comrade of the
Senate's high prosecutor).

He had prosecuted the Trial of 193. While Zasulich headed off to
shoot Trepov, her friend Maria Kolenkina, armed with the same kind of

revolver, went off to execute Zhelekhovsky. It was a coordinated terrorist act. Both women flowed from the wellsprings of the future Great Terror.

While Zasulich sat in Trepov's waiting room, Kolenkina rang the doorbell to Zhelekhovsky's apartment. A servant opened the door and she asked him to call the prosecutor. Zhelekhovsky's wife and children appeared in the entry, and she realized that she would have to shoot him in their presence. Kolenkina silently turned and left. The terrorists had not yet learned to kill in the presence of children.

Trepov was very lucky, too, that Zasulich's hand had shaken. At the time, many young men who did know how to shoot were planning to kill him. "Trepov's vicious act with Bogolyubov was the final drop that made the cup of bitterness overflow, in my heart and in the hearts of my comrades," wrote narodnik Nikolai Morozov, subsequently a bold terrorist. He had been preparing to kill Trepov. So was narodnik Alexander Barannikov, who had studied in a military school. An entire group of narodniki led by Mikhail Frolenko was also preparing an attack.

None of these people would have missed. They were soon to become heroes of Russian Terrorism. Zasulich's shot saved the city governor's life.

The case was very clear to the tsar, especially since Zasulich denied nothing. It was clear what a jury would decide. There was no point in passing the case to the Special Chamber of the Senate. On the contrary, Alexander wanted the would-be assassin and nihilist to be condemned publicly.

Zasulich's trial was to start on March 31 in the St. Petersburg District Court, in an open hearing. Anatoly Koni, chairman of the court, was to hear the case. Justice Minister Count Palen invited Koni to see him before the trial. He warned him, "In this case, the government has the right to expect special favors from the court and from you."

The liberal lawyer replied with dignity, "Permit me to remind you of the words of the French jurist addressed to the king who had also asked him for a favor: 'Your Majesty, the court does not perform favors, the court renders verdicts.'"

Palen had his reasons for asking Koni to help. The case, which had seemed so clear-cut, was producing anxiety. All the celebrated prosecutors turned down the state's offer to prosecute Vera Zasulich. In the end, K. I. Kessel, a mediocre lawyer and friend of the prosecutor general, agreed to do it. The legal stars all wanted to defend Zasulich, for it promised to be a case that would bring national fame (as had the Trial of 193). It was more fashionable than ever to be antiestablishment.

Petr Alexandrov, the brilliant orator who had defended the narodniki in the Trial of 193, took Vera Zasulich's case.

The date was March 31, 1878. Anatoly Koni recalled that he had not slept the night before. Huge crowds gathered outside the courthouse on Liteiny and on Shpalernaya, including many students. Long lines of police and gendarmes formed around the entrance to the court and at the gates of the House of Preliminary Detention nearby.

The courtroom was standing room only, filled with people from high society. In the VIP chairs behind the judges were the chancellor himself, Prince Gorchakov, State Comptroller Count D. M. Solsky, deputy head of artillery Count A. A. Barantsov, chairman of the Economics Department of the State Council A. A. Abaza, former governor general of St. Petersburg Prince A. A. Suvorov, and other members of the State Council. In the first row sat Minister of War Count D. A. Milyutin and generals and officers. In the press seats were Fedor Dostoevsky and the cream of Russian journalists.

Alexandrov used his right to veto jurors wisely and ended up with a jury with a predominance of midlevel and minor officials, the liberal part of the bureaucracy. Addressing them, Alexandrov expressed ideas that were surprising in a court session. "The face and shape of state crimes is often quite mutable. What yesterday was considered a state crime, today or tomorrow becomes a highly regarded act of civil courage. A state crime is often a homily on what is not yet sufficiently matured and for which the time has not yet come. All this, despite the severe punishment of the law that comes to a state criminal, does not allow us to see in him a despicable and rejected member of society, does not allow us to stifle sympathy for everything noble, honest, dear, and rational that remains in him outside the sphere of his criminal act."

He did not leave out the sensitive: "Bogolyubov's torturers needed the groan not of physical pain but the groan of a mocked human soul, a stifled, humiliated and destroyed man. The Russian apotheosis of the whip triumphant!"

In conclusion, Alexandrov said, "There have been women here in the defendant's bench who avenged themselves on their seducers with death. There were women who dirtied their hands in the blood of men they loved who had betrayed them or of their more fortunate rivals. For the first time there is a woman here who had no personal interests, personal revenge in her crime, a woman who with her crime connected the struggle for an idea to the name of someone who was only a fellow brother in misery throughout her young life."

The ovation was quelled with difficulty by the presiding chairman.

Addressing the jury, Alexandrov concluded in the spirit of Dostoevsky's novels: "Without rebuke, without bitter complaint, without hurt she will accept your decision and will find comfort in that perhaps her suffering, her sacrifice will prevent the possibility of a repetition of the event that caused her action. No matter how darkly we regard the act, we can see only honesty and nobility in the motives for it. Yes, she can come out of here condemned, but she will not come of here shamed."

Another ovation.

On her lawyer's advice, Zasulich refused to have a final word. It would have been stupid to ruin the effect of the brilliant speech that quickly made the rounds of Russia.

The time came for the sentencing. Koni described it in his memoirs.

With pale faces, the jurors crowded around the corner of the judges' table. There was total silence in the court, everyone had bated breath. The foreman of the jurors, an official in the Ministry of Finances, hurried rattled off the question: "Is Zasulich guilty of wounding . . ." and then loudly, so that the whole room could hear: "No! Not guilty!"

Anyone who did not witness it cannot imagine the explosion of sounds obliterating the foreman's voice, the movement that ran through the room like an electric shock. There were shouts of uncontrolled joy, hysterical weeping, rapturous applauses, foot stomping, cries of "Bravo! Hurrah! Well done! Vera! Verochka! Verochka!" all blurring into a single groan and howl. Many people in the downstairs seats blessed themselves; upstairs in the more democratic gallery, the public embraced; even in the seats behind the judges [the VIP seats] they applauded strongly. One was clapping right near my ear. I looked around. It was the deputy of the artillery general Count A. A. Barantsov, a gray-haired fat man, his face red, clapping wildly. Meeting my eyes, he stopped and smiled in embarrassment, but as soon as I turned around, he went back to clapping.

Vera Zasulich "had expected to be hanged after a staged trial." Instead, Koni declared, "You are acquitted! Go to the detention house and get your things. The order for your release will be sent immediately. The court is adjourned!"

Dostoevsky, moved, told the journalist G. K. Gradovsom, seated next to him, "Punishing that young woman is inappropriate, excessive. It should be put this way: go, you are free, but don't do it again. I don't think we have the judicial formula for that, and now they'll make a heroine out of her."

The crowd outside in the street was already making a heroine out of her. "A deafening 'Hurrah!' greeted Vera Zasulich, and shouts of 'Lift her onto your shoulders!' Another 'Hurrah!' and shouts of 'Long live Zasulich! Hail Zasulich!'"

Koni was about to leave the courtroom, but he was detained by A. I. Despot-Zenovich, a member of the Council of the Ministry of Internal Affairs. The old man with the St. Alexander Nevsky star pinned to his chest said, "This is the happiest day of my life, the happiest day!" And he shook Koni's hand.

But the elated admirers of that happiest day could see its results immediately. As the carriage carrying Zasulich approached Voskresensky

Prospect, gendarmes rushed toward it. Shots rang out. It was the revolutionary narodnik and student Grigory Sidoratsky, who thought that the gendarmes might arrest Zasulich again.

Koni was lunching with friends when a late guest announced, "Do you know what's going on in the street? They're shooting. A dead man is lying on Voskresensky Prospect." The shots and the dead gendarme were the bloody epigraph to what followed.

Thus Russia demonstrated that it was still in its juridical infancy. The trial by justice (by liberal lights) won a crushing victory over trial by law. It created a legal precedent for the right to shoot out of your convictions. From this moment of the great humiliation of the law, the clock of the revolution started ticking.

Just as the court had mocked the law, the tsar mocked the court. Alexander was incensed by the verdict. The director of the House of Preliminary Detention, Colonel M. Fedorov, was called in by Major General Kozlov (acting city governor in Trepov's place). He announced: "On the command of the tsar, for the premature release of Zasulich, you are to spend seven days in the brig." Kozlov was very embarrassed, since Fedorov had acted in accordance with the law, that is, he implemented the court decision and the written orders of the chairman of the court. But the tsar wanted justice, too.

The day after the trial, Kozlov issued another order: "I suggest the gentlemen of the district precincts take the most energetic measures to find and hold Vera Zasulich, who attempted to kill Adjutant General Trepov." But Zasulich had gone without a trace.

Western newspapers hailed her and the court's heroic decision, acting against autocracy. Zasulich's fame must have been contagious. Right after the trial came two attempts on the German emperor's life, an attempt on the Italian king, and one on the Spanish king.

Vera's shot was ricocheting all over Europe.

It ricocheted most loudly in Russia. Members of Land and Freedom began taking revenge. They shot at the prosecutor of the Kiev District Court, Kotlyarevsky, whose thick fur coat acted as a bulletproof vest.

Police agent Nikonov was killed. Gendarme officer Baron Geiking was shot in the street. In Kharkov, the governor general Prince Kropotkin was killed.

The government responded with arrests. During an arrest in Odessa, I. Kovalsky, another member of Land and Freedom, shot a policeman. He was captured and executed. The revolutionaries considered his sentence unjust and took commensurate action.

Terror came to St. Petersburg.

On the morning of August 8, N. Mezentsov, chief of the Third Department and the gendarmes, was returning home from church. His house was in the center of St. Petersburg on Mikhailovsky Square, near the Mikhailovsky Palace.

A young man was lying in wait for him there. He was athletic, with a dusky complexion, curly hair, and a fashionable curly beard à la Napoleon III. It was Sergei Kravchinsky, the aristocrat who was one of the first to resign from the army and go to the people. Kravchinsky had seen a lot in that time. He fled Russia, fought in the war against the Turks, fought with the rebel poor in Italy, and then returned to Russia to become one of the leaders of Land and Freedom.

He wrote a lot for their underground press, becoming a well-known author under the pseudonym Stepnyak. All Europe read his book *Underground Russia.* He entered Russian history under the name Stepnyak-Kravchinsky.

Stepnyak-Kravchinsky paced in front of Mezentsov's house with a mysterious package. Farther along on Mikhailovsky Square a second participant stood ready, a tall young man in an elegant navy blue coat. This was another failed officer, also athletic and also handsome.

He deserves a more detailed account as one of the main protagonists of terrorism. His name was Alexander Barannikov, and he came to St.

Petersburg from the provinces to study at the prestigious Pavlovsk military school. His family hoped that he would be an officer like his late father. As he left for the school, he promised to become a general.

Tall, with perfect military bearing, he was distinguished by great physical strength and glowing health. "If terror needed physical embodiment, there could be no better choice than the image of Barannikov," wrote the terrorist Vera Figner. "His dusky face without any trace of blush, hair like a raven's wing, and black eyes made him unlike a Russian: he could easily be taken for an Eastern man, most likely a man from the Caucasus." (His mother was Persian.)

But he also looked threatening. "When we needed to put a scare into someone, we sent Barannikov," she added.

Slow to change his mind, Barannikov did not accept revolutionary ideas quickly. But once he did, he became a fanatic. The lofty goal, freeing the people, elevated him above his classmates. What could be more important than that for a young man? He loved danger, it made him feel most alive.

In order to leave the Pavlovsk school and keep his mother from looking for him, Barannikov faked his suicide, leaving his uniform and a note to his mother on a riverbank. He went underground, living without documentation.

Naturally, Barannikov went to the people. With him went Maria Oshanina, one of the great beauties of the movement. She came from a family of wealthy merchants and had a brilliant education. "She was beautiful," recalled narodnik V. Chernov. "Delicate features, huge dark languid eyes." She became Barannikov's common-law wife, but not for long. The underground life required pretense of marriage in order to deceive the police, but with constantly shifting partners.

The many qualities Barannikov enjoyed made him intolerant of weakness. Such people do not value their own lives or the lives of others. Only the noose could stop him and the many like him. Barannikov would take part in all the attempts on Alexander's life. The terrorists called him the Avenging Angel.

At the house of gendarme chief Mezentsov, his carriage pulled up. With him was his old friend, a retired lieutenant colonel. Mezentsov got out, and Stepnyak-Kravchinsky rushed up to him. In front of stunned witnesses, he pulled a dagger from his package and jabbed it to the hilt into Mezentsov's belly. Calmly, to make sure, he twisted the dagger. Mezentsov's unarmed friend attacked Kravchinsky with his only weapon, an umbrella. Shots rang out in response. Alexander Barannikov was covering Kravchinsky's escape, and both leaped into a carriage. It was harnessed to a famous black horse called Barbarian, used three other times to help terrorists flee from prison.

The "sleepy tiger" Mezentsov had not been known for cruelty or bloodthirstiness. He was killed as a symbol, for being the head of the Third Department. Stepnyak-Kravchinsky wrote a proclamation entitled "Death for Death." It was dedicated "to the memory of Martyr Ivan Martynovich Kovalsky, shot by the secret police for defending his freedom, August 2, 1878, in Odessa."

"The chief of gendarmes, the leader of a gang that has all of Russia under its heel, has been killed," wrote Stepnyak-Kravchinsky. "Few have not guessed whose hands dealt the fatal blow. But in order to avoid any confusion, we announce for general information that gendarme chief Adjutant General Mezentsov was in fact killed by us, revolutionary socialists. . . . We tried the perpetrators and inciters of the brutalities done to us. The trial was as just as the ideas we are defending. This trial found Adjutant General Mezentsov deserving of death for his villainous deeds against us, and the sentence was carried out on Mikhailovsky Square on the morning of August 4, 1878."

This was the first instance of a new rule in Russian terror—claiming responsibility publicly for murder. At first, the athletic Kravchinsky had planned a much more horrible death for Mezentsov. He wanted to behead him on the street. But he decided against that piece of street theater because it would have been difficult to keep the sword hidden in advance.

Mezentsov's death, next to the Mikhailovsky Palace, which Alexander visited every Sunday to have tea with his cousin, was a shock for St. Petersburg. Land and Freedom had achieved its goal. Now people talked about the power of the terrorists. Kravchinsky's name was on everyone's lips. Most amazingly, Kravchinsky, who had attacked an unarmed, elderly man, became a kind of Robin Hood.

The tsar appointed a military general, sixty-year-old Alexander Drenteln, who had fought gloriously in the Balkan campaign, as the new chief of gendarmes. But soon General Drenteln discovered that the terrorists had eyes in his own office.

At the time, one of the most influential political salons in St. Petersburg was that of Alexandra Bogdanovich, wife of General Bogdanovich, who was a member of the Council of the Ministry of Internal Affairs, and a respected elder of St. Isaac's Cathedral, the greatest in St. Petersburg. The hospitable hostess gathered the cream of St. Petersburg's officials in her salon. She made precise notes in her diary of the conversations of the most famous guests.

She recounts how soon after Drenteln was appointed (in the middle of March), two of his friends had lunch at his house. "After lunch they went to the study where they saw the socialist journal *Land and Freedom* on his desk. The issue was not carefully printed . . . Drenteln commented on that but added that it was rather well written [even the chief of the gendarmes wanted to show his freethinking—it was the fashion]. The next day he received a letter from the socialists, thanking him for his review and promising to correct the deficiencies soon! That's the kind of people they are!"

Her exclamation is filled with the horror of impotence.

The chief of the Third Department only laughed then. He did not see what the wise Bogdanovich saw—the shameful impotence of the once almighty Third Department. A few days later he was taught a lesson.

On March 13 around one o'clock in the afternoon, Drenteln's carriage was driving past the Summer Garden headed for Palace Square and the Winter Palace. His carriage was passed by a young dandy, who had ridden on the general's path before. It was hard not to notice the young man. "A tall handsome fellow with exquisite manners on a magnificent English horse, and all the society ladies who rode by in open carriages stared at him through their lorgnettes," is how the revolutionary Nikolai Morozov described him.

This time the young man came back at full gallop. Passing Drenteln's carriage, he pulled out a revolver and shot at the chief of the gendarmes. He missed. Galloping on, he turned his horse around at full speed and came at the carriage. He shot at Drenteln again, and missed again. Then he galloped away.

The shooter was quickly found, through his rented horse. He was Leon Mirsky, an aristocrat, and also a member of Land and Freedom. Mirsky had studied at the mutinous Medical-Surgical Academy and even spent time in the fortress for distributing illegal literature.

The bizarre reason for his attempt was that his fiancée found Stepnyak-Kravchinsky's daring assassination very attractive. The image of the fearless revolutionary killing the chief of gendarmes in broad daylight obsessed the woman. The jealous Mirsky decided to recapture her affections by killing the new chief of gendarmes.

He got in touch with Nikolai Morozov, and the Land and Freedom group approved his idea. Mirsky did everything by the rules—he studied the general's usual route and found the place where the carriage usually slowed down. But he was a bad shot.

In prison Mirsky remained steadfast at first. He asked permission to have a frock coat made by an expensive tailor for the trial, which his fiancée was to attend. He was wearing it when he was sentenced to endless hard labor.

The tsar, just back from Crimea, wrote sarcastically about Mirsky. "He acted under the influence of women and writers." He was very angry because he had "not doubted that Mirsky would be hanged," he wrote to the minister of justice.

But the justice system knew what it was doing. The flirtatious young man could not stand incarceration and became an agent provocateur in prison. He started working for the secret police.

The security situation demanded extraordinary measures from the tsar, instantly. Governor N. D. Seliverstov wrote to Alexander II: "All the measures taken up to this time against antigovernment agitation have had no success and no good consequences. Evil is growing by the minute. . . . We need extraordinary measures."

The columnist M. N. Katkov suggested making all trials of terrorists closed. Open trials were too helpful to the terrorists. "Thanks to glasnost, the nihilists of the whole world could learn that using a long-range revolver if you want to hit someone in the head at close range, you must aim at the feet, and that you should not buy revolvers without testing them first."

The tsar knew that harsh punitive measures were already being taken, and that the openness of trials was already limited. But it wasn't enough, and the two-faced Janus was not prepared to curb any more of the freedoms he had himself granted. All he managed was to ask for help from owners of apartment buildings.

In his letter to the St. Petersburg Duma, he wrote: "I appeal to you, gentlemen. Building owners must keep an eye on their janitors and residents. You must help the police and not keep suspicious persons. . . . Look at what is happening in our country. Soon an honest man won't be able to show his face on the street. Look at the number of killings. All right, God spared me. But they sent poor Mezentsov to the other world. They shot at Drenteln. . . . I am counting on you. Your help is needed. It is your duty."

CHAPTER 13

War on Terror

A major schism occurred in Land and Freedom. Some still believed that the peasants had to be enlightened, to be prepared for an insurrection, and that they had to work in the countryside. They were still called narodniki or, disparagingly, country bumpkins. They were despised by the other camp, which was now called the politicals. The politicals considered work in the country useless: "You need centuries to make fighters against the regime out of illiterate, cowed peasants who can't read proclamations, are afraid to rebel, and often turn their enlighteners in to the police." A small group of heroes could put an end to tsarism much faster with the new weapon of the century—terrorism.

Terrorism against the regime's violence created respect in the public. That was shown by the shooting of Trepov and the murder of Mezentsov. They woke up Russia. Only terrorism could make the mighty regime tremble and make concessions. The heroism of the terrorists, they hoped, would force the regime to respect their ideas, and fear would force the average man to put pressure on the pathetic government. Power to the revolver and the bomb. Political terrorism must be the basic tool in the life of Land and Terror.

As Stepnyak-Kravchinsky, who had escaped abroad, declared: "Terror is a terrible thing. There is only thing worse than terror, and that is putting up with oppression docilely." This became the motto of the politicals. They began to put their ideas into practice.

By this time murder at all the steps of the social ladder had been achieved—the governor general was killed, the chief of gendarmes was killed. Only the very top of the Olympus remained untouched, the palace, the autocrat. Twelve years had passed since Karakozov shot at the tsar. It was time to try again. The country bumpkins disagreed, they felt it would lead to new, ruthless repressions.

While they argued in the capital, the decision was taken in the provinces. In the spring of 1879, Alexander Solovyov came to St. Petersburg. He was the son of the poor assistant to the paramedic on the estates of Grand Duchess Elena Pavlovna. She gave generous aid to their family. She paid for the education of all the children. Solovyov had attended high school and then law school at the university thanks to her money. But he dropped out, went to the people, and then joined Land and Freedom.

He was thirty-three, and as Christ did at that age, he understood his destiny. He headed for St. Petersburg. There he found Alexander Mikhailov, one of the leaders of the party. His comembers considered Mikhailov their Robespierre.

Alexander Mikhailov was from the aristocracy and also from the provinces, from Pskov, like Alexander Barannikov. They were friends in high school. Mikhailov was one of the numerous Russian boys who appeared at that time—"great critics" born in an era of freedom. Dostoevsky said of them, "If you give a Russian schoolboy a chart of the heavenly bodies, he will make corrections." In high school, he became obsessed with the idea of restructuring the imperfect world. He instantly felt "much higher than my peers" as a result. His peers acknowledged his leadership. Fat, clumsy, and nearsighted, Mikhailov was the leader in his friendship with the handsome and strong Barannikov, whom he brought to revolutionary ideas. Mikhailov naturally went to the people, but he grew disenchanted quickly. He came back to the capital as a proponent of ruthless terror. Alexander Mikhailov, who resembled Pierre Bezukhov in *War and Peace,* whose round fat face radiated kindness, became the leader of the politicals.

Alexander Solovyov came to his illegal apartment. Mikhailov recalled, "Knowing that I was close to the Land and Freedom party, he opened up his heart to me." It turned out that Solovyov wanted to kill the tsar and that was his reason for coming to the capital. Solovyov explained to Mikhailov: "The death of the emperor will make a turn in public life. The dissatisfaction that is expressed in quiet mumbling will explode in regions where it is most deeply felt. And then it will spread everywhere. It just needs an impetus for everything to rise up."

So twelve years later, he gave the same reasons to Mikhailov that had brought Karakozov to the gates of the Summer Garden. Kill the tsar and the rest will follow. He asked for the help of Land and Freedom.

Robespierre Mikhailov liked Solovyov's focus and he went out to buy a revolver for him. "We chose an American one with big barrels, they use them for hunting bear." The revolver was called Bear-hunter. The revolutionaries called the Russian tsar "The Bear." So they chose the appropriate weapon for the hunt.

But no sooner had Mikhailov gotten a gun for one regicide than another one came to him. Another provincial came to St. Petersburg, this time from Kharkov. Grigory Goldenberg was also a member of Land and Freedom, notorious for his assassination of the governor general of Kharkov, Prince Kropotkin. Buoyed by his success, Goldenberg now wanted to kill the tsar. He also asked for help from the capital's branch of Land and Freedom. It was hard to refuse such an experienced man, but Solovyov had come first. So Mikhailov reported on the situation to another of the politicals' leaders, Alexander Kvyatkovsky. They decided to arrange a meeting of the two candidates.

They met in a tavern, and over a shot of vodka Mikhailov and Kvyatkovsky discovered that they were meeting terrorists of a new type. Both men were willing to shoot, knowing that they were unlikely to escape from the tsar's bodyguards and therefore did not intend to try. They had both decided on their own to take poison as soon as they had killed the tsar. They would leave the world without revealing their identities.

This was a new type of terrorist—a suicide killer. Kvyatkovsky and Mikhailov were stunned. "We were not prepared at that time for self-sacrifice. The awareness of our situation between two men who had doomed themselves to death took away our moral right to help decide which of the two should do it," recalled Mikhailov.

But they had to take part in the decision. Goldenberg was Jewish and Mikhailov delicately explained to him that "we must avoid giving the government any excuse to oppress any particular estate or nationality . . . so that millions are spared new hardship." He then told Goldenberg that a Jew who kills the tsar would unleash a wave of pogroms across Russia. Solovyov picked up on the theme and added, "I'm the only one who meets all the criteria. I must go. It is my affair, Alexander II is mine, and I won't relinquish him to anyone." Goldenberg agreed without argument.

Solovyov's arrival was the detonator that blew up Land and Freedom. A secret meeting took place in an underground apartment. Alexander Mikhailov reported on Solovyov's mission. Nikolai Morozov recalled, "Alexander Mikhailov then asked for a horse for Solovyov to escape after the assassination and a member of the organization to act as coachman." Apparently Mikhailov decided to help the dead man remain alive.

The country bumpkins shouted that "no help should be given to the man who came to kill the tsar and Solovyov should be captured, tied up, and taken out of St. Petersburg as a madman."

The politicals rebutted angrily. The bumpkins screamed that in that case they would stop Solovyov themselves. A man named Popov yelled: "He is ruining the work of the narodniki, I'll kill him, if there's nothing else to be done with him." They understood the repression that would follow the murder of the tsar and that they would have to stop their work with the peasants.

The leader of the country bumpkins, the theoretician of the narodnik movement, Georgi Plekhanov, made a speech: "Because of your whims, our organization is going to be forced to give up old regions of activity one after the other, like Rome gave up one province after the other under the pressure of the barbarians. . . . The only change from that killing will be that after the name of Alexander there will be three lines instead of two. Alexander II will be replaced by Alexander III. And nothing more!"

But the majority believed otherwise. They declared that while they would not help Solovyov themselves in view of the differences of opinion, they would not forbid individual members from giving him help.

The meeting degenerated into shouts again. One of the country bumpkins declared that if a new Karakozov appeared, he was prepared to be the Komissarov. The political Kvyatkovsky shouted, "Are you planning to be an informer? Then we will deal with you the way we do with informers!"

Popov said to Kvyatkovsky, "Are you planning to kill us? If so, do not forget that we shoot no worse then you."

At that moment, when they were going to reach for their pistols, the doorbell rang.

"Gentlemen, it's the police!" cried Mikhailov. "We will defend ourselves, of course?"

"Naturally!" the rest said softly.

Each of the men took out his revolver and cocked it. Mikhailov slowly and calmly went to the entryway to open the door. It was a false alarm. Mikhailov returned with the news that it had been the janitor about some domestic problem.

"But that false alarm put an end to the stormy scenes. Soon afterward the meeting broke up quietly. Everyone left with the feeling that the good old unity of Land and Freedom was destroyed and now each direction would go its own way," wrote Plekhanov.

On April 2, 1879, after eight in the morning, Alexander set out as usual on his morning walk. The emperor's day followed an inviolable schedule. But on that day, a radical change was made in his plans. His traditional walk was canceled forever.

From the newspaper *Russkii Invalid,* April 5, 1879.

> On April 2, after 8:00 A.M., when the Sovereign Emperor deigned to take his usual walk in the area around the Winter Palace, on the sidewalk near the building of the headquarters of the troops for the St. Petersburg military region, a man, dressed quite properly, in a civil uniform with a cockaded cap, came toward His Imperial Majesty from the opposite side of the building. Coming closer to the Emperor, this man took out a revolver from his coat pocket and shot at His Majesty and took several other shots after that. People walking nearby as well as the police instantly threw themselves on the villain and detained him. God's Providence preserved our August Tsar's days, precious for Russia. The villain is arrested. The investigation is under way.

In fact, it was much more shameful. He was returning from his walk. He had passed Pevchesky Bridge and came out onto the square in front of the palace. Captain Kokh, the head of his bodyguards, followed at a distance so as not to disrupt his thinking. Not far from the arch of the General Staff building, a crowd of curiosity seekers had gathered, as usual. Here, the emperor saw a very tall young man in a long black coat and a uniform cap with a cockade (as worn by officials).

From the diary of Alexandra Bogdanovich, wife of a general: "Makov, who saw the tsar a half hour after the attempt on his life, told us that the tsar said that when the young man came even with the tsar, he stopped and saluted him. The man's face caught the tsar's attention. And when he turned back involuntarily, he saw a pistol pointed at him."

That turn of the head save his life. The bullet whistled past. "The bullet penetrated the wall of the palace and stuck there. The villain aimed again, the tsar bent to the left, the criminal aimed a third time, and the tsar bent again."

That was how Makov euphemistically described the tsar of all Russia running around the square. When Solovyov shot the first time, two steps away from him, he missed. Alexander ran from him like a boy. In front of the crowd, the tsar ran toward his palace. For the first time since his father's death, he had to obey another's will.

Solovyov ran behind him, shooting. Another shot. The emperor ran to the right. He ran in zigzags, as his army training had taught him. The sixty-year-old tsar had not lost his presence of mind. Another shot, he ran to the left. He could hear the assassin's breathing. Another two shots, but he swerved aside, and a bullet grazed his greatcoat. Finally, the last shot was near his legs. Solovyov shot as he fell, when Kokh caught up with him.

At first Kokh and the police had been stunned. Then they chased after Solovyov. He managed to get in five shots before Kokh caught him and knocked him down with his saber.

The huge pistol lay next to him. Solovyov was surrounded, kicked and beaten. But Solovyov was chewing on something. Kokh figured it out first. In his haste to force Solovyov to open his mouth, he scratched up his face. He had a nut with cyanide in his mouth, a powerful poison. But it must have been old and had deteriorated. Solovyov did not die.

Peter Shuvalov ran out of the palace. The retired chief of the Third Department continued to live in the palace. He persuaded Alexander to get into a passing carriage (one of "them" could still be on the square!) and brought him the remaining few yards to the palace.

The failed regicide was taken to the city governor's office.

Alexander returned triumphantly to the palace. He announced: "God saved me again!" The empress knew the whole story, and he ordered her not to talk about it. She did say, weeping, to her lady-in waiting, "There's no reason to live. . . . I can feel this killing me. Today the murderer hunted him like a hare. It's a miracle he survived."

The White Hall was filled with courtiers and officers of the guards' regiments. Mikhail, learning of the attempt, ran to the palace without his cap. Outside, a crowd gathered just as it had twelve years earlier. They shouted, "Hurrah!" when the tsar appeared to them. Someone helpfully calculated, "They shouted for an entire ten minutes." A church service was held. But Alexander sensed that something had changed drastically. Back then they had wept with joy. Now they tried to appear happy. They had grown used to assassination attempts.

He wrote dryly in his diary: "Out walking. An unknown assailant shot at me five times from a revolver outside the General Staff building. God saved me. The whole family gathered, one after the other. Spoke with Drenteln: the killer is arrested. Thanksgiving service. Many ladies and gentlemen. All the officers: hurrah!"

Then the bells rang and he went out on the balcony over the Saltykov Entrance. The crowd hailed him. Vassily Bilbasov, well-known journalist and historian (author of the *History of Catherine II*) was in the crowd and he later recounted to Mme Bogdanovich how someone in the crowd said loudly: "If you're a patriot, shout hurrah, if you're a socialist, keep quiet." "The words were spoken by someone dressed as a craftsman. The people around him heard him calmly and didn't do anything with the man."

A joke made the rounds: A janitor hearing the bells pealing, says: "Missed again?"

Many people came to the Guard's Staff Square (the name for that part of Palace Square near Pevchesky Bridge) to see the bullet marks on the southern facade of the Staff Building.

In the meantime, in the city governor's office the man everyone in Russia was talking about lay on a couch. He was thirty-three, he hadn't done a thing in his life, and he was a failure here, too. He couldn't shoot the tsar at three feet, he couldn't even poison himself with cyanide. Yet everyone in the country knew him now, after thirty-three years of no recognition at all. Suddenly everyone was bustling around him. He had made the giant leap from nobody to a major figure.

Fame was one of the motivations for terrorism. Stepnyak-Kravchinsky was famous. And now so was Solovyov. An eyewitness described the scene: "Next to the couch on the floor stood a washbasin with a lot of vomit (they had pumped his stomach). His first question when he came to was, Did I really not kill the tsar? After openly regretting it, he relaxed. He lay calm and important. Then, he causally asked for a cigarette. And someone with extraordinary courtesy jumped up and assiduously scratched matches. At the criminal's head, gracefully leaning on the arm of the couch and bending over him, stood a gentleman with court insignia on his uniform, who asked questions with an ingratiating voice: 'You are aware that in your position total frankness will lead to the good result where no innocent person will suffer, while otherwise . . .' But Solovyov kept silent regally."

Nonetheless, the investigators quickly learned everything about him.

Solovyov became chatty and happily told them that he had spent the night before the shooting "with a prostitute." (He liked shocking them.) Having enjoyed life's pleasures for the last time, he headed off to kill the emperor, not forgetting to put on a "clean shirt I had saved and threw the dirty one on the floor." He was going to his death.

Why did he do it? He was avenging his comrades. "Like ghosts, the martyrs for the people, who figured in many major political trials and who perished prematurely, pass through my imagination." He also explained the goals for which he was killing: "I belong to a Russian social-revolutionary party that recognizes the extreme injustice of the majority of the people laboring while the minority exploits their labor. We socialists declare war on the government. For the tsar, as an enemy of the people, I can feel only hostility."

He believed that his shot "brought closer the radiant future." He did not, however, have a very clear idea of that future: "I cannot clearly picture the new order, but I think that humanity must reach a perfection in which everyone will satisfy his own needs without harming anyone else."

The highest officials of the empire, dressed in epaulets and wearing orders, men who would not have permitted him to enter their waiting rooms, now hung on his every word and wrote down his thoughts. Even more important, Solovyov forced the tsar of all Russia and the entire royal family to change its life. The tsar would no longer take morning walks in the city. He now went out only with bodyguards. The grand dukes had to have bodyguards, as well.

The next day, the heir wrote in his diary: "Today I had to travel for the first time in a carriage with a convoy. Father, thank God, is also going to travel with a convoy, and now has, as I do, a Cossack sergeant next to the coachman and two Cossacks on horseback."

This was new for the populace, seeing the tsar protected by body-guards in his own capital. Neither Alexander I nor Nicholas I had needed them. Alexandra Bogdanovich wrote in her diary what everyone was saying: "It's painful to see that."

The Special Senate Court condemned Solovyov to death. He heard the verdict calmly. He was offered a chance to write a plea for pardon. He left the paper blank.

On May 28, 1879, he was brought to Semenovsky Square, where Dostoevsky and the Petrashevsky circle members had awaited execution. A crowd of four thousand people had gathered. The tall wooden scaffolding was surrounded by an iron fence on all sides. Two wooden pillars were connected by a bar, from which two nooses hung, swinging in the wind. Next to the scaffold stood a coffin covered by cloth but still obviously a coffin. There was something chilling about the sight of a coffin prepared for a still-living man. The cart pulled up. Solovyov sat facing away from the horses, his hands tied behind his back with rope. He wore a black coat of heavy army cloth and a big black sign hung on his chest: State Criminal. Soldiers formed several rings around the scaffold. The minister of justice and the prosecutor of the court entered the cordoned-off area.

The executioner Frolov went up on the scaffold. He was a criminal who took the job in exchange for a pardon. He was picturesque: tall, in a red shirt and black vest with a long golden watch chain. Frolov had many executions ahead of him.

Solovyov sneered as he stood by the pillory and listened to the sentence being read. Then a priest came up to Solovyov, but he shook his head. He had told them in the investigation that he did not believe in God. Frolov took over, helping him put on the white hooded garment that would hide his face and the sight of his suffering. Holding him by the shoulders, he led him to the gibbet. He threw on the noose, checked it, and then gave the sign. An assistant kicked away the support, and Solovyov fell through the trapdoor. The white hood jerked and remained swinging in the wind.

The next day a proclamation was distributed all over the city. "We have picked up the glove thrown at us, we are not afraid of struggle and death, and in the end we will blow up the government, no matter how many die on our side."

Real panic spread through the capital. A. A. Kireev, retired general, newspaper columnist, and acquaintance of Fedor Dostoevsky, noted in his diary: "The most fantastic rumors are spreading in the city that the nihilists will foment a revolution and that all of us will be killed. Some units of the army are on standby!!! The heir cannot live in Tsarskoye Selo and is moving to Peterhof . . . because it is too difficult in Tsarskoye Selo to protect against killers. That won't be a life, but hard labor! This is what things have come to!"

The lady-in-waiting Maria Frederiks (her mother, Cecilia, had been lady-in-waiting and best friend of Alexander II's mother), wrote in her *Reminiscences,* "Tsar Nicholas I knew that one could fight long and hard against innate [Russian] ungovernability and instability, but they can be conquered only by force and firmness. . . . He knew that for a Russian, strictness is more beneficial than laxness, which leads to no good. We can see that Emperor Nicholas I was right by what came after him. When, after the death of our wise tsar, there was weakness and laxness in the air, everyone breathed it in and rejoiced. . . . They gave us freedom of thought and freedom of action and freedom of the press; everyone rushed for everything at once, hoping to speed up Russia's development. The wild flow that was suddenly unblocked . . . poured over its banks quickly and wildly; it broke and burned everything in its path. And what was the end result? A handful of morally deformed degenerates who made their goal, under guise of loyalty to the Homeland, to change the entire order in Russia."

That was the manifesto of the court. It was an article of faith for a growing opposition of retrogrades, and the tsar could see it in the eyes of his son, the heir. The retrograde party rallied round his Sasha, the heir to the throne.

A fat leather-bound notebook with a metal lock contains the diary of the heir and his desperate notations of those years: "It's horrible, these times!" "Lord, give us the means and teach us how to act! What are we to do!" "The most terrible and disgusting years that Russia has ever lived through!"

Just as his father had been humiliated by his own fear during the Decembrist rebellion, Alexander was humiliated on Palace Square. To run like a hare (the empress's words were quickly repeated to him) at the age of sixty-one in full view of his court! And on the eve of his birthday: "A fine present that was," he said.

He tried to stay calm. But the mysterious "they" continued their work. They announced their name: the Executive Committee. Chief of gendarmes Drenteln, the city governor of St. Petersburg, and several other officials received letters by mail with the same message. Each was stamped with the oval seal of "the Executive Committee of the Russian Socialist-Revolutionary Party." The center of the seal bore a pistol, axe, and dagger.

"The Executive Committee has reason to think that Solovyov, arrested for his attempt on the life of Alexander II, might be subjected to torture and declares . . . that anyone who dares to stoop to that kind of interrogation method will be punished by death by the Executive Committee."

That was too much. He determined to be ruthless, to bring back the days of his father, which the court missed so much. The tsar decided to win by force. Barely finished with the war in the Balkans, he declared a new war in his own country. A war on terror. A ruthless war to complete victory.

Almost all of European Russia was divided into six temporary general provinces (Kiev, Moscow, Kharkov, St. Petersburg, Warsaw, and Odessa). So that there was no doubt that this was war, martial law was declared in all the territories. Battle generals, who had distinguished themselves in the last war, were appointed as governor generals, including the victor on the Caucasus front, Count Loris-Melikov; the hero of Shipka, General Gurko; and the victor at Plevna, General Totleben.

War Minister Dmitri Milyutin noted sadly in his diary: "All the cares of the highest government are now directed at increasing strictness, and all of Russia could be said to be in a state of siege."

The generals began with military precision: They exiled, they confiscated, they jailed. A new concept appeared in the public consciousness: "white terror." This was Alexander's determined attack on the determined young people.

Their response was to attack officials. A new way of life began. "Around the palace, at every step, there are police precautions; convoys of Cossacks. . . . You sense that the earth is shifting, that the building is in danger of falling, in every stratum of society there is a vague dissatisfaction gripping everyone."

"Dissatisfaction gripping everyone!" That was written by Minister Valuyev in his diary. "The masters sense it," he added. Naturally Alexander sensed it. Despite his reprisals, the tension in the country did not diminish. Moreover, there was anxiety in the air—something was coming.

The constant nervous tension changed him, and the disintegration of the magnificent and handsome man continued. Valuyev also wrote in his diary, "I saw Their Imperial Majesties. The tsar looks tired and spoke with nervous irritation which he tries to hide. She is a semi-ruin. In an era when he needs strength, clearly, she cannot be counted on."

Alexander had to make another difficult decision that cost him a lot of "nervous irritation."

He was tormented by fear for Katya. He would see her with the children at her mansion or in his father's study, where they were still brought secretly. And he would go down the inner stairs, which his father had used to go up to his mother, to see them. Every time she was transported to the palace, he was mad with worry. He could not give her Cossack bodyguards like the grand dukes had. It would have been excessively public. That meant that they could simply approach her carriage (as they had Drenteln's) and shoot or take her and the children hostage. And who were they? How many were there? Like many people in the capital, the tsar asked himself the unanswerable questions. He was seen frequently sitting apathetically in his study and then angrily flinging a candlestick at the wall, or grimly walking through the endless enfilade of rooms instead of his morning walk. A prisoner in his own capital.

A rumor spread through the city that during his "palace walk" he saw a guard at the entrance to the private apartments quickly hide something behind his back. The tsar shot him, only to discover it was a cigarette. This was the kind of rumor the court spread about him now. They did not like him—rather, they were no longer afraid of not liking him. And they hated Katya.

But he made the decision to move Katya and the children to the third floor of the Winter Palace, where the chamberlains and ladies-in-waiting lived, far from the apartments of the empress, who lived on the second floor. There was nothing new in this. His grandfather Paul, his uncle Alexander I, and his father had kept their mistresses in the palace. It was not considered improper because no one dared discuss it. But now they had glasnost and the ruler's life was on everyone's lips. Instantly, the story became that Katya and the children were living directly above the empress, and the miserable, sick, and old empress had to listen to the patter of his illegitimate children's feet over her head.

For all the gossip, the princess's presence in the palace was considered a secret. His minister of the court, Alexander Adlerberg (who had replaced his father in the post), had known the tsar all his life. Sasha Adlerberg and he grew up together. Only Adlerberg had the right to see the emperor without a report and to call him by name, something that even the grand dukes were not permitted. But the minister of the court, who was required to know everything that happened at the palace, had to pretend "out of modesty" that he knew nothing about Princess Dolgorukaya and her two children living in the palace.

As Adlerberg later told War Minister Milyutin, "When the tsar decided to move Princess Dolgorukaya to the Winter Palace, he called in the commandant, Major General Delsal, and gave him all the orders directly, adding that he should say nothing to me about it. It goes without saying that it could not be followed precisely (and the emperor knew that), but I was grateful to the tsar. . . . Out of some sense of decency, some refined tactfulness for all our, I may say, friendly relations since childhood, the tsar said nothing to me about that ticklish subject, and I pretended to know nothing."

The empress was now just skin and bones. Her illness advanced after the assassination attempt on April 2, 1879, and even more so after Katya was moved into the palace.

Alexander told her about it himself. She said nothing. Now she lived in isolation, surrounded by her ladies-in-waiting, who had grown old along with her. She spent days in bed, and when they tried to amuse her, she would laugh bitterly and say, "Why this picnic at the bier?"

She feared that they would bring up "that woman." To prevent it, she told them about how of one the late empress's favorite ladies-in-waiting hinted to her about the affair of Nicholas I with Nelidova. Her thin lips drawn into a smile, she added, "If I had heard a similar exposé, I would not have been able to see that lady-in-waiting again."

The words of the palace "saint" served as a lesson to them all.

The emperor saw her less frequently. Her apartments consisted of the formal alcove with crimson fabric on the walls and marble maiden faces of the caryatids above the couch where her desiccated, weightless body lay in the daytime; the lettuce-green dining room, where he rarely came to take coffee now; and the golden parlor, where she took walks leaning on the arm of a lady-in-waiting. The candles burned, reflected in the golden walls. She forgave him, she always forgave him and never complained or accused. She would take her suffering and humiliation, as befits the wives of the impetuous Romanovs, to her grave.

It was time to take stock. She had performed her duty, for which German princesses were brought to the beds of Russian tsars. She had borne him three sons, but her favorite had died. There was a curse of the

Hesse line, and as part of it, the heir was her least favorite son, an awkward giant with a peasant, flattened nose. A joke of nature. The Russian tsars had married German princesses for a long time in order to come up with a pure Russian. Everything about Sasha was peasantlike—his slow mind, his inhuman strength, his revulsion for Europe.

She was dying not of her disease but of the uselessness of her life. She had no one and nothing to live for. Upstairs, in the rooms of his mistress, there was noise, there was life. She was certain that they couldn't wait for death to take her.

Alexander managed to persuade Masha to listen to the physicians and go south for the winter. She was going "for a cure in San Remo" as the emperor put it, or "to die in San Remo," as she did. She knew that he wanted to be able not to think about her. He wanted to go the Crimea with Katya.

When the empress set out for San Remo, Tsarevich Sasha was on military maneuvers and came to the train station at Gatchina to bid her farewell. The imperial train arrived from St. Petersburg in deep twilight. "It was getting dark, and all the faces were grim, as if this were a funeral procession," recalled Count Sheremetyev, the tsarevich's adjutant.

The train approached the station. The tsar, tall and slender, in his usual white cap with broad brim, was at the window, pale and thoughtful. (He seemed to grow younger on the eve of her departure.) The empress stared out the window, her thin face resembling an icon. The tsarevich went into the car but came out quickly. It was a brief farewell. The train left. Like everyone else who saw her off, the heir thought he would never see his mother again.

Now Alexander could be with Katya every day. They set off for the Crimea, to Livadia. The tsarevich, tsarevna, and the grandchildren traveled with the tsar in his car. Katya and her children were in the other car.

The emperor spent the day in the Livadia Palace with the royal family and the visiting ministers. But he left the palace every night. He rode on horseback through the warm twilight to his other family. The whir of cicadas, the scent of warm wormwood, and the sound of the sea surrounded him. He had been with Katya thirteen years, but circumstances kept them from becoming a bored married couple. They were always passionate lovers.

Soon it was time to return to rainy, chilly St. Petersburg. The last days in the south were also filled with autumn rains. Sasha and his family left. Katya and the children moved into the palace for the last days in Livadia, and they could sleep together.

It was getting more difficult for Alexander Adlerberg to pretend not to notice, but he tried to play the game. Minister Milyutin came to report on the state of martial law: It wasn't working, and the assassination attempts continued.

At bedtime, Alexander made notes in his memorandum book. "12 November: Rose at 1/4 past 8. Walked, damp, warm, drizzle all day. Coffee with K[atya] in room. . . . Worked. At 11 Milyutin and Adlerberg. Walked. Dinner at 7, to bed at 1/4 to 2."

The departure for St. Petersburg was set for November 17. There were two ways to travel—by sea to Odessa and then by railroad via Moscow, where he always stopped en route from Livadia. The other was by carriage to Simferopol and then by railroad through Moscow to St. Petersburg. He chose the second route. They arrived in Simferopol in the evening, where the imperial train awaited.

When the train left, urgent telegrams were sent to Moscow and Odessa. The mysterious "they" were at work. The emperor did not know that this trip was supposed to be his last.

CHAPTER 14

The Mysterious and Great EC

The events that were not known to the tsar and that were to contribute to his death occurred before his trip to Livadia, in the summer of 1879. Everything connected to those events, at the time absolutely secret, is still debated by historians. This account relies as much as possible on original sources—the accounts of the fathers of Russian terrorism. They described the events after they were arrested, and the few who lived until the revolution in Russia wrote about them in their memoirs.

After Solovyov's shooting, the divided Land and Freedom party saw that the proponents and foes of terror could not coexist anymore. Neither side could forget the hysterical scene between Popov, who was against terrorism, and Kvyatkovsky, who supported it, and the unexpected knock at the door that kept the argument from turning into a shoot-out. The hardliners formed a secret society inside Land and Freedom with the expressive name Liberty or Death.

But the partisans, the terrorists and their supporters, did not stop at that. They demanded a congress to ratify terrorism officially as the party's central activity or to disband. The site for the congress was the city of Voronezh. But the secret society wanted to have its own secret congress in Lipetsk to prepare.

In June 1879, ten young men and a very beautiful young woman began arriving in the sleepy provincial town of Lipetsk, known for its medicinal mud. The spa was founded in the days of Alexander I, and its people were used to visitors, but the athletic young men bore little resemblance to invalids. Nevertheless they declared themselves patients when they checked into the hotel.

They came from all corners of Russia, the eleven people who wanted to turn around Russian history. Several came from the south. Unlike the aristocratic Land and Freedom chapter in St. Petersburg, the southern branches had children of poverty among the nobles. They would all become famous Russian terrorists.

From the southern port of Odessa, the Russian Marseille, came the peasant son Andrei Zhelyabov, a strong man with a dark beard. His father had been a serf, and Andrei was ten when Alexander II emancipated them. After high school he went to the law school at the university in Odessa. He was expelled and exiled from the city two years later for taking part in student riots. He went through many underground circles and student groups, prison and political trials. Eventually, he concluded that the only way to achieve his goals was terrorism.

From Kiev came the ideologue of terrorism, the nobleman Kolotkevich; from Kharkov came the always agitated son of a Jewish merchant, Grigory Goldenberg, who had killed the governor general of Kharkov.

Also from the south was Mikhail Frolenko, the son of a poor retired corporal. He had been accepted at the St. Petersburg Technological Institute, but he found it boring. Frolenko moved to Moscow to study at the Petrovsky Agricultural Academy, where Nechaev murdered the student Ivanov. It was much more interesting in Moscow, where Frolenko joined the revolutionary bohemians, began publishing proclamations, and participated in all the student meetings. In the end, he dropped out of the academy and lived illegally. During the back to the people movement, he went to the Urals to seek out bearers of the Russian revolutionary spirit. He expected to find them among fugitives from Siberian prisons and members of sects persecuted by the Russian Orthodox Church. Frolenko believed that the Urals would be crawling with rebels. Dressed in peasant clothes, Frolenko traveled through the area, mostly on foot. After three months, he returned, never having run across a single sectarian or fugitive from a chain gang, and joined Land and Freedom. He made daring attacks on prisons to free revolutionary prisoners. He was highly valued in the organization. Among his comrades with refined aristocratic, or intellectual, or typically Jewish faces, Frolenko looked like the average working-class Russian. He was their man on the street.

Another arrival was the aristocrat Stepan Shiryaev, a specialist in dynamite. He was a dandy in fashionable clothes. He had worked in Paris in the laboratory of Yablochkov, one of the inventors of the electric light bulb, and returned to Russia with expert knowledge in electricity. Shiryaev created an underground laboratory; with him worked a true genius, the future father of rocket engines Nikolai Kibalchich.

When Kibalchich joined the organization, he swore: "I promise that all my time and all my efforts will serve the revolution through terrorism. I will study a science that will help me and the comrades apply their efforts in a manner that is the most profitable for the revolution." With Shiryaev, they created the most advanced technology in Russia for making dynamite bombs. Prepared ahead of time for use in attacks, their bombs would spend long periods on the bottom of the Neva River and still work.

A good-looking married couple came to Lipetsk, Alexander Barannikov and his wife, Maria Oshanina. He was the Avenging Angel, with olive skin and raven hair, a worthy successor to the Jacobin aristocrats who killed their emperors. She, the daughter of a wealthy landowner, had ash-colored hair, dark eyes, and "a thirst for the blood of the oppressors." After his killing of chief of gendarmes Mezentsov, Barannikov returned to the countryside to inspire revolutionary fervor in the peasants. After the daring, danger-filled life he led in St. Petersburg, enlightening the peasantry seemed unbearably dull. As Mikhail Frolenko said, laughing at their life in the country, "Their boredom was immense, and they accepted the invitation to Lipetsk like liberation from the Tatar yoke." Thus, a beautiful young woman joined the ten men.

Nikolai Morozov, tall, thin, in spectacles, looked like a typical member of the intelligentsia. Orphaned young, he was the son of a landowner and a serf. His father's butler, whose wife was taken by the master, blew up both of his parents with a powder keg. Nikolai Morozov learned about explosions in his infancy, and now he planned to devote his life to them.

Another interesting character was Lev Tikhomirov, the main intellectual and brains behind Land and Freedom. He was twenty-seven, but because of his mind and erudition and also his middle-aged appearance (by contrast with the majority of the arrivals, who were strong, healthy, and handsome), he was called The Old Man. It became his party pseudonym. "L. A. Tikhomirov is the best exponent of our ideas and goals," Nikolai Morozov said. With time, this "best exponent" would become the staunchest foe of those same ideas and goals. But at first, as the terrorist Vera Figner put it, "Lev Tikhomirov was our acknowledged ideological representative, theoretician, and best writer."

The main organizers of the congress came before the rest. They were the founders of Liberty or Death and the dismantlers of the former Land and Freedom—Alexander "Robespierre" Mikhailov and Alexander Kvyatkovsky. They were an odd couple: fat, round-faced and amiable-looking Mikhailov, and sleek, tall Kvyatkovsky who had a refined face framed by a well-tended beard.

The son of a Siberian gold prospector, Kvyatkovsky had studied (like Frolenko) at the Technological Institute, took part in student riots, quit, and went to the people. He worked as a sharecropper, smith, laborer, and peddler in villages. He came back convinced of the primacy of terror. Like many of the other arrivals, he was exceptionally strong and courageous. He had taken part in attacks on prison convoys and had twice rescued prisoners.

The young people spent their time peacefully in the hotel, went to take mud baths, and spent a lot of time boating on the unpleasantly named Antichrist Pond. "In Lipetsk . . . behind the spa's gardens was a large pond or small lake with very clear water," recalled Frolenko, "but surprisingly, there were no fish. We often took a boat and rowed there. . . .

We asked the peasants and learned that the cause for the absence of fish was the weir built by the Antichrist. By Antichrist, they meant Peter I!"

During the reforms of Peter the Great, the people believed that Peter, who destroyed the Patriarchy in Russia and many ancient habits and customs, was the Antichrist, whose coming had been prophesied by church books. Many works appeared proving it through numerical calculations. Russia's Great Transformer dealt with these authors handily, sending them to the stake or to dungeons.

The boat rides were not recreational. On Antichrist Pond, far from prying ears, "many preliminary questions were raised and discussed." By mid-June, all eleven had arrived. On June 15 they went for their first historic meeting, in a very romantic spot.

Mikhail Frolenko wrote: "We found out from the bellmen that there was a forest outside town where people had picnics. We hired coaches, bought food, some wine, purified vodka, and set off." The summer weather was perfect. The eleven (almost all of whom would end up hanged or dying in isolation cells) were merry.

"The road outside town was an unending series of meadows. . . . Far ahead lay the forest, where we were headed. Andrei Zhelyabov showed us his strength. Along the way, he bet someone that he could lift a droshky with its driver by the rear axle." They saw a new carriage on the road. "Zhelyabov jumped down from our droshky, rushed over to the one approaching, grabbed its rear axle, and lifting it with the driver, stopped the trotting horse in its tracks." That's the kind of people they were.

They reached the spot, released the drivers, and "started looking for a place where we would not be readily seen from afar but from which we could see anyone approaching us. We found a place quickly. It was a group of trees and shrubs in a meadow, almost in the very center. Settling in that green island, we could see everything around us on the meadow, while we remained invisible and unheard. . . . We placed the bottles of wine, the food, and glasses on the grass, to make it look as if we had come to have a party, and immediately began our discussion."

At this first meeting Kvyatkovsky and Mikhailov read the program and bylaws of the new party. They were accepted unanimously. This was the first time political terror was part of a party program.

Two more meetings were held in the cheerful green glade. At the last one, they defined the main goal of the coming terror. "At the third meeting . . . Alexander Mikhailov read a long list of charges against Emperor Alexander II. . . . 'The emperor has destroyed in the second half of his reign,' said Mikhailov, 'almost all the good he permitted to be done by the progressive figures of the sixties.'"

"A vivid outline of the political persecutions of recent years ended that marvelous speech. . . . The listeners pictured long lines of young people sent to Siberian tundras for love of their homeland, the emaciated faces of prisoners, and the unknown graves of freedom fighters," wrote Vera Figner.

After the obligatory revolutionary bathos, concrete questions were raised. Should the good works at the beginning of his reign pardon Alexander II for "all the evil that he has already done and will do in the future?" The answer was a resounding "No!"

In that cheerful glade eleven people condemned the emperor of an enormous empire to death. After that, they had a long discussion about how the eleven of them would overturn that great empire with its huge punitive apparatus. Outwardly, it seemed like a meeting of madmen, but there already existed new technology that made the murder of rulers quite possible despite all safeguards. Moreover, it allowed them to kill the guards along with the guarded, and to get away unscathed. The pistol and dagger, the main weapons of nineteenth-century conspirators, were becoming obsolete.

Now there was dynamite, an advanced technology invented by the Swede Alfred Nobel in 1867, the year after the first attempt on the Russian tsar's life. Old Man Tikhomirov, the smartest of the lot, put it this way: "Terrorism is a very toxic idea, very terrible, which can create strength from impotence." Dynamite was the terrible power of the powerless.

As Goldberg later testified, it was at Lipetsk that "we first spoke of using dynamite in the work of the revolution." The idea of dynamite as a powerful weapon was already discussed by students in 1874. Europe was beleaguered by mysterious naval catastrophes that took many lives. They happened to old ships that exploded in the open sea once they left Dutch harbors. It turned out that shipowners were insuring old, useless ships and then blowing them up with newly invented dynamite and timing mechanisms.

Actually, besides the use of dynamite, another innovation arose in the Lipetsk meadow: a party of a new type. Robespierre Mikhailov was its creator. At the head was the Executive Committee. All the members gave their entire fortunes and lives to the committee. You could join it, but you couldn't leave. The decisions of the Executive Committee (EC) were not subject to discussion but had to be executed unquestioningly by the rest of the party. The all-powerful EC had agents of various categories working for it. They were the "revolutionaries of the second rank" that Nechaev had written about in his *Catechism for the Revolutionary*.

"Agents of the Executive Committee," recalled Maria Oshanina, "were appointed by the committee and had no rights, only obligations." They were the revolutionary capital to be spent by the EC. The eleven people in the meadow named themselves members of the EC: A. I. Barannikov, A. I. Zhelyabov, A. A. Kvyatkovsky, N. N. Kolotkevich, A. D. Mikhailov, N. A. Morozov, M. N. Oshanina, L. A. Tikhomirov, M. F. Frolenko, S. G. Shiryaev, and G. Goldenberg.

At the head of the EC stood the Administrative Commission. The members of the EC met and passed resolutions, and the commission supervised their execution. Between meetings, the commission had dictatorial powers and demanded absolute execution of its own decisions. It met almost daily. The Administrative Commission consisted of three people elected by the members of the EC from its members. At that time the three were Alexander Mikhailov, Lev Tikhomirov, and Alexander Kvyatkovsky.

An iron dictatorial discipline was maintained in the new party, from top to bottom. That is exactly how Vladimir Ulyanov-Lenin would build his party.

The bylaws described terror as the main means and the main goal of the party. There were several departments subordinate to the EC. The Military Department was headed by Andrei Zhelyabov, who formulated the first rule of future terrorism: its relentlessness. "The meaning of terror and all the chances of its success lie in consistency and relentlessness of action. . . . Under the blows of systematic terror autocracy will start to crack. The Government is not able to withstand such pressure for long and it will make actual, instead of virtual, concessions. Any deceleration is disastrous for us; we must go by forced march, straining our abilities." Ruthless, uninterrupted terror would blow up the existing order, as Nechaev had once dreamed. Nikolai Morozov and the chief ideologue Lev Tikhomirov were elected editors of their planned underground newspaper.

They moved on to a discussion of the first steps of the new party. It was decided to start with a bang—blowing up the tsar in a railroad car. It had to be done that very fall, when he was returning from his usual stay in Livadia. The Lipetsk congress was declared closed. The next day the participants left for Voronezh, two or three at a time, as they had arrived for this meeting.

The congress of Land and Freedom met in Voronezh and concluded with a schism. The former Land and Freedom was buried. Two months later, the terrorists of the Lipetsk congress announced the creation of their own organization. They called it the People's Will, as it is usually translated, even though the Russian word *volya* means both freedom and will.

The Voronezh congress added new members to the EC, including Vera Figner and Sofia Perovskaya. Now there were twenty-five members of the EC. The most famous new member would be Sofia Perovskaya, who changed the course of Russian history.

———

Sofia, known as Sonechka, always wore the favorite outfit of the "progressive college girls," a modest brown dress with snowy white starched
collar. Her round face, shining blue eyes, and light brown hair made her
look like a little girl. Only the too-large, sloping forehead spoiled the
delicate girl's face. With every year her forehead grew larger; it seemed to
take over her face. Lenin had that kind of forehead.

The People's Will members believed in Nechaev's definition: "The
revolutionary is a doomed person." They forswore a personal life until
the victory of revolution. But that vow was often broken, because youth
was stronger than promises.

The rock-hard revolutionary Sonechka Perovskaya became Andrei
Zhelyabov's mistress. They were a strange match: the handsome heroic
man and the little girl with the large forehead. He was the son of a serf
and she was the great-great-granddaughter of the hetman of Ukraine,
the great-granddaughter of a minister, the granddaughter of the governor of the Crimea, and the daughter of the governor of St. Petersburg.
The scion of serfs joined with the scion of the most outstanding aristocrats.

Sonechka Perovskaya came from the line of the Razumovsky counts.
Their distant ancestor was a simple Cossack and alcoholic. His son,
Alexei Rozum, had a beautiful voice and was brought to St. Petersburg
to sing. At the court church, the choirboy was seen by the future empress
Elizabeth, and she fell in love with him. When she ascended the throne,
Elizabeth gave her lover the title of count of the Roman Empire. The
former choirboy became Count Alexei Razumovsky, whom the court
jokingly called the Night Emperor.

Sober, he was good-natured and treated his title with self-deprecating
humor. But drunken (his father's blood!), he was combative and beat
Elizabeth's officials. The wives of these courtiers had services said in
church when their husbands went to dine with the hospitable Count

Razumovsky, praying that they would return without broken noses. Even Elizabeth felt his wrath, for he sometimes beat "his treasure," the empress of Russia. When he sobered up he crawled abjectly on his knees before the locked door of his mistress. But the empress could not go long without his nocturnal services. The count stayed out of court intrigues, had no great opinion of his own intelligence, and read only one book, the Bible. Instead of intrigues, he took care of his family. He brought his mother and brother from the village.

They dressed his mother in a court dress and brought her to the palace to meet the empress. There were no mirrors in the village. When the Cossack woman saw herself in a mirror, she dropped to her knees to bow—she thought it was the empress she was seeing.

He also brought his brother, Kirill, who was herding cows when they came to take him to St. Petersburg. He climbed a tree to hide from what he thought were recruiters for the army. At fifteen, Kirill was illiterate. But not much later he graduated from Goetingen University and eventually came to head the Academy of Sciences. Unlike his brother, Kirill Razumovsky was involved in court intrigues and conspiracies. Under Catherine the Great, he was the last hetman of Ukraine. He was Sonechka's great-great-grandfather.

His son, Count Alexei Razumovsky, minister of education under Alexander I, was married to one of the wealthiest brides in Russia, but did not live with her. He lived with his mistress and had ten children by her. They were all given the surname Perovsky, after the count's estate, Perovo. They were all granted noble status and some had brilliant careers under Alexander II. One was a minister, another a general, a third an influential tutor of the heir to the throne. They helped Sonechka's father, Lev Perovsky, become governor of St. Petersburg.

Following family tradition, Sonechka's father lived openly with a mistress while his own family was in financial need. All the other Perovskys lived in luxury, and the little girl saw it when she was taken to visit her famous and influential relatives. After the first attempt on Alexander II, Lev Perovsky was forced to retire, reducing the family circumstances even more.

This might have been when the very proud girl developed her hatred of inequality and her thirst for justice. In high school, she befriended girls who became revolutionaries. At sixteen, Sonechka Perovskaya left her parents' house; she participated in workers' circles, was arrested, and spent time in the fortress. Her father went to see Peter Shuvalov, chief of gendarmes, and she was released. Sonechka was sent to the Crimea, where her grandfather was governor. There she studied medicine to become a paramedic and work for the people. Then she was one of the defendants in the Trial of 193 narodniki. She was exiled to the Olonetsk Province. While she was being transported there, she slipped a sleeping draught into the gendarmes' tea and escaped. She began living without legal status. She took part in the armed attempt to free I. Myshkin, who gave the celebrated speech at their trial. They ambushed the wagon taking him to hard labor. They wounded the gendarme accompanying him, but Myshkin was in leg irons and could not jump down from the wagon.

She was iron-willed. Once she made up her mind to do something, she was implacable. Her comrades feared her. She did not forgive weakness. As Stepnyak-Kravchinsky, who assassinated Mezentsov, said about her, "That woman is capable of driving a party comrade to suicide over the slightest failure."

Upon their return from Voronezh, the EC went into action. An agent was sent to Switzerland to buy dynamite, which was smuggled into Russia. Shiryaev and Kibalchich started making bombs.

In late August at a secret apartment in Lesnoi near St. Petersburg, the EC had a meeting. The main point on the agenda was whether they should roll out numerous terrorist acts against top government officials or concentrate solely on killing the tsar.

The unanimous answer was to focus on killing the tsar. They formulated a pacifying theory of "the final killing" that would end the era of terror. They believed that the people would rise up in response, putting an end to the autocracy. Alexander Mikhailov, the de facto leader of People's Will, kept a written history of its work. "26 August 1879, the Executive Committee passed a death sentence on the Emperor of All of Russia, Alexander II."

At the time the forces of People's Will in the capital consisted of only a few dozen people, but with the new technology, that was enough. The power of the powerless worked.

In the fall, when Alexander II left for Livadia, the EC had enough dynamite to destroy his imperial train. There were only two ways by which he could return to St. Petersburg, by sea through Odessa and then by train to Moscow and St. Petersburg, or by coach to Simferopol, and then by train. In either case he had to pass through the small town of Alexandrovsk. Thus the Odessa-Alexandrovsk-Moscow triangle covered all possibilities. Whichever way he traveled, he had to go through one of those places. The dynamite would be stored in all three, and his train would be blown up wherever he went.

The members of People's Will went off to deliver their fatal presents for the tsar.

In September 1879, Vera Figner came to Odessa with the first portion of dynamite. Nikolai Kibalchich himself followed with explosives. Pretending to be a married couple, they rented an apartment on prestigious Ekaterininskaya Street.

Mikhail Frolenko arrived soon after. The trio started its dangerous work—they made fuses, dried pyroxylin, and tested the explosive mechanism. Dynamite was extremely sensitive and often blew up on its own, killing the dynamiters. That is what they were called, dynamiters, a new word for a new time.

The bombs were made. Now they had to place them on the tracks of the tsar's train. Vera Figner went to see Baron Ungern-Shternberg, son-in-law of Count Totleben, the governor general of Odessa. Her refined society manners and good looks enchanted the baron. Figner asked him to find a job as a railroad guard for her servant, because "the doctors prescribe outdoor work because of his lung disease." The baron was delighted to be able to help the aristocratic beauty, and he wrote a letter of recommendation to the head of the Odessa railroad. A new guard began work in the little village of Gnilyakovo, outside Odessa. He was Mikhail Frolenko, with his working-class looks.

But all the work in Odessa was in vain.

They had an agent in Simferopol, A. Presnyakov. At his youthful twenty-three, he had already been arrested, escaped, and lived abroad. But terror in Russia seemed much more attractive for the revolutionary than gay Paris or wealthy London. Presnyakov sent a coded telegram to Odessa to report that the tsar was not going there, he was traveling to Simferopol. Next his train would go through Alexandrovsk and Moscow.

In Alexandrovsk the terrorist group was headed by Andrei Zhelyabov, who assumed the role of a merchant come to the town to set up a leather factory. He bought land right next to the railroad tracks. This was at a point where the train traveled on a high embankment. They hoped it would be a bloody run.

Zhelyabov testified, "The place where the mine was laid was a huge ravine. The bomb was placed there with the intention of taking the entire train. . . . We knew how many cars there would be in the tsar's train." The chosen spot guaranteed the greatest damage. The cars would fall into the ravine. The victims would be not only the tsar and his family, but ordinary people, servants and guards. Of course, the former peasant Zhelyabov no longer worried about them. Revolutionary expediency meant that the end justified the means.

Every night Zhelyabov and his assistants, dressed in black, worked on the embankment. The ground was frozen, the cold had come early, and a cold autumn rain fell. But he dug tirelessly until the tunnel was ready. Then Zhelyabov did the most perilous part—he moved the armed mine into the tunnel, under the tracks. He had to carry it 200 meters, because the horse could not get any closer. He carried it, expecting it to blow up at any moment.

Everything was ready. Zhelyabov demanded the honor of connecting the wires for the explosion. His peasant hands would blow up the emperor's train.

It was November 18, the day the tsar's train was to travel through Alexandrovsk. A coded telegram informed Zhelyabov that the train with the tsar's retinue would come first, followed by the imperial train, and that the tsar would be in the fourth car. At nine that morning Zhelyabov and his comrades went to the embankment and down into the ravine. He dug out the buried ends of the wires and waited.

The first train roared above them. The imperial train came soon after. Three cars passed over the spot with the mine. Then came the fourth, with the tsar. One of his comrades shouted to Zhelyabov, "Go!"

Triumphantly, Zhelyabov made the connection. Nothing happened. The train rolled down the track and out of view. They stood there in furious frustration. So much effort for nothing. The EC created a special commission to investigate the reason for the failure. The peasant son Zhelyabov had connected the wires incorrectly.

The tsar's train rushed toward Moscow.

They followed the same scheme in Moscow. A pleasant married couple, the Sukhorukovs, came to the suburbs of the old capital. Stepnyak-Kravchinsky described it this way: "In one of the suburbs of the first Russian capital, where that half-Asian city, no less majestic than ancient Babylon or Nineveh . . . meets the gardens, orchards, and meadows that surround Moscow on all sides, in that almost rural part of the city stood a dilapidated one-story house with an attic, blackened by age and half in ruins."

The Sukhorukovs rented that house, just 150 meters from the Moscow-Kursk Railroad. They were Sofia Perovskaya and Lev Gartman. From their house they started to dig toward the tracks, to lay the mine. They told the owner of the house that they were going to do major repairs and boarded up the windows. Others came to dig: Mikhailov, Barannikov, Morozov, Shiryaev, and their comrades.

They did not know how to make a tunnel. "Manuals on sappers and mines did not give us anything useful," recalled Mikhailov. They learned as they went along. They had to dig a shallow tunnel because of the groundwater that quickly rose to the surface. But even at that depth, the floor was constantly damp. Week after week, on all fours, up to their necks in cold wet mud, they worked from early morning until late at night; they covered no more than two meters a day. They reinforced the tunnel with boards. In case the reinforcement didn't hold and there was a cave-in, they carried poison so that they would not suffer long.

The police posed a much greater threat. "All the participants knew what awaited them in case of arrest. A bottle of nitroglycerine was kept in the house, to be blown up if the police were breaking down the door," wrote Stepnyak-Kravchinsky.

Once, a fire broke out near their house. The neighbors knocked and offered to help carrying things out. They could not let them in, and quick-witted Sonechka Perovskaya saved the day. She grabbed an icon and ran outside, shouting, "Leave everything as it is, it's God's will. You can protect yourself from God's punishment only through prayer!" The neighbors treated that declaration with great respect and left them alone. The girlish figure stood outside holding the icon and blocking the way until the fire was put out.

"However, despite all the danger, the most sincere merriment reigned in the little house. . . . At meals, when everyone gathered, we chatted and joked as if nothing were out of the ordinary. Sofia Perovskaya's silvery laugh pealed most frequently, even though she kept a loaded revolver in her pocket, with which if necessary, she would blow up all and sundry," the members recalled.

And so they labored and sincerely made merry, listening to Sonechka's silvery laughter, before attempting to blow up a trainload of people. The tunnel went through the railroad embankment, right under the bed, and they could listen to the distant rumble of approaching trains. It would increase until the train roared right overhead, the tunnel roof shaking. "The wheels jumped from rail to rail. . . . Everything shook around you . . . earth rained down through the cracks onto your head, into your ears and eyes, and the candles guttered, and yet it was pleasant to greet that mighty force flying past you," recalled Nikolai Morozov.

At last, the time came to lay the mine. And here some of them worried that there wasn't enough dynamite, even though Kibalchich assured them it was more than adequate. They received a telegram from their tireless agent A. Presnyakov: "The price of wheat is two rubles, our price is four." They knew that the imperial train was traveling second, behind the retinue's train. And the tsar was in the fourth car. They had plenty of dynamite for one car.

Goldenberg, impatient for action, went to Odessa to take the unused dynamite from Vera Figner. He put it in a big suitcase and headed back to Moscow.

He blew his cover at the Odessa train station. Dressed like a dandy, Goldenberg dragged the big and clearly heavy suitcase along the platform himself. He did not use a porter, as an obviously wealthy man would do. This made one of the porters suspicious and he reported him to the police.

The police sent a wire to the next station, Elisavetgrad, and the police there were waiting for Goldenberg. He tried to run but was immediately surrounded. He pulled out a gun. From the report to the Third Department: "It was not possible to approach him and take him: he cocked his revolver and aimed at whoever came near . . . thereby outraging the crowd against him."

Finally, they got the gun away from him, and the crowd attacked poor Goldenberg. The gendarmes put an end to the beating. "However, even after that it took six men to tie his hands: he was so strong . . . and also angry, and he even bit."

Grigory Goldenberg's fate was horrible. At the Fortress of Peter and Paul, Goldenberg was given an experienced investigator, who quickly understood his main trait—monstrous conceit (a reaction to the endless humiliations he suffered as a Jewish child). Listening to Goldenberg's proud speech about the great and noble goals of the People's Will, the investigator proposed that he could save Russia. It would take very little—revealing to the government the true lofty aims of their party and describing the noble activists of the revolutionary party, after which, naturally, the government could not persecute such people. "The fault lies in our general confusion. But now he would lead the lost youth of Russia from the darkness of terror and the lost government toward the light of general reconciliation."

Goldenberg believed it and wrote one hundred fifty pages, giving names, addresses, events, facts, and brief biographies of one hundred forty-three "noble members of the People's Will." However, at one of the interviews he warned, "Bear in mind that if even one hair falls from the heads of my comrades, I will not forgive myself."

"I don't know about hair . . . but I can promise you that heads will fall for sure," the investigator said, laughing.

Goldenberg hanged himself in his cell.

In Moscow, the revolutionaries learned about Goldenberg's arrest, but they were sure that he would not inform on them. A new blow awaited them on November 18, when they heard that the train got through Alexandrovsk without problem. They attributed that to an arrest, as well. They thought that Zhelyabov and his comrades had been caught, which might mean that the police were on their trail. They expected them to show up at any moment. Sonechka's pistol was ready, and their nerves were strained to the limit.

Things were still quiet on November 19, when the train was to pass by. The arrival of the trains of the retinue and the tsar was expected at 10:00 and 11:00 P.M. All the diggers left the house. Nikolai Morozov took a rock from the deadly tunnel as a memento. "We discussed who should stay in the apartment to await the train and set up the explosion. We decided that Gartman and Perovskaya would stay to the end. The role of the person who would do the explosion was merely to make the connection," said Shiryaev.

Thus, Sonechka would keep watch outside, and as the tsar's fourth car came by, she would signal Gartman in the house, who would connect the wires. The mine would explode and the imperial train would fly into the air.

The historic moment arrived—the first train was barreling down the track. As the telegram had informed them, it was the entourage, and Sonechka let it go by. About half an hour later, the imperial train came into view. The cars rattled by, one at a time. There it was, the fourth car. She gave Gartman the sign. He connected the wires and a powerful blast shook the sleepy town of Rogozhskaya Zastava. The car was tossed into the air and it fell, wheels up. The other cars were derailed.

Perovskaya and Gartman quickly fled the scene. The tsar surely was dead.

War Minister Milyutin, who was in the imperial train, wrote, "The imperial train usually travels a half hour behind the other one, usually called the retinue train. This time it went ahead of the retinue train. It was due to mechanical problems with the retinue train. The tsar did not want to wait while they changed the locomotive, and the imperial train went first."

Perovskaya had let the tsar's train go by, and they blew up the retinue train. "The baggage car with fruit from the Crimea was blown up. There were no human casualties," Milyutin wrote.

It was dark when Alexander reached Moscow. Troops were lined up at the station, and music played. When he left the station, the echo of a distant explosion could be heard.

He stayed at the Nikolayevsky Palace in the Kremlin, where he had been born sixty-one years earlier.

Milyutin wrote: "Around ten that evening, we moved into the Kremlin palace and had not yet settled into our rooms when we learned that the second train, traveling a half hour behind the first, with part of the retinue, servants, and baggage, just as it reached the outskirts of Moscow crashed because of a secret mine. Obviously, this villainous attack had been intended for the tsar's train; a completely random circumstance (change of trains) led the villains into confusion. . . . The locomotive got past, but the two baggage cars behind it fell on their side; the other cars were also derailed, but fortunately were undamaged and not a single person was hurt."

The tsar was unpacking when minister of the court Alexander Adlerberg came in. He told the tsar that the retinue train had been blown up. "The fourth car of the retinue train has been turned into marmalade," Adlerberg said. "There was nothing in it but fruit from the Crimea."

The emperor must have turned white with the realization that his was the fourth car in the imperial train. He now knew that they knew everything, the order of the trains and even the secret number of his car. Someone who was very well informed was feeding them information. His helpless response was reported: "What do those scoundrels want with me? Why are they badgering me like a wild animal?"

From Moscow he sent a telegram to the empress: "Arrived safely in Moscow, where it is 14 below zero. I am saddened that you are in the same condition. I feel good and not tired. Tender kisses."

The next day the rumor spread through Moscow that the explosion was the work of students. A crowd rushed the university, but the police were already in place. At the Cathedral of the Assumption, a thanksgiving service was held for the health and miraculous rescue of the tsar. "God saved me again," Alexander said. He did not know that God had saved him twice on that terrible voyage.

"The event of November 19 brought a grim color to our entire stay in Moscow," wrote Milyutin. "We were still under that horrible impression during the trip to St. Petersburg. All measures were taken to protect the imperial train from new dangers. We did not let them know in St. Petersburg when the tsar would arrive. The troops of the imperial garrison, all the officers, officials, and even imperial family waited for several hours in the streets and at the station, in extremely and unusually cold weather. All telegraph service was suspended. To make matters worse, there was a blizzard in the night. The emperor got to St. Petersburg only around three in the afternoon. He was sad and serious."

His heir was waiting for him in the palace. He was grim. His eyes conveyed his desire, "Destroy sedition." He wrote in his diary: "22 November. Father back from Livadia, after two days in Moscow, where there was another attempt on his life. . . . It's horrible, what a sweet time we live in!"

Now not only the tsar's coach was guarded when he moved within his own capital, but also the entire railroad when the imperial train was traveling. Grand Duke Alexander Mikhailovich, who came to St. Petersburg with his father, the viceroy of the Caucasus, described his surprise: "The Moscow–St. Petersburg line, all 605 kilometers, was lined by troops. Throughout the entire journey we saw the glimmer of bayonets and soldiers' greatcoats. At night thousands of campfires lit our way. At first we thought this was part of the ceremony of greeting the Viceroy, but then we learned that the Tsar was planning to visit Moscow in the near future, and therefore the government was taking extreme measures to protect his train from attack by villains. This saddened us greatly. Apparently, the political situation was taking on an extremely tense character, if even the train of the Emperor of All Russia needed every inch of road between the two capitals guarded. This was very unlike the days when Emperor Nicholas I traveled almost without guards through the most remote areas of his vast empire. Our father was very troubled and could not hide his agitation."

In the meantime there was a police report. They had found the tunnel under the tracks. It led to the house of a certain Sukhorukov, which was only 150 meters from the railroad bed. The house was empty, but when the police arrived, the stove was filled with glowing embers, the samovar was still warm, and a candle was burning. The man who called himself Sukhorukov was not only a terrorist, he was also a con man. Just before the explosion, he borrowed a large sum of money from a widow, using the house he had rented as collateral.

The terrorists' proclamation was brought to the tsar. "On November 19 of this year, near Moscow on the Moscow-Kursk railroad line, on the orders of the Executive Committee, an attempt was made on the life of Alexander II by blowing up the tsar's train. The attempt failed. The reasons for the mistake and failure we do not find necessary to publish at the present time.

"We are certain that our agents and our entire party will not be discouraged by the failure, but will draw from this incident confidence in their strength and the possibility of successful struggle. Appealing to all honest Russian citizens for whom the road is free, for whom the people's will and the people's interests are sacred, we once again proclaim that Alexander II is the main representative of the usurpation of the people's sovereignty, the main pillar of reaction, the main perpetrator of court murders. . . . In order to break despotism and return to the people their rights and power, we need general support. We demand it and expect it from Russia."

The most inexplicable aspect of this story is the behavior of the tsarist police. On November 14, right after Goldenberg was arrested in Elisavetgrad, a telegram was sent to the Third Department: "Today at the Elisavetgrad Station the gendarmes arrested an unknown man arriving on the Odessa train. He resisted arrest. His baggage held more than thirty-six pounds of explosives. Under interrogation he declared himself to be a socialist. I am reporting this."

"Was he preparing for the imperial train?" wrote Drenteln, chief of the Third Department, on this information. But what a strange question. It's unlikely he was carrying dynamite for his own amusement. It was obvious that terrorists were preparing to blow up the imperial train. They should have telegraphed the train, perhaps stopped it, checked the railroad bed. They should have done something. But nothing was done. Only fate saved the tsar.

Stepnyak-Kravchinsky wrote: "The enormous dynamite conspiracy organized by the Executive Committee in 1879 in expectation of the tsar's return from the Crimea was perhaps the grandest affair ever undertaken and brought to a conclusion by conspiracy. The organization did not have the personnel to execute it and therefore we had to use the services of many outsiders selected from the populous world of sympathizers that always surrounds a popular organization like the one that the EC was running then. It is not surprising then that with so many partici-pants the rumors of the coming attempts spread very quickly literally throughout Russia. Of course, people did not know where the explosion was to take place. But all students, lawyers, and writers with the excep-tion of those on the police payroll, knew that the tsar's train would be blown into the air during the trip from the Crimea to St. Petersburg. People talked about it, as they say, everywhere. In Odessa one rather well-known writer (I. I. Svedentsov) ran a subscription for the explosion almost openly, and the fifteen hundred rubles he raised were delivered to the EC. The police knew nothing."

Knew nothing? With its numerous agents and gigantic staff of informers? Why not? We will never know.

The penultimate new year in Alexander's life, 1880, arrived with no greater sense of security. He had to admit that the executions and martial law had not pacified the country. Everyone expected reprisals, yet the emperor called Kostya. Grand Duke Konstantin Nikolayevich later related joyfully, "The tsar told me that he would like to show Russia a sign of trust for the 25th anniversary of his reign [February 19, 1881] by taking a new and important step toward completing the transformations he had undertaken. He would like to give society more participation than presently in the discussion of the most important affairs."

Instantly rumors of a constitution began. Alexander had a confer-ence, but when he announced his intention to continue reforms, the tsarevich's eyes filled with horror. He saw the same horror in the eyes of the courtiers and the members of the extended Romanov family. They wanted a continuation of reprisals, not concessions.

That evening he noted in his memo book: "29 January, conference with Kostya and others, we decided to do nothing." And once again he would spend hours plunged in deep thought in his study.

He suffered another humiliation. From the head of Russian foreign intelligence service came word that Lev Gartman had recently arrived by train in Paris, and he was the terrorist–con man Mr. Sukhorukov who was behind the bomb on the railroad. The Russian government demanded extradition.

Minister of Foreign Affairs Gorchakov appealed to the president of France: "The question is not about a Russian nihilist, but the principle of punishment. We must ask ourselves: is it possible to struggle with these new barbarians under these conditions?" He went on to say that they must not be given the opportunity to make "conspiracies freely, without any personal risk. It is enough for them to create a plan, dig a tunnel, set the mechanism for a certain time or send an electric spark from a distance" and then "vanish to another country to wait the results of their destructive work . . . under cover of the right to refuge that guarantees them security and freedom."

The Russian government demanded the return of the "new barbarian." But the French president's chancellery was engulfed by letters from the public outraged by the "Russian monarchist frenzy." The public campaign was headed by Victor Hugo, who sent an appeal to President Grévy. The French demanded Gartman be protected from "tsarist terror," and French newspapers printed articles by famous Russian radical émigrés—Georgi Plekhanov, Petr Lavrov, and Stepnyak-Kravchinsky. The Russian ambassador, Prince Orlov, was informed by mail that a death sentence had been passed on him by the "Russian Socialist Committee in Paris."

The president of France refused to extradite Gartman, and the tsar could do nothing but recall his ambassador from France.

Alexander decided to bring back the ailing empress, since the climate in Nice was not helping her. He thought she was afraid of dying alone in a strange land. It was winter. He sent Count Alexander Adlerberg to bring her back.

The empress had read in the newspapers about the new attempt on the Moscow railroad. This was another blow for her. It turned out she did not want to return at all, especially now after the attempt on his life.

She did not want to go to a country where the monarch was humiliated and where he in turn humiliated his empress.

"No one asked my opinion. This is a cruel decision. I think they would treat a sick housemaid better," she complained to her lady-in-waiting.

In preparation for departure, she wept and said that in her condition she would not be able to take a long winter journey. In fact, she was so ill on the trip that her ladies-in-waiting thought several times that they would not get her home alive.

Dr. Botkin explained to the tsar that it was important to keep her from being upset. So no one except a few family members was allowed to greet her at the station. She was brought to the Winter Palace, where she went to bed and did not get up again.

Unbeknownst to almost everyone, there was an assassin in the Winter Palace. Even the members of the "Great EC" (as Russian revolutionaries would subsequently call the committee) did not know about him. It was kept top secret. Only the Administrative Commission—Alexander Mikhailov, Lev Tikhomirov, and Alexander Kvyatkovsky—knew about the agent of the People's Will now in the home of the Alexander II.

The core belief of the People's Will, that once the tsar died, tsarism would fall, was becoming more popular in workers' circles. The laborer Stepan Khalturin decided that the tsar must fall at the hand of a worker. "Let all tsars know that we workers are not so stupid and we can evaluate the 'services' tsars afford workers." The thought that the tsar had betrayed the people and therefore must be killed by a worker became an idée fixe.

Having committed to regicide, Khalturin started on his path to the Winter Palace. He was an excellent carpenter with a wide network in the St. Petersburg labor market. He soon got a job working on repairs of the tsar's yacht. It was a good step, and he acquitted himself well enough to come to the attention of the palace administration. Stepan Khalturin got the position he wanted at the palace.

Then he got in touch with the People's Will. He offered to blow up the palace, with the entire royal family. He asked for cooperation from the EC, which would give him information, but most important, supply the dynamite.

The proposal was discussed by the Administrative Commission and accepted, naturally, but only as a backup. The commission was planning the attacks on the railroad, and they had neither the time nor the dynamite for a palace job. They told Khalturin to take the job at the palace and bide his time. In October 1879, under the name of Batyshkov, he began to work at the Winter Palace and to wait.

Khalturin was tall, with rosy cheeks, and the very sight of his always-happy young face was cheering. He became popular with the servants, especially the many females. The household services were on the first floor and in the vast cellars—kitchens, storerooms, workshops. Khalturin lived in the cellar with the other carpenters and his workshop was there, too. The royal family lived on the second floor. In the marvelous formal rooms, in the "reserve half," the luxurious private apartments of the many Romanovs, and in the rooms of the lord chamberlains and ladies-in-waiting, something was always in need of repair or replacement. The calls on the very good handyman "Batyshkov" were frequent.

Khalturin even made repairs in the Diamond Storeroom, which held the imperial regalia and treasures accumulated over the centuries of the Romanov dynasty. Famous diamonds were there, for only the monarchs of Russia, Germany, and Austria-Hungary bought large precious stones in those days. Later when the Bolsheviks confiscated the tsar's diamonds they found themselves in the position, as Grand Duke Alexander Mikhailovich wrote, of robbers "who got the commodity and destroyed the only possible purchasers."

Khalturin learned the layout of the Winter Palace.

The tsar was expected back from Livadia and the palace was getting a general sprucing up. Khalturin worked from morning till night, primarily in the tsar's rooms, renovating the valuable furniture. Portraying the peasant Batyshkov, Khalturin turned out to be a talented actor. He came up with a useful mask—the dull-witted, simple peasant. All the footmen laughed at his awkward manners and habit of scratching behind his ear while thinking. They tried to impress the unpolished country rube. Their boasting stories gave Khalturin a good picture of the palace schedule and the daily life. The fear that pervaded the reign of Nicholas I was long gone from the palace, as it was from Russian life. Only the oldest servants remembered the "reverent atmosphere, like church."

General Delsal, commandant of the palace, was in charge of security. The old general, wounded in Sevastopol, kept up the patriarchal, preterrorism mores. The lack of discipline and the lax habits of the innumerable staff amazed Khalturin. His coworkers had parties in the staff rooms, attended by dozens of their friends, who came and went at will.

"At a time when even the most high-ranking people could not pass through the main entrances of the palace, the back doors were open at all hours of the day and night for any tavern acquaintance of the lowliest palace servant. Sometimes the visitors stayed the night in the palace," Khalturin said.

The debauchery in the servants' quarters and the disorder in household management shocked Khalturin. There was widespread thievery, and Khalturin had to steal food in order not to seem suspicious.

The revolutionary was not making this up. The same petty thievery was rampant even during the magnificent balls at the Winter Palace. The situation was so typical that Leo Tolstoy described it in his novel *Anna Karenina*. At a ball, a grand duchess asks one of the officers to show his new helmet to the Italian ambassador, who is interested in Russian army equipment. The cavalry guardsman begs off with some excuse. The grand duchess insists, and he takes it off. The grand duchess "turned over the helmet and—bam, a pear fell out, followed by two pounds of chocolates," wrote Tolstoy. The officer had stolen it from the dinner tables.

As soon as the Moscow bombing failed, Khalturin became the main player in the tsar's murder. His connection with the EC was Kvyatkovsky. Now he met with Khalturin daily, to pass along some dynamite, which he brought into the palace in small portions.

Kvyatkovsky's apartment was turned into a dynamite laboratory. He kept detonators and other parts there. But the apartment had to appear to be an ordinary family home. Thus, Kvyatkovsky was given a "wife," played by Vera Figner's younger sister. The elegant Kvyatkovsky and his wife, a typical aristocrat with flawless manners, looked good together.

At one point, Khalturin had an opportunity to get the deed done with one blow. He was called into the tsar's study to polish the furniture. The tsar was there, with his back to him, by his desk. A blow to the head with his hammer, and the tsar would be dead. But he was not prepared to kill an unarmed old man from behind. When Kvyatkovsky learned of the lost chance, he cursed Khalturin roundly.

But time was on the side of the EC. Khalturin figured out that the cellar where he and the other carpenters lived was right under the tsar's dining room. He would kill them all there.

Between the cellar and the second-floor dining room was the guards corps, where the sentries lived. A good fifty men, they were peasants beloved by the revolutionaries. They would be doomed by an explosion in the cellar. Khalturin said coolly to Kvyatkovsky: "It'll kill fifty without doubt . . . so it's better to put in more dynamite, so that they don't die in vain, so that it definitely gets him."

In order to blast through the mighty granite vaults of the Winter Palace, Shiryaev and Kibalchich calculated that over 300 pounds of dynamite would be needed.

Khalturin continued bringing it in to the palace. "Every morning," Khalturin recounted, "after work, I went out [to meet Kvyatkovsky] and came back with a small portion of dynamite, which I hid under my pillow. I was afraid to bring in more, which would attract attention. There were frequent searches, but they were so superficial that no one ever thought to lift my pillow (my luck!), which would have destroyed me. Of course, I had instilled absolute confidence in me with my good behavior."

Sleeping on dynamite takes its toll. Nitroglycerine is highly volatile and highly toxic. Inhaling the vapors poisons the blood. It made Khalturin's eyes strain out of their orbits, and his rosy complexion turned to clay. He had terrible headaches.

He came up with a clever idea—he purchased a large trunk, which was delivered to the cellar. He told his roommates that he was getting married and was buying his bride's dowry. He had gotten a bonus for good work, and he intended to keep the dowry in the trunk.

Beneath the dresses and lingerie, he kept a large amount of dynamite. The explosives-filled trunk was to play the role of an infernal machine. Until November 24, that is, when Kvyatkovsky did not bring the next portion of dynamite and did not appear at their meeting place. He also failed to show up for the daily meeting on November 25.

Unbeknownst to Khalturin, Kvyatkovsky was in a detention cell, arrested, and his apartment was being searched. The trusting sister of Vera Figner had given illegal literature to a friend, who showed it to her lover, who immediately reported it. The police came to the apartment.

A strange turn of events ensued. The police found a green glass jar filled with nitroglycerine and magnesium, necessary components of dynamite. They found vessels with fulminate of mercury, used for detonators. These were all parts of destructive explosives.

It became clear what they were to be used for. The police confiscated a paper that Kvyatkovsky vainly tried to burn. It was a building plan, with an X marking one of the rooms. The police determined that it was a plan of the Winter Palace and that the X marked the royal dining room.

The palace should have been searched thoroughly, and all the staff should have been checked, particularly the new people. Someone from inside had given the terrorists the building plan.

None of it was done. They settled for searching the rooms adjacent to the dining room. They also did perfunctory searches of workers returning from leave. They did not bother Khalturin, who had already brought 250 pounds of dynamite into the palace.

He even continued adding to his stores, because now Andrei Zhelyabov brought it to him.

Both of the great actions of the Great EC—the bomb on the railroad

track and the bombing in the Winter Palace—could have, rather, should
have, been averted. But the police were strangely inactive. The question
arises again: why?

The trunk now held close to 280 pounds of dynamite. Khalturin suggested blowing up the dining room. The Administrative Commission
held a special meeting, asking their chief dynamiter to speak.

"What would be the effect of exploding that charge?" they asked.

"The tsar will be scared, but unharmed," Nikolai Kibalchich replied
firmly. "My calculations remain in effect—you need 320 pounds. Even
better would be 360 pounds." (Serpokryl, a member of People's Will,
later recounted this.)

Khalturin was nervous. Free access had been limited, and residents of
the palace had to wear a brass badge identifying them. Nonetheless, he
continued to bring in the dynamite in small pieces, "Inventing various
subterfuges to avoid being searched or to trick the vigilance of the
searchers."

In other words, even after Kvyatkovsky's arrest, there still was no
mandatory search of everyone. The security check was clearly easy to
foil, but Khalturin was tired and pushed for a quick move. Zhelyabov
also wanted to use the dynamite as soon as possible. So the Administrative Commission, despite Kibalchich's opinion, gave the order to set off
the bomb.

Now, Zhelyabov waited for Khalturin every evening on Palace
Square. As he walked past, Khalturin would say, without stopping,
"No." The explosion was postponed.

Khalturin wanted the whole family to be there, and he learned that
on February 5, Alexander of Hesse, the empress's beloved brother, would
be visiting the Winter Palace. In honor of the occasion, a six o'clock family dinner would be held. The tsar would attend with his sons, the heir
Alexander and Vladimir. The empress, it was said, would not be able to
join them, for she did not leave her bed.

On February 3, agents of the EC lured a typesetter in their underground printing house, Zharkov, an informer, onto the ice of the Malaya Neva River. Stunned by a bludgeon, Zharkov fell. Young Presnyakov finished him off by stabbing him with a dagger.

On February 5, Khalturin had to get the carpenters who lived with him out of the cellar by six o'clock. It was not difficult. He invited them to a restaurant to celebrate his engagement. The restaurant was not far from the palace, and just before six, he told them that he wanted them to meet his fiancée and would go get her. He left them in the restaurant and hurried back to the palace.

The clock struck six. He could tell by the bustle among the staff that the prince had arrived. Khalturin went down to the cellar and connected the wires. He had fifteen minutes to get out of the palace.

St. Petersburg was in a blizzard. For three days heavy snowflakes fell on the city. The bridges and buildings drowned in snow and the street lights could barely be seen. It was disquieting and lovely. The Egyptian sphinxes on the Neva lay under a blanket of snow. The lights of the Winter Palace merely flickered in the distance.

Zhelyabov, covered in snow, waited for Khalturin on Palace Square. Khalturin appeared out of the swirling snow. "With amazing calm he greeted Zhelyabov and said, as if it were an ordinary conversation, 'It's ready,'" recalled Lev Tikhomirov. A few second later a thunderous explosion rang out in the square. The palace seemed to shudder, and the lights went out in the windows.

The dark palace vanished in the white blizzard.

The emperor had been waiting for Prince Alexander of Hesse. The blizzard had blocked the roads; even the horse-drawn trolley wasn't working. He sent his sons, Sasha and Vladimir, to meet the train. It was delayed by snowdrifts, and the prince arrived just in time for dinner.

It was just after six when the emperor, his sons, and their guest approached the Yellow Dining Room (named for the color of the walls). Suddenly, the floor began to rise beneath their feet, and there was a heavy, monstrous thud below. "The floor rose as if in an earthquake, the gas lights in the gallery went out, there was total darkness, and the air was filled with the disgusting odor of gunpowder or dynamite," recalled the prince of Hesse.

"We all ran to the Yellow Dining Room, from where the noise came, and found all the windows burst open, the walls showing cracks in several places, almost all the chandeliers out, and everything covered with a thick layer of dust and plaster," the heir wrote in his diary.

There was smoke in the dining room. The windows were blown open by the shock wave, but even the freezing wind could not dissipate the thick, sulfurous smoke. Only one chandelier was still lit, and at the table two barely visible footmen, covered in plaster, stood at attention. The table service was covered with plaster, the candelabras rising above it. The palms decorating the table were also white with plaster. This suddenly white space, with the immobile, ghostlike footmen and the devilish smell of sulfur, was like a vision from the Apocalypse.

The heir's diary records: "There was total darkness in the big courtyard, and terrible screams and noise came from there. Vladimir and I immediately ran to the main guard house, which was not easy, since all the lights were out and the smoke was so thick that it was hard to breathe."

Terrified servants ran around with candles in the dark. The palace was in a state of panic. They could not find the commandant. He was stuck between floors. Because of his leg injury, Delsal usually used the lift. He had entered it and was on his way up when the blast occurred. The lights went out and the lift stopped.

"The poor general, not understanding the reason for the halt, hung in the air for twenty minutes, which must have seemed an eternity to him. He was surrounded by complete darkness on all sides," recalled lady-in-waiting Tolstaya.

The fire bell rang in the square and fire engines hurried to the palace.

The firemen ran up the marble stairs to the corps de guards. As a newspaper described it, "It was hell in there. Ashes, smoke . . . impossible to breathe . . . flares barely showed through the smoke . . . the firemen's helmets shone. . . . They brought more flares. Now the site of the catastrophe was illuminated. The granite floor, made of very heavy slabs, had been tossed up like a toy ball by the horrifying force of the explosion. A mound of broken slabs, rocks, plaster. . . . Beneath the ruins we heard moans. . . . Among the mounds in the smoke lay figures. It was impossible to walk—there were arms, legs, and other body parts strewn everywhere. . . . And in the light of the flares, we could see dark spots on the walls. . . . The wretched guards were literally blown apart. Wounded and dying men, groans and pleas for help that the firemen, crazed with horror and darkness, could not give. The only medic on duty that evening in the palace, and the nurse, rushed among the wounded."

Sasha and Vladimir entered the sentries' space. "When we ran in, we found a terrible scene: the entire large guards room where people lived was blown up and everything had collapsed more than six feet deep, and in that pile of brick, plaster, slabs and huge mounds of vaults and walls lay more than fifty soldiers covered with a layer of dust and blood. It was a heartbreaking picture, and I will never forget that horror in my life!" wrote the heir.

If not for the granite slabs, there would have been nothing left of the dining room or of the royal family. They were saved by the room full of murdered sentries.

While his sons ran down to the sentry room and a footman came out of the darkness to lead the frightened prince of Hesse away, the emperor ran upstairs. All the gas lights in the corridors had gone out and the halls were plunged into darkness. What if they were in the palace? He ran through the black, smoke-filled space. An illuminated face floated out of the dark—a lackey with a candelabra. He grabbed it and ran to the third floor. Beyond the chamberlain's rooms he saw a weak strip of light. She was in the doorway with a candle. She was waiting for him.

The empress was the only person in all of St. Petersburg who knew nothing about it. She had slept through it. She slept almost all the time. The tsar would not permit her to be told.

In the evening the church bells rang dutifully about yet another miraculous escape. This was the fifth attempt on his life. If there really had been a gypsy who told his fortune, he should have been counting.

First they kept him from walking around his city, then from riding the train in his country, and now he could not live peacefully in his own house.

The next day, as usual, he received the war minister Dmitri Milyutin.

He tried to be calm, as usual.

Milyutin wrote in his diary: "The tsar called me to his study. As in the previous similar incidents, he maintained total presence of mind, seeing in this case a new manifestation of God's Finger saving him for the fifth time from villainous attack."

That was a lovely explanation. However, the minister, like the rest of Russia, could not get rid of this thought: "This incident was particularly amazing. Everyone has to think—where can one seek peace and safety, if villains can lay mines in the royal palace itself?!"

The minister was right, where could one seek peace and safety? St. Petersburg was in even greater panic than before. As the newspaper *Golos* put it: "Dynamite in the Winter Palace! An attempt on the life of the Russian tsar in his own dwelling! This is like a nightmare. Where is the limit and when will there be an end to this barbarity?"

Or, as Grand Duke Konstantin Nikolayevich wrote in his diary, "Nerves are so taut that you expect to be blown up into the air at any moment. We are living through the Terror [of the French Revolution] with the difference that the Parisians could see their enemies face to face, while we not only do not see them or know them, we do not even have the slightest idea of their numbers."

Later, Grand Duke Alexander Mikhailovich repeated the same sentiment: "It would be too weak a comparison for me to say that we lived in a besieged fortress. At war you know your friends and enemies. Here we did not know. The chamber footman serving morning coffee could be working for the nihilists . . . every chimney sweep who came in to work now looked like the bearer of an infernal machine."

Apparently, this was the consensus in the Romanov family and in St. Petersburg. A letter to the Third Department warned, "Beware your chimney sweeps, they've been ordered to put gunpowder into your chimneys. Avoid theaters, masquerade balls, because there will be an explosion soon in the theaters, in the Winter Palace, in the barracks."

Rumors were rife, as Alexandra Bogdanovich wrote in her diary: "They said that under the Small Church of the Winter Palace they found a hundred pounds of dynamite." . . . "Now they check the cellars daily in St. Isaac's Cathedral—you never know, they might put some dynamite there, too, since they do it so easily." . . . "They threaten to blow up all of St. Petersburg on February 19." . . . "Some say that they will ruin the water pipes in St. Petersburg and we will be left without water, others that printed leaflets were sent the barracks of the Preobrazhensky, Horse Guards, and 8th Fleet that they will be blown up; they say that there was another incident at the palace, that they are still finding dynamite."

Another writer feared death from the air. "At the time wild rumors spread in the city that the entire center was mined. . . . Balloons with dynamite would be sent at the city. Panic and fear spread like the plague through St. Petersburg."

The People's Will discussed the incident in an illegal apartment. Khalturin was terribly depressed, not because he had killed and maimed fifty people, but because the tsar was not killed.

"The news that the tsar was safe had an oppressive effect on Khalturin. He collapsed, and only tales of the enormous impression made by February 5 on Russia could console him a bit, although he never could accept his failure," wrote Tikhomirov.

The Great EC did express its regrets over the death of the sentries. Here is the Proclamation of the Executive Committee of the People's Will dated February 7, 1880.

"With deep sympathy we regard the death of the wretched soldiers of the tsar's guard, those forced guardians of the divine villain. But as long as the army is a bastion of tsarist absolutism, until it realizes that in the interests of the homeland its sacred duty is to be with the people against the tsar, such tragic conflicts are inevitable."

So it was their own fault and a lesson for others.

They concluded with a new threat. "We declare once more to Alexander II that we will continue this fight until he abdicates his power to the people, until he offers societal restructuring to a national Constituent Assembly."

The sentries were buried on February 7. The tsar was in the church for the funeral service. There were ten coffins on the catafalque and Alexander said, "It feels as if we are still at war, back in the trenches near Plevna."

After he returned to Russia and published *The Devils*, which was panned by the avant-garde critics, Dostoevsky turned to newspaper column writing. He started publishing *Diary of a Writer*, in which he told the reader, with frenzied frankness, everything that worried him about Russia right then. He wanted to be extremely sincere and he recognized no political correctness. His "biting thoughts" were often against everyone. His timely and topical diary was read eagerly even by those who disagreed with him. Only work on his last novel, *The Brothers Karamazov*, interrupted the diary.

In those years, the usually solitary writer had a few close friends— Konstantin Pobedonostsev, the journalist Alexei Suvorin, and other leaders of the retrograde party were his circle. But they should have been wary of him, too. No matter how conservative he was, he could never become officially affiliated. While he was against the nihilists, he was simultaneously against reprisals against them and executions. "I cannot consider moral the man who burns heretics. I have only one moral model and ideal—Christ. I ask: would he have burned heretics—no. That means that burning heretics is an immoral act," he wrote in a letter to Professor K. Kavelin.

It is why he had wanted an acquittal for Vera Zasulich. Fidelity to Christ was more important to him than fidelity to his convictions. If one day he was more retrograde than all the retrogrades, the next day he was suddenly more liberal than all the liberals. He wrote in his notebook,

"Our conservative part of society is no less full of shit than any other. So many scoundrels have joined it." In conversation he would call himself a Russian socialist.

He was in constant debate with himself. This was a struggle between "Yes" and "No" that often sounded simultaneously in his soul.

The Brothers Karamazov is a gigantic fresco depicting the battle between God and the Devil in the human heart. It is a testament imbued with forebodings of an apocalyptic catastrophe moving toward Russia. *The Brothers Karamazov* was printed in 1879–80 to the accompaniment of terrorist shots and bombs. The novel was enormously successful with readers.

Naturally the most topical of Russian writers was stunned by February 5. Soon after the explosion in the Winter Palace, Dostoevsky had a curious conversation. He was visited on February 20 by Alexei Sergeyevich Suvorin, a man known to reading Russia. He was owner and editor of *Novoye Vremya* (*New Times*), the most influential (and a semiofficial) newspaper.

Suvorin came in from the cold, tall and thin in his always unbuttoned beaver coat and ever-present walking stick. There was something vulpine and demonic about his face. Suvorin could easily have been a character in a Dostoevsky novel. He had made his way from grueling poverty to fame as a journalist whose feuilletons were read throughout Russia. He lived through a tragedy that almost cost him his mind: His wife was shot by her lover in a hotel room. Suvorin was brought there and she died in his arms. All this was newspaper fodder. But he rose from the ashes and concentrated on work. He bought *Novoye Vremya,* a failing newspaper, and soon made it famous.

The paper's basic line was patriotism for the nationalist party, hatred of liberalism, and anti-Semitism. "The motto of Suvorin's *Novoye Vremya*," wrote Russia's greatest satirist Saltykov-Shchedrin, "is to go inexorably forward, but through the anus." Nevertheless, this brilliant and terrible man was the friend of two great writers, Dostoevsky and, later, Chekhov.

Suvorin wrote a detailed account in his diary of his conversation with

Dostoevsky. It is essential reading for an understanding of what was going on in Russia at the time. "Dostoevsky lived in a poor little flat. I found him at a round table in the living room, filling *papirosy* with tobacco." He had just had an epileptic fit, and "his red face looked like the face of man fresh out of a steam bath."

They started to talk about what the whole country was discussing, February 5, the bomb in the Winter Palace. Dostoevsky offered Suvorin a scenario. "Just imagine that we are standing in front of the windows of the Datsiaro [a store on Nevsky Prospect that sold artworks] and looking at the paintings. Next to us is a man who is pretending to be looking. He is waiting for something and keeps looking around. Suddenly another man hurries up to him and says, 'The Winter Palace will be blown up now. I set the mechanism.' We hear it. What would we do? Would we go to the Winter Palace to warn them of the bomb or go to the police, to the constable on the beat, to have them arrest these people? Would you go?"

In other words, Dostoevsky asked Suvorin: If you and I knew what would happen on February 5, would we have reported it? The editor of the semigovernmental newspaper replied, "No, I wouldn't go." And Dostoevsky, the author of *The Devils,* says, "Neither would I. But why? It's horrible, it's a crime. We might have been able to prevent it." He explains why: "I was filling my *papirosy* and thinking, going over the reasons why it should be done: serious, important reasons of state significance and Christian duty. The reasons for not doing it were totally insignificant. Simply—the fear of being known as an informer. I pictured how I would arrive, how they would look at me, start questioning me, making me look at suspects, probably offering me a reward, or even suspecting me of being part of the conspiracy. They would publish: Dostoevsky fingered the criminals. Is that my business? It's the business of the police. That's what they're for, that's what they get paid to do. The liberals would not forgive me. They would torment me and bring me to despair. Is that normal? Everything is abnormal in our country."

Suvorin continued, "Dostoevsky talked on the theme for a long time, and he spoke animatedly."

The worst had happened: The liberal part of Russian society sympathized with the terrorists. They had become heroes, sacred cows that could not be touched. In the eyes of the progressive Russian intelligentsia, the killers had become fighters against the regime, which had once seduced the country with reforms and had now rejected reforms for ruthless repression. It was no accident that famous writers, journalists, and lawyers were friends of the terrorists. For example, the writer Gleb Uspensky was a close friend of Vera Figner; another EC member, the terrorist Nikolai Morozov, hid in 1879 in the apartment of the writer Vladimir Zotov. Vera Figner wrote then, "We are surrounded by the sympathy of the greater part of society."

As if to confirm this, Dostoevsky concluded his conversation with Suvorin by telling him that "he would write a novel in which Alyosha Karamazov would be the hero. He wanted to take him through a monastery. And make him a revolutionary. He would commit a political crime. He would be executed. He sought truth and the search would, naturally, make him a revolutionary," noted Suvorin in his diary.

The "political crime" punishable by execution was terrorism.

Thus, Dostoevsky, who had censured "Russian nihilism" in *The Devils,* now declared that he would make his beloved character, the holy Alyosha Karamazov, a revolutionary terrorist (that is, a devil).

Grand Duke Alexander Mikhailovich would later write in his memoirs that allegedly Dostoevsky told Suvorin that day a terrible prophetic thing: "Wait for the sequel. Alyosha will leave the monastery and become an anarchist. And my pure Alyosha will kill the tsar."

It may seem incredible, but the existence of that apparently impossible plot line was published three months later in the Odessa newspaper *Novorossiiskii Telegraf.* On May 26, 1880, it reported rumors "in St. Petersburg literary circles on the further content of *The Brothers Karamazov.* In the continuation of the novel, Alexei Karamazov, under the influence of some special psychological processes in his soul, is brought to the idea of regicide."

This was the truth of life that Dostoevsky could not avoid: The Alyosha Karamazovs, the best young people, were becoming terrorists and regicides. That was the tragic result of the last decade of Alexander II's reign. It was the revenge of the society seduced by his reforms. This suggests the frightening paradox that the tsar of all Russia was in some way the father of Russian terrorism.

The writer's fantasy and prophecies soon became the reality of his own life. Just a few months later, in November 1880, an amazing young man moved into the apartment on the same landing as Dostoevsky's. He would walk up the same narrow staircase and go up to the same floor. Dostoevsky lived in apartment 10, his apartment was 11. He was on the other side of the wall. It would have been impossible for Dostoevsky not to notice him. He was tall and handsome, with the demeanor of a guardsman, olive skin and raven hair. It was Alexander Barannikov, participant in the murder of chief of gendarmes Mezentsov, member of the EC of the People's Will, part of the plot to blow up the imperial train, the Avenging Angel.

Next door to Dostoevsky, the truth-loving Alyosha-Karamazovs-turned-terrorist would meet. The people sought all over Russia, the leaders and members of the Great EC, met to plan regicide, the final attempt on Alexander II. They would all face what Dostoevsky planned for his unwritten sequel—regicide and death by execution or in a prison cell.

But that would happen later. Let us return to Dostoevsky's apartment and his interesting conversation with Suvorin. Dostoevsky would not go to report a bombing at the palace because "the liberals would torment" him. But why wouldn't the retrograde Suvorin go to save the tsar? He was not afraid of liberal torment, he tormented the liberals himself.

He was afraid of the conservatives. In 1880 certain letters came to Moscow from St. Petersburg. Their recipient was former lady-in-waiting Ekaterina Fedorovna Tyutcheva (sister of now also retired lady-in-waiting Anna Tyutcheva). This is what was in the letters:

"God's fates sent him to the misfortune of Russia. Even the healthy instinct for self-preservation has dried up in him: the only instincts left are of dull love of power and sensuality.." . . . "Pathetic and miserable

man!." ... "I am pained and ashamed, it sickens me to look at him.." ...
"It is clear that he has lost his will: he does not want to hear, does not
want to see, does not want to act. He only wants to live by the mindless
will of the belly."

The man reviled in those letters was Alexander II, emperor of Russia.
The writer was neither a revolutionary nor a liberal, but a key antiliberal
and antirevolutionary. Those antitsarist remarks came from one of the
most influential Russian officials, Konstantin Pobedonostsev, tutor of
the heir to the throne and soon to become head of the Holy Synod of
the Church. He was the true head of the retrograde party.

His office had an oversized desk with bronze lions. The desk was
always piled with papers and was surrounded by bookshelves. His ascetic
face, so like the Grand Inquisitor's, rose above the desk. The high forehead ended in a bare skull, his ears stuck out, and his nose was beaklike.
His constant scornful gaze rattled his interlocutors.

From this office came the ideas that fed all the retrogrades in Russia,
then and now. Many statements were attributed to Pobedonostsev: "In
Russia all things must be done without hurry. I always tell the coachman, 'I pay extra to drive slowly.' That way I know the coach won't overturn on our terrible roads. . . . We have a great legend about the spirit of
the robber Stepan Razin, trapped in a cliff. Only autocracy and strict
laws keep the rebel spirit of the Russian people in that wall. You want
reforms? A constitution? Then the cliff will split open and the wild man
will come out with a bludgeon into the boundless Russian field. At liberty, our wild man who has not known liberty, is frightening . . . he will
destroy the world around him . . . and then himself. . . . Things are simple with a European, it is all in his face. He hates you, you can see it, he
loves you, you see that, too. Our muzhik will greet you and then, with
the same kind face, grab you by the throat and choke you to death, after
which he'll cross himself."

Pobedonostsev dreamed of freezing Russia in order to save it. But for
that, he needed a leader. When the tsar appointed him tutor of the new
heir, Alexander, after the death of Niks, Pobedonostsev said, "I will bring
him to the other pole." And he did.

———

At the Anichkov Palace, where the heir resided, nothing had changed since the days of Catherine the Great. It was winter, and the conservatory was lit by the cold low sun. Inside the conservatory were marble statues, an Italian fountain with gurgling water, and evergreen trees. Outside there was snow. Anichkov Palace had been the residence for Sasha's grandfather and father when they were crown princes. His brother Niks should have lived here. But Niks was in the grave, in the Cathedral of Peter and Paul, and the waters of the Neva had probably seeped into the coffin by now. Instead of handsome Niks, he lived here: His Imperial Highness Tsarevich Alexander Alexandrovich. He was thirty-six, almost the age when his father became tsar.

After February 5, Pobedonostsev came to see him at Anichkov Palace almost daily. Dmitri Milyutin laughingly called Pobedonostsev "the nymph Egeria of Anichkov Palace." The nymph had counseled a Roman king in law. Of course, there was nothing nymphlike about the skeletal and tall Pobedonostsev. The gigantic heir was so fat he could not see his own boots because of his belly.

Count Witte, the most famous minister of the future tsar's government, left an intellectual portrait of him: "Of a totally ordinary mind, perhaps even a below average mind, with below average abilities, and a below average education." The piercingly brilliant Pobedonostsev had no difficulty in "bringing him to another pole," turning the tsarevich into an embodiment of the National Idea, a colossus of unwavering autocracy.

The heir was best suited for this role. That direct descendant of a Holstein prince (Emperor Peter III) and an Anhalt-Zerb Princess (Catherine II), who thanks to the efforts of so many German princesses had 99 percent German blood, had a very Russian appearance. "He looked like a big Russian muzhik . . . a sheepskin jacket, long coat, and bast shoes would have suited him; in manner, he was more or less bearlike," Witte continued.

The tsarevich knew this and he adored everything Russian. His habits were those of a middle-class landowner. He liked to drink and could hold his liquor. He was as anti-Semitic as many Russian landowners. He acknowledged his own limitations and respected intelligent people, so he obeyed Pobedonostsev. But his real comrade was Adjutant General Petr Cherevin, who was the deputy of the chief of the Third Department. Of medium height, neckless, and with the face of a bloodhound, the general was at heart a servant, a batman. He adored Alexander, the next tsar, the real tsar. And even though he owed his career to Alexander II, he considered him a false tsar, a Western tsar. In general, the world was divided into two categories for Cherevin: On one side were the heir and Cherevin who served him, and on the other "various scum."

He loved sharing the heir's simple pleasures, fishing, hunting, and drinking. The tsarevna did not approve of the last amusement and tirelessly fought against it. But Cherevin came up with a solution: He had boots made with very wide tops and a pocket for a flat flask that could hold a bottle of cognac. He later recalled, "Maria Alexandrovna was near us and we sat quietly, such nice boys. The minute she moved away, we'd give each other a look—one, two, three!—we'd pull out the flasks, suck on them, and then look innocent again. We used to call it mother of invention."

They kept up the game even when the heir became tsar.

At home, the tsarevich was nice, simple, kind, and cozy, very moralistic and religious. He had a "wonderful heart, good humor, and fairness," according to Witte. An excellent family man and monogamous, he hated infidelity and struck out against it, often in a childish way. He never missed an opportunity to tug on the skirts of the mannish suit worn by his aunt Masha, princess of Leichtenberg, who was secretly married to Stroganov. And then he would apologize innocently.

He could not bear his father's affair with Princess Dolgorukaya.

The heir's most dangerous trait was his habit of developing crushes. First he adored his brother Niks and was under his influence, then it was his

wife. Now it was Pobedonostsev who influenced him. The tsarevna supported this attachment. The presence of the tsar's favorite in the Winter
Palace, her illegitimate children, as well as the dying empress, and the
threat of a marriage between the tsar and Dolgorukaya after the
empress's death, hung over the tsarevich and tsarevna. She was happy
when Pobedonostsev began gathering the party that Grand Duke Konstantin called retrograde around the heir. It should have been called the
nationalist opposition.

Here are a few of the postulates Pobedonostsev instilled in the heir
and that the nationalist opposition espoused. They are not forgotten in
Russia even now.

"A constitution and parliament are the great lie of our times."

"The great truth is the autocracy of tsars."

"Old institutions, old proverbs, old customs are great and the people
must value them as the Ark of their ancestors' covenant."

"Elections are merely an art with its own strategy and tactics, like the
art of war. The crowd listens to whoever shouts loudest and who is best
at pretending through banality and flattery to suit the concepts and
inclinations popular in the masses. In theory, the voter gives his vote to
the candidate because he knows him and trusts him, whereas in practice . . . he does not know him at all, but the voter is told about him in
speeches and shouts from the interested party."

"The winner of an election is, as a rule, the favorite of the well-
organized minority, while the majority remains impotent."

The nationalist party was supposed to protect the rights of the future
real Russian tsar, Tsarevich Alexander Alexandrovich. All the opponents
of reform were part of it. In the late 1870s, General P. A. Fadeyev and
Adjutant General I. I. Vorontsov-Dashkov wrote a manifesto of the
counter-reformers. It was a book called *Letters on the Contemporary State
of Russia*. It juxtaposed "living popular autocracy" to Western constitutions: "The tsar must be an autocratic tsar and not the head of the executive branch." It criticized the "unproportionately large bureaucratic

mechanism, infected with nihilism" and called for the "restitution of pre-Petrine government forms."

The heir brought the manuscript to his father, and the emperor permitted it to be published, but only abroad.

Opposition was growing. People of passionate conviction took part in the constant meetings at Anichkov Palace, including such ideologues of nationalism as Prince Meshchersky and the columnist Katkov, who promoted the idea of the Great Slavic Empire. At the head of this union of the most conservative elements stood the heir to the throne. But the power behind him was Konstantin Pobedonostsev.

They declared themselves to be the party that protected the foundations of society, the party of order. More and more people with power joined their ranks. Thus began the battle between Anichkov Palace and the Winter Palace. All the officials of St. Petersburg knew about it. That is why Suvorin would not have rushed off to report his suspicions about a bomb at the Winter Palace. His newspaper was the voice of the retrogrades. He would not try to save the tsar, about whom Pobedonostsev had said, "God's fates have sent him to the misfortune of Russia."

The liberals were against the emperor because the reforms had stopped and the retrogrades were against him because there had been reforms. But these were politicians, leaders of public opinion. What about the ordinary people, what did they think? They were unhappy, too. "The basic underpinning of that dissatisfaction was obvious: the general economic downturn with individual artificial exceptions," wrote the contemporary historian Klyuchevsky.

The half-measures of the reforms, and particularly the unfinished agrarian reform, coupled with robber-baron capitalism, had done their work. There appeared "the impoverishment of the masses and general dissatisfaction" that always accompanied Russian reforms. Against the background of this impoverishment, Klyuchevsky continued, "the persistent work of the old guard continued." The retrograde party tried to persuade the public that all the ills were due to the reforms and that the only way out was back to Muscovite Russia, the reign of Nicholas, and autocracy. They successfully insisted on the favorite Russian contradiction: Forward means going back.

"As a result, the apathy of the days of Nicholas I ceded to general grumbling" and "wan docility to fate was replaced by malicious rejection of the existing order," wrote Klyuchevsky. War Minister Milyutin wrote in his dairy: "No one supports the government now."

Fedor Dostoevsky described the situation in Russia as "vacillating on the brink."

Right after the bomb, the emperor called in the leaders of the military and security ministries. He wanted proposals, but they sat in total confusion and said nothing.

"Saw generals Drenteln and Gurko. Both behave as if they are observers of what is going on. Yet one is chief of gendarmes and the other governor general and commander of the troops! Halfwits!" recorded Valuyev in his diary on February 6.

Grand Duke Konstantin Nikolayevich, Kostya, became a frequent visitor at the Winter Palace. The camarilla knew how dangerous his influence could be. An instant rumor spread through the court that he was behind the terrorism. No wonder he was out of St. Petersburg when the bomb went off in the palace. Mme Bogdanovich recorded, "There is always something to take Konstantin Nikolayevich from St. Petersburg whenever something happens."

From a denunciation to the Third Department: "Protect the tsar from Konstantin's intrigues, the rebels are in his hands, a screen and weapon for his aims." All this talk was passed on to the tsar.

In the meantime, the carriage bearing the desiccated Pobedonostsev pulled up at Anichkov Palace every day. He spent time with the heir in his study, after which the tsarevich would go to the Winter Palace. "I see Father every evening," he wrote in his diary. Anichkov Palace had begun its campaign.

On February 8, the tsar convened a big meeting. The halfwit ministers were still stunned, but the heir spoke loudly. He spoke as one who had the right and power, and Alexander could hear Pobedonostsev in his speech.

He mocked the idea of a constitution, "which someone might propose now. Even in Western states constitutions bring disaster. I asked their ministers in Denmark, and they all complained that because of parliamentary blowhards they cannot accomplish a single beneficial measure. In my opinion, we need to be thinking not about constitutional ideas but something completely different."

The heir continued: "My idea is very simple. I find that we are in an almost impossible position now. There is no unity in the administration; everyone is going in different direction, not thinking about a common connection." He said there was a war going on. A war with the barbarians. *A la guerre, comme à la guerre.* They needed a supreme commander who could unite all power in his hands. They needed a dictator who could deal with the homeland's enemies.

The tsarevich recalled how after the first attempt on the emperor's life in 1866, General Muravyev (the Hangman) was given extraordinary powers, and he dealt with the nihilists.

The ministers were silent. But the tsar spoke. He did not agree. They must continue thinking. Everyone left in their original confusion. "This morning there was a lengthy but almost resultless conference with the tsar. . . . The tsarevich, ministers—military, court, internal affairs, chief of gendarmes, and me," recorded Interior Minister Valuyev in his diary on February 8.

But that evening a letter from the heir was delivered to the Winter Palace. Full of filial gratitude for being allowed to speak, Sasha stubbornly proposed forming a punitive commission. It was not hard to guess who had dictated the letter to him.

The decisive night fell. It's unlikely that the emperor got any sleep. It was a miserable night in the life of rulers—when you have to tell yourself what you least want to hear. The reprisals did not work. The fourteen executions, the trials, the exile—nothing came of it. It had not worked. Freedom below and autocracy above was not feasible. It was the path to perdition. There was only one way out, and that was to create harmony. Freedom below and above. They needed reform above, reform of the regime. But that would be a turn toward a constitution. Otherwise nothing would work. Kostya was right when he repeated the words of Count Geiden. That liberal bureaucrat wrote: "Autocracy today is the path to revolution. The only possibility of preserving the monarchy is to limit it."

Alexander had to make a decision. It is hard to betray your father's testament, but he had to reject the tight fist holding Russia. That meant overcoming the opposition of the halfwits that included the court, the ministers, his son—all of whom expected more reprisals, his father's fist. But that was the usual fate of a great tsar in Russia. The writer Pososhkov put it brilliantly in the sixteenth century: "When it's uphill, the tsar has to drag ten himself. Downhill, there are millions."

Alexander came up with a way, a devious, eastern path. He needed someone to execute it. A devious, clever man, not tied to the court. He was surrounded by confused halfwits. Yet sometimes, the right man appears in a key historical moment, and there was such a man available. His name came to Alexander that night.

The next morning all the ministers were recalled to the Winter Palace. Once again they discussed what to do, and once again, there were more vague speeches, to which the tsar listened attentively. And then to the astonishment of the rest, the emperor announced that he was going to do what he had rejected the day before: He was establishing a Supreme Administrative Commission for the War on Sedition. It would have extraordinary powers, and the chairman would have power that only sovereigns had in Russia. All the highest institutions in the state, including the Third Department and the Gendarme Corps, would be responsible to him.

Thus, a dictator was being appointed. They all believed that Alexander had given up and was accepting the heir's proposal. They froze in anticipation of the dictator's name. They were stunned when they heard it: General Count Loris-Melikov.

He was Armenian, one of the most brilliant generals of the Balkan war. But he had fought in the periphery, in the Caucasus, so that he was basically unknown in St. Petersburg.

From Valuyev's diary: "February 9: In the morning another command to be at the palace. A change in the tsar's views (as Count Adlerberg surmises, as a result of yesterday's letter from the tsarevich); a Supreme Commission is being established here. To be headed by Count Loris-Melikov. The tsar's will was announced unexpectedly for everyone. The unexpected impression was expressed on every face."

The members of the Supreme Administrative Commission were senators, generals, and officials of all rank responsible for preserving order. Among them were two people very close to the heir—member of the State Council Senator Pobedonostsev and Deputy Chief of the Third Department Major General Cherevin. Everyone at the first meeting decided that the unknown General Loris-Melikov was merely a pseudonym and that the heir would be in charge.

Even the simple heir thought so. On February he wrote in his diary, "Today Count Loris-Melikov took on his new position; may God grant him success, strengthen and guide him!" The tsarevich was triumphant.

Now everyone in St. Petersburg was interested in the Armenian who did not even keep a house in the capital. He had to rent an apartment on aristocratic Bolshaya Morskaya Street.

Count Mikhail Tarielovich Loris-Melikov, age fifty-six, came from the Armenian aristocracy; that is, he did not belong in any way to the St. Petersburg elite. He was an outsider. He had served thirty years in the Caucasus, fighting in 180 battles with the mountain tribes and Turks. He was courageous and cunning. He handled his soldiers gently and cruelly, as needed, earning the nickname "the Fox Tail and the Wolf Jaw." But Loris-Melikov's outstanding trait, which distinguished him from other generals, was a gift for administration. He managed not only his army but the civilian population.

The tsar remembered how during the war Loris-Melikov not only took the impregnable forts of Ardagan and Kars but also managed the impossible. During military action he persuaded the local populace to accept Russian chits instead of gold rubles. He used them for the war, saving a lot of gold. Once peace was established, he was made a count and continued his dangerous exploits. He dealt successfully with an outbreak of plague in Astrakhan Province, and even more amazingly, returned unspent funds to the treasury—a totally unexpected gesture in Russia.

During the war on terror, Loris-Melikov had been appointed governor general of Kharkov. He ruled the province harshly but without excess. He used repression, but he also made concessions to public opinion. As a result, he was the only military governor general to have ended terrorism in his province.

PART IV

The Return of the
Tsar Liberator

CHAPTER 15

Fox Tail and Wolf Jaw

The two-faced Janus was now looking only forward. Tsar Alexander II was great once again, he was his former self, just as in the days when he emancipated the serfs. But this time there was much more maneuvering: He had to soothe his heir and deceive the opposition rallied around the tsarevich and the court.

The tsar would be behind all the actions of Loris-Melikov. At first Loris-Melikov wagged his fox tail. In those sweet days, the heir, who hated the liberal bureaucracy of St. Petersburg, was delighted by the provincial war general who seemed prepared to follow his (or rather Pobedonostsev's) every instruction.

The general did not tire of assuring him: "From the first day of my appointment as head of the Supreme Administrative Commission," he wrote flatteringly to the tsarevich, "I vowed to act only in the same direction with High Highness, finding that the success of the work entrusted to me and the calming of the homeland depend on it."

The young nihilists also believed in Loris-Melikov's total subordination. One of them decided to act, soon after his appointment. It was February 20, the very day that Dostoevsky had his conversation with Suvorin, after 2:00 P.M. Two gendarmes were at the entrance to the count's house and a policeman was patrolling nearby. Nevertheless, and despite the recent acts of terrorism, none of the guards paid attention to the suspicious "bedraggled and dirty young man" (as *Novoye Vremya* described him) hanging around the building. Loris-Melikov's carriage pulled up, with Cossacks on horseback. The count got out, and the young man rushed toward him. He pulled out a pistol from his coat and shot.

The bullet grazed the count's overcoat, tearing the coat and his uniform. Expecting a second shot, the count fell to the ground and just as quickly jumped up. Before the eyes of the stunned guards, he attacked the shooter and knocked him down. The Cossacks helped, and the bold count handed over his attacker.

St. Petersburg applauded a representative of the regime for the first time in quite a while. The public liked his bravery. But the general did note the strange blindness of the guards who had not noticed the lurking terrorist. "They were saluting instead of grabbing the villain and noticing others in the vicinity," wrote *Novoye Vremya* on February 22. The shooter was Ippolit Mlodetsky, a petty bourgeois Jew from the town of Slutsk in Minsk Province. It was later determined that Mlodetsky acted on his own, without sanction from the People's Will. But at the time, naturally, everyone assumed the mighty EC was involved. The foreign newspapers wrote about the imminent fall of the dynasty.

Loris-Melikov ordered Mlodetsky hanged immediately, without a trial, the way it is done in war. But the emperor commanded him to follow the law. New military legislation required everything completed within twenty-four hours. The investigation was completed that evening, the trial was in the morning, and Mlodetsky was taken to the gibbet later that morning.

The writer Vsevolod Garshin, who had fought as a volunteer in the Balkan War, came to see Loris-Melikov right after the attempt. To the general's surprise, Garshin begged him to forgive Mlodetsky, saying that his forgiveness would "save everything." The general could not understand that reasoning.

Mlodetsky was executed on Semenovsky Square. It was a wet, sleety February. Fedor Dostoevsky came to watch the execution. The writer was planning a novel about a young terrorist who dies in the noose and he could not miss this. Looking at Mlodetsky as he awaited his death, he thought of another young man who faced death on that very square. He had loved life so much, and he had consoled another of the condemned men with the words, "We will be together with Christ."

Kostya's second son, Grand Duke Konstantin Konstantinovich (who published poetry under the pseudonym K.R.) later spoke with Dostoevsky and recorded their conversation in his diary: "Dostoevsky went to Mlodetsky's execution. Perhaps he wanted to relive his own impressions. . . Mlodetsky looked around and seemed indifferent. Dostoevsky explained that at such a moment a person tries to chase away thoughts of death and he recalls mostly happy pictures, and he is transported to a garden of life, filled with springtime and sunshine. But the closer it gets to the end, the more persistent and tormenting is the idea of inexorable death. The coming pain and suffering are not frightening: what is terrifying is the transition to another, unknown form."

The young Dostoevsky had gotten a reprieve. This time, there was no pardon: The drumming began, Mlodetsky was dressed for the execution, and the executioner, with a friendly arm around his shoulders, led him to the noose dangling in the wind.

The emperor made this notation: "Mlodetsky was executed. Everything is in order."

As the anniversary of the emancipation of the serfs, February 19, approached, crazy rumors spread like wildfire, and people fled the city. It passed peacefully. Yet, something strange did happen. Loris-Melikov appealed to the residents of the capital. The government had decided to trade polemics with the revolutionaries. "Preaching freedom, they are trying by threats and anonymous letters to oppress the freedom of those who are performing their duty. Fighting for the principles of their personal inviolability, they stoop to murder by ambush." The government called "for help from all strata of the Russian people for a united front in the effort to uproot evil."

The regime was turning for the first time to support from the public, which the autocrats had never considered. The count explained tirelessly: The Supreme Commission is a dictatorship, but it was a dictatorship of good, of reason and law. The skeptics referred to the count's ideas ironically as the "dictatorship of the heart."

During the first two months of the work of the Supreme Administrative Commission, Loris-Melikov met several times a week with the heir. They had very amiable relations and corresponded continually. On February 21, 1880, the heir wrote. "Gracious Count, if you are not too busy and if it is possible, I ask you to drop by to see me at 8:30 this evening—I would like to speak with you."

Their meeting was very successful. That same night, on the 21st, the heir noted in his diary that he and Loris-Melikov "talked over an hour about the current situation and what to do."

The Loris-Melikov archive has many notes from the heir with the same invitation, to drop by. Their number increased as Loris-Melikov started visiting less frequently, and the heir had to send more reminders. On February 27 the heir wrote, "I haven't seen or talked with you in a long time. If you are busy and don't have time, please, don't be shy, I can set another day." He wanted to see the count because Loris-Melikov was preparing a report to the tsar with a proposed program of action. In April 1880 the report—"the plan of government actions that should put an end to the turmoil and promote bringing order in the Russian state"—was ready.

To the heir's joy, Loris-Melikov called "untimely" and "harmful" the "proposals to create national representation in forms borrowed from the West" (that is, a constitution). The heir wrote to Loris-Melikov on April 12, 1880: "Now we can go forward boldly and calmly . . . implement your program for the fortune of our beloved homeland and the misfortune of the Messrs. ministers, who will probably be very upset by the program . . . the hell with them!"

But the program upset not only the ministers. To the heir's great surprise, Pobedonostsev did not like it, either. Pobedonostsev sadly noted numerous points that Loris-Melikov made in his report. For instance, the count proposed liquidating the Third Department, which was loyal to the heir and of which one of the main administrators, Cherevin, was fanatically loyal to the tsarevich. (The files of the Third Department were transferred to the Ministry of the Interior, to form a special Police Department.)

Pobedonostsev knew that the Third Department was more than an institution, it was a symbol of the era of Nicholas I, the era of true autocracy and national fear. The simple-minded heir, intoxicated by the count's flattery, did not understand. The fox tail was doing its work.

There were many points in the program that made Pobedonostsev wary. For instance, it spoke of a "new management of the periodic press, which has an influence here that is not comparable to Western Europe, where the press is merely the expression of public opinion, whereas in Russia the press forms it." Other proposals included giving rights to sects, a review of the passport system, an easing of peasant migration, and so on. Pobedonostsev felt this was a very dangerous beginning.

The policies implemented by Loris-Melikov bore fruit right away. February ended in peace; so did March. April came, and there were still no attacks from the People's Will. Even more important, the liberal intelligentsia was changing its attitude toward both the terrorists and the regime. Success!

But the more successful Loris-Melikov was, the more he forgot his original intentions, which had pleased the tsarevich so much. Before shutting down the Third Department, Loris-Melikov did a review of the institution hated by liberals. As a result many victims of the secret police were freed from surveillance, returned from exile, and even from abroad.

The tsar was behind all of Loris-Melikov's actions. The emperor did not forget about nods in the direction of the retrogrades. He commanded Loris-Melikov to appoint Pobedonostsev chief procurator of the Holy Synod.

The tsar had felt a tangible drop in the influence of the Russian Orthodox Church. The recent trip of the Protestant Evangelical missionary Granville Waldegrave (Lord Radstock) was proof of that. The tall middle-aged Englishman, with large forehead, tufts of blond hair around his mostly bald head, and short red side-whiskers, dressed in a dull gray suit, had created a furor in the Orthodox capital. He inspired faith. After his sermons, rich men gave away their fortunes and donated thousands to charity. He was invited to every fashionable salon. Four dozen of the most aristocratic homes opened their doors to him. Count Alexei Bobrinsky, minister of transport, a man from the tsar's inner circle, and Prince Vassily Pashkov, a well-known millionaire, became Protestant.

"I found the Lord!" Bobrinsky told the tsar. Alexander thought this a dangerous symptom. The tsar believed that Orthodoxy was the main bastion of Russia's tsars, and he decided to strengthen the Church with Pobedonostsev, a wise and conservative man. He also hoped that the problems of the Church would distract Pobedonostsev from fighting reforms.

It was time to fight, because the tsar had landed a palpable blow. In late April, Loris-Melikov forced into retirement a living symbol of the retrograde movement, an active member of the Anichkov Palace party, Minister of Education Count Dmitri Tolstoy. He exemplified the official as slave. Hating the tsar's reforms, he still kissed his hand, the only minister to do so. A fervent opponent of emancipating the serfs, who whipped his serfs personally and forced serf girls into marriage and sometimes into his bed, Dmitri Tolstoy espoused the most liberal ideals in the presence of the tsar. Appointed head of education after the first attempt on Alexander's life, he invented a system that would lead young people away from dangerous modern ideas. It called for a predominantly classical education, with high school students focusing on dead languages (Latin and Ancient Greek) and memorizing long ancient works.

At long last, the round little man on stubby legs, greedy and cruel, fell. The liberals were thrilled. They called it the third emancipation: First the tsar freed the peasants from their masters, then the Bulgarians from the Turks, and now education from Tolstoy. Even an underground leaflet of the People's Will spoke favorably of Tolstoy's firing.

Loris-Melikov worked well with the press, and he set up a special commission to explore the repeal of censorship. But the press continued its favorite activity—berating the regime. Loris-Melikov was accused of breaking promises and making empty promises, of hypocrisy. When he could not stand the attacks anymore he acted in accordance with a discerning understanding of the Russian character. He did not shut down the papers, he did not fine them, the way his predecessors had. Instead, he called in the editors of the top newspapers, and waving his fox tail, he made a speech about the significance and might of the Russian press, the opinion-maker, and how he wanted to work in conjunction with it. After which he asked them not to rush the regime and not to rile the already aggravated public. He told them his long-range plans and listened to their opinions.

For once, the regime was taking advice from the press instead of persecuting it. The omnipotent minister of the autocrat asked for help and was extremely frank. He told them the most bitter truth: At present Russia could not have anything like a European parliament. Nevertheless, the editors liked him, because he did what Russians value most: He showed respect. The tone of the liberal press changed, the newspapers became moderate, and the opposition relaxed, because there would be no constitution.

The Anichkov Palace finally became upset when Loris-Melikov started flirting with the most volatile part of society, its youth. The students saw all their demands met: the right to organize mutual aid associations, to form literary and scholarly clubs, to have reading rooms and meetings. Of course, the students still wanted to rebel; they had gotten used to the thrill.

When the executor of these reforms, the new minister of education Andrei Saburov, showed up at the auditorium of St. Petersburg University, he heard a passionate antigovernment speech that called him "lying and vile." Leaflets fell from the balcony onto his head. During the confusion, a student rushed up to the poor minister and slapped him.

The next day the students had come to their senses and repented. At a noisy meeting where they were selecting guests for their university ball, they chose Minister Saburov and Count Loris-Melikov to head the list. Other names on the list included the terrorist Vera Zasulich, and People's Will member Gartman and the Pole Berezovski, who both had tried to kill the tsar.

No one persecuted them for that. The terrorist Rusakov wrote in a letter found by the police: "Count Loris-Melikov gives us all forms of freedom; this is not life, but heaven."

Alexander and Loris-Melikov had tamed Russia. The murderous attacks ceased. It was quiet.

Expressing the sentiments of the opposition, Pobedonostsev wrote to Ekaterina Tyutcheva in Moscow. "Things have quieted down thanks to him, but we'll see for how long. . . . He raises up and releases forces that will be difficult to handle. His recipe is simple . . . the students are rebelling, let's give them freedom and self-regulation. The press is going mad—free it!" He predicted: "These tricks will cost Russia dearly. O, woe!" And he warned: "The time will come when the champions of the healthy forces of truth and national life find themselves in opposition to the government. I fear that soon I will find myself in that situation. I expect great ordeals for myself from that. I cannot be silent."

Pobedonostsev could not be silent, and so he cursed. But would he stop at that? Had the time come for him to act?

The tsar's second family life was still a secret. An open secret, naturally. But this *secret de Polichinelle* continued romantically. Wherever he was, Katya and children moved nearby.

For instance, when he moved to one of his residences outside the city, Peterhof or Tsarskoye Selo, he would go out for a drive in a carriage with his children, his daughter and sons. The carriage would stop in the park and he would get out for a walk. At an agreed-upon meeting place in the park, his adjutant waited with a horse. "And the emperor rides in the direction known well to the public. . . . The second half of the walk ends in the society of his secret friend. That maneuver was repeated daily," wrote lady-in-waiting Tolstaya.

It was a very risky maneuver in view of the many attempts on his life, but love was stronger than fear. More often, a procession would appear on the palace grounds—a lady with children, accompanied by a male servant. They were brought through a hidden door into the palace. He could not exist without her and the children.

The prayer of one of the empress's ladies-in-waiting was understandable: "Lord, protect our empress, because as soon as her eyes are closed, the tsar will marry the odalisque!"

The prayer was refused. "Translucent, ethereal—there seemed nothing earthly left to her. No one could look at her without tears," remembered lady-in-waiting Alexandra Tolstaya. It hurt him to see her "all-forgiving" (accusing) eyes. "For God's sake, don't mention the empress to me, it hurts," he asked his brother Kostya.

She did not get out of bed or leave her apartment. In bed, the empress brought her affairs into order and dictated her last letters and her will to her ladies-in-waiting. Not long before her death, she thought of a poor Englishwoman she had been aiding for many years and "sent her money in an envelope, with difficulty addressing it herself with trembling hand: 'For Miss Lundy from a patient,'" Tolstaya wrote.

In her will she asked to be buried in a simple white dress without the royal crown. "I also wish, if it is possible, to have no autopsy." Most of the time, she slept. She also began having hallucinations, seeing beloved faces and talking to them. She would realize that it was her imagination and stop.

On the night of May 21, the tsar wanted to go to Tsarskoye Selo, where Katya and the children were living. He visited the empress and her condition worried him. He spoke with Dr. Botkin, wondering whether he should stay in town. "The revered Botkin declared with the confidence typical of doctors that he vouched for the tsaritsa's life for that night. . . . However, it was during that night that the angel of death came for her very quietly, while the palace slept. . . . A solitary death was the final chord in a life so far from vanity and earthly fame," wrote Tolstaya.

No one was with her when she died. Her chamber lady Makushina came in at eight and found the empress. The emperor was informed that she had died quietly, without pain, in her sleep.

In the morning War Minister Milyutin came for his daily report to Alexander in Tsarskoye Selo. He learned that the tsar had just been told of the empress's death and had left for St. Petersburg by special train.

"I hurried back to town, where I was commanded to come to the Winter Palace. It was after eleven when I entered with my report. The tsar was sad and nervous, but he had the patience to listen to my usual report."

During his conference, Makushina came in "with various rings and other pieces of jewelry that the empress usually wore. The tsar went through them himself and decided which to place on the corpse and which he wanted to keep as mementos."

After her death, besides her will, they found just one letter, addressed to the tsar and written long ago. She had saved it. In it, she thanked Alexander for her happy life with him.

Mourning was declared in St. Petersburg. While the members of the Romanov family waited to see Alexander's next steps, there was agitation in Moscow—but for another reason. The long-anticipated unveiling of a monument to Pushkin approached, and the organizers feared that the ceremonies and festivities would have to be postponed because of the mourning. In the end, the mourning period was not long or strict (for which there were good reasons), and the tsar permitted the festivities in Moscow.

Besides writers, professors, and representatives of the press, ambassadors from almost every public organization in the country, including choral societies, came to Moscow. There were numerous deputations with church banners and wreaths, and the halls were filled with crowds of admirers of the famous authors participating in the events.

The political spring that began with the appointment of Loris-Melikov had reinvigorated society, and the Pushkin festivities were a sign of that awakening. The occasion took three days. On the third, final day,

Fedor Dostoevsky gave a speech about Pushkin. It remains one of the greatest and loveliest legends in the history of Russian literature.

Reading the speech today is not the same as experiencing what occurred in the auditorium. "When he finished his speech, there was a moment of silence, and then, like a dam bursting, came unprecedented elation. Applause, shouts, banging of chairs—it all blended into one sound. Many wept, turning to strangers with exclamations and greetings; many rushed to the stage, where lay a young man who had passed out from the overwhelming emotions he experienced. Almost everyone was in a state that if the orator had called on them, they would have followed him anywhere. This must have been the effect Savoranola had on crowds in the distant past."

The reminiscences of all witnesses are the same: "When he concluded, something incredible began . . . there wasn't a person who wasn't clapping, banging, or shouting 'bravo' in a frenzy . . . women waved their hankies hysterically . . . people jumped up on chairs, the better to shout and wave their kerchiefs from there . . . hats and top hats flew into the air. People embraced universally. A young man in ecstasy rushed to Dostoevsky on the stage and fell in a nervous faint. . . . Then several charming college girls came out with a huge laurel wreath . . . God knows where they got it."

"After Dostoevsky the head of the Moscow Slavophiles, Ivan Sergeyevich Aksakov, was supposed to speak. But he . . . announced that he was in no shape to speak after Fedor Mikhailovich."

What created this triumph? First, it was Dostoevsky himself, "a hypnotic man." He came out to speak, with rounded shoulders, not very tall, head bent, tired eyes, hesitant gestures, and quiet voice. His face was unattractive and sickly pale, with a sparse reddish beard. The light chestnut hair with a reddish cast was thin and soft, carefully slicked back with pomade.

He began dryly, as if wound tight, with no movements, not a single gesture; only his thin, bloodless lips moved nervously when he spoke. But gradually, he was completely transformed. His small light brown eyes expanded and glowed. His arm moved imperiously. The audience, entranced by the hypnotic power of his words, could not pull away from those eyes, from the gesturing hand of the prophet.

The magnificent moment of that speech is not all that has vanished. The other component of his outstanding success is also gone—the burning topicality of the speech. It was desperately needed by the society divided by enmity; it was a uniting speech, so rarely popular in Russia. Speaking about Pushkin, Dostoevsky naturally spoke of his own times. He addressed a crazed Russia vacillating at the brink. He spoke of the tragedy of Aleko, the protagonist of Pushkin's narrative poem *The Gypsies,* the proud murderer who dreamed of freedom and who (as Dostoevsky wrote in *Diary of a Writer*) "needed universal happiness . . . he would not accept anything less." The audience knew that he was addressing other murderers who also believed that they were killing for the sake of freedom and who also dreamed of universal happiness.

He entreated them: "Humble yourself, proud man, and only then will you be free!" "Labor, idler!" He addressed those wretches who had forgotten what productive labor was, devoting their talents and youth to revenge and killing.

"These young wastrels who every day eat bread made with another's labor, do they have the right to any pride? If you take any of those possessed people and ask them what, finally, are their contributions to society, what tangible efforts permit them to live this way, there will be none. The great majority of them are parasites or semiparasites," wrote a contemporary meanly about the young terrorists.

But that was the point: In Dostoevsky's speech there was no anger. No reproach. Only love for the lost, only one fervent prayer—to repent, to unite, and love one another.

With this love he appealed to the two ever-hostile camps, the Westernizers and Slavophiles, who called their war "holy." He told them there was no point in fighting each other, since there were no contradictions in their views. "'We must be Russian and be proud of it,' the Slavophiles say. But to become a true Russian, you must be the brother of all men . . . for the destiny of the Russian is indubitably European, universal, as the Westernizers dream. . . . Oh, the nations of Europe, they do not even know how dear they are to us!"

Uniting all in love, forgiveness, and humility before God was what the writer begged Russia to do. This stunned the audience, used to endless arguments, debates, and malice. The Pushkin speech was Dostoevsky's anointment as a prophet in the eyes of Russians.

At the end of the year, Pobedonostsev tried to bring Dostoevsky into the Anichkov Palace party. He arranged a meeting of the writer with the tsarevich and tsarevna.

On December 16, 1880, Dostoevsky came to the palace. While there, Dostoevsky consistently violated all the rules of court etiquette. He stood whenever he wanted, he spoke first, and in departure he turned his back on the tsarevich, instead of backing out of his presence. "This is probably the only instance in the life of the future Alexander III that he was treated like an ordinary mortal," Dostoevsky's daughter wrote.

It's unlikely that this "inner freedom" would have pleased the heir. And it's unlikely that Dostoevsky did not know that. The writer remembered the words of his beloved Pushkin: "Spare us more than all sorrows the master's wrath and the master's love." A wild steed cannot live in a political enclosure. It was impossible for free thought. It was impossible for the writer who wrote, "I have only one moral model—Christ."

The denouement of Alexander's private intrigues came sooner than expected in St. Petersburg. The tsar waited until after the memorial services on the fortieth day after the empress's death and then he summoned Adlerberg. The minister of the court heard what he had feared. The tsar announced that he had decided to marry Katya. The games between the tsar and the minister, the secret of Polichinelle, were over.

Adlerberg tried to persuade him against it: The official year of mourning had only begun, this was a challenge to the Romanov family, to religion, to custom. The response was, "I am the sovereign and the only judge of my actions." The tsar ordered him to organize the wedding and to take part in the ceremony.

He was in a hurry to wed. He valued every day he lived without an assassination attempt. What if they killed him or he died on his own? Katya and the children would be left with nothing.

One romantic element remained: They married in secret.

The wedding took place on July 6, 1880, at 3:00 P.M. in Tsarskoye Selo. He led the bride into the room where a field altar had been set up. The senior priest of the Winter Palace, Father Ksenofont Yakovlevich Nikolsky, officiated. There were only a few people present, the tsar's closest associates, Adlerberg and two adjutant generals, Eduard Baranov and Alexander Ryleev. They held the wedding crowns over the heads of the bride and groom during the ceremony.

The guests were uncomfortable, but the tsar was in excellent spirits, joking and clearly happy. He wore the pale blue Hussars uniform and she a formal wedding gown.

The witnesses signed the marriage certificate: "On the sixth of July eighteen hundred eighty, at three o'clock in the afternoon, in the field church of the Tsarskoye Selo Palace, His Imperial Majesty of All Russia Alexander Nikolayevich deigned to enter a second time into a legal marriage with lady-in-waiting Princess Ekaterina Mikhailovna Dolgorukaya. We, the undersigned, were witnesses to the marriage and have written this certificate and confirm it with our signatures, July 6, 1880."

It was signed: "Adjutant General Count Alexander Vladimirovich Adlerberg. Adjutant General Eduard Trofimovich Baranov. Adjutant General Alexander Mikhailovich Ryleev."

After the ceremony, the tsar invited his wife for a carriage ride. The weather was perfect and he felt at peace. Now he did not have to worry about the future.

By the next morning, of course, the court knew. The ladies-in-waiting of the late empress were stunned and angered. The witnesses had to justify their behavior by explaining they were commanded to do so. The news traveled instantly from Tsarskoye Selo to St. Petersburg. Mme Bogdanovich recorded her "profound indignation" in her diary. The general reaction was "the old emperor has immediately forgotten his poor wife and married a young debauched woman."

The two-faced Janus didn't get it, yet again. The despot Peter the Great could marry a cook and make her an empress—precisely because he was a despot. Alexander, who wanted to rule European-style, had to think about public perception all the time. But he had been brought up by his father, and he could not get used to the idea of public accountability.

That night she slept in the palace, in his bed, and he sat at his desk and finalized formalities. He signed the necessary decree: "To the Government Senate: Having entered a second time into a legal marriage, with Princess Ekaterina Mikhailovna Dolgorukaya, we command her to be named Princess Yuryevskaya with the title Serene Princess. We command that the same name with the same title be given to our children: our son, Georgii, our daughters Olga and Ekaterina, and also to any others that might be born subsequently, and we confer upon them all the rights of legitimate children in accordance with art. 14 of the empire's basic laws and art. 147 of the Statutes on the Imperial Family.

"Alexander.

"Tsarskoye Selo 6 July 1880."

Their children, Georgii, Olga, and two-year-old Ekaterina, born in 1878, became serene princes. But according to the Statutes on the Imperial Family, "Children of a marriage between a person of the imperial family with a person without the appropriate qualifications, that is, not of royal or ruling family, do not have the right to the throne." The rules for morganatic marriage were clear. That should have appeased the court and the heir.

But they all knew that this was an autocratic state and the laws were changed by the sovereigns. "There is no will but the tsar's," as General Cherevin, friend of the heir, liked to say.

The next morning Loris-Melikov was summoned to Tsarskoye Selo. Alexander informed the count of his new marriage and told him it had to be kept secret for now. He added, "I know how loyal you are to me. From now on you must be just as loyal to my wife and my children." Then Alexander switched to current affairs. But after that, Katya, now the serene princess Yuryevskaya, was often present during their meetings.

The count understood that the tsar was showing him that this was the future empress. The title of serene princess was only the first step. Wise Loris-Melikov sometimes consulted with her before his meetings with the tsar—he knew how much it pleased him.

The heir, who had been at a spa in Gapsal, Estonia, returned to St. Petersburg, where he was immediately told the "secret." He was stunned. Deeply religious and monogamous, he never did understand his father's sinful life, but now, for Alexander to marry before the mourning period was over was too much.

Three days later the emperor summoned his son to Tsarskoye Selo. He told him about his marriage and explained his reasoning. The heir found the reasons shameful. The autocrat of Russia was afraid of being killed by a band of villains he was unable to control. They had forced the divinely anointed ruler to violate church laws. They were controlling his actions.

The heir was told that the marriage would be kept secret until the year's mourning was over. And that Princess Yuryevskaya and her children naturally had no rights to the throne and that she would never overstep her modest role.

At their first meeting, the wife of the emperor, Serene Princess Yuryevskaya, kissed the hand of the tsarevna, as was required by the etiquette for morganatic spouses.

The summer of 1880 passed tranquilly. August began, and there were still no attempts on his life. But there was trouble brewing at court and in the Romanov family. The grand duchesses, the wives of his brothers, were old women and they remained outraged by his marriage. Clearly they feared it would set a bad example. Their ladies-in-waiting and those of the late empress kept inventing terrible stories about "the odalisque." They even managed to find that the great beauty wasn't beautiful at all— and poorly brought up, at that.

Things got worse. Adlerberg told them that she dared to discuss state affairs with Loris-Melikov, and this gave rise to the rumor that would find its way into their memoirs and move into the works of many historians: The emperor had turned into a useless old man who was bossed by his young and stupid wife and the sly Armenian general.

The rumor grew stronger as it became more evident to the camarilla which way the emperor was leading the country. Princess Yuryevskaya was turned into a forerunner of Rasputin. Like Rasputin, she divided the Romanov family, and the opposition used her image to undermine the tsar's prestige.

Alexander ignored the family rebellion because his main goal had been achieved. He stopped the country from going over the brink into the abyss. His decision to bank on reform had been justified. Loris-Melikov reported the joyous tidings: It was time to disband the Supreme Administrative Commission.

The news was announced on August 6. Russia was returning to normal life and Count Loris-Melikov was giving up his dictatorial powers. At the same time the main symbol of oppression of public life, the Third Department of His Majesty's Chancellery, was being destroyed.

To replace it, the powerful Ministry of Internal Affairs was created, with a Police Department within it. The functions and personnel of the Third Department were moved there. Count Loris-Melikov was appointed as the new minister of internal affairs, of course, and he also became chief of the Gendarme Corps.

It was mid-August. The tsar was preparing to leave the city for his traditional vacation in the Crimea, in the Livadia Palace. Before leaving, he accomplished an extremely important separation of his son from the opposition. Loris-Melikov and the emperor met with the heir. Alexander knew that for all his stubbornness, the heir was a weakling, easily broken.

Loris-Melikov had the floor, and he explained to the tsarevich that reprisals only led to an increase in the influence of the revolutionaries, while the new policy had made the public turn toward the regime. The Fox Tail knew how to put things extremely simply, unlike the complex perorations of Pobedonostsev. The emperor was menacingly and significantly silent. That evening Loris-Melikov wrote to Mme Shebeko, Dolgorukaya's dearest friend, "As far as I can judge, the report I made today to the heir did not make a poor impression on him. Thank the Lord!"

Loris-Melikov was too modest. The tsarevich had once again become the obedient heir, as had been his father, his grandfather, and his great-grandfather. He was the executor of his father's will.

Now Alexander could leave St. Petersburg to the tsarevich's care. The emperor took Loris-Melikov with him. In Livadia they would work on the greatest transformation, the final goal. In blessedly gorgeous surroundings, far from the capital fraught with strife, he wanted to think through his most risky project. He wanted to make reality out of Count Geiden's phrase: "To preserve autocracy you must limit it." It was the lifelong dream of Kostya and the liberal bureaucrats.

On the morning of August 17, the emperor returned to St. Petersburg from Tsarskoye Selo, planning to leave for Livadia that evening. A carriage awaited him at the train station, and surrounded by an escort of Cossacks, the tsar set off for the Winter Palace. The usual journey took the imperial cavalcade over the Kamenny Bridge.

Certain young people had started boating frequently under that bridge. They included fat, round-faced Alexander Mikhailov (who after Kvyatkovsky's arrest had become the sole leader of People's Will), the tall and bearded Zhelyabov, who was head of the fighters, and the pleasant intellectual in pince-nez, the chief dynamiter Kibalchich. Mikhailov had come up with this plan. He felt pressured to act fast, because it was clear that Loris-Melikov was moving public opinion in favor of the regime. Terrorism was losing its popularity.

Kibalchich himself made the calculations: 250 pounds of dynamite were placed under the supports of the bridge. This would lift the tsar's carriage into the air, along with the bridge itself. In waterproof rubber cushions, the dynamite had been lowered to the bottom of the river. The wires were brought out to the plank dock by the shore where women did laundry. There, the terrorists would join the wires of their latest gift for the tsar.

On August 17, the royal carriage approached the bridge, completely surrounded by the Cossack escort. The horses galloped, and the carriage and men on horseback seemed to fly over the bridge. There was no explosion.

This time the explanation was quite prosaic: One of the main team members had overslept. The terrorist Teterka had no watch, and he reached the bridge after the carriage had passed over it.

God had saved the tsar once again. If the gypsy's prediction were to be believed, two attempts on his life stood between the tsar and his death.

Late in the evening of August 17, the imperial train left for the Crimea. Princess Yuryevskaya and the children were brought to the station. Since their marriage, she went everywhere with him, to Tsarskoye Selo and Peterhof. She told him that after the explosion on the train, she would not let him go alone. If he were to die, they would all die with him. Previously, she had traveled in a separate railroad car, and the officials accompanying the tsar pretended not to know who the lady was.

But now a tiny revolution occurred—the princess and children were escorted to the tsar's car. She took the compartment that had been the empress's. The retinue was flabbergasted. The marriage was supposed to be kept secret for a year. An even greater surprise occurred in Livadia. The princess did not depart, as usual, for the small villa in Byuk-Sarai. Instead, she moved into the Livadia Palace with the tsar. He had her move into the apartments of the late empress. Now, the retinue realized what Loris-Melikov had seen earlier. There would be a new empress.

They were together all the time in Livadia. They went for rides in his carriage, they rode horseback, they played with the children on the grounds, and in the evening they sat together on the upper veranda, cuddling and gazing at the sea.

They were together when Loris-Melikov came to discuss the coming constitution and the end of autocracy. On August 30, the main executor of the reform, its public face, cavalry general, adjutant general, and minister of internal affairs, Count Loris-Melikov was given the empire's highest honor, the Order of St. Andrew.

The emperor strengthened his loyal associate before the outrage of the court and the powerful retrogrades descended upon him.

They worked on the project every day. Ministers were summoned to Livadia. It was a plan for elected representatives from the zemstvos and towns to participate in the legislative work of the State Council. This was what he had long ago asked Minister Valuyev to elaborate, what he had discussed with Kostya before the Winter Palace bombing, and had not done. But now, he was ready.

This reform, modest by European standards, was revolutionary for Russia. For the first time a European principle was being introduced into the highest state institution—the principle of popular representation. A principle hated by his father. For the first time, elected representatives would be able to participate in the discussion of new laws.

Elections would undermine the very concept of autocracy, the holy of holies. The transformed State Council could not be considered a parliament, but it could be the embryo and forerunner of one. In Russian history, this reform came to be known as the Constitution of Loris-Melikov.

It was not yet a constitution, but as the emperor would tell the heir, "We are moving toward a constitution." This is how they prepared for the next blow against their Asiatic past. It was the path toward Europe.

But once he had decided on this project, the tsar began his old game, vacillating, hesitating, tormenting himself and everyone around him. But Loris-Melikov had figured out his psychology. The tsar wanted everyone to insist and force him. Loris-Melikov and Katya kept after Alexander.

The tsarevich came with his family to visit the tsar in Livadia, and saw that Katya had been moved into his late mother's rooms. The tsarevich was offended, and the wise tsarevna understood that something serious was afoot. These were the hateful princess's first steps to the throne. The tsarevna made the heir even more upset, so that he told his father that the situation was intolerable. He was going to Denmark to stay with the tsarevna's family. Alexander replied like a true autocrat: "Then you will no longer be the heir to the throne."

The son's rebellion was quelled. The tsarevich, gritting his teeth, had to be polite to the princess. His father took pity on him and spared his feelings. Every Sunday the emperor had the ministers brought to Livadia to dine with him. That Sunday his son and the tsarevna sat next to the tsar. But the following Sunday the tsarevich and tsarevna were sent for a long walk to visit the grand dukes, whose palaces were nearby, while Princess Yuryevskaya sat next to the tsar at the dinner table. The tsar introduced her to the ministers. She was becoming more of an empress every day.

The heir took his family back to St. Petersburg.

Everything was going well, but premonitions disturbed him. Despite all of Loris-Melikov's success, there was something ominous in the quiet. The closer they were to returning to St. Petersburg, the more he thought of death.

On September 11, the emperor sent instructions from Livadia to have 3,302,900 rubles transferred to the State Bank for the account of Ekaterina Mikhailovna Dolgorukaya. He wrote: "I give the right to her alone to use this capital in my lifetime and after my death."

In early November he wrote from Livadia to his son, who had left. "Dear Sasha, In the event of my death I entrust my wife and children to your care. Your friendly disposition toward them, which you displayed from the very first and which was a true joy for us, makes me believe that you will not abandon them and will be their patron and kind advisor. . . . In my wife's lifetime, our children must be only under her guardianship. But if Almighty God calls her before they reach their majority, I wish General Ryleev, or another person of his choice and with your approval, to be appointed as their guardian. My wife did not inherit anything from her family. Thus, all property that she now owns, including real estate, has been acquired by her personally, and her family has no rights to this property. . . . Until our marriage is announced, the capital I put in the State Bank for her, belongs to my wife by force of the document I gave her.

"This is my last will, and I am certain that you will execute it diligently. God's blessings upon you! Don't forget me and pray for your Pa, who loves you tenderly."

He knew that his son was kind, and that after receiving that letter, would take care of her and the children.

On November 12, the emperor decided to return to St. Petersburg. Loris-Melikov's department was on the alert and the police found an infernal machine under the railroad bed near the Lozovaya station. The People's Will were still active, but Russia's police were finally improving.

The tsar was leaving Livadia for the last time. As usual, he stopped over in Moscow. Princess Yuryevskaya lived with him in the Niko-layevsky Palace, where he was born.

On November 21 at noon the imperial train arrived from Moscow in St. Petersburg. Usually, he was greeted by the whole Romanov family upon his return from the Crimea. But the ceremony prescribed for such an official welcome required his morganatic wife to follow in the procession behind all the grand duchesses. He did not permit her to be humiliated this way. The formal welcome was canceled. He commanded the train to be stopped at a small station near St. Petersburg, and he had his meeting with the Romanovs in his car.

When they reached the capital, the emperor, the princess, and their children left the train, got in a carriage surrounded by Cossacks, and headed for the Winter Palace. A new present awaited her there. Instead of the pathetic three rooms in which she had lived, now a magnificent apartment was made ready for her—a habitat fit for an empress.

Work on the project proceeded quickly. In January 1881 the tsar received a report from Loris-Melikov with a draft. He read it and expressed no objections. That meant it was almost done. The tsar decided to convene a secret commission for a special session to polish the text.

"My dear Ekaterina Fedorovna," wrote Pobedonostsev hopelessly to Tyutcheva. "Another year has passed, a difficult and terrible one, leaving lots of broken pieces. Loris is a master at manipulating and charming. . . . He created two bases for himself with amazing speed—both in the Winter Palace and in Anichkov Palace. He became indispensable to the tsar, a security screen. He eased access to the tsar for the heir and gave him ready answers to all his questions, Ariadne's thread to follow out of any labyrinth. Upon the death of the empress, he grew even stronger, because he untangled an even more difficult knot in the tangled family and found a third base of support in that woman. . . . This fateful reign is pulling toward a fatal fall into an abyss. Forgive this man, O Lord, he knows not what he does, and now he knows even less. Now you can't see anything in him except [debauched Assyrian King] Sardanapal . . . I am pained and ashamed, it sickens me to look at him, and I sense that he does not like or trust me. I hurry to conclude this letter so to give to someone for you. . . . May God preserve you."

Such letters could not be trusted to the post. Loris-Melikov had instituted total surveillance. The police read all mail, even spoiling a chess game played by mail between Moscow and St. Petersburg, because they thought the chess moves were code. Letters like this had to go with trusted travelers, and there were many trusted people around Pobedonostsev.

The tsar continued introducing his wife to the high officials. Madly in love, he could not imagine that everyone else did not share his delight in her. He invited Pobedonostsev. Naturally, a description of the meeting was sent to Ekaterina Tyutcheva in Moscow. "She wore a black silk dress, only slightly open, with a diamond star on a velvet ribbon around her neck. The tsar looked pleased and happy and was voluble. She sat on the tsar's right and I on his left. Next to her was Loris-Melikov, with whom she kept talking in a low voice. . . . I found her unpleasant and very vulgar. I see no beauty in her. However, her complexion is very fine. The eyes, by themselves, would be attractive, I suppose, only her gaze has no depth—the kind in which transparency and naïveté meet with lifeless-ness and stupidity. . . . How it irks me to see her in the place of the dear, wise, and graceful empress!"

He managed to find the beautiful woman vulgar and ugly, as did all the elderly ladies-in-waiting of the late empress. "How it irks me to see her in the place of the dear, wise, and graceful empress!" That was the refrain of the aging court of Alexander II. But the besotted emperor con-tinued bringing the Romanov family together with the princess.

The tsar's brother, Grand Duke Mikhail Nikolayevich, viceroy in the Caucasus, was invited to one of the family receptions. Later his son, Grand Duke Alexander Mikhailovich, recalled: "On Sunday evening the members of the imperial family met at the Winter Palace around the dinner table to meet Princess Yuryevskaya. The voice of the master of ceremonies after he banged three times with the ivory-handled staff was uncertain: 'His Majesty and Serene Princess Yuryevskaya.'

The grand duchesses were not warmly welcoming. "My mother looked to one side, the tsarevna Maria Fedorovna looked at the floor. The emperor walked in quickly, leading a pretty young woman by the hand. He nodded cheerfully at my father and looked searchingly at the mighty figure of the heir.

"Counting on the complete loyalty of his brother (our father), he had no illusions regarding the views of the heir on his second marriage.

"Princess Yuryevskaya graciously responded to the polite bows from the Grand Duchesses and Dukes and sat next to the Emperor in the chair of the late empress.

"The many years of living together had not decreased their mutual adoration. At sixty-four, Emperor Alexander II behaved with her like an eighteen-year-old boy. He whispered words of encouragement in her small ear. He asked whether she liked the wines. He agreed with every-thing she said. He watched us all with a friendly smile, as if inviting us to rejoice in his happiness, he joked with me and my brothers. . . .

"Full of curiosity, I did not take my eyes off Princess Yuryevskaya. I liked the expression of her sad face and the radiant glow from her light hair. It was obvious that she was nervous. She turned to the emperor frequently, and he patted her arm soothingly. She certainly would have conquered the hearts of all the men, but the women were watching them, and all her attempts to take part in the general conversation were met with polite, cold silence. I pitied her and could not understand why they treated her scornfully for falling in love with a handsome, jolly, and kind man who to her misfortune was the Emperor of All Russia.

"At the end of the meal the governess brought in their three children.

"'And here's my Goga!' the emperor exclaimed proudly, picking up a merry little boy and putting him on his shoulder. 'Tell us, Goga, what is your name?'

"'My name is Prince Georgy Alexandrovich Yuryevsky,' Goga replied and started playing the emperor's side-whiskers, tugging at them with his little fingers.

"'I'm pleased to make your acquaintance, Prince Yuryevsky!' joked the tsar. 'And wouldn't you like to become a grand duke, young man?'

"'Sasha, for God's sake, drop it!' the princess said anxiously.

"With that joke, Alexander II rather clumsily tested his relatives on the question of adopting his morganatic children. Princess Yuryevskaya was extremely embarrassed, and for the first time forgot court etiquette and called the tsar, her spouse, by a diminutive in the hearing of others.

"On the trip back from the Winter Palace, we witnessed a new argument between our parents: 'Whatever you may say,' my mother declared, 'I will never recognize that adventuress. I hate her! She is despicable. How dare she in the presence of the entire imperial family call your brother Sasha.'

"My father sighed and shook his head in despair. 'You still do not wish to understand, my dear,' he replied meekly, 'good or bad, she is married to the sovereign. Since when have women been forbidden to use a diminutive for their legal husbands in the presence of others? Do you call me Your Imperial Highness?'

"'How can you make such stupid comparison!' said my mother with tears in her eyes. 'I haven't broken anyone's family. I married you with the consent of my parents and yours. I am not planning the destruction of the empire!'"

They would later accuse Rasputin of the same evil intentions.

The Romanov family understood his question, "And wouldn't you like to become a grand duke, young man?" They knew Alexander's character; he would not put up with the current situation, when the emperor's wife had to give way to grand dukes and duchesses and sit at the end of the table between the prince of Oldenburg and Duke Nicolas of Leichtenberg. He would have to crown her empress. And that would make his son a grand duke. And if that happened, would the next step follow? Would he want to give Russia a new heir instead of the son he did not love?

Their fears were not groundless. The daughter of Grand Duchess Elena Pavlovna, whose name was also Ekaterina Mikhailovna, like Katya, soon related that the tsar, playing with little Goga, said, "This is a real Russian. He, at least, has only Russian blood flowing in him."

Then came more troubling information. Allegedly the tsar said, "At least there will be a tsar with Russian blood on the Russian throne." They also repeated Loris-Melikov's servile words: "When the Russian people meet Your Majesty's son, they will say as one, 'This is our man.'"

Aware of the danger, the tsarevich became even more obedient. During a discussion of the Loris-Melikov project, the tsarevich expressed his total agreement with the will of his father. On January 17, Loris-Melikov returned from a conversation with the heir at Anichkov Palace and told Princess Yuryevskaya triumphantly: "Now the heir is completely with us."

The tsar appointed the heir head of the secret special session that would complete the elaboration of the project. As he had in the days of the emancipation, Grand Duke Konstantin Nikolayevich took a very active part in this project, becoming chairman of the State Council, where the reform was to take place.

But the tsar was frightened by the combination of Kostya's enthusiasm and Loris-Melikov's energy. He was wary of their dangerous impatience. Alexander planned to watch carefully the elections of the representatives of the zemstvos and cities to the State Council. He said, "All of Louis XVI's problems began when he convened the notables. The notables were rebels."

Despite all his doubts, on February 17, Alexander II approved the report of the special session and wrote: "Execute." The new reform would live.

On February 19, they celebrated the anniversary of his first major reform. A quarter century had passed since he had emancipated the serfs. There were more rumors of terrorist actions, and many wealthy people left St. Petersburg. The festivities were unmarred. The tsar appeared with his children on the balcony, the band played "God Save the Tsar." Then came the artillery salute, followed by the tsar's Grand Entrance. The five hundred people of his retinue awaited Alexander.

He saw how his court had aged over the quarter century. The sagging powdered flesh of the ladies-in-waiting, draped in diamonds and pearls, the quivering fat jowls of the officials drooping onto their golden epaulets. The women were dry and comically tall, the gentlemen had slumped under the weight of their years. And all those old people could not forgive Katya's youth or his youthful happiness.

Preparations for a dynastic revolt continued apace. It was not a simple matter. Empresses were crowned when their husbands were crowned, with only one exception. The second wife of Peter the Great, Catherine (the cook of Pastor Gluck), was crowned separately. After the coronation, her children born before their marriage were legitimized and took on the rights of Peter's legitimate children. Her daughter Elizabeth later became empress. This precedent and the ceremony were studied closely on Alexander's command.

Tertii Filippov, an acknowledged expert on Church history, was sent to Moscow to search in the archives for material on the coronation of Catherine I. He had to hurry, because court rumor put the coronation of Princess Yuryevskaya in August 1881.

Alexandra Tolstaya, a lady-in-waiting, wrote: "Alexander II spent the last fourteen years of his life outside the laws of God and morality. . . . It was definitely known that the tsar was thinking of the coronation of Princess Yuryevskaya, the model and precedent for the coming event was the coronation of Catherine! The archives were rummaged in the search of promising documents. . . . Everyone kept silent, but in their hearts they all thought approximately the same way: what would happen to the tsarevich and his wife, whose position was already intolerable? Could they accept the humiliating role intended for them when even we, myself included, tried to avoid her, not knowing where to apply but determined not to put up with the offensive new order. The situation was more than tragic. It seemed hopeless—no way out or salvation ahead."

Pobedonostsev and the retrograde party, abandoned by the heir, watched events unfold in desperation. The heir may have been broken now, but he might return to them—in his heart he was with them. But now they saw that he might no longer be the heir. If these members of the great Byzantine autocracy wanted to continue to exist, they had to act fast.

The sentiment that the princess was destroying the empire was repeated more and more frequently in society and especially in the St. Petersburg salons. The Armenian count Loris-Melikov, they said, was using her to push his destructive projects on the tsar in exchange for supporting the terrible idea of crowning her empress. The retrogrades saw nothing but the tsar's weakness, his old man's whining, his trembling hands, his continual sadness, and how his aides were managing him.

But it was just the opposite. He had become powerful again. If the war had aged him, love had returned his youth. Grand Duke Alexander Mikhailovich had commented that he behaved like an eighteen-year-old and that she had fallen in love with a handsome, cheerful, kind man. Pobedonostsev himself had said, "The tsar looked pleased and happy and was voluble."

To the retrogrades, their fears meant that it was time to change the ruler. Quickly.

The old ladies-in-waiting were quitting en masse, rather than serve the "odalisque." The poet Tyutchev had a third daughter, Daria, who also was a lady-in-waiting. She left "so as not to spit in the face of Princess Yuryevskaya," who dared to settle into the rooms of the "sainted" late empress. When she was leaving the palace, she had a conversation with Alexandra Tolstaya, who also "suffered from hopelessness." Daria Tyutcheva, sister of Pobedonostsev's correspondent Ekaterina Tyutcheva, said something amazing to Tolstaya: "Remember what I tell you: I have an accurate premonition that everything will change. I don't know what will happen, but you will see that in three or four months all the dirt will be swept out of the Winter Palace."

Since her enormous prophecy did take place, we can only wonder whether she had inside information. The information could have come from her sister, who had confidential letters from Pobedonostsev.

The sudden death of Dostoevsky marked the rapidly advancing end of a great era. He had welcomed 1881 happily, and his health was markedly good in the first weeks of January. He had had no epileptic fits, and his wife, Anna Grigoryevna, was sure that the winter would pass well.

Anna Grigoryevna was "the nicest and most rare of writers' wives," as a contemporary called her. The young woman had borne everything—the death of her first two children and their terrible financial situation. She was his secretary and stenographer, and she dealt with their creditors. "She followed him like a nanny, like the most caring mother. Their adoration was mutual," a woman who knew them recorded. The dawn finally broke for them. The publication of *The Brothers Karamazov* brought him national fame, which reached its apogee with the Pushkin speech. Now his every appearance on stage for fundraisers or readings drew endless ovations. There was hope for material well-being. And then . . .

On the night of January 25, as Anna Grigoryevna later related, Dostoevsky's pen holder fell to the floor and rolled behind the bookcase. "He loved that pen holder not only because he wrote with that pen, but he also used the holder to fill his *papirosy* with tobacco. . . . To get it, he had to move the bookcase, which was very heavy. He had to strain, which caused the pulmonary artery to burst and blood poured out of his mouth."

It was over in three days. On January 26, they called the doctor, and the writer seemed to improve. But at 4:00 P.M., he hemorrhaged again severely and lost consciousness for the first time. When he came to, he said, "Anya, please get a priest immediately, I want to say Confession and take Communion."

His state improved again after Communion and the night passed quietly. On January 27, there was no bleeding. But on January 28, he woke his wife at dawn and said, "You know, Anya, I've been awake for three hours, thinking, and it's become clear to me that I will die today." Poor Anna Grigoryevna tried to calm him down, but he interrupted, "No, I know that I am to die today. Light a candle, Anya, and give me the New Testament."

This was the New Testament given to him by the wives of exiled Decembrists. He often used it for predictions. In the dark winter morning, she lit a candle and he let the book fall open. It was book three of Matthew: "But John forbad him, saying, I have need to be baptized of thee, and comest thou to me? And Jesus answering said unto him, Suffer it to be so now: for thus it becometh us to fulfill all righteousness."

Dostoevsky said very calmly to his wife: "Do you hear—'suffer it to be so.' That means I will die."

At eleven, the hemorrhage resumed, and he began to die. According to his daughter, he called her and his son Fedya at six. He handed them the New Testament and asked her to read the parable of the prodigal son. Afterward, he said, "Children, never forget what you just heard here. Keep your free faith in God and never despair of His forgiveness. I love you very much, but my love is nothing compared to the endless love of God for all people created by Him. . . . And remember, if you should ever commit a crime in your life, still do not lose hope in God. You are His children, be as humble before him as before your father, pray to Him for forgiveness, and He will rejoice in your repentance as He rejoiced in the return of the prodigal son."

At eight, the death agony began. He lay on the couch in his study, a dark, unattractive room. The church of St. Vladimir, where he was a parishioner, was visible through the window. The writer Boleslav Markevich, who was there for the last minutes of his life, wrote: "He lay fully dressed, with his head back on a pillow. The light from the lamp on a table near the divan fell directly on his forehead and cheeks, white as paper, and the dark-red spot of blood on his chin. . . . His breath came from his throat in a weak whistle through his feverishly open lips. His eyes were half-shut. He was totally unconscious. The doctor . . . suddenly bent over him, listened, then unbuttoned his shirt, slipped his hand beneath it and shook his head at me. . . . It was over . . . I looked at my watch: it was 8:36."

The news of his death traveled through St. Petersburg, and a pilgrimage began to his apartment. Russia's most famous jurist, Koni, who had been chairman at the trial of Vera Zasulich, came to pay his respects. "In the dark, uninviting stairs of the house on the corner of Yamskaya and Kuznechny, where the deceased had lived on the third floor, there were quite a few people headed toward the door with an insulating covering of worn oilcloth. Fedor Mikhailovich lay on a low catafalque, so that his face was visible to all. What a face! It was unforgettable. . . . It was not the seal of death upon it, but the dawn of a new, better life . . . I could not tear myself away from contemplating that face, the expression of which seemed to say: 'Well, yes! It is so—I had always said that it must be, and now I know that it is.'"

His funeral was an unprecedented event in Russian history. A human sea, thirty thousand people, followed the coffin, seventy deputations carried wreaths, and fifteen choirs took part in the procession. His wife and other witnesses of his death recounted it in detail. But they did not recount the most mysterious aspects of his death.

If we had followed Koni up the dark uninviting staircase of Dostoevsky's house to the third floor and went not into the writer's apartment but the one opposite, number 11, we would have learned about the amazing events that took place there the very same days that Dostoevsky was dying.

Back in early November 1880, when Dostoevsky was thinking about a sequel to *The Brothers Karamazov* in which Alyosha Karamazov would become a terrorist, a new tenant had moved into apartment 11, a raven-haired, olive-skinned young man. In the large, seven-room flat, he chose the room that shared a wall with Dostoevsky's apartment. He was one of the most dangerous Russian terrorists, Alexander Barannikov, the Avenging Angel.

The EC had selected the apartment for a reason. Dostoevsky had many visitors—galleys were delivered, manuscripts were picked up for printing houses. The revolutionaries coming to see Barannikov were lost in the flow of people headed for the writer's apartment.

The author of *The Devils* now served as a smoke screen for the new "devils," who were, in fact, the heroes of his next novel. The visitors to Barannikov's apartment would have been of great interest for this book. The most frequent visitor was Alexander Mikhailov, the head of the People's Will. He kept track of all the terrorist acts they committed. Another visitor was one of the great beauties of the organization, a tall brunette often dressed in an expensive fox-lined silk pelisse and white goose down and wool scarf, Alexandra Korba, the one who wrote a letter to Dostoevsky before heading to the Balkan war. Despite the general ban on romantic entanglements among members until the revolution, Korba started an affair with chubby Mikhailov, following the example of the passionate relationship between Perovskaya and Zhelyabov.

And finally, the narrow staircase led the most mysterious member of the People's Will, whom they called the Guardian Angel, to the apartment of the Avenging Angel. His name was Nikolai Kletochnikov. He was gaunt, with sunken cheeks, not tall, with a duckbill nose, thinning hair, and a muffled voice. To use an image of the times, he was a typical "chancellery rat," or to use a contemporary one, a cubicle drone.

"Kletochnikov came to St. Petersburg in late 1878 from Simferopol, where he held a second-rate position in the district court. Before leaving, Kletochnikov had suffered some personal drama. He never told anyone what it was. But his suffering was so bad that he wanted to commit suicide. However, the political events in St. Petersburg in 1878, Vera Zasulich's shot and her acquittal by a jury, the assassination of the gendarme general Mezentsov—all this so agitated Kletochnikov that instead of suicide he decided to offer his services in a terrorist act to the revolutionaries," recalled Alexandra Korba.

Like the failure Mirsky, Kletochnikov was seduced by the fame of the terrorists. The office worker decided to change his life radically. Instead of "the sticks of the provinces and life among clerks who quarreled and drank," he wanted the danger of an "interesting life." What could be more interesting than hunting down people, especially in the name of the lofty ideal of the people's happiness?

He came to St. Petersburg where he knew two women from home who were enrolled at the higher courses for women at the liberal educational institution created for women when the universities admitted only men. Through them he met Alexander Mikhailov and Alexander Barannikov. "In his eyes they stood on an unattainable peak, and he worshipped them, hoping that they would be models of life and behavior for the rest of humanity. . . . He regarded Mikhailov and Barannikov as giants who could only be worshipped and whose influence had to be obeyed," Korba continued.

Chance sealed Kletochnikov's fate. His landlady had a close relative who worked in the Third Department. The "giant" Mikhailov came up with a plan. But instead of asking him to fight dangerous battles, Mikhailov asked (rather, ordered) Kletochnikov to try to get a despised office job at the Third Department.

This was the first mole, an agent of the revolutionaries, in the secret police. For two years (1879 and 1880), Kletochnikov worked in the chancellery of the Third Department—in the very important Third Expedition, which was in charge of political detection.

When those functions were moved to the Police Department, Kletochnikov became a junior file clerk of that department in December 1880.

He had a fine calligraphic hand and he was entrusted with the copying of secret papers, and he was put in charge of file cabinets with top secret documents. His coworkers teased him for his assiduousness, his readiness to stay after hours and to do work for his colleagues. Deep into the night, alone in the empty building, Kletochnikov familiarized himself with the files on the desks of his coworkers and in the file cabinets. Thus, the quiet office rat "knew all the political cases in St. Petersburg and all of Russia."

His hard work was noted. On April 20, 1880, he was awarded the Order of St. Stanislav. As a chevalier of the order, he told the People's Will about the plan to send agents provocateurs into their ranks. Thanks to Kletochnikov, Presnyakov stabbed to death Alexander Zharkov, who had been recruited by the Third Department. Kletochnikov also warned them of the betrayal by the miserable terrorist Grigory Goldenberg. They took measures that kept the police from using "Goldenberg's list."

Kletochnikov never took notes at the department. He did not need to. He carried home in his phenomenal memory dozens of names, numbers, and addresses every day, and he reported it all during his meetings with the revolutionaries. At those meetings, Kletochnikov wrote down his information, which Alexander Mikhailov immediately copied, destroying the originals. Kletochnikov visited the apartment of Barannikov, on the other side of Dostoevsky's wall. There he relaxed after his office work.

Such interesting people lived next door to Dostoevsky. In December, the heroes of his unwritten novel began preparing for the final act of the Russian drama of the nineteenth century—the murder of Tsar Alexander II.

Every morning in December, Barannikov left his apartment. Like a dandy flaneur, he wandered around the center of St. Petersburg, looking for something. He found it on Malaya Sadovaya Street—the basement apartment in a building owned by Countess Megden was for rent. Every Sunday the tsar turned down this street—Malaya Sadovaya—toward the Winter Palace from the Mikhailovsky Manege, where he watched the guards parade.

That fall rumors circulated about the constitution being prepared. Later, Stepnyak-Kravchinsky, the killer of Mezentsov, wrote that the People's

Will had not known of the reform. This was his attempt to justify their action before European public opinion. Only he, who was living abroad, might not have known about it. The members of People's Will living in St. Petersburg knew all about it. In fact, they feared it. This was the great paradox—two opposing forces were equally afraid of reform. The retrograde-nationalists feared the reform that would put an end to autocracy. The revolutionaries feared that Loris-Melikov's reform would lead the country away from revolution.

The interests of two hostile parties coincided. They both had to hurry.

The Trial of the 16, all members of the People's Will, took place in October 1880. Five were sentenced to death. The explosions had stopped and the public seemed reconciled. The tsar should have pardoned all five, but Alexander pardoned only three. Two were condemned to the noose. They were Kvyatkovsky, who was involved in the deadly explosion at the Winter Palace, and Presnyakov, who killed the agent Zharkov. Presnyakov, in a shoot-out during his arrest, also killed a doorman, who was an innocent bystander.

This was the first execution since Mlodetsky had been hanged. Mlodetsky, a terrorist who shot publicly, had been executed right after the monstrous explosion at the palace. But now with the attacks stopped, even those who had demanded blood were no longer furious. People got used to quieter times and forgot attacks and executions. This was a reminder. Kvyatkovsky and Presnyakov were executed publicly on Semenovsky Square.

Several years earlier, Kvyatkovsky helped Presnyakov escape from prison, and then did not see him again. Now they met on the scaffold. "Both took Communion, both embraced, first with the priest, then, their hands tied, they kissed each other and bowed to the troops. . . . When Kvyatkovsky was hanged, Presnyakov had tears in his eyes. The same fate awaited him a minute later. . . . A horrible impression! I'm not very sympathetic to the nihilists, but such a punishment is terrible," wrote Alexandra Bogdanovich, the general's wife, in her diary.

She was seconded by the mistress of another St. Petersburg salon.

Elena Shtakenshneider, whose literary coterie included Dostoevsky, wrote, "A sad and bad impression comes from that execution, even for nonliberals."

The public execution was the signal the People's Will was waiting for. The tsar would not play by the new rules, and that gave them the moral right to act. An eye for an eye! "I think we'll finish him off now," Alexander Mikhailov declared. The Great EC went into action.

After their failure on Kamenny Bridge, Mikhailov decided to continue the general scheme: blow up the tsar on one of his habitual routes. The new team included Sofia Perovskaya and two very young men, both students, Ignati Grinevitsky and Nikola Rysakov. "Our team had to determine the time and the streets . . . the tsar used for his travels in the city," according to Perovskaya.

They learned that he traveled by carriage, surrounded by six riders from His Majesty's Cossack Convoy. They traveled at great speed. The routes during the week changed frequently. But the Sunday route was inflexible. At noon, the tsar went to the Mikhailovsky Manege for the changing of the guard and parade. The time of his departure was fixed and he was always punctual. Then he returned to the Winter Palace, and there were only two ways: via Malaya Sadovaya Street and via the Catherine Canal.

At a meeting in late November, the observers summed up the situation. The emperor could be killed easily on a Sunday during his regular return from the Manege. Sofia Perovskaya noted that when he used the Catherine Canal, the driver had to slow the racing horses down to a walk when they reached the turn. "That's the best place. A bomb can be thrown accurately at that moment. . . . As for his return through Malaya Sadovaya Street [which was more frequent], that is in the center of town and there are many police agents about. It is better to mine the basement of one of the buildings on that street, and blow up the tsar's carriage from there."

That was why Barannikov looked for a basement on this street. They decided to turn the rented basement into a cheese store, and to start digging under the street. The parts of the married owners of the store were

played by a nobleman and former landowner in Pskov named Semyon
Bogdanovich and another member of People's Will, Anna Yakimova.

Bogdanovich looked like a Russian merchant, with a reddish beard
and broad red face. He called himself Evdokim Kobozev, a merchant
from Voronezh, and he and his wife moved in to the flat on Malaya
Sadovaya, where they started selling cheese.

Settled in their store, the revolutionaries decided to start digging in January. That same month an event occurred that would have been of great
interest to Dostoevsky. The heroes of his unwritten novel got a letter
from the protagonist of a published novel: "The devil" Nechaev wrote a
letter to the People's Will. The letter was momentous and they debated it
hotly.

He had been resurrected from oblivion, buried in a solitary cell several years earlier. This amazing person had managed to influence the
guards—the guards of the main prison citadel of Russia, the secret Alexeyevsky ravelin in the Fortress of Peter and Paul. Through the tiny window of the cell door, Nechaev talked to the bored guards. The former
teacher of religion knew how to speak to simple soldiers. He explained
that he was a holy martyr, suffering for the people and obeying Christ's
commandment to serve the poor. He did not fail to instill belief in his
mysterious power, either. He demonstrated it, when he slapped the chief
of gendarmes, the adjutant general Alexander Potapov, who then
kneeled before him. After that, Nechaev could tell the soldiers stories
about his high protectors, that the heir himself was behind him, and that
Nechaev belonged to the heir's party and that was why he was being persecuted. He told them this was just a temporary setback and the party of
the true, Orthodox tsarevich would soon vanquish the Antichrist
Alexander II.

The guards began referring to their prisoner as "our eagle."

Nechaev sent the soldiers to deliver his letter to the People's Will.
They believed that they were bringing it to associates of the crown
prince's party. It arrived in January, the last month of Dostoevsky's life.

"One crackling frosty night," Vera Figner recalled, they read the letter in a secret apartment. Nechaev addressed it "as a revolutionary fallen from the ranks to comrades still at liberty." Figner said, "Nechaev's letter was very businesslike—simply and directly Nechaev raised the question of his liberation."

"Let's free him!" everyone there cried with "extraordinary spiritual enthusiasm." They discussed fantastic scenarios for his escape: through the sewers during outdoor recreation for prisoners or after the guards loyal to Nechaev kidnapped members of the royal family during services at the Cathedral of Peter and Paul near the graves of the Romanov dynasty. They wrote back to him with their plans. The "Alyosha Kara-mazovs" began corresponding with "The Devil."

When Nechaev learned that they were planning to kill the tsar, he wrote: "Forget about [my escape] for the time being and get on with your work, which I will watch from afar with the greatest interest." Like the members of the People's Will, he believed that the people would rise up after the death of the tsar.

Vera Figner recalled, "That letter had an amazing impact: everything that had lain on Nechaev's character like a dark spot . . . all the lies that enfolded Nechaev's revolutionary image had vanished. [The lies were the death of the student Ivanov, his provocations with proclamations that sent many young people to prison, his use of compromising materials for blackmail, and so on.] What remained was his intelligence, undimmed by many years of isolation; his will remained, unbent by the weight of the punishment; his energy, unbroken by the misfortunes of his life."

They now saw him as a hero. Once they had been impossibly far from Nechaev, but now they had grown closer. They had been executing the program of his *Catechism* for some time. As he had dreamed, they created a terrorist organization, based on total subordination. As he had called for, they learned to kill the innocent along with the guilty, persuading the enemies of the revolution with dynamite, and as he had taught, they had penetrated "all institutions and even the Winter Palace."

Nechaev's reasoning, "The worse life is for people, the better it is for the revolution," had become their morality. That was why Loris-Melikov's transformations frightened them, and why they were in a hurry to kill the tsar.

On the eve of the death of the author of *The Devils,* the novel's protagonist mocked its creator. The novel's epigraph about demons that were cast out from people and into pigs now seemed like a joke. The devils had possessed Russia's youth, and the Bolshevik revolution was not far off.

On the morning of January 25, an icon of St. George and a votive light were displayed in the window of the cheese shop. The next window, of the shop owner's apartment, was tightly shuttered.

This was a significant morning—they were starting to tunnel under the street. Taking off the wooden cover, they exposed the brick and mortar wall. The revolutionaries picked up sledgehammers and went at it: Andrei Zhelyabov, Semyon Bogdanovich, and Alexander Barannikov, who came to do the honors. After breaking through the wall, Barannikov went to visit Fridenson, another member of the group. But Fridenson had been arrested the night before, and the police had set up a trap in his rooms.

Barannikov was caught when he entered. Once they got his identification, the police searched his room, next door to Dostoevsky. They set up a trap there, as well.

Dostoevsky, a man of nocturnal habit, was usually awake after midnight. The walls were not very thick in the cheap building, so he had to have heard the noise of the search. It was during the search on the other side of the wall that Dostoevsky's pulmonary artery burst, causing the hemorrhage.

The next day, January 26, as Dostoevsky suffered, the first victim was caught in the police trap next door—a People's Will member named Nikolai Kolotkevich. There is a police report on his noisy arrest: "In house 5/2 on the corner of Yamskaya Street and Kuznechny Alley, apartment No. 11, on this date at 4 o'clock an unknown man arrived. . . . He was asked by officer Yakovlev to go to the police precinct. . . . After which the unknown man asked to be let go, offering money. At the precinct the unknown man refused to identify himself or his residence."

Kolotkevich's being taken away in the police coach could be seen from Dostoevsky's study. Dostoevsky's severe hemorrhaging began just at that time.

Thus, the first signs of Dostoevsky's fatal illness appeared during the search of Barannikov's apartment, and the main symptoms occurred right after Kolotkevich was arrested. Are these things coincidental? Many theories are possible.

One is that the search and arrest of the young revolutionaries were a vivid reminder of his own arrest in his youth. The impressionable and ailing Dostoevsky began to hemorrhage.

There is another theory, very dark and even fantastic.

Dostoevsky, who was planning a novel about a terrorist, knew about his neighbor. He met the People's Will group even before Barannikov had moved in. The archives of the People's Will have a residency permit issued by the police to another member of the Great EC, Alexandra Pavlovna Korba. It stipulates that she was issued a permit to live in building 5/2 in November 1879. The People's Will beauty lived in Dostoevsky's building a year before Barannikov moved in.

It might be that Dostoevsky met the revolutionaries in 1879, through Korba, who had written to him years ago. There would not have been anything particularly unusual in this. The People's Will members maintained amicable relations with some liberal writers. But could young radicals be friends with the author of *The Devils?*

Even though they hated the novel, revolutionary young people always treated Dostoevsky with great trust. The writer E. P. Letkova-Sultanova, part of revolutionary and narodnik circles, explained that despite *The Devils,* radical youth perceived Dostoevsky as "a former revolutionary and convict, a humanist artist of genius, the defender of the humiliated and injured. . . . They acknowledged his right to be a teacher and to address society as its judge." That was why the narodnik and future terrorist Korba wrote to him. Young radicals attempted to carry leg irons in Dostoevsky's funeral procession, but the police confiscated them.

But would the author of *The Devils* have dealt with the young madmen?

Dostoevsky, who had almost paid with his life for his convictions, understood the tragedy of these noble young people. "Sacrificing yourself and everything for the truth is the national trait of this generation. May God bless it and send it an understanding of the TRUTH. For the question is exactly that: what is to be considered the truth."

He fought with them for their own sake, "for a correct understanding of the truth." That was why he wrote *The Devils,* for which they came to hate him. That was why he wanted to write a sequel to *The Brothers Karamazov,* in which the story of Alyosha, whom they loved, would open their eyes. That was why he needed to know the heroes of his new book personally. And that was why the young radicals and the writer who planned to write about them were quite likely to meet. That may even be why Barannikov rented an apartment in Dostoevsky's building.

The handsome idealist turned terrorist who had fought in Montenegro's war against the Turks (a war Dostoevsky considered holy)—how interesting Barannikov must have been for the writer. But once Dostoevsky got to know them, he might have accidentally learned their plans to blow up the Winter Palace. If that were the case, then his odd conversation with Suvorin becomes explicable. He had said, "Just imagine that we are standing in front of the windows of the Datsiaro [a store on Nevsky Prospect that sold art] and looking at the paintings. Next to us is a man who is pretending to be looking. He is waiting for something and keeps looking around. Suddenly another man hurries up to him and says, 'The Winter Palace will be blown up now. I set the mechanism.' We hear it. What would we do? Would we go to the Winter Palace to warn them of the bomb?" He had answered his own question: "I would not." And explained it this way: "The liberals would not forgive me. They would torment me and bring me to despair."

This is a very weak and unimaginative explanation for the mutinous Dostoevsky. He had gone against the current all his life and he never tired of fighting the liberals. He served "only Christ." There may have been another reason that he did not dare give in: He could not send the young people who trusted him to their death. It would explain why he was tormented during his conversation with Suvorin and why he told him that he was going to write a novel about Alyosha Karamazov as a terrorist.

If Dostoevsky had had some of the People's Will literature in his study, for his research, the nighttime search in Barannikov's apartment would have made him destroy it hastily. He would have moved heavy furniture, which might have brought on the hemorrhage. The arrest of Kolotkevich, too, would have shaken the former prisoner completely. The possibility of exposure of his ties to the terrorists would mean a new and final collapse of his life. It might have caused the fatal hemorrhage. Of course, all this is pure speculation, that the "devils" on the other side of the wall directed the death of their creator. What is indisputable is that Dostoevsky's death was a prologue to a fateful turn in Russian history.

During the frighteningly successful work of the Executive Committee, people kept wondering how they were getting away with it and why the police could not capture them. As Vera Figner recalled, the EC in fact had twenty-four members plus five hundred active party members. They were up against the famous Third Department with its huge staff, plus the army and the prison system.

The most popular answer was that this was the first time that the tsarist police had to deal with professionals, instead of mere students. The professional revolutionaries proved the might and invulnerability of terrorism.

But General Loris-Melikov apparently attributed the success of the terrorists to other causes. After studying the two sensational actions of the EC—the explosion on the railroad and the explosion in the Winter

Palace—he correctly assessed the suspicious carelessness of the Third Department. He did not trust the Third Department and wanted to reform it. That is why he created a structure that duplicated the work of the Third Department.

In the spring of 1880, the city governor was given the right to search and arrest people for political crimes in St. Petersburg on the same terms as the Third Department. Now the Third Department (and after its transformation. the Police Department) learned about searches and arrests post-factum.

Suddenly, the "great conspirators" stopped succeeding. On July 24, 1880, officials captured the elusive Alexander Presnyakov, who participated in blowing up the royal train and had murdered an agent of the Third Department. Later the "poet of conspiracy," the head of the party Alexander Mikhailov, was arrested. Mikhailov was the party's historian. Here is how his lover, Alexandra Korba, described his failure. "He sought out pictures of everyone who died for the liberty and happiness of the people. He gathered material on them, he did not want them to remain unknown in the history of the revolutionary movement in Russia. . . . He was arrested when he went into a photographer's shop to pick up the photos he had ordered of the arrested members of People's Will Kvyatkovsky and Presnyakov. The shop was on Nevsky Prospect. Its owner was an agent of the secret police. When Alexander Mikhailov had come the day before to find out about the photos, the wife of the photographer and spy stood behind her husband's chair, gave Mikhailov an anxious look and moved her hand across her neck, to let him know that he was in danger of being hanged. . . . That same day the Administrative Commission met and the members of the Commission were indignant and made him promise that he would not return to the dubious photography shop. He gave his word." Yet he went. "He probably thought that not picking up the photos would be cowardly," wrote Korba, who knew him well.

He was arrested at the shop. The childish fecklessness of the Genius of Conspiracy is astonishing. But that strange fecklessness was typical of other "professionals" as well. Here is how Kibalchich, the chief dynamiter of the People's Will, behaved: "During the organization of the explosion of the royal train, he was carrying the explosive in a worn suitcase. He was sleepy. While waiting for the train, he fell asleep on a bench in the waiting room. . . . Martial law was in effect, and in anticipation of the tsar's return from Yalta, there were all kinds of officials at the train station; spies were everywhere, peering into people's faces. Kibalchich was illegal then, and it was easy to recognize him from photographs, since he had already served time in prison. He lay there, face upward, noticeable because of his pose and his suitcase under his head. . . . That time, fortunately, nothing happened," recounted a People's Will member named Deich.

They seemed strikingly unprofessional, those outstanding professionals from a secret organization. No sooner had Loris-Melikov created another institution doing the work of the Third Department than their "luck" went away. They were caught one after another, quite unprofessionally.

The police set a trap in Fridenson's apartment. The conspirators, it turned out, had no sign to warn of danger, a commonsense precaution. So the previously elusive EC member Barannikov showed up there and was arrested. They immediately set up a trap at Barannikov's. There were no secret signals there, either. The next terrorist fell into the trap—also a member of the Great EC, Kolotkevich. This professional carelessly carried around secret documents. They confiscated the top secret bylaws of the People's Will, the program of the Executive Committee, and his address book with notations on how to make explosives.

Now there was a trap at Kolotkevich's apartment, which also lacked danger signals.

As Alexandra Korba wrote, "Our comrades had become lax about using warning signs. Neither Barannikov nor Kolotkevich had their signals in order, and that led to the loss of Kletochnikov."

The legendary Kletochnikov, the Guardian Angel of the People's Will, was in danger. Kolotkevich, who had been arrested, was his contact. Kletochnikov gave him information from the Police Department. Kolotkevich had been arrested by the city governor's agency, and the news of the arrest reached the Police Department only after the fact. The EC knew that Kletochnikov would not be aware of the arrest and would come to Kolotkevich's apartment, only to be arrested.

He had to be warned. Someone would have to go to the Police Department and wait for him to come out. Someone would have to hurry to his apartment, someone would have to wait for him along the way to the Kolotkevich's place. Their invaluable Guardian Angel had to be protected. They had Alexandra Korba go to his house.

"His maid told me that he had not come home yet." Korba dropped by again later, and since he was still out, left him a note. Nothing more was done. (She may have been too concerned with the arrest of her lover, Mikhailov, to worry about Kletochnikov.) Kletochnikov went to Kolotkevich's apartment, where he was arrested.

On February 27, the head of the fighters, Andrei Zhelyabov, was captured at the apartment of Mikhail Trigoni. They fell, one by one. Which raises the question, how had they survived so long? In countries with a long tradition of autocracy, as soon as there is a threat to the autocratic regime, the most conservative forces form a union with the secret police. Could some conservatives have been using the terrorists as a cat's paw? The idea of making the People's Will concentrate on killing the tsar would have suited them. Was that why the police were so useless and why the terrorists lived so freely? Was Russia the first place where terrorists were used by others to destroy an unsuitable monarch?

Once Loris-Melikov created a parallel police structure, the helplessness of the police instantly stopped. Only the terrorists were helpless. Is my theory correct? I don't know. But I do know that the strange behavior of the police continued.

By March, Loris-Melikov had arrested the leadership of the People's Will. The count had found out about the apartment on Malaya Sadovaya Street. A delegation came to the cheese store: It was headed by a gentleman in a fur coat with a red lining and a general's cap. He was General Mrovinsky, the inspector of the Police Department and a specialist on explosives. Behind him came a police inspector and the janitor. Their appearance suggested that someone had informed on the plot.

Bogdanovich, pretending to be a cheese merchant, thought it was the end. There was a barrel in the store filled with earth from the tunnel they were digging and covered with a layer of cheeses. Mrovinsky headed straight for the barrel and asked what it contained. Told it held cheese, he did not even look inside.

Then the inspector went into the living quarters, where the tunnel began. When the revolutionaries went into the tunnel, they removed the wooden panel of the wall from floor to window, and then replaced it. Mrovinsky went to the wall. Just knocking on it would show that it was a hollow wall. The experienced inspector knocked, so inexpertly (or so expertly?) that there was no telltale hollow sound. He also looked in the back rooms of the store, where there were mounds of dirt, covered with sacking. Here, too, the inspector general found nothing unusual.

The explosion of the train and the bomb in the Winter Palace were to be repeated. The Third Department was still doing its job. The tsar was doomed.

Daria Tyutcheva apparently did have basis for her prediction that in three or four months the Winter Palace would be swept clean. The tsarevich's closest friend, formerly deputy director of the Third Department and now deputy minister of internal affairs, Adjutant General P. A. Cherevin, would later say, "I owe my entire career to Alexander II, but I still say: it's a good thing they got rid of him, otherwise where would he have led Russia with all his liberalism!"

Getting rid of unsuitable tsars was a tradition that went back to the palace coups of the guards. Usually the people closest to the sovereign were involved in the conspiracies.

There was an Iago in the Winter Palace. Minister of the Court Alexander Adlerberg held a hereditary position. His father had been minister of the court under Nicholas I and remained in the position when Alexander II ascended to the throne. His son, the tsar's childhood friend, succeeded him when he retired. Both Alexanders enjoyed recalling their childhood and their tutor Zhukovsky. Adlerberg was the only one at court to enjoy the privilege of calling the tsar by his diminutive name, Sasha, and to see him without being announced.

But politics and the tsar's love came between them. Adlerberg and Peter Shuvalov had taken a passionate part in the counter-reforms, and Alexander's inability to suppress sedition irritated Adlerberg. The appearance of Loris-Melikov, the coming reform, and Princess Dolgorukaya ended the friendship. Adlerberg joined the camarilla and had been against the tsar's marriage. The tsar did not forgive him.

Adlerberg's career was coming to an end. As War Minister Milyutin subsequently recorded in his diary: "Count Adlerberg told me, 'Even if the catastrophe of March 1 had not occurred, I still would not be minister of the court now. . . . The late tsar was completely in the hands of Princess Yuryevskaya, who would have led the tsar to the most extreme irrationality, to shame."

The count's behavior had become quite strange. After the attack by Solovyov, Alexandra Bogdanovich recorded the words of the historian Vassily Bilbasov in her diary: "Five days before the attempt, a German agency sent coded telegrams. . . . They ended up on Adlerberg's desk and he never bothered to unseal anything." The shots took place.

Before the explosion in the Winter Palace, Governor General Gurko, who knew about the lax discipline at the palace, wanted to take the supervision of the palace out of Adlerberg's hands. But Adlerberg told the tsar that Gurko wanted to enforce military order at the palace, knowing that the tsar would immediately think of the "delicate circumstances" (i.e., the presence of Princess Dolgorukaya, then his mistress) and would not permit the general in the palace.

On the eve of March 1, the minister's actions were very surprising. A. I. Dmitriev-Mamonov (later governor general of Omsk) was head of the bodyguards of the tsar and his family, subordinate not to the Ministry of Internal Affairs, but personally to Minister of the Court Count Adlerberg. Only he and Dmitriev-Mamonov knew the routes the tsar took on his travels.

Dmitriev-Mamonov later told the story to a relative of his, A. Spassky-Odinets, who recorded it. "There was no lack of reports on preparations for an attack, but they were all anonymous. However, on the morning of fateful March 1 there was a signed warning that gave the place and circumstances, which turned out to be completely accurate. Dmitriev-Mamonov, in his words, took the letter to Adlerberg and reported on the need to change the usual route that day. Adlerberg replied: 'No later than yesterday after dinner and in the presence of the heir, the tsar said in a stern voice, almost shouting, "Listen, Adlerberg! I've told you before and I command you now: do not dare tell me anything about attempts being planned on my life. Leave me in peace. Take whatever measures you and Dvorzhitsky think necessary, but I want to live whatever life God has left me in peace!" How could I, after that command, given in such harsh tones, report to His Majesty and insist on changing his trip?'"

Apparently not everyone in the camarilla was convinced of the need to get rid of the tsar, and there was a struggle in its ranks. The State Archive of the Russian Federation has letters that were received by Princess Yuryevskaya starting in May 1880. The first letter tells the princess that a secret organization of defenders of the monarchy had been created in St. Petersburg that intended to fight with secret organizations of revolutionaries. The organization called itself The Secret Anti-Socialist League, with the Russian acronym TASL. The author of the letter, the Great Leaguer, was its head. He would not tell her his name or the names of the league members. "We swore that no one would ever know our names."

Instead, the Great Leaguer gives detailed descriptions of TASL's ceremonies, which resembled Masonic ones. After a brief service, the members gathered in a hall, dressed in black with silver medallions of the order on their chests and their faces behind black hoods. This would seem no more than game playing if not for the author's knowledge of the work of the People's Will.

The Great Leaguer told her about the structure of the People's Will, and gave an accurate number of members of its top secret Executive Committee and the number of fighters. This was information only at the disposal of the Administrative Commission of the People's Will. In May 1880, the Great Leaguer begged Princess Yuryevskaya to persuade the tsar not to attend the changing of the guard and parade in the Mikhailovsky Manege on Sundays. He told her that "probably, a bomb will be thrown at the tsar or the road will be mined." But it was only in May that the Executive Committee, according to Vera Figner, "came up with the project to rent a store in the part of St. Petersburg where the tsar travels most frequently and to lay a mine to blow him up."

Princess Yuryevskaya got the last letter in December 1880. Who wrote those letters? And what was this secret organization that surfaced so mysteriously and vanished as mysteriously?

Probably there was no TASL; it was just an invention of the writer. And the writer was most likely someone from the Third Department. He was one of the people who intended to use the People's Will as a cat's paw to remove the tsar, hence his knowledge of underground Russia. For some reason, he betrayed his fellow conspirators and tried to save the tsar. We can only imagine his reasons.

The notebook of Captain K. F. Kokh, the chief of the tsar's convoy, records all the routes taken by Alexander II. They did not change after the May warning from the Great Leaguer. Apparently Alexander II did not take the letters seriously.

CHAPTER 16

Death of the Tsar

Following a tradition established by his murdered great-grandfather, Paul I, the emperor observed the changing of the guard and parade every Sunday, in the enormous Mikhailovsky Manege, which could hold several cavalry squadrons. Often it was attended by the grand dukes, adjutant generals of the retinue, and ambassadors (if they had military titles). As February came to an end, the whole route traveled by the emperor's carriage was lined by police guarding him and by observers from the People's Will.

Almost all the participants of the assassination would later be arrested and give detailed testimony. Their words shed light on the event, which is still not clear in many respects.

The tunnel from the cheese shop on Malaya Sadovaya was completed by late February, and required only the mine to be laid. Four volunteers were found to throw bombs if the tsar took the route via the Catherine Canal. They were Nikolai Rysakov, a student at the Mining Institute (he was only nineteen, a minor under tsarist law), the aristocrat Ignati Grinevitsky, a student at the Technological Institute, twenty-four, and two young workers, Timofei Mikhailov and Ivan Emelyanov.

The four met at an illegal apartment, where the chief dynamiter Kibalchich explained how the bombs worked. Rysakov stated, "As he left, Kibalchich asked us not to frequent places where we might be arrested. . . . Usually, at such moments, arrests are more likely somehow, he explained."

Mikhailov, Barannikov, and Kolotkevich were already behind bars. Andrei Zhelyabov was now in charge of the People's Will. He sensed approaching danger. Rysakov continued, "I noticed a feverishness in the actions of my comrades, which was explained by the frequency of arrests. Zhelyabov told us, 'We must hurry.'"

In late February Zhelyabov told them, "You must come to the conspiracy apartment on Sunday March 1, to get the mines and necessary instructions." They understood that the assassination was set for that day, and that it would probably be the last day of freedom for them, and perhaps of their lives.

They never saw Zhelyabov again. The next day, February 27, the police came to the room of Mikhail Trigoni, who rented a room on Nevsky Prospect, and arrested him and Andrei Zhelyabov, who was visiting him. The giant did not even have time to reach for his revolver. In prison, Zhelyabov repeated his line, "If you kill us, there will be others . . . lots of people are being born these days."

The next morning at the Winter Palace, the tsar received Loris-Melikov and Milyutin (he saw them daily) and Nikolai Girs, head of the Asian Department (who was expected to replace elderly Gorchakov as minister of foreign affairs). Loris-Melikov proudly reported the arrest of Zhelyabov and Trigoni. Later the tsar told Milyutin, "Congratulate me twice: Loris told me that the last conspirator has been captured and that they will persecute me no more!"

That evening, the tsar made notes as usual: "28 February. 11:00 A.M. reports of Milyutin, Girs, Loris. Three important arrests: including Zhelyabov."

Those were the happy results of the penultimate day of his life.

On that same day, the remaining members of the Executive Committee met in an illegal apartment near Voznesensky Bridge. None of the original leaders was left. They were all in the Fortress of Peter and Paul. The organization was in disarray. "And on top of it, we learned to our horror that not one of the four bombs was ready. The next day was March 1, Sunday, and the tsar might drive along Sadovaya, where the mine was still not placed in the tunnel," wrote Vera Figner.

Sofia Perovskaya led the meeting. The petite young woman took charge of the bewildered men. She believed that a popular rebellion would follow the death of the tsar, and then Zhelyabov, who was in prison, would be saved. It would be a complete misunderstanding, however, to think that his release was her primary motivation. She wanted to achieve the party's main goal, their maniacal dream, to kill the tsar, so that the revolution would begin.

With her rampant faith and fierce energy, Perovskaya fired up the men's spirits. The women turned out to be the ones with the greatest courage at this meeting—Alexandra Korba, Alexandra Mikhailova, and Vera Figner, who all wanted to free Russia.

After Perovskaya's inspiring speech, the men perked up. "Agitated, we were imbued with one feeling, one sentiment. . . . Everyone present declared unanimously: 'Act. Tomorrow no matter what, we act!' The mine had to be placed. The bombs had to be ready by morning," Figner wrote.

It was around three in the afternoon on Saturday. They had under twenty-four hours.

Only the ones with work to do remained in the apartment by five. Three dynamiters led by Kibalchich and Vera Figner labored until morning, making the bombs. It was very dangerous work, especially done in haste. These sensitive bombs often went off by themselves. Figner wrote, "I persuaded Sofia Perovskaya to lie down, to gather strength for the next day, and I helped the workers, wherever they needed a hand, even though I was inexperienced; I cut up kerosene tins I had bought to serve as wrappers for the bombs. Our lamps and the fireplace were lit all night. At two in the morning I left the comrades, because my services were no longer needed."

That same night, the student Ignati Grinevitsky (nicknamed "Kotik") wrote his last will and testament. "Alexander II must die. His days are numbered. He will die and we, his enemies, his killers, will die with him. . . . History will show that the luxuriant tree of freedom demands human sacrifices. . . . Fate has doomed me to an early death, and I will not see victory, I will not live a single day, a single hour in the radiant time of triumph. . . . But I believe that with my death I will have done everything I had to do, and no one in the entire world can demand more of me."

Perovskaya and Figner slept. "When Perovskaya and I awoke at eight, the men were still working, but two bombs were ready, and Perovskaya took them [to the other apartment where the bomb throwers were supposed to get them]." Figner helped fill the other two bombs, and Kibalchich took them to the apartment. That is how they greeted the morning of March 1.

Rysakov's apartment, early on the morning of March 1. His landlady testified, "That morning he got up after 7:00: hearing noise in his room, I got up, too. He came to the kitchen and said, 'See how early I got up today; I should get up this early on weekdays.' . . . He was so touching, he started talking to me, before he almost never spoke."

He was small and round-shouldered, with a pale fuzz on his upper lip. He looked like a high school student. Rysakov testified: "Around 9:00, I came to the conspiracy apartment to get the bombs and for the explanation of the assassination plan. At about the same time Kotik, Ivan Emelyanov, and Timofei Mikhailov showed up. Then came a blonde, who had carried a rather big parcel. . . . Those were the bombs. She first handed them out and then explained the action plan, sketching on an envelope the approximate location. And who should be where."

The final plan had two versions. The first was if the tsar returned from the Manege along Malaya Sadovaya Street. Then the mine in the tunnel near the cheese shop would go off. This part of the operation was called Central Blow.

At the same time all four bomb throwers were to be at both ends of Malaya Sadovaya Street. If the explosion was unsuccessful (that is, if it went off too soon or too late), they had to throw their bombs at the carriage. The plan had also called for Zhelyabov to attack the tsar bodily, and stab him to death with his dagger, if the bombs all failed. But now Zhelyabov was in prison, Sofia Perovskaya was in charge, and they had to give up on the stabbing.

The second version was if the tsar went back to the palace via the

Catherine Canal. Then it was up to the bomb throwers alone. All four had to leave Malaya Sadovaya Street and hurry to the canal, on the signal that would come from Perovskaya.

"The signal was a light flutter of a ladies' lace hankie," Vera Figner wrote poetically, many years later. That fluttering lace hankie became part of many works of history and poetry. But in fact, as Rysakov testified during the investigation, the historic signal was much more prosaic. "The blonde [Perovskaya] would take out a handkerchief and blow her nose, and that would show us we had to go to the canal."

Usually, when Alexander took the Catherine Canal, he stopped along the way to visit his cousin at the Mikhailovsky Palace. That would give them time to take their places on the canal.

March 1, early morning in the Chancellery of the city governor. A. I. Dvorzhitsky, the chief of police who accompanied the tsar to the Mikhailovsky Manage, explained what happened: "At nine in the morning of the horrible day of March 1, 1881, the city governor General Fedorov gathered all the police chiefs of the district precincts and told us that everything was going well, that the main activists of the anarchists, Trigoni and Zhelyabov, were arrested, and only two or three people remained to be captured to end the war on sedition, and that the emperor and the minister of internal affairs were totally satisfied with the work of the police. Despite this faith on the part of the city governor on the success of suppressing anarchy, many of us remained in great perplexity. I personally did not share the city governor's conviction, based on the information that was continually reported to him, and I felt it my duty right after General Fedorov's speech to go to see my acquaintance chamberlain Count Perovsky, a man who was close to the Imperial Highnesses Grand Dukes Vladimir Alexandrovich and Alexander Alexandrovich."

Dvorzhitsky, like many other police chiefs, knew of troubling information that was continually reported to the city governor, who ignored it. Did that mean that the governor was also working with the people opposed to the coming reforms?

The information was so terrifying that the police chief was willing to risk his career and go over the heads of his superiors to see Count Perovsky. "Having told the count of the worrying situation in the capital, I asked Count Perovsky to inform Grand Duke Vladimir Alexandrovich [note, not the heir] that in what I perceived the present situation to be, we could not guarantee the safety of the tsar. The count gave me his word to do so that very day."

So Count Perovsky promised to speak with the tsar's son Vladimir, even as his niece, Sofia Perovskaya, had turned over the bombs to the throwers. In the meantime, Dvorzhitsky went to the Winter Palace to accompany the tsar to the Mikhailovsky Manege.

At the Winter Palace, the tsar no longer took walks in the morning—the assassination attempts had curtailed them. On March 1, after the service in the Small Church, the tsar had coffee in the lettuce-green dining room with Princess Yuryevskaya and went to his study.

He received Loris-Melikov, who brought a government announcement on the new reform. The tsar commanded a meeting of the ministers to be convened on March 4, because the draft had to be promulgated in the name of the government. He was irritated by the thought that the "opposition would speak in the name of Pobedonostsev" again. But it was done, Alexander had approved the draft. They had started down the road to a constitution. The day would be remembered in history, he hoped.

The tsar was wearing the uniform of the Sapper Battalion, the one that saved his father and the palace during the Decembrist uprising. His father had brought him out to greet them in his child-size uniform.

Now he was wearing their uniform and taking his last trip. He went to say good-bye to his wife. She pleaded with him not to go, she wept, she had a foreboding, not because of the prediction of the gypsy or the letters from TASL, but because she loved him.

He overcame her nervous objections. As the all-knowing Suvorin would record in his diary, repeating what the tsar's doctor Botkin told him, "Before leaving for the guards parade on March 1 . . . the tsar toppled the princess onto the table and took her. She told this to Botkin herself."

That was the way a passionate and powerful man of the Romanov dynasty was supposed to calm a woman. Neither of them knew it would be their farewell.

The Winter Palace was not the only place where wives pleaded with their husbands—a similar scene took place at the palace of Grand Duke Mikhail Nikolayevich, Alexander's brother, at 12:30. He was seen off to the Manege as if he were going to war. "The fact that my father always had to accompany the tsar during these Sunday parades drove my mother terribly crazy. 'I'm not afraid of the officers or the soldiers,' mother would say, 'but I don't trust the police. . . . The road to Mars Field is long, and all the local nihilists can see you travel down the streets,'" recalled Alexander Mikhailovich in his memoirs.

But the grand duke went to the Manege.

At the Winter Palace, at 12:45, police chief Dvorzhitsky drove up in a sleigh, in order to accompany the tsar to the Manege. Dvorzhitsky testified: "At a quarter to one I was at the Winter Palace, when Count Loris-Melikov was leaving the palace. When I came into the entry, I met Minister Count Adlerberg, who in conversation with me sadly spoke of the difficult times as a result of the activity of the anarchists. During this conversation we heard a joyous "Health to you, Sire!" from the guards in response to His Majesty's greeting. After that, the tsar came into the covered entry, greeted everyone there, as was his custom, got in the carriage and told the coachman Frol Sergeyev, 'To the Manege over Pevchesky Bridge.'"

The tsar was traveling via the Catherine Canal.

Alexander II traveled in a closed carriage. He was accompanied by six Cossacks and a seventh sat on the coachman's left. The carriage was followed by two sleighs with police chief colonel Adrian Ivanovich Dovrzhitsky and the chief of the tsar's guards Captain Kokh with policemen.

They reached the Manege, and the tsar was greeted with the guards' "Hurrah!" The tsar entered the Manege. The battalion of the Life Guards of the reserve infantry regiment and the Life Guards of the Sapper Battalion were in formation. The tsarevich and the tsar's brother Grand Duke Mikhail Nikolayevich joined the tsar.

At the cheese store on Malaya Sadovaya Street, at 1:00 P.M., according to the plan developed by the Executive Committee, Bogdanovich and his "wife," Yakimova, prepared to leave the cheese store. They would be replaced by an experienced dynamiter, Frolenko. He had volunteered to join the wires. Frolenko would most likely die under the ruins of the building from the blast he would create. "When he came to the store," Yakimova recounted, "I was surprised to see him take out a sausage and a bottle of red wine from the package he had with him, put it on the table, and get ready to eat. 'What is this?' I asked, almost in horror, seeing the materialistic intentions of a man doomed to certain death under the collapsed building. 'I have to be strong,' [he replied] and Frolenko calmly set about eating."

He and the bomb throwers had already said good-bye to life.

Frolenko could see through the window that gendarmes on horseback had appeared at both ends of Malaya Sadovaya in preparation for the tsar's carriage. At both ends of the street, mixing with passersby, were the four bombers. It was time for the tsar to leave the Manege.

Yakimova left the cheese store with only Frolenko in it. The last thing she saw was Frolenko at the table by the window. Before him on the table was a vessel with the solution that would conduct electricity, and one wire. All he had to do was lower the other wire into it.

The guards parade ended at the Manege. "The guards parade went very well. The tsar was pleased by everything and was, apparently, in a good mood, joking. . . . When it was over, he spoke a bit with the persons around him and then left the Manege," Milyutin recalled.

Alexander got into the carriage with its convoy and commanded, "To the Winter Palace, by the same route."

At the cheese store, Frolenko saw the gendarmes leave, which meant that the tsar was taking the other route. He realized that he would live. Frolenko quickly left the store. The four bomb throwers also left their posts at Malaya Sadovaya. They went down Mikhailovskaya Street in the direction of the Catherine Canal.

Sofia Perovskaya was waiting for them on Mikhailovskaya Street and gave them the signal that meant they should head to the Catherine Canal.

On the way home to the Winter Palace, the tsar stopped at Mikhailovsky Palace. His cousin Grand Duchess Ekaterina Mikhailovna (with the same name as his wife) lived here. She was the daughter of Grand Duchess Elena Pavlovna, who was the tsar's associate in his reforms, and of the martinet Grand Duke Mikhail Pavlovich. She took after her father and did not approve of either his reforms or his wife.

The tsar's brother, Grand Duke Mikhail Nikolayevich, pulled up in his carriage right after the tsar. The two brothers tried yet again, unsuccessfully, to bring peace between the two Ekaterina Mikhailovnas. Tea was served in the formal reception room of the palace. It was the last tea of the tsar's life.

The bomb throwers took their places on the canal. Perovskaya later related that at 2:00 P.M. the student Grinevitsky, "passing her, headed for the fatal place, smiled quietly at her, barely noticeably. . . . He did not exhibit a shadow of fear or agitation and went to his death with a completely calm mind."

"Don't consider sacrifice a sacrifice, and live only for the sacrifice," wrote the Decembrist Alexander Yakubovich, who had planned to kill Alexander II's father, Nicholas I.

Most of them sought a joyous death. But only three bomb throwers took their places at the canal. The one who was to meet the carriage first, the worker Timofei Mikhailov, had vanished. He "felt that he could not throw the bomb and he went home without even reaching the place." Now, Rysakov was first.

Rysakov testified, "Around two o'clock I was on the corner of Nevsky and the canal, and before that time I walked around Nevsky or connecting streets, so as not to call attention to myself from the police on the canal."

While the men took their places, Perovskaya had crossed the Kazansky Bridge to the opposite side of the Catherine Canal. She waited for the denouement, a grateful spectator of bloodshed.

At 2:10 P.M., the tsar said good-bye to Grand Duchess Ekaterina Mikhailovna, after spending his customary half hour with her. Apparently, he had not persuaded her, so Grand Duke Mikhail Nikolayevich stayed on.

At 2:15 P.M., Alexander went to the carriage. It turned onto the canal, followed by two sleighs carrying Dvorzhitsky, Captain Kokh, and the policemen.

The coachman whipped the horses and the carriage speeded up along the street—a fence and narrow sidewalk on the left and on the right, the wall of the grounds of the Mikhailovsky Palace and the sidewalk. There were not many people on the street: a boy with a big basket with meat, two young apprentices carrying a couch, and a young woman.

Walking toward the carriage from Konyushenny Bridge came a very young man, blond, short, and wearing a black overcoat, holding a white package the size of a box of chocolates. It was a bomb wrapped in a white handkerchief. He swung his arm.

Rysakov went on: "After a moment's hesitation, I threw the bomb. I sent it under the horses' hooves in the supposition that it would blow up under the carriage. . . . The explosion knocked me into the fence."

There was a deafening blast, and a cloud of white smoke enveloped the carriage. When it cleared, the carriage was past the bomb, which had blown up behind it. Only the back of the coach had been damaged. The imperial cavalcade stopped. One of the Cossacks lay dead behind the carriage. The man who had sat on the coachbox with the driver had a concussion and was convulsively clutching at the empty air. On the sidewalk, the dying boy groaned, his basket of meat next to him. A few steps away, a wounded pedestrian leaned against the fence and a wounded policeman struggled to his feet.

It was a street scene previously unknown in St. Petersburg.

Rysakov started to run, shouting, "There he goes! Get him!" pretending to be chasing the criminal. But they were after him already. A workman who was doing some repairs nearby threw his crowbar at his feet, tripping him. The police and Cossacks forced his head down, holding him tight in a crouching position. Rysakov must have seen a familiar face in the crowd and shouted, "Tell my father they got me!"

They disarmed him: He had a pistol and a dagger under his coat.

As soon as the carriage had stopped, the emperor opened the door and climbed out, with the help of one of the Cossacks. Colonel Dvorzhitsky was already out of his sleigh and he ran up to the tsar.

Dvorzhitsky recalled, "The tsar crossed himself; he was a bit unsteady and understandably upset. When I asked him about his health, he replied, 'Thank God, I am not wounded.' Seeing that the tsar's carriage was damaged, I decided to offer His Majesty a ride in my sleigh to the palace."

Dvorzhitsky heard Rysakov shout at someone in the crowd and realized that there was someone else nearby, also with a bomb. He asked the tsar to leave without delay. The coachman understood, also, and made the same request. "The coachman Frol also asked the tsar to get back in the carriage and go on." Only the back wall was damaged.

The tsar understood, too, but . . . "But His Majesty, without a word in response to the driver's request, turned and headed for the sidewalk on the Catherine Canal side. He walked along the sidewalk; I was to his left, behind him was the Cossack who had been on the coachbox and four convoy Cossacks who had dismounted and led their horses. They surrounded the tsar. After a few steps, the tsar slipped on a cobblestone, but I helped to steady him."

The tsar was headed toward Rysakov. The would-be assassin was about twenty paces from the site of the explosion; he was held by four soldiers, and Captain Kokh, chief of the bodyguards, was there. A junior lieutenant, who did not recognize the tsar at first, asked, "How is the tsar?" and the tsar, approaching Rysakov, replied, "Thank God, I'm fine, but look . . ." and he pointed to the dead Cossack and the dying boy. Rysakov replied immediately, "Is it thanks to God?"

The tsar approached Rysakov. Relieved to learn that he was from the bourgeoisie and not a nobleman, the tsar berated him: "A fine one!" He shook his finger at Rysakov and walked back toward the carriage.

Colonel Dvorzhitsky once again pleaded with the tsar. "Here I permitted myself a second time to speak to the tsar with a request to get in the sleigh and leave, but he stopped, thought for a bit, and then replied, 'All right, but first show me the site of the explosion.'"

A platoon of the Eighth Naval Equipage, returning from the guards parade, approached. Completely surrounded by the guards and the Cossacks, the tsar headed on the diagonal toward the hole in the street. He was pacing the canal, apparently waiting for something. "Obeying the tsar's will, I turned at an angle toward the explosion site, but I had not taken three steps when . . ." A young man who had stood sideways by the canal fence had waited for the tsar to draw near. He suddenly turned, lifted both arms, and threw something at the tsar's feet.

That was Ignati Grinevitsky. The tsar and the officers and Cossacks surrounding him, the young man who threw the bomb, and the people nearby all fell at once, as if mowed down. Above their heads a big white cloud of whitish smoke formed and, swirling, dissipated and settled.

"I saw how the tsar fell forward, leaning on his right side, and behind and to the right of him fell an officer with white epaulets. That officer tried to stand up, but rising slightly, he pulled the tsar over on his back and looked into his face," an eyewitness reported.

The officer with white epaulets was Dvorzhitsky, who said, "I was deafened by the new explosion, burned, wounded, and thrown to the ground. Suddenly, amid the smoke and snowy fog, I heard His Majesty's weak voice: 'Help!' Gathering what strength I had, I jumped up and rushed to the tsar. His Majesty was half-lying, half-sitting, leaning on his right arm. Thinking that he was merely wounded heavily, I tried to lift him, but the tsar's legs were shattered, and the blood poured out of them.

"Twenty people, with wounds of varying degree, lay by the sidewalk and on the street. Some managed to stand, others crawled, still others tried to get out from beneath bodies that had fallen on them. Through the snow, debris, and blood you could see fragments of clothing, epaulets, sabers, and bloody chunks of human flesh." The cap had fallen from the tsar's head; his tattered coat slipped from his shoulders; his pale face was bloodied and bruised. In a weak voice, he repeated: "Cold, I'm cold." His head was covered in wounds. One eye was shut and the other stared ahead without expression. Not far from the tsar, Grinevitsky lay dying in a puddle of blood. "The explosion was so strong that all the glass was blown out of the gas light and the post itself was bent," an eyewitness said.

A crowd had gathered around the tsar, dying on the bloody street, in dirty snow and tatters of clothing. They were Junkers from the Pavlovsk school, passersby, police, and the surviving Cossacks. Colonel Dvorzhitsky stood, swaying, above him. Grand Duke Mikhail Nikolayevich came racing up in his carriage. He had heard the explosion in the Mikhailovsky Palace and hurried to the scene. The grand duke kneeled on the street. He heard his brother say, "Take me home quickly!"

The tsar lost consciousness as the blood pulsed out of his body.

If they had taken him to the military hospital nearby, they might have stopped the bleeding and saved his life. But in a panic, without binding his wounds, they took him to the palace.

It was impossible to carry the bleeding body into the carriage, so a dozen hands carried the emperor to Dvorzhitsky's open sleigh. Among the helpers was the third bomb thrower, Ivan Emelyanov. He had a briefcase under his arm, with the bomb he would have used to kill the tsar if the first two had failed.

The sleigh moved toward the palace. The horse pulling it was the famous Barbarian that had long served the People's Will. The police had confiscated him and now he worked for the police. Once upon a time Barbarian had helped Stepnyak-Kravchinsky and Barannikov escape after killing Mezentsov. Now he was bringing the dying tsar to the palace. The Cossacks stood in the sleigh and supported the unconscious body. Their coats were drenched in his blood.

They brought him to the Saltykov Entrance. The doors were too narrow for the crowd to carry him in. There was no stretcher in the palace. They broke down the doors and all carried Alexander II up the steps of the marble staircase to his study, where twenty-five years earlier he had signed the emancipation proclamation and where that day he had laid the path to the Russian constitution. The marble steps and the hallway were covered in his blood.

This was how the seventh attempt on his life ended.

Doctor F. F. Markus said, "When I ran into the study, I found the tsar in a semirecumbent position on the bed, which had been brought out from the alcove and placed almost next to the desk, so that the emperor's face was turned to the window. He was wearing a shirt without a tie, he had a Prussian order around his neck . . . his right hand was in a suede glove, splattered in blood. Grand Duke Mikhail Nikolayevich, in tears, stood at the head of the bed in full parade uniform. When I ran up to the bed the first thing I noticed was the terrible disfigurement of the lower limbs, especially the left leg, which from the knee down was a shattered bloody mass; the right leg was also damaged, but less than the left. Both shattered limbs were cold to the touch. . . . I started pressing as hard as possible on both femoral arteries, where the pulse was almost imperceptible, thinking this way to preserve at least some of the blood. The tsar was completely unconscious. All the efforts of the doctors who came after me were in vain—the tsar's life had been extinguished."

The tsar died leaving us this last puzzle—why did he not leave immediately, knowing full well the danger in staying? Why did he walk for such a long time along the deadly canal? Was it weariness of fighting with the camarilla, and his son, and with the madmen who hunted him like a wild animal, which made him lose the will to live? Or was it absolute faith that God would always protect him and that he was invulnerable? Did he decide to prove that to himself and those around him one more time?

The sound of the first bomb on the canal had traveled far, and it resembled the noon cannon shot at the Fortress of Peter and Paul. But it was past two. An extraordinary agitation enveloped the city after the second blast. Crowds of excited people filled Palace Square and Catherine

Canal. Held back by armed guardsmen, the crowd blocked the narrow space of the canal embankment, creating a bottleneck. The sidewalk was a mess of dirtied snow mixed with debris and blood.

An officer sent by Grand Duke Mikhail Nikolayevich rushed along Nevsky Prospect to Anichkov Palace, to inform the heir. He had been present at the guards parade at the Manege and then had gone back to his palace. The tsarevich and tsarevna had just finished lunch: He was at his desk and she was looking out the window onto Nevsky, when two distant booms reached them. They were trying to guess what it could have been when she saw the sleigh racing down Nevsky, with the officer standing up in it. The tsarevich ran down the stairs, Maria Fedorovna running after him.

The messenger could only manage: "The tsar is terribly wounded!"

The gigantic tsarevich in a general's topcoat and his petite wife next to him rushed to the Winter Palace in a two-seat sleigh. They were slowed by the human bottleneck by the Palace Square.

In the meantime, at the palace of Grand Duke Mikhail Niko-layevich, who had gone to the Manege, his youngest sons planned to go ice skating with thirteen-year-old Nicky, son of the tsarevich. (Nicky was what the future Nicholas II was called in the Romanov family.)

Grand Duke Alexander Mikhailovich recalled, "We were supposed to pick him up, when we heard a loud explosion and then a second one. Soon a panting servant ran into the room. 'The tsar has been killed!' he shouted. 'And so is Grand Duke Mikhail Nikolayevich! Their bodies have been taken to the Winter Palace.'

"Mother ran out of her room upon hearing his screams. We rushed to the carriage at the entrance and hurried to the Winter Palace. We were passed on the road by a battalion of the Life Guards of the Preobrazhen-sky Regiment, who were running, rifles over their shoulders, in the same direction.

"The big spots of black blood on the marble steps and then along the corridor showed us the way to the tsar's study. Father stood in the door-way, giving orders to the servants. . . . Mother, shocked to see him unharmed, fainted. . . . Emperor Alexander II lay on a couch by the desk. He was unconscious. . . . He looked horrible. . . . One eye was shut, the other stared ahead without expression. . . . Members of the Imperial Family came in one after the other. The room was overflowing. . . . The heir came in and wept, saying, 'This is what we have come to,' and embraced the grand dukes, his brother, Vladimir Alexandrovich, and his uncle, Mikhail Nikolayevich.

". . . Princess Yuryevskaya, half-dressed, ran in. They said that some overzealous guard tried to stop her from entering. She fell on top on the tsar's body, covering his hands with kisses and shouting, 'Sasha! Sasha!' It was unbearable. The grand duchesses began weeping. Dr. S. P. Botkin examined the dying man. . . . In answer to the tsarevich's question of how long the tsar would live, he replied, 'Up to fifteen minutes.'"

A boy in a sailor suit was being led up the marble steps. It was the new heir, thirteen-year-old Nicky. He tried to avoid stepping into his grandfather's blood, but it was hard. The blood of Alexander II was everywhere. Nicky became the heir in blood. And in blood, he would cease being tsar.

The spiritual advisor of Their Majesties, Father Bazhenov, gave the tsar Communion and Extreme Unction. The death agony began. The doctor, who was taking the tsar's pulse, nodded and released the bloody wrist. "The emperor has passed away!"

"Princess Yuryevskaya cried out and fell to the floor. Her pink and white peignoir was soaked in blood," recalled Grand Duke Alexander Mikhailovich. At around 3.30, the standard of Alexander II was lowered at the Winter Palace.

The entire Romanov family kneeled around the late emperor. "To my left," wrote Grand Duke Alexander Mikhailovich, "stood the new emperor. A strange change came over him in that instant. This was not the same tsarevich Alexander Alexandrovich, who liked to amuse the small friends of his son, Nicky, by tearing a deck of cards in half or bending an iron rod into a knot. In the course of five minutes he was completely transformed. Something incomparably greater than the simple consciousness of the duties of the monarch illuminated his heavy figure. A fire burned in his tranquil eyes."

It was the regal gaze, the heavy, pitiless gaze of Nicholas I. They had all waited for that ruthless gaze, they had all believed that it would return peace and great power to the country. "He made a sign with his hand to Maria Fedorovna, and they left together. Her miniature figure highlighted the mighty build of the new emperor."

The grand dukes looked down from the windows of the late emperor's study with such hope, as they watched the giant tsar Alexander III make his way through the crowds below to his sleigh. He strode and his little wife barely kept up.

The crowd shouted "Hurrah!" But the new tsar responded angrily to the crowd's greeting. He was awesome. Surrounded by a hundred Don Cossacks, his sleigh moved. The spears glinted red in the setting March sun.

The unconscious body of Princess Yuryevskaya was taken from the study to her rooms. After everyone left, they brought in Konstantin Makovsky, Alexander's favorite painter. He started to work in the fading light. He looked closely at the emperor's face, covered in tiny wounds. "I worked on his final portrait through my tears," he wrote.

The court grieved loudly, while many remembered quietly. They remembered numerous ill omens of the reign. The orb that fell from Gorchakov's hands during the coronation, and the crown that fell from the empress's head. About two weeks before his death Alexander kept finding mutilated pigeons on his bedroom window every morning. A falcon had settled on the palace roof. It was so unusually large that they had it stuffed for the museum after it was killed.

People talked about the mystical coincidence of his last day. After the guards parade at the Mikhailovsky Manege, the tsar had tea with Grand Duchess Ekaterina (Catherine) Mikhailovna; he died on the Catherine Canal; and he was married to another Ekaterina Mikhailovna. His affair with her began in 1866, as did the era of assassinations. "The criminal affair seemed to open an era of attacks on his life. This gives a large field for considerations of a mystical bent, but they creep into your heart

whether you want them or not," said lady-in-waiting Alexander Tolstaya.

The tsar had married Princess Dolgorukaya at 3:30 in the afternoon,
and he took his last breath at 3:33 P.M. To the court it was evident that his
death was a reprisal for his sin and preposterous reforms. "And everything was saved by God's hand, which cut the Gordian knot in time,"
Tolstaya concluded.

Postlude

The terrorists achieved their immediate goal, but it was a stunning failure. "The people were completely indifferent to the fact of regicide. There was nothing else—no barricades, no revolution. A dreary longing for our failed dream entered my heart," wrote a revolutionary named Dmitrieva. After the death of Alexander II the secret police suddenly became both wise and powerful. The Great EC was ended quickly. Sofia Perovskaya and almost all the other members were arrested.

When the prosecutor at the trial began to speak of the tsar's blood and the innocent victims of the bomb, the courtroom was filled with the peals of Zhelyabov's laughter. The prosecutor responded with a phrase that all Russia would repeat: "When people weep, the Zhelyabovs laugh."

Five were sentenced to hang. During the investigation, one of the condemned men, Nikolai Kibalchich, worked furiously on his real work (which he had been too busy with bombs and tsar hunting to do when he was at liberty). "When I came to see Kibalchich," wrote his defense attorney, "I was struck, first of all, that he was working on something completely unrelated to the trial. He was immersed in research that he was doing on some air-traveling apparatus; he desperately wanted to be given time to write his mathematical research on this invention. He did write it and he presented it to the authorities."

The air-traveling apparatus was a fantastic invention: a jet-propelled flying machine. But the head of the police department decided, "Giving this to scientists for examination would hardly be timely and could elicit inappropriate comment."

Kibalchich's project, one of the boldest technological ideas of the centuries, lay unknown, gathering dust in the archives. The scientist Konstantin Tsiolkovsky, who later developed the same idea, was stunned when he was shown the terrorist's concept. On the eve of his hanging, Kibalchich had opened the way to the space age. Terrorism had taken away brilliant minds.

Before the execution, Kibalchich told his lawyer, "I keep trying to come up with a philosophical formula [. . .] that would persuade me that it is not worth living. No matter how hard I try, I can't convince myself! I so want to live! Life is so good! Yet I must die! And what of my air ship? Is it safe?"

Terrorism had taken away brilliant minds.

On April 3, 1881, Andrei Zhelyabov, Nikolai Kibalchich, Sofia Perovskaya, Timofei Mikhailov, and Nikolai Rysakov were hanged on Semenov Square. The same unfortunate incompetence attended their execution as had plagued the execution of the Decembrists. Huge and heavy Timofei Mikhailov's noose tore. He fell onto the platform. He was picked up. "Mikhailov was still alive and conscious, so he moved his feet and walked along the platform," recalled an eyewitness. He was hanged a second time, and once again the noose did not hold and he fell to the ground. The wretch was hanged three times, and on the third attempt, the rope started to wear so the executioner Frolov added a second noose, from the gibbet next to his. Just to make certain, he himself hung from the victim's legs.

Five people were hanged, wearing white shrouds and hoods covering their faces, on the square crowded with troops and onlookers.

It did not get better. Zhelyabov and Rysakov had to suffer for a long time, because their nooses were not placed properly. They were too close to the chin, which prolonged the onset of death.

Alexander Mikhailov, Alexander Barannikov and Nikolai Kletochnikov condemned to life sentences in solitary confinement, would die in the cells of the Fortress. Prison care was very different under Alexander III. Nechaev died of dropsy in the Fortress in 1882, surviving the emperor very briefly.

Stepan Khalturin did not spend much time as a free man. He was hanged in 1882 for the murder of the Odessa military prosecutor. He was hanged under an alias, and the police did not know that they were executing the author of the bomb at the Winter Palace.

The writer and terrorist Stepnyak-Kravchinsky did not avoid a violent death, even in peaceful England. He died under the wheels of a train.

Of the celebrated terrorists, two survived in solitary confinement—Vera Figner (twenty years) and Nikolai Morozov (twenty-three). Theirs was a different punishment. They lived to see 1917, the "luxuriant tree of freedom" and the "radiant time" of revolution in Russia that Grinevitsky wrote about before going to die killing the tsar. They would also see the entire party of Socialist Revolutionaries, the favorite successors of the People's Will, die in Stalin's camps, with famous revolutionaries up against the wall in execution yards. They would see the Russian peasantry perish in Stalin's collectivization.

Stalin did not touch them. They were there as living museum exhibits, dying of natural causes in the 1940s. Alexandra Korba died at the age of ninety in 1939, also condemned by fate to observe the joys of civil war and the Stalinist terror.

The new tsar did not betray the hopes of the Anichkov Palace party. It triumphed at the very first discussion of the reforms signed by his father on March 1. Konstantin Pobedonostsev gave a denunciatory speech. "Your Majesty, the duty both of my position and my conscience obliges me to tell you everything that is in my heart. I am not only perplexed, I am in despair. Just as in previous times they said before the death of Poland, 'Finis Poloniae,' now we are almost forced to say, 'Finis Russiae.' . . . My heart contracts at the sight of the project presented for your confirmation. I hear falsehood in this project, I'll say it more strongly: it breathes falsehood. . . . They want to introduce a constitution in Russia, if not right away, then at least to take a first step in that direction. And what is a constitution? The answer comes to us from Western Europe.

The constitutions that exist there are weapons of all kinds of lies, weapons of all kinds of intrigues."

Zhukovsky had taught little Alexander II: "Revolution is a fatal effort to leap from Monday right into Wednesday. But the effort to leap from Monday back to Sunday is just as fatal." Alexander III would leap back into Sunday. To use his words, he "would put an end to the lousy liberals." Count Loris-Melikov, along with the liberal bureaucrats, was forced to retire. Grand Duke Konstantin Nikolayevich lost his position as chairman of the State Council and all his other positions. The great family liberal would be a "private person" until his death.

That was the end of his father's great reform using the Loris-Melikov Constitution. "Constitution? They want the emperor of all Russia to swear to cattle?" said Alexander III.

At a historic crossroads, Russia (once again) took the wrong path. And Pobedonostsev began to rule Russia behind the broad back of the emperor. They would freeze Russia for decades. The nationalist party triumphed, with strict censorship and state anti-Semitism. It was the apotheosis of majestic autocracy.

When Alexander III, occupied with his favorite pastime, fishing, was asked to sign some papers dealing with urgent European matters, the tsar responded proudly, "Europe can wait while the Russian tsar catches fish." The aphorism was repeated around the globe.

Europe could wait, but history would not.

At the end of his reign, Alexander III felt the results of his successful return to the ways of his ancestors. Not long before his death, the emperor spoke with one of his most trusted people, Adjutant General Oleg Rikhter. "I feel that things in Russia are not going as they should," the tsar said and asked Rikhter to give his views.

"I have thought about it for a long time," Rikhter replied, "and I envision the country as a colossal kettle in which fermentation is taking place, and people with hammers are around it. When the smallest crack appears in its walls, they rivet it. But one day the gases will break though such a large chunk that it will be impossible to rivet it shut, and we will all suffocate."

"The tsar moaned, as if in suffering," Rikhter recalled.

The boy Nicky who ran up the bloody steps would see that for himself when he was Nicholas II. He and his family and most of the grand dukes who had looked at Alexander III with such hope would die in 1917 and its aftermath. And Grand Duke Alexander Mikhailovich, living as an émigré abroad, would write bitterly, "Of all of us who had gathered at the emperor's bed, only I am alive."

Might there have been a way out? Not long before his death, Dostoevsky wrote, "Solidity will come not to those who shed blood but to those whose blood is shed. There it is, the law of blood on earth." Both the regime and the terrorists had shed blood generously, so neither side ended up solid.

The first one to attack the tsar, Karakozov, wrote to Alexander II from his death cell. In prison he had prayed constantly and had come to understand many things. In his letter he asked the tsar to pardon him, "as man to man and Christian to Christian."

Karakozov was executed.

After the unsuccessful attempt on Count Loris-Melikov by Mlodetsky, the writer Garshin begged the count to pardon him and to imagine the effect of that pardon now that the count had announced the dictatorship of conscience.

He, too, was executed. Alexander II wrote: "Mlodetsky was executed. Everything is in order."

Then Alexander II was killed. The great philosopher Vladimir Solovyov, reputedly the inspiration for Alyosha Karamazov, said in a public lecture: "As the representative of a Russian Orthodox nation that does not accept capital punishment, the tsar must pardon his father's assassins." He wrote to the new tsar. Alexander III's reaction was: "Psychopath."

Rysakov was only nineteen. He had a conversion at the canal. He saw with his own eyes how his bomb killed innocent people. And how Grinevitsky's bomb blanketed the snow with bloody human fragments.

He saw the painful death of Grinevitsky, his friend Kotik. Now he wanted, as he wrote, "to do everything against terror."

He appealed to the tsar. "Pleading for mercy, I refer to God, in whom I had always believed and believe now. . . . I am not thinking at all of the ephemeral suffering that accompanies capital punishment, I have come to terms with that thought during the month of my incarceration, but I fear only appearing before God's terrible judgment without having cleansed my soul through long repentance. Therefore I beg not for the gift of my life, but for a postponement of my death."

He was executed.

In 1905, Ivan Kalyaev killed one of the sons of Alexander II, Grand Duke Sergei Alexandrovich. Grand Duchess Elizaveta Fedorovna, his widow and sister of Alexandra, the last tsaritsa, and the wisest person in the Romanov family, came to Nicholas II and begged him to forgive Kalyaev.

He was executed.

This Law of Blood in Russia was a hellish circle. No one wanted to break the circle. Lubricated by the blood of the dead, the wheel of Russian history rolled swiftly toward revolution and 1917.

I often wonder, "What if?" What if (which has no place in history, but does in the human heart) they had just once forgiven a repentant killer. What if they had just once followed the parable of the prodigal son, which Dostoevsky had entreated his children to remember.

Who knows, perhaps Russia's sad history would have been different.

Selected Bibliography

Archival Material

STATE ARCHIVES OF THE RUSSIAN FEDERATION (GARF)

Emperor Alexander II — 678 (some material is in the collection 8 of the Winter Palace, created during Alexander II's lifetime)

Emperor Alexander II — 677

Empress Maria Alexandrovna — 641

Empress Maria Fedorovna — 642

Grand Duke Konstantin Nikolayevich — 722

Grand Duke Konstantin Konstantinovich — 722

Investigative Commission and Supreme Criminal Court on the case of the attempt on Alexander II of 1866 — 272

Investigative Commission of 1862 on the case of disseminating revolutionary calls and propaganda (1862–71) — 95

"People's Will" — 122

Supreme Administrative Commission on the Preservation of State Order and Public Calm, 1880 — 94

Police Department of the Ministry of Internal Affairs (1880–1917) Fond 109 (materials on People's Will, Nechaev, attempt on life of Trepov, and the bomb in the Winter Palace in 1880)

Loris-Melikov, M. T. — 569

Secret Archive of the Third Department — 109

Staff of the Separate Gendarme Corps — 110

Directorate of the Caucasus Gendarme District 1173 (telegrams and circulars about the attempts on the life of Alexander II in St. Petersburg, 1866, and Paris, 1867)

COLLECTIONS OF DOCUMENTS

Alexander II. *Vospominaniia, dnevniki* (Reminiscences and diaries). St. Petersburg, 1995.

Alexander III. *Vospominaniia, dnevniki* (Reminiscences and diaries). St. Petersburg, 2001.

Arkhiv "Zemli i voli" i "Narodnoi voli" (Archives of Land and Freedom and People's Will). Moscow, 1932.

Venchanie s Rossiei. Perepiska velikogo knizia Aleksandra Nikolaevicha s Nikolaem I (Betrothal to Russia: Correspondence Between Grand Duke Alexander Nikolayevich and Nicholas I). Moscow, 1999.

Doznanie o tainoi tipografii "Narodnoi voli" (Testimony on the People's Will secret printing press). *Byloe,* 1907, No. 3.

1 marta 1881 goda. Po neizdannym materialam (March 1, 1881. Unpublished Materials). Petrograd, 1918.

Delo 1 marta. Protsess Zheliabova, Perovskoi i dr Pravitel'svennyi otchet (The March 1 Case. The trial of Zhelyabov, Perovskaya et al. Government report). St. Petersburg, 1906.

Delo 1-go marta 1881 g. So stat'ei i primechaniiami L'va Deicha (The March 1, 1881, case, with article and commentary by Lev Deich). St. Petersburg, 1906.

Zvenia. Sbornik materialov i dokumentov po istorii literatury, iskusstva i obshchestvennoi mysli (Links. Collection of Materials and Documents on the History of Literature, Art, and Social Thought), Vol. 6. Moscow-Leningrad, 1936.

Organy politicheskogo rozyska, razvedki i kontrrazvedki tsarskoi Rossii i ikh agentura: Sbornik dokumentov (Agencies of Political Investigation, Intelligence and Counterintelligence in Tsarist Russia and Their Agents: Collection of Documents). Moscow, 1957.

1 marta 1881. Stat'i i vospominaniia uchastnikov i sovremennikov (March 1, 1881. Articles and Reminiscences of Participants and Contemporaries). Moscow, 1931.

1 marta 1881. Kazn' imperatora Aleksandra II. Dokumenty i vospominaniia (March 1, 1881. The Execution of Emperor Alexander II. Documents and Reminiscences). Leningrad, 1991.

1 marta. Proklamatsii i vozzvaniia, izdannye posle tsareubiistva (March 1. Proclamations and Appeals Published after the Regicide). Moscow, 1920.

Pererpiska Imperatora Aleksandra II s velikim kniazem Konstantinom Nikolae-vichem. Dnevnik velikogo kniazia Konstantina Nikolaevicha (Correspondence of Emperor Alexander II with Grand Duke Konstantin Nikolayevich. Diary of Grand Duke Konstantin Nikolayevich). Moscow, 1993.

Revoliutsionnoe narodnichestvo 70-kh godov XIX veka (sbornik dokumentov i materialov v dvukh tomakh, pod redaktsiei S. S. Volka) (Revolutionary Narodnik Movement of the 1870s, collection of documents and materials in two volumes, edited by S. S. Volk). Moscow-Leningrad, 1965.

Literature

A. V. Amfiteatrov, E. Anichkov. *Pobedonostsev.* St. Petersburg, 1907.

Andrei Ivanovich Zheliabov i Sof'ia L'vovna Perovskaia (Biograficheskie ocherki) (Andrei Ivanovich Zhelyabov and Sofia Lvovna Perovskaya [Biographical Sketches]). Rostov-on-Don (Russian historical library, No. 16).

N. P. Asheshov. *N. I. Rysakov: Materialy dlia biografii i kharakteristiki* (N. I. Rysakov: Materials for a Biography and Character Assessment). Petrograd, 1920.

M. A. Bakunin. *Narodnoe delo. Romanov, Pugachev ili Pestel'?* (The Narodnik Work. Romanov, Pugachev or Pestel?). London, 1917.

V. N. Balezin. *Samoderzhtsy* (Autocrats). Moscow, 1999.

A. I. Barabanova, E. A. Iamshchikova. *Narodovol'tsy v Peterburge* (People' Will in St. Petersburg). Leningrad, 1984.

A. A. Baranov. "Rossiia—induktor terrorizma. Togda i seichas" (Russia—Inductor of Terrorism. Then and Now), *Rossiia: put' v tret'e tysiacheletie* (Russia: Path to the Third Millennium). Moscow, Kaluga, 2000.

E. Beliakova. *Detstvo i iunost' imperatora Aleksandra II: Ocherk* (Childhood and Youth of Emperor Alexander II: A Sketch). St. Petersburg, 1911.

Bezumstvo khrabrykh (Russkie revoliutsionery i karatel'naia politika tsarizma 1866–1882 gg.) (Madness of the Brave [Russian Revolutionaries and the Punitive Policies of Tsarism 1866–1882]). Moscow, 1978.

E. Biriukov. "Konstantin Pobedonostsev—gosudarstvennyi deiatel', iurist" (Konstantin Pobedonostsev, state figure, jurist), *Zakonnost'*, 1994, No. 12.

Otto von Bismarck, *Vospominaniia* (Reminiscences), Vols. 1–2. Moscow, 2002.

A. A. Bogdanovich. *Tri poslednikh samoderzhtsa* (The Last Three Autocrats). Moscow, 1990.

Iu. I. Bokan'. *Evraziiskii antiterrorizm* (Eurasian Antiterrorism). Moscow, 2001.

A. Bokhanov. "Iavlenie Ekateriny III. Dinasticheskii skandal 1880 goda (Appearance of Catherine III. The Dynastic Scandal of 1880)," *Rodina*, 1998, No. 2.

O. V. Budnitskii. *Terrorizm v rossiiskom osvoboditel'nom dvizhenii: ideologiia, etika, psikhologiia* (Terrorism in the Russian Liberation Movement: Ideology, Ethics, Psychology). Moscow, 2000.

O. G. Bukhovets. *Sotsial'nye konflikty i krest'ianskaia mental'nost' v Rossiiskoi Imperii nachala XX veka* (Social Conflicts and the Peasant Mentality in the Russian Empire in the Early Twentieth Century). Moscow, 1996.

B. I. Chicherin. *Moskovskii Universitet* (Moscow University). Moscow, 1929.

G. I. Chulkov. *Imperatory. Psikhologicheskie portrety* (Emperors. Psychological Portraits). Moscow-Leningrad, 1928.

A. de Custine. *Nikolaevskaia Rossiia* (The Russia of Nicholas). Moscow, 1990.

V. A. Danilov. "Iz perezhitogo" (Experiences), *Byloe*, 1907, No. 10.

Iu. Davydov. "Nikto i nikogda ne uznaet nashikh imen" (No One Will Ever Learn Our Names)," *Prometei*, No. 11. Moscow, 1977.

V. Debagorii-Mokrievich. "K voprosu o peregovorakh IK 'Narodnoi voli' s 'Dobrovol'noi okhranoi'" (On the Negotiations Between the EC of the People's Will with the Volunteer Guards), *Byloe*, 1907, No. 4.

L. Deich. "O sblizhenii i razryve s narodovol'tsami" (On Approaching and Breaking with the People's Will)," *Proletarskaia revoliutsiia*, 1923, No. 8.

L. G. Deich. "Iz otnoshenii G. V. Plekhanova k narodovol'tsam" (The Attitude of G. V. Plekhanov Toward People's Will), *Katorga i ssylka*, 1923, No. 7.

A. G. Dostoevskaia. *Vospominaniia* (Reminiscences). Moscow, 1971.

L. F. Dostoevskaia. *Dostoevskii v izobrazhenii ego docheri* (Dostoevsky in the Depiction of His Daughter). Moscow-Petrograd, 1922.

F. M. Dostoevskii. *Polnoe Sobranie sochinenii v 30 tomakh* (Complete Works in 30 volumes). Moscow, 1983.

———. *Pis'ma* (Letters), Vol. 4. Moscow, 1959.

"Neizdanny Dostoevskii" (Unpublished Dostoevsky), *Literaturnoe Nasledstvo*, Vol. 86. Moscow, 1978.

Dostoevskii. Materialy i issledovaniia (Dostoevsky. Materials and Research). Leningrad, 1980.

A. Dvorzhitskii. "1 marta 1881 g." (March 1, 1881), *Istoricheskii Vestnik,* 1913, No. 1.

I. P. Eroshkin. "Vystrel u Letnego sada" (The Shot Near the Summer Gardens), *Voprosy istorii,* 1993, No. 7.

S. L. Evenchik. "Narodovol'cheskaia propaganda sredi krest'ian" (People's Will Propaganda Among the Peasants), *Obshchestvennoe dvizhenie v poreformennoi Rossii.* Moscow, 1965.

V. N. Figner. *Zapechatlennyi trud* (Labor Depicted). Moscow, 1964.

——. *Shlissel'burgskie uzniki. 1884–1905 gg.* (Prisoners of Shlisselburg, 1884–1905). Moscow, 1920.

N. P. Giliarov-Platonov. *Nechto o russkoi tserkvi i ober-prokurororstve Pobedonostseva* (Something About the Russian Church and the High Procuracy of Pobedonostsev). Leipzig, 1887.

N. Golubev (Father). *Vospominaniia o tsare-osvoboditele Aleksandre II* (Reminiscences about the Tsar-Liberator Alexander II). Pskov, 1882.

Iu. V. Got'e. "K. P. Pobedonostsev i Naslednik Aleksandr Aleksandrovich" (K. P. Pobedonostsev and the Heir Alexander Alexandrovich), *Publichnaya biblioteka SSSR,* Vol. 2. Moscow, 1928.

L. Grossman. *Dostoevskii.* Moscow, 1965.

——. *Zhizn' i trudy Dostoevskogo. Biografiia v datakh i dokumentakh* (Life and Works of Dostoevsky. Biography in Dates and Documents). Moscow-Leningrad, 1935.

A. I. Herzen. *Byloe i dumy* (My Past and Thoughts). Moscow, 1969.

A. V. Iakimova. "Gruppa 'Svoboda ili smert'" (The Freedom or Death Group), *Katorga i ssylka,* 1926, No. 3.

B. L. Ikhlov. *Sovremennyi terrorizm v Rossii: otsutstvie natiosnal'nogo i konfessional'nogo soderzhaniia* (Contemporary Terrorism in Russia: Absence of National and Religious Content). Omsk, 2000.

Illiustrirovannaia istoriia tsartvovaniia imperatora Aleksandra II (Illustrated History of the Reign of Emperor Alexander II). Moscow, 1904.

V. S. Intenberg. *Aleksandr II I graf M. T. Loris-Melikov* (Alexander II and Count M. T. Loris-Melikov). Moscow, 1996.

V. S. Intenberg, A. Ia. Cherniak. *Zhizn' Aleksandra Ul'ianova* (The Life of Alexander Ulyanov). Moscow, 1966.

S. Ivanova. "Vospominaniia o Perovskoi" (Reminiscences about Perovskaya), *Byloe,* 1906, No. 3.

P. S. Ivanovskaia. "Pervye tipografii 'Narodnoi voli'" (The First Printing Presses of the People's Will), *Katorga i ssylka,* 1926, No. 3.

"Iz arkhiva Tikhomirova" (From Tikhomirov's Archive), *Katorga i ssylka,* 1924, No. 6.

"K istorii narodovol'cheskogo dvizheniia sredi voennykh v nachale 80-kh godov" (For the History of the People's Will Movement in the Military in the Early 1880s), *Byloe,* 1906, No. 8.

"K istorii pobega S. L. Perovskoi" (For the History of the Escape of S. L. Perovskaya), *Istoricheskii arkhiv,* 1961, No. 3.

K. P. Pobedonostsev: pro et contra: Lichnost', obshchestvenno-politicheskaia deiatel'nost' i mirovozzrenie K. P. Pobedonostseva v otsenke russkikh myslitelei i issledovatelei (K. P. Pobedonostsev: Pros and Cons: The Personality, Socio-political Activity and World View of K. P. Pobedonostsev in the View of Russian Thinkers and Researchers). Moscow, 1996.

S. V. Kalinchuk. "Psikhologicheskii faktor v deiatel'nosti 'Zemli i voli' 1870-kh" (The Psychological Factor in the Work of Land and Freedom in the 1870s), *Voprosy istorii,* 1999, No. 3.

R. M. Kantor. "'Ispoved'" Grigoriia Gol'denberga" (Grigory Goldenberg's "Confession"), *Krasnyi arkhiv,* 1928, Vol. 5.

———. "Avtobiograficheskaia zapiska i pis'ma S. G. Shiriaeva" (Autobiographical Notes and Letters of S. G. Shiryaev), *Krasnyi arkhiv,* 1924, Vol. 7.

M. Kheifets. "Vystrel iz 'Ada'" (Shot from "Hell"), *Znanie—sila,* 1996, Nos. 6, 7.

F. A. Kibal'chich. *Nikolai Kibal'chich.* Moscow, 1986.

A. F. Koni. *Vospominaniia o dele Very Zasulich* (Recollections of the Vera Zasulich Case). Moscow-Leningrad, Akademia, 1933.

A. A. Kosmodem'ianskii. *Konstantin Eduardovich Tsiolkovskii.* Moscow, Nauka, 1987.

V. A. Kovalev. *Zalozhniki zabluzhdeniia: Istoriia pokushenii na Aleksandra II* (Hostages of Misapprehension: History of the Attempts on the Life of Alexander II). Moscow, 1995.

E. N. Koval'skaia. "Moi vstrechi s S. L. Perovskoi" (My Meetings with S. L. Perovskaya), *Byloe,* 1921, No. 16.

E. I. Kozlinina. *Za Polveka* (Over the Course of a Half Century). Moscow, 1913.

P. A. Kropotkin. *Zapiski revoliutsionera* (Notes of a Revolutionary). Moscow, 1988.

A. A. Kunkl'. *Pokushenie Solov'eva* (Solovyov's Assassination Attempt). Moscow, 1929.

L. M. Liashenko. *Tsar'-osvoboditel': Zhizn' i deianiia Aleksandra II* (The Tsar-Liberator: Life and Works of Alexander II). Moscow, 1994.

F. Lif. "Glava 'Avgusteishego' romana" (A Chapter of the "Most August" Novel), *Argus,* 1917, No. 8.

N. D. Litvinov. *Rol' idei v razvitii antigosudarstvennogo terrorizma* (The Role of the Idea in the Development of Anti-State Terrorism). Voronezh, 1999.

———. *Terroristicheskie organizatsii: formirovanie i deiatel'nost'* (Terrorist Organizations: Formation and Activity). Voronezh, Moscow, 1999.

Literatura partii "Narodnaia volia" (Literature of the "People's Will" Party). Moscow, 1930.

F. M. Lur'e. *Khraniteli proshlogo* (Keepers of the Past). Leningrad, 1990.

———. *Nechaev.* Moscow, 2001.

M. Masson. " 'Tashkentskii' velikii kniaz': Iz vospominaniia starogo turkestantsa" (The "Tashkent" Grand Duke: From the Reminimisces of An Old Turkestani), *Zvezda Vostoka,* 1991, No. 12.

K. K. Merder. "Zapiski 1826–1832" (Notes 1826–1832), *Novyi zhurnal,* 1995, No. 3.

D. A. Miliutin. *Dnevnik* (Diary), Vols. 1–4. Moscow, 1947–50.

K. K. Mogil'ner. "Radikal'naia intelligentsia pered litsom smerti" (The Radical Intelligentsia Facing Death), *Obshchestvennye nauki i sovremennost',* 1994, No. 5.

N. A. Morozov. *Povesti moei zhizni* (Tales of My Life). Moscow, 1947.

G. D. Nagaev. *"Kaznen neopoznannym . . .": Povest' o Stepane Khalturine* ("Executed Unidentified . . .": A Tale about Stepan Khalturin). Moscow, 1970.

"Narodnaia volia" i "Chernyi peredel." Vospominaniia uchastnikov revoliutsionnogo dvizheniia v Peterburge v 1879–1882 gg. (The People's Will and Black Redistribution. Reminiscences of Participants in the Revolutionary Movement in St. Petersburg in 1879–1882). Leningrad, 1989.

"Narodniai volia" pered tsarskim sudom (The People's Will in the Tsarist Court), 2nd ed. Saratov, 1983.

Narodovolets Barannikov v ego pis'makh (People's Will Member Barannikov in His Letters). Moscow, 1935.

Narodovol'tsy posle 1 marta 1881 (People's Will after March 1, 1881). Moscow, 1928.

"Neizdannye zapiski L. Tikhomirova" (Unpublished Notes of L. Tikhomirov), *Krasnyi arkhiv,* 1928, Vol. 4.

"Neizvestnye zametki Sof'i Perovskoi" (Unknown Notes of Sofia Perovskaya), *Sovetskie arkhivy,* 1983, No. 3.

M. Paleolog. *Aleksandr II i kniaginia Iur'evskaia* (Alexander II and Princess Yuryevskaya). Moscow-Petrograd, 1924.

V. Pankratov. "Iz deiatel'nosti sredi rabochikh v 1880–84" (From the Work among Laborers in 1880–84), *Byloe,* 1906, No. 3.

Z. I. Perfudova. *Politicheskii sysk Rossii (1880–1917)* (Political Investigation in Russia [1880–1917]). Moscow, 2000.

V. L. Perovskii. *Vospominanie o sestre* (Reminiscences of My Sister). Moscow-Leningrad, 1927.

I. A. Persianov. "'Spasitel' Imperatora: O. I. Komissarov-Kostromskoi" (The Emperor's "Savior": O. I. Komissarov-Kostromskoi), *Iz glubiny vremen,* 1997, Issue 8. St. Petersburg, 1997.

"Petrashevtsy." *Sobrnik materialov* ("The Petrashevsky Circle." Collection of Materials), Vol. 3. Moscow-Leningrad, 1928.

N. Pirumova. *M. Bakunin.* Moscow, 1970.

K. P. Pobedonostsev. *Sochineniia* (Works). St. Petersburg, 1996.

———. *Velikaia lozh' nashego vremeni* (The Great Lie of Our Time). Moscow, 1993.

"Podvig Nikolaia Kletochnikov" (The Exploit of Nikolai Kletochnikov), *Prometei,* Vol. 9. Moscow, 1972.

Iu. Z. Polevoi. *Stepan Khalturin.* Moscow, 1979.

A. Iu. Polunov. "K. P. Pobedonostsev—chelovek i politik" (K. P. Pobedonostsev—Man and Politician), *Otechestvennaia istoriia,* 1998.

M. O. Popov. *Zapiski zemlevol'tsa* (Notes of a Member of Land and Freedom). Moscow, 1933.

M. A. Popovskii. *Pobezhdennoe vremia: Povest' o Nikolae Morozove* (Conquered Time: Tale of Nikolai Morozov). Moscow, 1975.

I. V. Preobrazhenskii. *K. P. Pobedonostsev, ego lichnost' i deiatel'nost' v predstavlenii sovremennikov* (K. P. Pobedonostsev, His Personality and Activity in the Perception of Contemporaries). St. Petersburg, 1914.

A. V. Pribylev. *Zapiski narodovol'tsa* (Notes of a Member of the People's Will). Moscow, 1925.

A. P. Pribyleva-Korba. "'Narodnaia volia'. Vospominaniia" ("The People's Will." Reminiscences), *Arkhiv "Zemli i voli" i "Narodnoi voli."* Moscow, 1932.

Problemy terrorizma (Problems of Terrorism), collected articles. Moscow, 1997.

Protsess shestnadtsati terroristov (1880 g.) (Trial of Sixteen Terrorists [1880]). St. Petersburg, 1906.

P. A. Sadikov. "Obshchestvo 'Sviashchennoi druzhiny'" (Society of the "Holy Squad"), *Krasnyi arkhiv,* 1927, Vol. 2.

A. N. Sakharov. "'Krasnyi terror' narodovol'tsev (O pokusheniiakh na Aleksandra II)" (The "Red Terror" of the People's Will [On the Attempts on the Life of Alexander II]), *Voprosy istorii,* 1966, No. 5.

N. P. Salamanov. "Tsiolkovsky i Kibal'chich" (Tsiolkovsky and Kibalchich), *Ogonek,* 1961, No. 8.

K. N. Salimov. *Sovremennye problemy terrorizma* (Contemporary Problems of Terrorism). Moscow, 2000.

A. N. Savin. "Svatovstvo tsesarevicha Aleksandra Nikolaevicha" (Matchmaking of Tsarevich Alexander Nikolayevich), *Institut istorii.* Anthology, Issue 1. Moscow, 1926.

M. G. Sedov. *Geroicheskii period revoliutsionnogo narodnichestva* (The Heroic Period of the Revolutionary Narodnik Movement). Moscow, 1966.

E. A. Segal. *Sof'ia Perovskaia* (Sofia Perovskaya). Moscow, 1962.

S. M. Serpokryl. *Podvig pered kazn'iu* (Exploit Before Execution). Leningrad, 1971.

P. E. Shchegolev. *Alekseevskii ravelin* (The Alexeyvsky Ravelin). Moscow, 1989.

V. B. Shklovskii. *Lev Tolstoi* (Leo Tolstoy). Moscow, 1963.

E. A. Shtakenshneider. *Dnevnik i zapiski* (Diary and Notes). Moscow-Leningrad, 1934.

E. Sidorenko. "1 marta 1881 g. (Vospominaniia uchastnika)" (March 1, 1881 [Reminiscnces of a Participant]), *Puti revoliutsii,* 1926, Nos. 2–3.

Sof'ia L'vovna Perovskaia (Sofia Lvovna Perovskaya). St. Petersburg, 1906.

S. M. Stepniak-Kravchinskii. "*Podpol'naia Rosiia*" ("Underground Russia"). Moscow, 1960.

A. S. Suvorin. *Dnevnik A. S. Suvorina* (Diary of A. S. Suvorin). Moscow, 2000.

Tainy tsarskogo dvora (iz zapisok freilin) (Secrets of the Tsar's Court [from the Notes of Ladies-in-Waiting]). Moscow, 1997.

S. S. Tatishchev. *Imperator Aleksandr II, ego zhizn' i tsarstvovanie* (Emperor Alexander II, His Life and Reign), 2 Vols. Moscow, 1996.

Terrorizm: sovremennye aspekty (Terrorism: Contemporary Aspects). Anthology. Moscow, 1999.

L. Tikhomirov. *Pochemu perestal ia byt' revoliutsionerom* (Why I Stopped Being a Revolutionary). Paris, 1888.

———. *Zagovorshchiki i politsiia* (Conspirators and the Police). Moscow, 1930.

L. A. Tikhomirov. *Teni proshlogo* (Shadows of the Past). St. Petersburg, 1995.

———. *Vospominaniia* (Reminiscences). Moscow-Leningrad, 1927.

Anna Tiutcheva. *Vospominaniia* (Reminiscences). Moscow, 2000.

P. N. Tkachev. *Sochineniia* (Works), Vols. 1–2. Moscow, 1975.

A. A. Tolstaia. *Zapiski freiliny* (Notes of a Lady-in-Waiting). Moscow, 1996.

A. Torgashov. "Zapiski narodovol'tsa. 1878–1883" (Notes of a Member of People's Will, 1878–1883), *Golos minuvshego*, 1914, No. 2.

Iu. V. Trifonov. *Neterpenie* (Impatience). Moscow, 1973.

N. A. Troitskii. *Tsarskie sudy protiv revoliutsionnoi Rossii* (Tsarist Courts Against Revolutionary Russia). Saratov, 1976.

V. A. Tvardovskaia. "Krizis 'Zemli i voli' v kontse 70-kh godov" (The Crisis in "Land and Freedom" in the late 1870s), *Istoriia SSSR,* 1959, No. 4.

———. "Voronezhskii s"ezd zemlevol'tsev" (The Voronezh Conference of the Land and Freedom Group), Scholarly Papers of the Higher School. *Istoricheskie nauki,* 1959, No. 2.

S. S. Usherovich. *Smertnye kazni v Rossii* (Executions in Russia). Kharkov, 1933.

S. N. Valk. "Avtobiograficheskoe zaiavlenia A. A. Kviatkovskogo" (Autobiographical Statement of A. A. Kvyatkovsky), *Krasnyi arkhiv,* 1926, Vol. 1.

———. "Iz narodovol'cheskikh avtobiograficheskikh dokumentov" (From the People's Will Autobiographical Documents), *Krasnyi arkhiv,* 1927, Vol. 1.

———. "Iz pokazanii N. I. Rysakova" (From the Testimony of N. I. Rysakov), *Krasnyi arkhiv,* 1926, Vol. 6.

———. "Vokrug 1 marta 1881 g." (Around March 1, 1881), *Krasnyi arkhiv,* 1930, Vol. 3.

P. A. Valuev. *Onevnik,* Vols. 1–2. Moscow, 1961.

L. Vasil'eva. "Terpelivaia imperatritsa, ili Korona na dvoikh" (The Patient Empress, or a Crown for Two), *Nauka i religiia,* 1999, Nos. 3–6.

D. G. Venediktov. *Palach Ivan Frolov i ego zhertvy* (The Executioner Ivan Frolov and His Victims). Moscow, 1931.

"Viktor Giugo i revoliutsionnaia Rossiia 1870–1880-x godov" (Victor Hugo and Revolutionary Russia of the 1870–1880s), *Izvestiia AN,* 1986, No. 1.

G. A. de-Volan. "Ocherki proshlogo" (Sketches of the Past), *Golos minuvshego,* 1914.

I. L. Volgin. *Poslednii god Dostoevskogo* (Dostoevsky's Last Year). Moscow, 1990.

S. S. Volk. *"Narodnaia Volia" 1879–1882* ("The People's Will," 1879–1882). Moscow-Leningrad, Nauka Publishers, 1966.

Vospominania o K. Markse i F. Engel'se (Recollections of K. Marx and F. Engels), Vols. 1–2. Moscow, 1983.

L. G. Zakharova. "Aleksandr II," *Voprosy istorii,* 1992, Nos. 6–7.

L. S. Zalkind. "Vospominaniia narodovol'tsa" (Reminiscences of a Member of the People's Will), *Katorga i ssylka,* 1926, No. 3.

"Zaveshchanie Marii Oshaninoi" (The Will of Maria Oshanina), *Sovetskie arkhivy,* 1964, No. 3.

V. A. Zhukovskii. "Podrobnyi plan ucheniia gosudaria velikogo kniazia naslednika tsesarevicha" (Detailed Teaching Plan for His Highness Grand Duke the Heir Tsarevich), *Obrazovanie i obshchestvo,* 1999, No. 1.

———. *Proza poeta* (The Poet's Prose). Moscow, 2001.

I. O. Zhukovskii-Zhuk. *Aleksandr Ivanovich Barannikov.* Moscow, 1930.

Index

"Raid, The" (Tolstoy), 87
Railroads, 122, 205–6, 250
Rasputin, Grigory, 164, 216, 371, 380
Rastrelli (architect), 8
Razin, Stepan, 211
Razumovsky, Alexei (nephew), 313
Razumovsky, Alexei (uncle), 5, 224, 312–13
Razumovsky, Kirill, 313
Rebel, The (Camus), 222
Revolution, cultural decline in wake of, 228–29
Revolutionaries:
    assassination efforts of, 174, 175–84, 274–76, 280–81, 284–85, 289–97; see also People's Will, regicide conspiracies of
    coordinated terrorist actions of, 275–76
    criminal prosecutions of, 36–37, 139–40, 144–44, 161–62, 175, 184, 210, 225, 226–27, 256–57, 274–74, 276–81, 285–86, 296, 314, 356–57
    Decembrists, 28–34, 36–37, 38, 39, 49, 51, 62–63, 104, 125, 145, 182, 298, 384, 409
    falsehoods employed by, 176, 219, 223, 226
    ideological discourse of, 206–13, 217–18, 220, 221–22, 412
    literature of, 143, 144, 152–53, 154, 159, 160–61, 162–64, 174–75, 221–22, 254
    in London, 206–9
    militant transformation of, 221, 257
    nihilists vs., 154
    personal life forsworn by, xii, 312
    as police informants, 286, 320, 333, 388
    political reprisals against, 142, 181–84, 298–99, 350–51, 357–58, 371
    as professionals, 396, 398

    rural activism of, 134–35, 251–56
    socialist goals of, 175–76, 229–30, 251, 258
    student protests of, 135–38, 139–40, 141, 181, 205, 218, 221, 275
    terrorist tactics employed in, see Terrorism
    see also Land and Freedom; People's Will
Revolution of 1917, vii, 152–53, 425, 42
Rikhter, Oleg, 426–27
Robespierre, Maximilien-François-Marie-Isidore de, 21
Romania, independence of, 270
Romanov, Mikhail, Tsar of Russia, 61–62, 178
Romanov dynasty:
    sole Soviet survivor of, 248–49
    start of, 61–62
Rostopchina, Countess, 37
Rostovtsev, Count, 26–27, 119, 125–26
Rozum, Alexei, 312
Rubenstein, Anton, 75
Rurik dynasty, 61, 193
Rusakov (revolutionary), 362
Russia in 1839 (Custine), 81
Russian-American Trading Company, 187–88
Russian Empire:
    capitalist development in, 250–51
    ceremonial pomp in, 122–24, 130, 236–37
    court system of, xi, 103, 149, 269–70, 280
    Decembrist rebellion of, 28–34, 36–37, 38, 39, 49, 51, 62–63, 104, 125, 145, 182, 298, 384, 409
    European views of, 79, 80–83
    foreign influences on upper class in, 44, 77, 128, 134
    guards regiments of, 3, 4–5, 6, 8, 9, 10–11, 15–17, 20–21, 25–34, 37, 38, 74

About the Author

Edvard Radzinsky is a celebrated Russian historian, playwright, and talk show host. Always fascinated with the mystery surrounding the fate of the Romanovs, for twenty-five years he labored to produce the international bestseller *The Last Tsar,* which was published to critical acclaim in 1992 and was on the *New York Times* bestseller list for twelve weeks. He is also the author of *Stalin* (1996) and *The Rasputin File* (2000). He lives in Moscow, and has been lecturing to sold-out auditoriums and prime-time television audiences on Alexander II for the past two years.